Conversations with Leading Economists

T0327498

To Jean and Christine; and to Phil Vane who died on 5 July 1998

Conversations with Leading Economists

Interpreting Modern Macroeconomics

Brian Snowdon

Principal Lecturer in Economics, School of Social, Political and Economic Sciences, University of Northumbria, UK

Howard R. Vane

Reader in Economics, School of Social Science, Liverpool John Moores University, UK

Edward Elgar
Cheltenham, UK • Northampton, MA, USA

Published by
Edward Elgar Publishing Limited
The Lypiatts
15 Lansdown Road
Cheltenham
Glos GL50 2JA
UK

Edward Elgar Publishing, Inc.
William Pratt House
9 Dewey Court
Northampton
Massachusetts 01060
USA

This book has been printed on demand to keep the title in print.

A catalogue record for this book is available from the British Library

Library of Congress Cataloguing in Publication Data
Snowdon, Brian.
    Conversations with leading economists : interpreting modern
macroeconomics / Brian Snowdon, Howard R. Vane.
    Interviews with 14 economists conducted between February 1993 and
May 1998, with a majority of 12 between 1996–1998.
    Contents: 1. Interpreting modern macroeconomics : from Tobin to
Romer — 2. James Tobin — 3. Gregory Mankiw — 4. Milton Friedman–
– 5. Robert Lucas — 6. Alberto Alesina — 7. Robert Clower —
8. John Taylor — 9. David Colander — 10. Olivier Blanchard —
11. Franco Modigliani — 12. Edward Prescott — 13. Robert Solow —
14. Paul Romer — 15. Mark Blaug [comments on the interviews].
    1. Macroeconomics. 2. Economists—United States—Interviews.
3. Economists—Great Britain—Interviews. I. Vane, Howard R.
II. Title.
HB172.5.S648   1999
339—DC21   99–12890
                                                      CIP

ISBN 978 1 85898 942 6 (cased)
        978 1 84064 149 3 (paperback)

Contents

Figures

Tables

Acknowledgements

The editors wish to thank the following who have kindly given their permission to reproduce the interviews undertaken with Greg Mankiw, Milton Friedman, Robert Lucas and Alberto Alesina respectively, which appear as part of fuller journal articles, namely:

The International Honor Society in Economics for: 'New-Keynesian Economics Today: The Empire Strikes Back', *The American Economist*, Vol. 39, No. 1, Spring 1995, pp. 48–65.

MCB University Press for: 'Modern Macroeconomics and its Evolution from a Monetarist Perspective: An Interview with Professor Milton Friedman', *Journal of Economic Studies*, Vol. 24, No. 4, 1997, pp. 192–222.

Routledge for: 'Transforming Macroeconomics: An Interview with Robert E. Lucas Jr.', *Journal of Economic Methodology*, Vol. 5, No. 1, June 1998, pp. 115–46.

The International Honor Society in Economics for: 'The New Political Macroeconomics', *The American Economist* (1999, forthcoming).

The editors also wish to thank Professor Paul Romer for permission to use their interview with him, the copyright on which is held by Professor Romer.

Preface

The idea of bringing together this collection of interviews into a single volume has had a long gestation period and owes a debt of gratitude to the inspiration first provided by Arjo Klamer's (1984) fascinating conversations with new classical economists and their opponents. Since the publication of Klamer's book macroeconomics has witnessed a number of important developments including a real business cycle revolution, a new Keynesian counter-revolution and a renaissance of interest in economic growth. Six years ago when preparing the manuscript for our book *A Modern Guide to Macroeconomics: An Introduction to Competing Schools of Thought* (Snowdon, Vane and Wynarczyk, 1994) we decided to include at the end of each chapter short interviews with some leading exponents of the main schools of macroeconomic thought. Our purpose in doing so was to help bring the subject matter alive and capture the imagination of the reader, most notably intermediate undergraduates at which that book was primarily aimed. We ourselves found the interviews revealing and were somewhat frustrated that, due to constraints of time and finance, a number of the interviews had to be conducted by correspondence. Having completed that project we vowed that whenever possible we would seek to interview our chosen victims face-to-face. The present volume brings together 14 interviews undertaken with leading economists over the period February 1993 to May 1998. Between them, with varying degrees of influence, these economists have made a profound contribution to the ever-changing and ongoing debates witnessed in the field of macroeconomic theory and policy, the way macroeconomics is taught and the history and methodology of macroeconomic research. Above all else their answers to our questions shed light on, and provide interesting insights into, the origins, development and current state of modern macroeconomics.

The interviews are presented in chronological order and were all conducted in person with the exception of that undertaken with Alberto Alesina who, due to unforeseen circumstances, was unable to meet up with us at the *AEA* Conference in New Orleans in January 1997. Twelve out of the fourteen interviews were undertaken in the period January 1996 to May 1998. The remaining two interviews, with James Tobin and Gregory Mankiw, were originally conducted in February 1993. However, in the latter two cases we have included five additional questions which were answered by correspondence at the beginning of 1998. It should also be noted that none of the economists that we interviewed in person had any advance notice of the questions we asked. In our view the illuminating and at times starkly contrasting answers to our questions demonstrate that macroeconomics is an exciting, controversial and important subject. We hope that the readers, whether they be students or fellow academics, enjoy reading the interviews as much as we enjoyed organizing and conducting them. In order to help place the interviews in context, in the opening chapter we provide a *brief* overview of the major developments which have taken place in modern macroeconomics since the Great Depression. The chapter, which assumes familiarity with a level of analysis on par with that contained in an intermediate undergraduate macroeconomics textbook, contains extensive references enabling the interested reader to pursue more detailed reading at his or her leisure.

The reader might be interested to learn that the geographical location of the venues for the interviews turned out to be as diverse as many of the views expressed by the economists themselves, ranging from San Francisco, New Orleans, Chicago, Charleston, New Haven, Middlebury, and Cambridge USA, to Durham and Leeds UK. In addition several episodes are imprinted on our memories. Milton Friedman, for example, kindly allowed us to interview him in his study at his apartment in San Francisco – at one point during the course of the interview Milton left the study to answer a telephone call in another room and on his return quite remarkably, without any prompt or reminder, picked up the conversation at the exact point, mid-sentence, where he had been interrupted ten minutes earlier. In contrast we interviewed Bob Clower in the lobby of the Francis Marion Hotel in Charleston at the start of the History of Economics Society annual conference. Throughout the interview a constant stream of conference participants checked-in to the hotel, many passing on their greetings to Bob as they went by. The entire interview was also carried out against a background noise of piano music. Nevertheless, mesmerized by the charm and wit of Bob, who turned out to be capable of holding several conversations simultaneously, our interview was successfully completed, though not without a great deal of laughter at various points. Our visit to Yale and Harvard in February 1993 to interview James Tobin and Greg Mankiw also led to a memorable experience of a different kind in that it brought home to us just how cold winters in New England USA can be compared to those we experience in the North of England UK. Driving back from Boston to New York on ice-covered roads at night, in a blinding snowstorm, is one experience that we shall never forget. A more enjoyable experience was the series of seminars we conducted with David Colander's students at his house following our interview with David at Middlebury College. The combination of stimulating discussion combined with plentiful supplies of beer and pizza in front of an open log fire are warmly remembered. Finally we had our usual share of mislaid airport luggage which resulted in Brian having no alternative attire other than a polo neck sweater and denim jeans for our interview with Robert Lucas.

We would like to express our thanks to all the interviewees for the time and care they took in answering our questions and in particular Mark Blaug. With his extensive knowledge of the history of economic thought and interest in methodology we asked Mark to read all the interviews we had conducted and be interviewed on the interviews. His answers to our questions provide a far more illuminating interpretation of the views expressed than we could have provided.

Brian Snowdon and Howard R. Vane

Interpreting Modern Macroeconomics: From Tobin to Romer

Economic knowledge is historically determined ... what we know today about the economic system is not something we discovered this morning but is the sum of all our insights, discoveries and false starts in the past. Without Pigou there would be no Keynes; without Keynes no Friedman; without Friedman no Lucas; without Lucas no ... (Blaug, 1991a)

Macroeconomics is an applied economic science concerned with the analysis of economy-wide phenomena such as unemployment, inflation and economic growth. These are fundamental issues which have profound implications for human welfare. It is difficult to overstate just how important satisfactory macroeconomic performance is for the well-being of the citizens of any country. While the general public are constantly made aware of such macro issues through their everyday experience, as well as the constant attention paid to these issues by both the media and politicians, it is difficult for the non-economist to make sense of what are extremely complex problems. Nevertheless if economists can design a policy framework capable of improving macroeconomic performance, the benefits to humanity, in the form of improvements in living standards, are potentially enormous. Conversely, large policy errors, such as those made during the early 1930s, can have disastrous economic, social and political consequences. The economic failure experienced in Europe during the inter-war period contributed greatly to the political extremism characterizing that era which ultimately led to war in 1939. There seems little doubt that the course of world history would have been very different if somehow Germany could have avoided the hyperinflation of the early 1920s and mass unemployment of the early 1930s (De Long, 1999).

The design of coherent economic policies, aimed at achieving an acceptable rate of economic growth and reduced aggregate instability, depends on the availability of internally consistent theoretical models of the economy which can explain satisfactorily the behaviour of the main macro variables and are not rejected by the available empirical evidence. Such models provide an organizing framework for reviewing the development and improvement of institutions and policies capable of generating reasonable macroeconomic stability and growth. The knowledge that macroeconomists have today about

1

the way that economies function is the result of a prolonged research effort often involving intense controversy and an ever-increasing data bank of experience. As Olivier Blanchard (1997a) points out 'Macroeconomics is thus the result of a sustained process of construction, of an interaction between ideas and events. What macroeconomists believe today is the result of an evolutionary process in which they have eliminated those ideas that failed and kept those that appear to explain reality well.' Taking a long-term perspective our current understanding of macroeconomics, at the end of the twentieth century, is nothing more than another chapter in the history of economic thought. However, we should recognize from the outset that the evolution of economists' thinking on macroeconomics has been far from smooth. So much so that many economists are not averse to making frequent use of terminology such as 'revolution' and 'counter-revolution' when discussing the history of macroeconomics (Johnson, 1971; Tobin, 1981, 1996; Blaug, 1997a; Snowdon and Vane, 1996, 1997a).

UNEMPLOYMENT, INFLATION AND GROWTH

In this introductory chapter we seek to highlight the interface between economic ideas and economic policy. During the twentieth century the world has witnessed three outstanding economic events, namely, the 'Great Depression', the 'Great Inflation', and the 'Diffusion of Economic Growth' across the world's economies. In each case the ideas of economists have been profoundly influenced by what has occurred and economic policy has been shaped by the experience illustrating James Tobin's (1996) point that 'it takes big events and their interpretation to discredit ideas and replace them with new ones'.

First, during the 1930s the world economy witnessed the Great Depression which some economists have suggested was *the* defining moment in twentieth-century economic history (Bordo et al., 1998). The 1930s slump in economic activity was perhaps the most unexpected macroeconomic event in US economic history (Gordon, 1998). Although debate still rages over the origins and consequences of this particular cataclysmic event there is general agreement that it constituted the main impetus which inspired John Maynard Keynes (1936) to write *The General Theory of Employment, Interest and Money*. The catastrophic impact of economic failure on unemployment is clearly illustrated for the US and UK economies in Figures 1 and 2. It was this magnitude of economic failure, and the immense waste of scarce resources, which led Keynes (1933a), in a moment of utter frustration, to write 'The decadent international but individualistic capitalism in the hands of which we found ourselves after the First World War is not a success. It is not

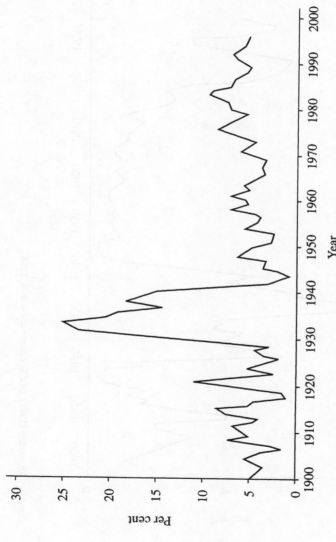

Source: Mankiw (1997a)

Figure 1 Unemployment in the US economy, 1900–1995

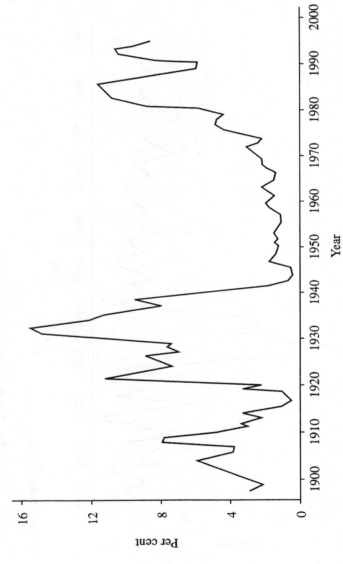

Sources: Broadberry (1991); OECD *Economic Outlook*, 1998

Figure 2   Unemployment in the UK economy, 1900–1995

4

intelligent, it is not beautiful, it is not just, it is not virtuous – and it does not deliver the goods. In short, we dislike it and we are beginning to despise it.' It is also certainly the case that many of the older generation of macroeconomists first became involved with economics because they were students during the 1930s and recognized the relevance that a better understanding of economic forces had for the future political and economic stability of the world. This comes through clearly in the interviews we conducted with Milton Friedman and James Tobin, as well as in several autobiographical essays and interviews published elsewhere with other Nobel Laureates, such as Maurice Allais, Lawrence Klein, Paul Samuelson and Jan Tinbergen (Blaug, 1990; Szenberg, 1992; Breit and Spencer, 1997). William Zakha (1992) lists 13 Laureates, including Franco Modigliani and Robert Solow, who specifically refer to the Great Depression 'as a prime factor that led them to study economics'. In Samuelson's words '1932 was a great time to be born an economist ... (it) was the trough of the Great Depression and from its rotten soil was belatedly begot the new subject that today we call macroeconomics'.

In the United States the trough of the depression, as measured by real GDP, was reached in March 1933 just as Franklin D. Roosevelt began the first term of his Presidency. Lorie Tarshis, one of Keynes's students, recalls that six months earlier, on 10 October 1932, 'Keynes began the first of his eight lectures and in effect announced the beginning of the Keynesian Revolution' (Skidelsky, 1996). To economists such as Tobin, who has described himself as an 'old Keynesian' who 'won't quit', the essential message of the *General Theory* remains valid and he continues to articulate the case for Keynesian-style policies and against the nostrums of the 'classical counter-revolution' in its many forms (Tobin, 1996).

The second important event which had a huge impact on the course of macroeconomic analysis was the experience of what John Taylor (1998a) calls the 'Great Inflation' of the 1970s. While inflation is certainly not a rare phenomenon in economic history it is the case that until the post-1939–45 period previous inflationary episodes tended to be followed by periods of deflation. Taking a long historical view it is striking how in the case of the US and UK economies the years since the end of the Second World War have been the longest continuous period of inflation on record. In addition, the inflation of the post-1945 era has constituted the only major prolonged *peacetime* experience of continuously rising prices in the major industrial economies (of course the Korean, Vietnam and 'Cold' wars all played their part in adding to inflationary pressures during specific periods). These features are evident in Figures 3 and 4 which trace the path of inflation in the US and UK economies over the past century. However, it was the *acceleration* of inflation during the 1970s, combined with stagnating output and rising unemployment, that provided fertile ground for the anti-Keynesian ideas promoted by

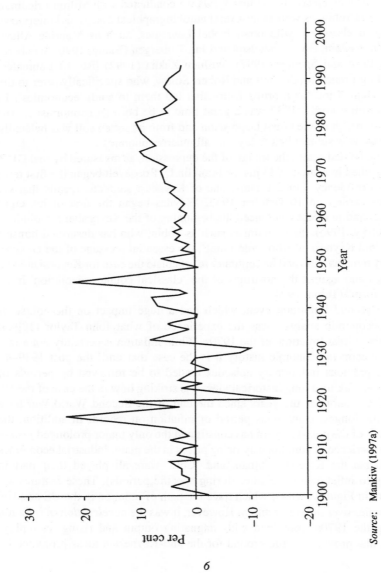

Source: Mankiw (1997a)

Figure 3 Inflation in the US economy, 1900–1995

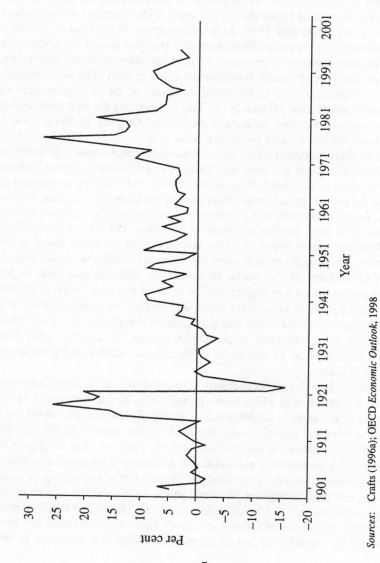

Sources: Crafts (1996a); OECD *Economic Outlook*, 1998

Figure 4 Inflation in the UK economy, 1900–1995

both Milton Friedman and Robert Lucas. Again, in Tobin's (1996) words 'Just as the Great Depression of the 1930s was an environment favourable to the Keynesian revolution the Great Stagflation of the 1970s inclined both economists and the general public to welcome the counter-revolution'. The 'two types of monetarism', monetarism mark I associated with Friedman and monetarism mark II associated with Lucas, began to exert an increasingly powerful influence on the development of macroeconomics from the late 1960s. In the case of Friedman his influence in the macroeconomics sphere following his celebrated 1968 'Role of Monetary Policy' paper has been predominantly on the policy front, whereas Lucas has played *the* pivotal role in redirecting theoretical research. As is made clear from the interviews, either explicitly or implicitly, the influence of one or both of these economists played a significant role in the research efforts of the new generation of macroeconomists after the mid-1970s. This is especially the case with respect to the work of Edward Prescott, John Taylor, Gregory Mankiw, Olivier Blanchard, Alberto Alesina and Paul Romer.

The third phenomenon which has dominated the macroeconomic history of the twentieth century has been the 'Diffusion of Economic Growth' among the economies of the world. Prior to this century and 'over the vast course of history, the process of economic growth was sporadic and inconsistent' (Jones, 1998). In the eighteenth and nineteenth centuries growth had been largely confined to a small number of countries (Pritchett, 1997; Maddison, 1997). The dramatic improvement in living standards that has taken place in the advanced industrial economies since the industrial revolution is now spreading to other parts of the world. However this diffusion has been highly uneven and in some cases negligible. The result of this long period of uneven growth is a pattern of income per capita differentials between the richest and poorest countries of the world that almost defies comprehension. Even small differences in growth rates of per capita income, if sustained over long periods of time, lead to significant differences in relative living standards between nations.

During the last 15 years economists have returned to the issue of economic growth, a research area which in the period 1956–70 was dominated by the influence of the seminal contributions of Robert Solow who pioneered work on the neoclassical growth model. Research on the *theoretical* front in this field 'effectively died' in the 1970–85 period. This was due mainly to its perceived lack of empirical relevance, the diversion of economists' research interests towards business cycle analysis in the wake of the aggregate instability experienced throughout the world in the 1970s and the impact of the rational expectations 'revolution' within academia (Barro and Sala-i-Martin, 1995). The resurgence of interest in growth since the mid-1980s has been stimulated by a number of factors but the availability of a rich array of new data for a large number of countries (for example Summers and Heston, 1991) together with new theoretical insights inspired by the research of Paul Romer (1986; 1987a; 1989; 1990) and Robert Lucas (1988; 1990; 1993) have been of paramount importance. For *some* economists, such as Edward Prescott (1996) the renewed interest in growth stems from their belief that business cycle fluctuations 'are not costly to society' and that it is more important for economists to worry about 'increasing the rate of increase in economywide productivity and not smoothing business fluctuations'. This position had been publicly expressed earlier by Lucas in May 1985 when delivering his Yrjo Jahnsson lectures. There he argued that post-1945 economic stability had been a relatively 'minor problem' especially in comparison 'to the costs of modestly reduced rates of growth' (Lucas, 1987).

In 1984 Arjo Klamer's fascinating conversations with new classical economists and their opponents were published. In the period since Klamer's interviews were conducted (1982/83) macroeconomics has witnessed a real business cycle revolution, a new Keynesian counter-revolution and a renaissance of interest in economic growth. Our interviews with 14 leading economists can be regarded as complementary to Klamer's contribution and help locate our interviewees' opinions on the evolution of macroeconomic ideas and recent developments. In the remainder of this opening chapter we aim to provide a brief overview of the major developments which have taken place in macroeconomics since the Great Depression. Our aim is the modest one of providing the reader with a frame of reference in which to place the conversations with 14 leading economists which follow. Between them, with varying degrees of influence, these economists have made a profound contribution to the ever-changing and ongoing debates witnessed in the field of macroeconomic theory and policy, the way macroeconomics is taught and the history and methodology of macroeconomic research. Above all else their answers to our questions shed light on, and provide interesting insights into, the origins, development and current state of modern macroeconomics.

Before moving on to look at the three outstanding events which have influenced the development of macroeconomics we should note that economics alone among the social sciences is the only field of study to be recognized with the award of a Nobel Prize. Since 1969 the Central Bank of Sweden has awarded a 'Prize in Economic Science in Memory of Alfred Nobel' to be given 'in accordance to the same principles and rules as the original Nobel Prizes' (Lindbeck, 1985). The statutes prescribe that 'the prize shall be awarded annually to a person who has carried out a work in economic science of the eminent significance expressed in the will of Alfred Nobel drawn up on November 27, 1895'. To date the work of five of our interviewees has been recognized with this prestigious award, namely, Milton Friedman, 1976; James Tobin, 1981; Franco Modigliani, 1985; Robert Solow, 1987 and Robert Lucas, 1995. For contemporary surveys of the contributions made by these five economists, for which they received their award, the reader should consult Thygesen (1977), Purvis (1982), Kouri (1986), Prescott (1988) and Svensson (1996).

In many of the conversations which follow we asked a variant of the following question: If Keynes had still been alive in 1969 (aged 86) when the first Nobel Prize was awarded, would he have received the Prize? Since Keynes is widely recognized as the founding father of macroeconomics, and his most famous work, *The General Theory*, was written as a response to the economic events resulting from the Great Depression, we hope the reader will find the answers to that question most illuminating!

THE 'GREAT DEPRESSION'

The story of modern macroeconomics begins with the Great Depression, an event which continues to influence economists' research agendas. Finding an explanation of the worldwide collapse of output in the 1929–33 period still throws out a stimulating intellectual challenge to economists. As we shall see the modern fascination with the macroeconomics of the Great Depression received a massive stimulus following the publication in 1963 of *A Monetary History of the United States* by Milton Friedman and Anna Schwartz and the response to that book by Peter Temin (1976) *Did Monetary Forces Cause the Great Depression?*

The inter-war period (1918–39) remains an epoch fascinating to economists and economic historians alike because of the unprecedented experience of deflation, extreme business cycle volatility and a poor average rate of economic growth among the most developed countries in the world. This era also showed beyond doubt the power that perverse economic policies can have in creating an international disaster for the world economy (Hall and Ferguson, 1998). For nearly 70 years economists have attempted to provide a coherent explanation of how the world economy suffered such a catastrophe. Ben Bernanke (1995) has even gone so far as to argue that 'To understand the Great Depression is the Holy Grail of macroeconomics'. In addition the period is one where the aftermath of the First World War and the 'economic consequences of the peace' (Keynes, 1919) devastated and 'laid waste to the emergent global capitalist system for more than half a century' (Sachs and Warner, 1995). Another significant inter-war development was the rise of state planning, political instability and authoritarianism following the Bolshevik revolution in Russia (October 1917) and the rise to power of fascist governments in Italy (October 1922) and Germany (January 1933).

It is now some 70 years since the Wall Street Crash of 1929 heralded one of the most dramatic and catastrophic periods in the economic history of the industrialized capitalist economies. In a single week from 23–29 October the Dow Jones Industrial Average fell 29.5 per cent with 'vertical' price drops on 'Black Thursday' (24 October) and 'Black Tuesday' (29 October). Controversy still rages over the causes of the crash and its connection with the Great Depression in economic activity which followed. It is important to remember that during the 1920s the US economy, unlike many European economies, was enjoying growing prosperity during the 'roaring twenties' boom. Walt Rostow's (1960) 'age of high mass consumption' seemed to be at hand. The optimism visible in the stock market throughout the mid to late 1920s was reflected in a speech by Herbert Hoover to a Stanford University audience in November 1928. In accepting the Republican Presidential nomination he uttered these 'famous last words':

> We in America today are nearer to the final triumph over poverty than ever before in the history of any land. The poorhouse is vanishing from among us. We have not yet reached the goal, but, given a chance to go forward with the policies of the last eight years, we shall soon with the help of God be in sight of the day when poverty will be banished from this nation. (see Heilbroner, 1989)

In the decade following Hoover's speech the US economy (along with the other major industrial market economies) was to experience the worst economic crisis in its history, to such an extent that many began to wonder if capitalism could survive! Controversy continues relating to whether or not a speculative bubble formed in the US stock market during the latter stages of the rapid economic expansion of the 1922–29 period. In 1954 John Kenneth Galbraith's (1972) classic account of *The Great Crash* was published. Galbraith placed a great deal of emphasis on the 'vested interest of euphoria' creating herd-like investor sentiment (Keynes's 'animal spirits') which he claims took over in the bull market after March 1928. This created what economists now refer to as a 'speculative bubble'. Olivier Blanchard and Mark Watson (1984) find that bubbles are a distinct possibility when the market finds it difficult to measure 'fundamentals' (defined as the present value of expected dividends). The rapid structural and technological changes taking place in the US economy during the 1920s certainly created the possibility that 'fundamentals became difficult to judge' (White, 1990). Hence Blanchard (1997a) argues that 'the source of the crash was almost surely the end of a speculative bubble'. Other economists are not convinced by these arguments claiming that the evidence does not show any substantial overvaluation of shares in terms of price–earnings ratios. They also argue that economic fundamentals in the US at this time were sound (Cecchetti, 1992a; Hamilton, 1986).

Whatever the cause of the stock market boom, when the crash came it was not because anyone anticipated the Great Depression. The market crashed when investors lost confidence and this was almost certainly the consequence

of a change in the monetary regime involving a substantial tightening of
monetary policy, beginning in 1928, combined with the impact of repeated
pronouncements and warnings by the Federal Reserve, and other public
officials (including President Hoover), that the price of stocks was 'unduly
high' (Friedman and Schwartz, 1963; Hamilton, 1987). James Hamilton's
(1987) evidence suggests that 'there should be no doubt that the US adopted
a policy of tight money at the beginning of 1928 ... and the major factor
influencing monetary policy during 1928–29 was the stock market'.

In the US economy the cyclical peak of economic activity occurred in
August 1929 and a decline in GDP had already begun when the stock market
crash ended the 1920s bull market. Given that the crash came on top of an
emerging recession it was inevitable that a severe contraction of output would
take place in the 1929–30 period. But this early part of the contraction was
well within the range of previous business cycle experience. It was in the
second phase of the contraction, generally agreed to be between early 1931
and March 1933, that the depression became 'Great' (Dornbusch et al., 1998).
Therefore, the question which has captured the research interests of economists is: 'How did the severe recession of 1929–30 turn into the Great
Depression of 1931–33?'

Everyone now seems to agree that the catastrophic collapse of output and
employment after 1930 was in large part due to a series of policy errors made
by the fiscal and monetary authorities in a number of industrial economies,
especially the US where the reduction in economic activity was greater than
elsewhere (Aldcroft, 1993). In the US, unemployment, which was 3.2 per
cent in 1929, rose to a peak of 25.2 per cent in 1933, averaged 18 per cent in
the 1930s and never fell below 10 per cent until 1941. Real GDP fell by a
third in the 1929–33 decline and this was accompanied by a 24 per cent fall
in the price level (Gordon, 1998). After March 1933, although output began
to recover rapidly, real GDP did not return to its August 1929 level until
1939! Events in Europe were also disastrous and closely connected to US
developments. Between April 1929 and August 1932 real GDP fell by 20 per
cent in Germany; from March 1930 until July 1932 real GDP fell by 16 per
cent in France; and from July 1929 until August 1932 real GDP fell by 6 per
cent in the UK (Abel et al., 1998). The impact of these developments on
unemployment was equally dramatic.

How can we explain such a massive decline in economic activity? Economists looking to the prevailing conventional wisdom contained in the work of
the classical economists and their followers could not find a coherent plausible answer to the causes of such a deep and prolonged decline in economic
activity. The vision of *laissez-faire* capitalist market economies provided by
the classical economists was one where an efficiently working price mechanism enables the economic system to restore full employment equilibrium,

following a shock, within a reasonable time frame. This self-adjusting vision emerges from a theoretical framework built around Say's Law of markets, the maximizing behaviour of agents armed with perfect information, competitive goods and labour markets and the quantity theory of money. Such a vision was in deep trouble by 1933. As Robert Gordon (1998) argues 'economics had lost its intellectual moorings, and it was time for a new diagnosis'. By 1932 Keynes had decided that the mass unemployment plaguing industrial capitalism was clear evidence of the intellectual bankruptcy of classical economics.

Although it is important to remember that economists prior to Keynes discussed what we now call macroeconomic issues such as business cycles, inflation, unemployment and growth, as we have already noted, the birth of modern macroeconomics as a coherent and systematic approach to aggregate economic phenomena can be traced back to the publication in February 1936 of Keynes's book *The General Theory of Employment, Interest and Money*. In a letter written on 1 January 1935 to a friend, the writer George Bernard Shaw, Keynes speculated that 'I believe myself to be writing a book on economic theory which will largely revolutionise – not, I suppose, at once but in the course of the next ten years – the way the world thinks about economic problems'. That Keynes's bold prediction should be so accurately borne out is both a comment on his own self-confidence and a reflection of the inadequacy of classical economic analysis to provide an acceptable and convincing explanation of the prevailing economic situation in the early 1930s. Keynes recognized that the drastic economic situation confronting the capitalist system in the 1930s threatened its very survival. In his famous essay *The End of Laissez-Faire* Keynes (1926) argued that capitalism was a system that could be made more efficient for attaining economic ends 'than any alternative yet in sight' but that it needed to be purged of its defects. As Don Patinkin (1978) notes, the 1930s was a period of 'fear and darkness as the western world struggled with the greatest depression that it had known. ... There was a definite feeling that by attempting to achieve a scientific understanding of the phenomenon of mass unemployment, one was not only making an intellectual contribution, but was also dealing with a critical problem that endangered the very existence of Western civilisation'. Given the context surrounding its creation it is hardly surprising that the *General Theory* would become a book notable for its polemical tone.

The most plausible explanation of the Great Depression is one involving a massive decline in aggregate demand. Both Patinkin (1982) and Tobin (1997) have argued forcefully that Keynes's major discovery in the *General Theory* was the 'Principle of Effective Demand'. According to the classical macroeconomic system a downward shift of aggregate (effective) demand will bring into play corrective forces involving failing prices so that the final impact of a reduction in aggregate demand would be a lower price level with real output and employment quickly returning to their full employment levels. In the classical world self-correcting market forces, operating via the price mechanism, restore equilibrium without the help of government intervention. While the US economy behaved in a way consistent with the classical model during the 1920s, it certainly did not in the decade after 1929. The classical model could not account for either the length or depth of the economic decline experienced by the major economies of the world. Indeed those economists belonging to the Mises–Hayek–Robbins–Schumpeter Austrian school of thought believed that the depression should be allowed to run its course, since such an occurrence was the inevitable result of overinvestment during the artificially created boom. In their view the Great Depression was not a problem which policymakers should concern themselves with and intervention would only make things worse. The choice was between depression now or, if governments intervened, even worse depression in the future (see Chapter 8 of Snowdon et al., 1994).

The current consensus views the behaviour of economies during this period as being consistent with an explanation which focuses on aggregate demand deficiency. However, this deficient aggregate demand explanation is one that a well-trained classical economist, brought up on Say's Law of markets and slogans of equilibrium, would find hard to either understand or accept. For those economists determined to find an explanation for the economic catastrophe which had befallen the economic systems of the Western world the Great Depression had a depressing impact on their enthusiasm for *laissez-faire* capitalism.

To recognize that fluctuations in aggregate demand lie at the heart of the matter is only the starting point. To understand the Great Depression it is necessary to discover what the main sources of aggregate demand failure were, and to what extent the theories developed in the wake of the Keynesian revolution can account for the magnitude of the aggregate demand shock which hit the US economy in the 1929–33 period. Recent research has also returned to the worldwide character of the Great Depression and the nature of the international propagation mechanism.

Intermediate macroeconomics textbooks by Mankiw (1997a), Dornbusch et al. (1998) and Gordon (1998) provide summary tables of the relevant data relating to the precipitous fall in output and employment, together with data on the behaviour of the 'main suspects' in this story. This data shows that over the 1929–33 period there was a decline in both consumption and investment spending, as well as a severe contraction of the nominal money supply and a falling price level. It is also evident that 'fiscal policy not only failed to help but actually further depressed aggregate demand' (Mankiw, 1997a). In addition most economists believe that the adoption by many countries of tariffs aimed at protecting domestic producers from international competition was counterproductive. These 'beggar-thy-neighbour' policies simply added to the dramatic decline in worldwide economic activity and trade (Crucini and Kahn, 1996).

Disputes over the interpretation of these 'facts' led to an extended controversy relating to which of the above components or factors played the most important role in reducing aggregate demand and in which phase of the decline they were particularly important. For the experience of the US economy this debate has tended to focus on three main hypotheses, namely: (i) the non-monetary/non-financial hypothesis; (ii) the monetary hypothesis and (iii) the non-monetary/financial hypothesis (Fackler and Parker, 1994). During recent years economists have begun to stress another important influence, namely, (iv) the constraints and deflationary impulses imposed on economies by the operation of the gold standard (Temin, 1989; Eichengreen, 1992a, 1992b).

The Non-monetary/Non-financial Hypothesis

With reference to the US economy economists who adhere to this hypothesis have emphasized a variety of real forces, such as a collapse of investment and/or consumption expenditure, demographic factors, a decline in housing construction and the adverse impact on trade arising from the Smoot–Hawley Tariff Act of 1930. In 1931 Keynes argued that it was 'the fall in investment ... I find ... and without doubt or reservation whatsoever ... the whole explanation of the present state of affairs'. In terms of the familiar Hicks–Hansen IS–LM analysis this view emphasizes the destabilizing effects on aggregate demand of shifts in the IS curve. Later on, in the *General Theory*, Keynes placed a great deal of emphasis on a decline in investment spending as a cause of slumps 'occasioned by a cyclical change in the marginal efficiency of capital' as the source of the problem. He further developed this theme in his 1937 paper 'The General Theory of Employment', written in response to a number of critical reviews of his new theory. Here Keynes argued that 'given the psychology of the public the level of output and employment as a whole depends on the amount of investment' a variable 'prone to sudden and wild fluctuations'. An important feature of the early years of the 'Keynesian Revolution' was the prominent place it gave to the instability of investment expenditure as a source of business cycle fluctuations. By 1955 Paul Samuelson declared in his best selling textbook that 'All modern economists are agreed that the important factor causing income and employment to fluctuate is investment'.

More recently, Temin (1976) has challenged the monetary interpretation of the Great Depression provided by Friedman and Schwartz (1963) and put forward an alternative thesis that the main disturbing factor was a shift of the IS curve caused by an *autonomous* decline in consumption. Temin claims that the observed decline in the nominal money supply was an *endogenous* response to declining economic activity. Subsequent attempts to account for the decline in consumption, relying on wealth or liquidity effects, or pessimistic consumer expectations, proved unsatisfactory. In a re-examination of this theme Christina Romer (1990) has argued that the Great Crash depressed consumption by creating uncertainty. This hypothesis suggests that the 1929 crash and subsequent gyrations of stock prices in 1930 made people 'nervous about the future of the economy'. In particular consumers became very uncertain about their future income. This uncertainty 'caused consumers to postpone purchases of irreversible durable goods'. In effect consumers began to use the stock market as a predictor of the future likely path of real variables. Temin also argues that the monetary explanation of the downturn is implausible given that there is no evidence of monetary stringency as measured by a decline in the *real* money supply or high nominal interest rates.

The Monetary Hypothesis

In their monumental and highly influential study, *A Monetary History of the United States, 1867–1960*, Friedman and Schwartz (1963) argue that *exogenous* contractions of the money supply were largely responsible for the Great Depression. Friedman and Schwartz provide a persuasive and well-documented argument that the huge decline in real output, employment and prices during 1929–33 was due to an unprecedented decline in the nominal money supply (Bordo, 1989; Hammond, 1996; Steindl, 1996). *A Monetary History* changed economists' views of the causes of the slump which until 1963 had been dominated by the Keynesian interpretation which emphasized a collapse of investment spending and business confidence. That in turn led to a steep decline in real economic activity via the familiar multiplier–accelerator mechanism. The 'analytical core' of the Friedman and Schwartz interpretation of events consists of a careful historical documentation of monetary data for the 1929–33 period, a narrative tracing the policy decisions of the Federal Reserve, and an explanation of the monetary mechanisms which linked the Fed's actions to the monetary aggregates (Steindl, 1996). A key element of the Friedman and Schwartz thesis is that the Fed could have prevented the collapse of the quantity of money which would have mitigated and shortened the Great Depression (Schwartz, 1981; Bordo et al., 1995). In effect the 1929–30 recession was transformed into the Great Depression due to monetary mismanagement by the Federal Reserve and 'the story of the powerless Central Bank acting valiantly but in vain in order to contain the economic storm has been effectively exposed as a myth' (Brunner, 1981). Rather than demonstrating the weakness of monetary policy, which was the orthodox Keynesian view at that time, Friedman and Schwartz argue that this whole episode is 'a tragic testimonial to the importance of monetary forces'. The successive waves of bank failures, beginning in October 1930 and ending in March 1933 led to the closure of one third of US banks. This caused a substantial reduction in the money supply which the Fed failed to offset and Friedman and Schwartz treat these banking crises as *exogenous* shocks to the money supply.

Many economists are now prepared to accept the main thrust of this argument for what happened in the 1931–33 period, in particular the view that the Fed could have done much more to prevent the monetary collapse which had such a drastic impact on the banking and financial system. A detailed investigation by Robert Gordon and James Wilcox (1981) suggests that monetary factors did not play a major role in the first phase of the downswing in 1929–31 but were more important in the 1931–33 period. This eclectic position suggests that both the extreme monetarist and non-monetarist interpretations are unsatisfactory. More recent research has also drawn attention to the constraints imposed on the Fed's action by adherence to the Gold Standard. This limited the Fed's ability to react to adverse shocks originating elsewhere in the economy (Eichengreen, 1992a, 1992b; Calomiris and Hanes, 1995).

An alternative monetary hypothesis, revived and given more emphasis in recent years, concentrates on the destabilizing effects of deflation. If a contraction of the money supply causes an *unanticipated* fall in prices this will lead to a redistribution of wealth between debtors and creditors as the real burden of nominal debt increases. Since the former group can be expected to have a higher propensity to spend, the *debt–deflation theory* predicts that an unanticipated deflation of the price level will depress spending and cause a contractionary shift of the IS curve (Fisher, 1933; Hamilton, 1992). Debtors will also find it increasingly difficult to service their outstanding debts because of the high *ex post* interest rates. Robert Dimand (1995) has described Irving Fisher's theory as his 'one potentially great contribution to macroeconomic theory in the 1930s'. Keynes (1931, 1936) also clearly recognized that price deflation could be very destabilizing and the impact of falling prices on debt was one of many mechanisms he discussed in relation to this. In his view a severe decline in money values threatens the whole financial framework and with it the viability of the whole economic system.

An alternative hypothesis examines the consequences of an *anticipated* deflation (Cecchetti, 1992b). In this case the *ex ante* real interest rate (r) will increase for any given nominal interest rate (i) since, from the Fisher equation, $r = i - \dot{P}^e$ (where $\dot{P}^e$ = the expected rate of inflation/deflation). The basic equations of the IS–LM model can now be written as (1) and (2) below.

$$IS \qquad Y = C(Y - T) + I(i - \dot{P}^e) + G \qquad (1)$$
$$LM \quad M/P = L(i, Y) \qquad\qquad\qquad\qquad (2)$$

Where Y = GDP, C = consumption, I = investment, G = government expenditure, T = taxes, M/P = supply of real money balances, $L(i, Y)$ = money demand.

Since $\dot{P}^e$ enters as a variable in the IS equation the increase in the *ex ante* real interest rate, caused by anticipations of deflation will shift the IS curve down as planned investment expenditures are curtailed. This assumes the IS–LM diagram is drawn with the nominal interest rate on the vertical axis (Mankiw, 1997a). If the diagram is drawn with the real rate of interest on the vertical axis the LM curve will shift up (Blanchard, 1997a). In effect the changes which take place in the expected rate of deflation break the link between shifts in the nominal and real interest rate. Thus it is possible to argue that low nominal interest rates are not a reliable indicator that monetary policy was 'loose'. Even if nominal interest rates are low, if deflation is anticipated real rates will be high. This is one of the dilemmas facing Japanese monetary policy in the recession of 1998.

Following the Friedman and Schwartz v Temin debate and subsequent contributions (for example Brunner, 1981; Hamilton, 1987) a consensus view has emerged that although non-monetary forces played an important role, especially in the first phase of the slump, monetary forces were paramount in the later stages. Christina Romer (1993) has also provided convincing evidence that the 'spectacular' recovery of output in the US economy after 1933 was induced by monetary expansion. This monetary expansion was caused by the combined effects of devaluation and a 'tremendous' inflow of gold, beginning in 1933, which reflected the deteriorating political situation in Europe. These developments led to a conventional aggregate demand stimulus via lower real interest rates and their consequent impact on investment and consumer durables expenditures, as well as a recovery in the construction sector of the US economy (Romer's calculations show that real interest rates were negative in the period 1933–37). Romer's simulations also suggest that fiscal policy was 'of little consequence' in the recovery and she also rejects any notion that 'the recovery from the slump was due to the self-corrective powers of the economy'. The economic recovery in the US from the Great Depression was quite dramatic with industrial production growing at an average annual rate of 13.5 per cent between March 1933 and June 1942. Although that recovery can be understood as a monetary phenomenon, Frank Steindl (1998) has recently shown that no economist in the 1930s used the quantity theory of money to explain the course of events. Since Keynesian economics did not become 'normal science' until much later and the quantity theory remained the dominant macroeconomic paradigm during the 1930s, it remains somewhat of a puzzle as to why Chicagoans at the time did not offer a monetary interpretation of the unfolding rapid recovery as well as the sharp 1937–38 depression.

With respect to the evolution of macroeconomic analysis the monetary explanation of the Great Depression has played a crucial role in persuading many economists that the Keynesian neglect of monetary forces was in need of considerable reappraisal. In Lucas's (1994b) 30-year review of the impact of *A Monetary History* he recalls that 'the book played an important – perhaps even decisive – role in the 1960s debates over stabilization policy between Keynesians and monetarists'.

The Non-monetary/Financial Hypothesis

During the 1930–33 period the financial system in the US was thrown into chaos with high default rates, bankruptcies and waves of bank failures being important features. While the research of Friedman and Schwartz provides an important monetary explanation of how financial factors can influence the path of real variables, Bernanke (1983) has argued that the reductions in the money supply identified by Friedman and Schwartz are quantitatively insufficient to explain the magnitude of the decline in output experienced during the early 1930s. The 'new view' developed by Bernanke suggests that the deflation of the 1929–33 period was *unanticipated* and this led to a debt–deflation problem which in turn caused a breakdown of the financial intermediation process thereby deepening the depression. By drawing on the emergent literature on imperfect capital markets Bernanke bases his argument on a theoretical model of credit allocation under conditions of asymmetric information. This approach shows how severe turmoil in financial markets reduces the ability of financial sector institutions to efficiently channel funds from savers to borrowers, raising the real cost of intermediation and thereby reducing investment. Bernanke's research suggests that the shock inflicted on the US financial technology deepened and lengthened the depression (Calomiris, 1993).

The 'Structurally Flawed' Gold Standard Hypothesis

Although much progress has been made on the sources of aggregate demand failure in the US, there still remains the *'aggregate demand puzzle'*, namely, why did strong declines in nominal aggregate demand take place, nearly simultaneously, in so many countries in the early 1930s? In recent years a new consensus has emerged concerning this question which emphasizes a 'structurally flawed and poorly managed international gold standard' (Bernanke and Carey, 1996). Although C. Romer (1992, 1993) has argued that demand shocks internal to the US were the main reason for both the US and world slump, a satisfactory analysis of the Great Depression needs to explain why this catastrophe was a worldwide phenomenon and how deflationary forces were transmitted from one country to another. The new consensus has grown from research conducted since 1980 (Choudri and Kochin, 1980; Temin, 1989, 1993; Eichengreen, 1992a, 1992b). During the period 1870–1914 the gold standard operated relatively successfully as a pegged exchange rate system. This system was suspended when the First World War broke out and then restored on much shakier foundations during the 1920s. The gold standard story of the Great Depression begins by noting that several countries, most importantly the US, shifted to contractionary monetary policies in the late 1920s. The deflationary impact of these policies was transmitted worldwide by a combination of policy errors and the operation of a technically flawed gold standard which by 1929 had been re-established by most of the major market economies. The only way to escape the deflationary forces unleashed on the world in the late 1920s was to leave the gold standard/fixed exchange rate system so that monetary and exchange rate policy could be directed towards the needs of the domestic economy. Ehsan Choudri and Levis Kochin (1980) found that countries which left the gold standard in 1931 suffered less contraction of output than those who remained tied to the system. Barry Eichengreen and Jeffrey Sachs (1985) have shown how devaluations in the early 1930s allowed countries to pursue expansionary monetary policies. This was certainly the case in the US. The initial choice of deflation rather than devaluation was the most important factor in the international transmission of the depression and this whole experience provides some important lessons for policymakers in the evolving European Monetary Union (Temin, 1993). There is overwhelming evidence that the slavish adherence to the rules imposed by the Gold Standard had drastic economic consequences in the 1930s.

During the last 25 years economists' research, conducted in the wake of Friedman and Schwartz's contribution, has clarified many issues relating to the causes of the Great Depression. Perhaps the most important lesson from this research is that a whole set of factors in combination produced the 1929–33 debacle, confirming Gottfried Haberler's (1958) view that 'explanations which run in terms of one single cause have been more and more discredited and should be regarded with suspicion'. Obstfeld and Rogoff (1996) argue that there is 'still no fully satisfactory explanation of the Great Depression's remarkable duration'. Whatever the causes of the 1929–33 catastrophe Michael Bordo, Claudia Goldin and Eugene White (1998) present a persuasive case that the Great Depression was the 'defining moment', a watershed in US economic history, in terms of the relationship between the government and private sector. The Great Depression generated a 'flood' of 'New Deal' legislation relating to agriculture, industry, finance and banking, and the labour market. It also changed in many important ways the conduct of macroeconomic policy.

KEYNES AND KEYNESIANISM

In a paper celebrating the fiftieth anniversary of the publication of Keynes's *General Theory* Robert Solow (1986) commented that:

> Like it or not, it has certainly been the most influential work of macroeconomics of the 20th century, and Keynes the most important economist. The *General Theory* was more than the original statement of Keynesian economics. In that book Keynes also invented what we now call Macroeconomics. So, in a significant sense the story of macroeconomics begins with the *General Theory*.

Even Pigou, who came in for a huge amount of criticism from Keynes (much of it unjustified) was prepared to backtrack on the position taken in his original review of the *General Theory* (Pigou, 1936). In his 1949 Marshall lectures Pigou admitted that he had 'failed to grasp its significance and did not assign to Keynes all the credit due for it'. Pigou went on to argue that nobody before Keynes 'had brought all the relevant factors, real and monetary at once, together in a formal scheme, through which their interplay could be coherently investigated' (see Solow, 1986). Only a classic work is the subject of frequent reappraisal and the topic of symposia after 25 years, 50 years and so on. The enormous influence of Keynes is also reflected in the titles of many books such as *The Age of Keynes* (Lekachman, 1969); *Keynes and After* (Stewart, 1986); *Great Economists Before Keynes* (Blaug, 1997b) and *Great Economists Since Keynes* (Blaug, 1998). Therefore, as we have argued elsewhere (Snowdon et al., 1994), we feel that in any broad discussion of the evolution of macroeconomic thought it is important to remember that the work of Keynes remains the main reference point, *either positive or negative*, for all that has subsequently followed. All the schools of thought in macroeconomics define themselves in relation to the ideas originally put forward by Keynes in the *General Theory*, 'either as a development of some version of his thought or as a restoration of some version of pre-Keynesian thought' (Vercelli, 1991). The unifying theme in the evolution of macroeconomics has been an ever-evolving classical/Keynesian debate (Gerrard, 1996). Although economists are still divided about the ideas of Keynes, the fundamental issue which led to the Keynes v Classics debate is still *the* central question for those macroeconomists who endeavour to understand aggregate instability, that is, does a capitalist market economy lead to the full utilization of its scarce resources and, when subjected to shocks, will it return to an equilibrium 'full employment' state within an acceptable time frame without help from the visible hand of government intervention? (Tobin, 1996, 1997). Those wedded to the classical tradition answer yes, those who accept the central message of the *General Theory* say no. As such Keynes will always remain either a villain or a hero (Blaug, 1994a).

As we have already noted, in January 1935 Keynes made a bold prediction to George Bernard Shaw about the ideas contained in his new book. He believed that his new ideas would 'largely revolutionise' the way the world thinks about economic matters 'in the course of the next ten years'. Mark Blaug (1992) reminds us that this prediction was remarkable for its accuracy because the revolution in economic thought created by the *General Theory* 'was a sea change unparalleled in the history of economic thought: never before had a new research programme conquered the economics profession so quickly and so completely'. By writing the *General Theory*, Keynes converted the 'vast majority of economists throughout the western world ... to the Keynesian way of thinking within the space of about a decade' (Blaug, 1994a). Herbert Stein (1986) recalls that by the late 1930s the 'Washington economics industry' was Keynesian in a 'loose, eclectic, pragmatic sense'. How can we account for the speed of this success?

Harry Johnson (1971) in his Richard T. Ely Lecture to the American Economic Association meeting in 1970 attempted to provide reasons for the rapid propagation of the Keynesian revolution. According to Johnson the two factors which explain the speed with which the *General Theory* swept the field in the immediate period after 1936 relate to (i) the '*objective social situation*', and (ii) '*the scientific characteristics of the new theory*'. The favourable objective social situation was the existence of an established orthodoxy which was 'clearly inconsistent with the most salient facts of reality', that is, the Great Depression and the persistent unemployment associated with it. The scientific characteristics of Keynes's ideas relate to certain features of his new theory which gave it mass appeal, especially among the new generation of economists (Moggridge, 1995). These features relate mainly to the internal dynamics within academia which provide a favourable climate for the acceptance of new ideas among professional economists, for example it is very helpful for the career development of young economists if a new idea is 'article laden' (Blinder, 1988a; Colander, 1988; Snowdon and Vane, 1996).

An additional factor, accounting for the speed with which Keynesian ideas spread, has been provided by David Colander and Harry Landreth (1996). It is generally accepted that there were two aspects to the Keynesian revolution; first, a revolution in economic theory and second, a revolution in economic policy. However, Colander and Landreth also identify a third feature of the Keynesian revolution which helped to contribute to the rapid spread of

Keynesian ideas. This third influence was the pedagogical or textbook revolution. An important reason for the rapid success of the Keynesian revolution was that Keynesian thinking was reducible to simple textbook models. Crucial to this 'pedagogical revolution' at the introductory level was the contribution made by Samuelson with the publication of the first edition of his classic textbook in 1948 (Pearce and Hoover, 1995). It was here that Samuelson utilized the famous 45 degree cross diagram and, until recently, the majority of introductory textbooks continued to present the Samuelson model (Mankiw, 1997b, does not use this model). At the intermediate level the Hicks–Hansen IS–LM model did not play an important role in the transmission of Keynesian ideas to students until much later, even though it lay at the heart of professional discussion. Therefore, if a body of ideas or vision can be conveyed to students at beginning and intermediate levels, its final influence will be greatly enhanced. As Colander (1988) argues, 'only theories which are teachable will be integrated into the textbooks'. However, an important feature of the Keynesian pedagogical revolution was the typical separation within textbooks of neoclassical microeconomic analysis from Keynesian macroeconomics. This cohabitation was to prove an uneasy arrangement in the long run.

The elimination of mass unemployment during the Second World War had a profound influence on the spread and influence of Keynesian ideas concerning the responsibility of governments for maintaining full employment. In the UK, William Beveridge's *Full Employment in a Free Society* was published in 1944 and in the same year the government committed itself to the maintenance of a 'high and stable level of employment' in a White Paper on *Employment Policy*. At the same time, in the US, the Employment Act of 1946 dedicated the Federal Government to the pursuit of 'maximum employment, production and purchasing power' (Tobin, 1987). Similar commitments to full employment as a priority objective emerged in Australia, Belgium, Canada, France, the Netherlands, New Zealand and Norway (Beaud and Dostaler, 1995). With varying degrees of enthusiasm virtually all advanced democratic capitalist economies embraced strategies of demand management after 1945 (Tobin, 1987). Bradford De Long (1996) argues that the important effect of the 1946 Employment Act was that it represented a signal that 'henceforth an administration that failed to achieve acceptable macroeconomic performance was a failed administration'. These commitments in the US, UK and elsewhere were, therefore, of great symbolic significance even if they lacked specific discussion of how such objectives were to be attained in practice.

One of the most important results of the Employment Act in the US was the establishment of the Council of Economic Advisers (CEA) to act as an independent professional body within the Executive Office of the President.

The CEA consists of a small team of three economists, of whom one acts as Chairman. In addition the CEA is supported by a professional staff of about ten senior staff economists (generally Professors on leave from University), ten junior staff economists (usually advanced graduate students), and four permanent economic statisticians (Feldstein, 1992). The main task of the CEA is to supply the President with advice relating to economic matters which reflect the mainstream views of the profession (Schultze, 1996). According to Martin Feldstein (1997a) 'the worldview of the leading economic thinkers when the CEA was created in 1946 can be summarized as "macroeconomic instability and microeconomic insensitivity" ... Today, for most economists, that worldview has been reversed.' Herbert Stein (1996) suggests that the view of CEA members towards Keynes largely reflects their age 'Those born before 1915 were not Keynesians. Those born between 1915 and 1940 were Keynesians or had strong leanings in that direction. For most of those born after 1940, Keynesianism was a minor and unreliable tool.' Given that the two most recent Chairmen of the CEA, Joseph Stiglitz and Janet Yellen, are prominent members of the new Keynesian school, Stein's view is perhaps exaggerated! (see Table 1). Undoubtedly, the Heller–Tobin–Gordon CEA has been the most Keynesian, with Walter Heller being credited with coining the term 'fine tuning' (Stein, 1996). Since the 1970s economists have undoubtedly become more sceptical about the potential stabilizing role of the fine-tuning approach. Feldstein (1997a), CEA Chairman 1982–84, believes that demand management is now viewed with 'suspicion' and activist fiscal policy is more likely to be 'destabilizing than stabilizing'. Given this change in 'worldview' the 'responsibility for stabilization policy has therefore effectively shifted to the Federal Reserve'. Solow (1997a), a former CEA staff member under Heller, admits that most of the opportunities for the CEA to do good are in the microeconomic rather than the macroeconomic sphere. In his review of the consequences of the 1946 Employment Act De Long (1996) argues that the contribution of discretionary fiscal policy over the postwar period has been limited with the clear exception of the Kennedy–Johnson tax cut in 1964. The stabilizing role of fiscal policy has mainly come from the impact of automatic stabilizers. De Long concludes that the US 'lacks the knowledge to design and the institutional capacity to execute a countercyclical discretionary fiscal policy in a response to any macroeconomic cycle shorter than the Great Depression itself'.

From the end of the Second World War until 1973 the industrial market economies, on average, enjoyed a 'golden age' of growth combined with low inflation and unemployment (Maddison, 1991, 1997). Although countercyclical fiscal policy became an acceptable instrument of stabilization policy in the UK throughout this 'golden age', in the US it was not until the 1960s, under the Kennedy–Johnson administrations, that 'avowedly Keynesian policies

Table 1   Council of Economic Advisers

Chairs of the Council of Economic Advisers		
Name	Oath of Office date	Separation date
Edwin G. Nourse	9 August 1946	1 November 1949
Leon H. Keyserling	10 May 1950	20 January 1953
Arthur F. Burns	19 March 1953	1 December 1956
Raymond J. Saulnier	3 December 1956	20 January 1961
Walter W. Heller	29 January 1961	15 November 1964
Gardner Ackley	16 November 1964	15 February 1968
Arthur M. Okun	15 February 1968	20 January 1969
Paul W. McCracken	4 February 1969	31 December 1971
Herbert Stein	1 January 1972	31 August 1974
Alan Greenspan	4 September 1974	20 January 1977
Charles L. Schultze	22 January 1977	20 January 1981
Murray L. Weidenbaum	27 February 1981	25 August 1982
Martin Feldstein	14 October 1982	10 July 1984
Beryl W. Sprinkel	18 April 1985	20 January 1989
Michael J. Boskin	2 February 1989	12 January 1993
Laura D'Andrea Tyson	5 February 1993	22 April 1995
Joseph E. Stiglitz	28 June 1995	10 February 1997
Janet L. Yellen	18 February 1997	

Source: Council of Economic Advisers Homepage

were followed' (Dornbusch et al., 1998). These policies were given the name *'New Economics'* and emphasized the activist use of fiscal policy to expand the US economy in order to achieve the administration's explicitly declared 4 per cent unemployment target. It was during this era that the Kennedy administration's economic advisers, including James Tobin and Robert Solow, made increasing use of concepts such as 'potential output', 'GNP gap' and the 'full employment budget surplus'. It was also during this period that Arthur Okun (1962) introduced his 'Law' showing how variations in GNP have a close inverse relation with variations in unemployment. When the Kennedy–Johnson administration implemented the famous 1963–64 tax cut (which Stein, 1996, calls the 'Oscar on the shelf of the CEA') even though the actual budget was in deficit, it was evident that the New Economics had won through. Stein (1969, 1994) went on to label the Kennedy–Johnson policy package a 'fiscal revolution'. A portrait of Keynes even appeared on the front cover of *Time* magazine on the last day of 1965!

The expansion of the US economy during the 1960s remains (to date) the longest on record and Keynesian-style policies were given the credit for this. However, with the US becoming increasingly involved in Vietnam after 1965 at a time when President Johnson was launching his 'Great Society-War on Poverty' programmes, the strain on the economy of trying to have more guns and butter at a time when the economy was fully employed led inevitably to increasing inflationary pressure. Although Johnson's Keynesian advisers recommended tax increases to contain these pressures they were not forthcoming until 1968–69 by which time it was too late. Although unemployment fell to 3.4 per cent in 1969 inflation climbed to 5.4 per cent (see Figures 1 and 3). The US economy was about to experience the 'Great Inflation'.

In the decade or so following the publication of the *General Theory* economists engaged in the Keynes v Classics debate sought to clarify the arguments of Keynes and the counter-arguments of his critics (Snowdon et al., 1994). A major theme of Modigliani's (1944) paper was to show that, except for the case of extreme wage rigidity, Keynes's system did allow for a restoration of full employment equilibrium via price flexibility, apart from some special limiting cases. Furthermore, Modigliani argued that monetary policy should take on the main role as a stabilizing device, not fiscal policy (Breit and Spencer, 1997). By the mid-1950s Samuelson (1955) declared a truce. He argued that 90 per cent of American economists had ceased to be anti- or pro-Keynesian but were now committed to a 'neoclassical synthesis' where it was generally accepted that neoclassical microeconomics and Keynesian macroeconomics could sit alongside each other. The classical/neoclassical model remained relevant for microeconomic issues and the long-run analysis of growth, but Keynesian macroeconomics provided the most useful framework for analysing short-run aggregate phenomena. This historical compromise remained the dominant paradigm in economics until the 1970s.

Reflecting on the theoretical developments of this period Modigliani (1986) has identified the 'Keynesian system' as resting on four building blocs: the consumption function; the investment function; the demand for and supply of money; and the mechanisms for determining the movement of prices and wages. Major contributions to our understanding of these building blocs were made in the 1940s and 1950s including those by Modigliani (1944), Modigliani and Brumberg (1954), Patinkin (1956), and Tobin (1958). By the early 1960s, following the publication of Phillips's (1958) influential article, the mainstream macroeconomic model was one which could be described as a Hicks (1937)–Hansen (1949) IS–LM model, augmented by a Phillips curve relationship. The MPS–FMP macroeconometric model constructed by Modigliani and his associates in the 1960s is probably the best practical example of the consensus position during this era. Meanwhile Solow (1956, 1957) provided the theoretical tools for analysing long-run growth by developing the neo-classical growth model (Beaud and Dostaler, 1995; Blaug, 1998).

What are the central propositions of Keynesian economics? Given the varieties of Keynesianism on offer, due in large part to different interpretations of the *General Theory* and the amendments to and elaboration of Keynes's contribution in the postwar period, this is not an easy question to answer. Allan Meltzer (1988) delineates six possible interpretations of the *General Theory* each of which tends to focus on one or two chapters of that book, for example Modigliani, Hicks and Patinkin focus on chapter 19 as having particular significance while post Keynesians such as Paul Davidson tend to concentrate on chapters 12 and 17 (see Blaug, 1994a). In his book *The Economics of Control*, Lerner (1944) set out his interpretation of Keynesianism in terms of the principles of *'functional finance'*. According to Lerner budget deficits/surpluses should be judged only with reference to their impact on macroeconomic stability. How far that accorded with Keynes's own views is debatable (Colander, 1984; Meltzer, 1988). However, Tobin, who is generally recognized as the most vigorous defender of orthodox Keynesian ideas in the profession, has on numerous occasions set out what he considers to be the central propositions of 'old' neoclassical synthesis-style Keynesianism (Tobin, 1977, 1987, 1993, 1996). These propositions are as follows:-

First proposition: Modern industrial capitalist economies are subject to an endemic flaw in that they are prone to costly recessions, sometimes severe, which are primarily caused by a deficiency of aggregate (effective) demand. Recessions should be viewed as undesirable departures from full employment equilibrium and are generally the result of demand shocks.

Second proposition: Keynesians believe that an economy can be in either of two regimes. In the Keynesian regime aggregate economic activity is *demand constrained*. In this regime we observe what Robert Clower (1994) has referred to as 'Hansen's Law' where demand creates its own supply. In the classical regime output is *supply constrained* and in this situation supply creates its own demand (Say's Law). The 'old' Keynesian view is that the economy can be in either regime at different points in time, whereas new classical economists such as Lucas and Prescott model the economy as if it were always in a supply-constrained regime. In the Keynesian demand-constrained regime employment and output will respond positively to additional real demand from whatever source.

Third proposition: Unemployment of labour is a major feature of the Keynesian regime and a major part of that unemployment is *involuntary* in that it consists of people without work who are prepared to work at wages that employed workers of comparable skills are currently earning (Solow, 1980; Blinder, 1988b). This contrasts sharply with the view of many monetarist, new classical and real business cycle economists who view unemployment as a voluntary phenomenon (Lucas, 1978a).

Fourth proposition: 'A market economy is subject to fluctuations in aggregate output, unemployment and prices, which *need* to be corrected, *can* be corrected, and therefore *should* be corrected' (Modigliani, 1986). The *discretionary* and coordinated use of *both* fiscal and monetary policies have an important role to play in stabilizing the economy. These macroeconomic instruments should be dedicated to real economic goals such as real output and employment. By the mid-1960s the early 'hydraulic' Keynesian emphasis on fiscal policy had been considerably modified among Keynesian thinkers, particularly Modigliani and Tobin in the US. However, fiscal policy remained the preferred instrument of demand management among the majority of orthodox Keynesians.

Fifth proposition: In modern industrial economies prices and wages are not perfectly flexible and therefore changes in aggregate demand, anticipated or unanticipated, will have their greatest impact in the short run on real output and employment rather than on nominal variables. Given nominal price rigidities the short-run aggregate supply curve has a positive slope, at least until the economy reaches the supply-constrained full employment equilibrium.

Sixth proposition: Business cycles represent fluctuations in output which are undesirable deviations below the full employment equilibrium trend path of output. Business cycles are not symmetrical fluctuations around the trend.

Seventh proposition: The policy makers who control fiscal and monetary policy face a non-linear trade-off between inflation and unemployment. Initially, in the 1960s, many Keynesians thought that this trade-off relationship was relatively stable.

Eighth proposition: More controversial and less unanimous, some Keynesians, including Tobin, have on occasions supported the temporary use of incomes policies ('Guideposts') as an additional policy instrument necessary to obtain the simultaneous achievement of full employment and price stability (Solow, 1966; Tobin, 1977). The enthusiasm for such policies has always been much greater among European Keynesians than their US counterparts, especially in the 1960s and 1970s.

Ninth proposition: Keynesian macroeconomics is concerned with the short-run problems of instability and does not pretend to apply to the long-run issues of growth and development.

Although these propositions reflect the vision of the mainstream Keynesian camp, and formed the basis of policy advice, during the 1960s there was growing dissatisfaction with the neoclassical synthesis interpretation of Keynes's *General Theory* at the theoretical level. During the period of the neoclassical synthesis the consensus view of Keynes's *theoretical* contribution was that he had failed to demonstrate satisfactorily that market economies, subject to aggregate demand shocks, were not self-equilibrating providing all prices are fully flexible. Keynes's theory was therefore a 'special case' and the classical model the more 'general' theory. Since Keynes's special case happened to be the one relevant for short-run policy it was argued that 'the classics won the intellectual battle; Keynes won the policy war' (Hines, 1971). In the mid-1960s a number of economists reacted against the neoclassical synthesis position which tended to minimize Keynes's status as an economic theorist. In 1965 Clower offerred a very influential re-interpretation of Keynes's contribution to economic theory which was quickly followed by the supporting work of Axel Leijonhufvud (1968). The seminal contributions of these two economists have been variously referred to as the 'non-market clearing paradigm', 'disequilibrium Keynesianism' or 'reconstituted reductionism' (Coddington, 1976). Clower's re-interpretation of the *General Theory* suggests that Keynes's revolt was against the Walrasian general equilibrium tradition within neoclassical economics. In the Walrasian paradigm all markets continuously clear thanks to the work of the fictional auctioneer. Building on the insights of Patinkin (1956) Clower's work emphasizes the dynamic disequilibrium nature of Keynes's work. Clower argues that Keynes's objective was to kill off the auctioneer myth in order to raise the profile of information and intertemporal co-ordination difficulties within real economies. The cumulative declines in output in Keynes's *General Theory* result from massive co-ordination failures as agents respond to wrong (false) price signals. Once the assumption of instantaneously adjusted prices is abandoned there is no longer any guarantee that a decentralized price system will co-ordinate economic activity at full employment. Once again the classical model is shown to be a 'special case' and Keynes's theory the more 'general'. Clower has continued to be highly critical of all the mainstream macro schools for not taking market processes seriously. To do so involves recognizing that markets and monetary institutions are *created* by firms, individuals and governments. In Clower's view in order to really understand market processes economists need to create a 'Post Walrasian Macroeconomics' based on Marshallian rather than Walrasian microfoundations (Clower and Howitt, 1996; Colander, 1996). While Keynes had a profound influence on the development of macroeconomics his anti-formalist approach was swept away by the 'Walrasian formalism' of mainstream theorists in the post-1945 period (Backhouse, 1997a).

In the 1970s several economists inspired by Clower's insights went on and developed neo-Keynesian quantity constrained models (Barro and Grossman, 1976; Malinvaud, 1977). This work served to remind economists that conventional Keynesian models lacked solid microfoundations (Barro, 1979). This was a theme the new classical economists were to exploit throughout the 1970s but in a very different way than that favoured by Clower. During the 1970s the new classical approach prospered while the neo-Keynesian models gradually fell out of favour, not least because high inflation made fix-price models appear 'unrealistic' (Backhouse, 1995).

As we have seen, early Keynesian analysis tended to emphasize fiscal policy, rather than monetary policy, as the means of avoiding recessions and maintaining capitalist economies at high and stable levels of employment. Furthermore, while Keynes had written about the post First World War inflations (see Keynes, 1923), quite understandably given the circumstances at the time of the Great Depression, he paid little attention to inflation in the *General Theory*. The price pathology in the 1930s was deflation (Tobin, 1997). While Keynesian economics swept the field in the 1940s and 1950s the relative neglect of consideration given to microfoundations, the analysis of inflation, the impact of monetary forces on the economy and the importance of the supply-side considerations proved to be the Achilles heel of Keynesian economics which was exposed by the inflationary events which began to unfold in the late 1960s. Enter Milton Friedman and Robert Lucas!

THE 'GREAT INFLATION', FRIEDMAN AND LUCAS: TWO TYPES OF MONETARISM

In the same way that the Great Depression in large part paved the way for a Keynesian revolution in macroeconomic thought the Great Inflation of the 1970s fully opened the door for a monetarist, and subsequent new classical, counter-revolution. Throughout the 'age of Keynes' Friedman's publications on monetary and fiscal policy (1948, 1953c), monetary theory, history and policy (1956, 1982; Friedman and Schwartz, 1963) and the Phillips curve (1968, 1975, 1977) have been highly influential in downgrading economists' faith in the ability of government to achieve desirable goals with respect to output and employment by using interventionist means based on activist demand management policies. In 1968 Karl Brunner christened the ideas associated with Friedman 'monetarist' and thereafter began the decisive period in what Friedman (1970a) and Johnson (1971) refer to as the 'monetarist counter-revolution'. During the 1960s the Phillips (1958) curve had been quickly taken on board as an integral part of the then-dominant Keynesian paradigm, not least because it was interpreted by many orthodox Keynesians as implying a stable long-run trade-off which provided the authorities with a menu of possible inflation–unemployment combinations for policy choice (Leeson, 1994a). Within academia the textbook interpretation of the Phillips curve came to be presented as a proposition that *permanently low levels* of unemployment could be realistically achieved by tolerating *permanently high levels* of inflation. As James Galbraith (1997) points out, in 1968 mainstream American Keynesians were 'committed to Samuelson and Solow's (1960) version of the Phillips curve'. According to Robert Leeson (1994a, 1997a, 1997b) this is not how Bill Phillips himself ever viewed the relationship he had discovered. His 1958 paper was an attempt to locate the level of unemployment consistent with price stability and Richard Lipsey has confirmed that Phillips had 'no tolerance for accepting inflation as the price of reducing unemployment' (Leeson, 1997a). However, up to at least the late 1960s the prevailing Keynesian economic orthodoxy used the Phillips curve to predict the rate of inflation which would result from different target levels of unemployment being attained by activist aggregate demand policies, with particular emphasis on fiscal instruments.

The prevailing Keynesian consensus view was overturned by ideas and events in the 1970s (Mankiw, 1990). A central component of the new thinking involving a critique of the trade-off interpretation of the Phillips curve was first provided by Friedman (1966) in his debate with Solow (1966) over wage and price guideposts but had been outlined much earlier in conversation with Lipsey in 1960 (Leeson, 1997a). However, the argument was developed more fully in his famous 1967 Presidential Address to the American Economic Association on 'The role of monetary policy' (Friedman, 1968). Here Friedman denied the existence of a permanent long-run trade-off between inflation and unemployment and put forward the natural rate of unemployment hypothesis. He argued that the original Phillips curve, which related the rate of change of *money* wages to unemployment, was misspecified and that the Phillips curve should be set in terms of the rate of change of *real* wages. By augmenting the basic Phillips curve with the anticipated or expected rate of inflation as an additional variable determining the rate of change of money wages, a distinction was made between the short-run Phillips curve, which depicts the relationship between inflation and unemployment that exists for a *given* expected rate of inflation, and a vertical long-run Phillips curve at the natural rate of unemployment. Interestingly, it seems that Friedman was profoundly influenced by 'Phillips's adaptive inflationary expectations formula' (Leeson, 1998, 1999). The adaptive expectations equation implicit in Friedman's analysis of the Phillips curve, and used in *Studies in the Quantity Theory of Money* (1956) appears to have been developed by Friedman in conjunction with Phillip Cagan, following a discussion he had with Phillips which took place on a park bench somewhere in London in May 1952 (Leeson, 1994b, 1997a). In fact Friedman was so impressed with Phillips as an economist that he twice (in 1955 and 1960) tried to persuade him to move to the University of Chicago! (Hammond, 1996).

According to Friedman (1968) the natural rate of unemployment is not fixed but is dependent upon 'the actual structural characteristics of the labour and commodity markets, including market imperfections, stochastic variability in demands and supplies, the cost of gathering information about job vacancies and labour availabilities, the costs of mobility and so on'. The notion of a permanent long-run trade-off between inflation and unemployment was also challenged by Edmund Phelps (1967, 1968) who provided a similar analysis to Friedman but from a non-monetarist perspective (Cross, 1995).

Following the Friedman–Phelps papers the natural rate of unemployment has been defined in a large variety of ways. As Richard Rogerson (1997) shows the natural rate has been equated with 'long run = frictional = average = equilibrium = normal = full employment = steady state = lowest sustainable = efficient = Hodrick–Prescott trend = natural'. Such definitional problems have led sceptics such as Solow (1998) to describe the 'doctrine' of the natural rate to be 'as soft as a grape'. When discussing the relationship between unemployment and inflation many economists prefer to use the 'NAIRU' concept (non-accelerating inflation rate of unemployment), a terminology first introduced by Modigliani and Papademos (1975) as 'NIRU' (non-inflationary rate of unemployment). While the majority of economists would probably admit that it is 'hard to think about macroeconomic policy without the concept of NAIRU' (Stiglitz, 1997), others remain unconvinced that the natural rate concept is helpful (Galbraith, 1997; Arestis and Sawyer, 1998; Colander, 1998a).

Notwithstanding these difficulties, Friedman's (1968) paper marked a crucial turning point in helping to change the landscape of modern macroeconomics, so much so that it has been described by one of his most eloquent, effective and longstanding critics as 'very likely the most influential article ever published in an economics journal' (Tobin, 1995). In a similar vein Friedman's paper has been described by Robert Gordon (1981) as probably 'the most influential article written in macroeconomics in the past two decades'; by Paul Krugman (1994a) as 'one of the decisive intellectual achievements of postwar economics' and by both Mark Blaug (1997a) and Robert Skidelsky (1996) as 'easily the most influential paper on macroeconomics published in the post-war era'. Between 1968 and 1997 Friedman's paper has approximately 924 citation counts recorded by the Social Sciences Citation Index and continues to be one of the most heavily cited papers in economics (Snowdon and Vane, 1998). In particular Friedman's insights were to have a dramatic impact on the ongoing debate concerning the role and conduct of stabilization policy. Here we note four implications of his natural rate hypothesis. First, the authorities can reduce unemployment below the natural rate in the short run by engaging in expansionary monetary policy only because the resulting inflation is not fully anticipated. As soon as inflation is fully anticipated it will be incorporated into wage bargains and unemployment will return to the natural rate. Second, any attempt to *maintain* unemployment permanently below the natural rate will result in accelerating inflation. Third, to reduce the natural rate requires supply-side policies to improve the microeconomic structure and functioning of the labour market and industry. Fourth, the natural rate is compatible with any rate of inflation which 'is always and everywhere a monetary phenomenon in the sense that it is and can be produced only by a more rapid increase in the quantity of money than in output' (Friedman, 1970a).

Undoubtedly the influence of Friedman's (1968) paper was greatly enhanced because he anticipated the inflationary events of the 1970s. In particular he predicted the emergence of accelerating inflation as a consequence of the repeated use of expansionary monetary policy geared to an over-optimistic employment target. The failure of inflation to slow down in both the US and UK economies in 1970–71, despite rising unemployment and the subsequent simultaneous existence of high unemployment and high inflation (so-called stagflation) in many countries following the first adverse OPEC oil price (supply) shock in 1973–74, destroyed the idea that there might be a permanent long-run trade-off between inflation and unemployment. Lucas (1981b) regards the Friedman–Phelps model and the verification of its predictions as providing 'as clear cut an experimental distinction as macroeconomics is ever likely to see'. In the philosophy of science literature Imre Lakatos (1978) makes the prediction of novel facts the *sole* criterion by which theories should be judged, a view shared by Friedman (1953a). While Blaug (1991b, 1992) has argued that the principal novel fact of the *General Theory* was the prediction that the size of the instantaneous multiplier is greater than one, he also argues that the prediction of novel facts emanating from Friedman's 1968 paper were enough to make Mark I monetarism a progressive research programme during the 1960s and early 1970s. As Roger Backhouse (1995) notes, 'the novel facts predicted by Phelps and Friedman were dramatically corroborated by the events of the early 1970s'.

In his Nobel Lecture Friedman addressed the issue of the positive relation between inflation and unemployment observed in the 1970s. He put forward an explanation for the existence of a temporary positively-sloped Phillips curve for a period of several years, which is compatible with a vertical long-run Phillips curve at the natural rate of unemployment. In Friedman's view the positive relationship between inflation and unemployment results from an unanticipated increase in the rate and volatility of inflation which damages the efficient working of the price mechanism and causes adverse real effects (see Friedman, 1977).

Before Keynesian economics could fully recover from the concerted attacks of Friedman and other leading monetarists it was subjected to an even greater challenge in the mid-1970s by an emerging group of economists who, in large measure inspired by the work of Robert Lucas, initiated a new classical counter-revolution in macroeconomic thought. Indeed by the late 1970s/early 1980s monetarism was no longer regarded as the main rival to Keynesianism within academia although monetarism was exercising a significant influence on the policies of the Thatcher government in the UK and the Fed in the US. Indeed the Keynesian–monetarist debate within academia reached a climax in the early 1970s when Friedman, in response to his critics, set forth his 'Theoretical framework for monetary analysis' (Friedman 1970b, 1972; Tobin, 1970, 1972). In opening up the monetarist 'black box' for theoretical scrutiny Friedman's statement turned out to be a generalized IS–LM model which helped contribute to the absorption of the monetarist approach within the mainstream (Gordon, 1975; Hammond, 1996). According to Thomas Mayer, (1990a, 1993, 1997) the seeming demise of monetarism can be explained by a number of factors including: (i) a change in the methodological preferences of economists away from positivistic methodology; (ii) the absorption of certain 'credible' ideas of the monetarist doctrine into mainstream macroeconomics (for example the hypothesis that the Phillips curve is vertical in the long run) resulting in a Keynesian–monetarist synthesis (Snowdon and Vane, 1997b); and (iii) a number of flaws in the monetarist paradigm itself. In the latter case, of particular significance was the sharp decline in trend velocity in the 1980s in the US and elsewhere. The deep recession experienced in the US in 1982 has been attributed partly to the large and unexpected decline in velocity (B.M. Friedman, 1988; Modigliani, 1988a; Poole, 1988; Mankiw, 1997a). If velocity is highly volatile the case for a constant growth rate monetary rule as advocated by Friedman (1959, 1968) is completely discredited. There is no question that the collapse of the stable demand for money function in the early 1980s proved to be very damaging to what James Pierce (1995) calls 'hard core' monetarism. As a result monetarism was 'badly wounded' both within academia and among policy makers (Blinder, 1987).

During the 1970s Robert Lucas became 'without question the most influential economic theorist' (Krugman, 1994a) and the development of new classical economics dominated the macroeconomics research agenda (Hoover, 1992). Lucas's 'new classical' macroeconomics began as a development of the Friedman–Phelps natural rate hypothesis as he sought to formalize the contention that there is no long-run trade-off between inflation and unemployment, while simultaneously accounting for the observed non-neutrality of money in the short run (see Lucas, 1994a, 1996). In both Friedman's and Phelps's analyses expectations of inflation played a key role in explaining why there would be no long-run trade-off between inflation and unemployment. The assumption underlying orthodox monetarist analysis is that expected inflation adjusts to actual inflation only gradually in line with the so-called 'adaptive' expectations hypothesis. The existence of a short-run trade-off, which allows the authorities to temporarily reduce unemployment below the natural rate, depends on the lapse in time between an increase in the actual rate of inflation and an increase in the expected rate. Once inflation is fully anticipated the economy returns to its natural rate of unemployment. In his 1972 paper on 'Expectations and the neutrality of money' Lucas combined the Friedman–Phelps natural rate hypothesis with the assumption of continuous market clearing and the rational expectations hypothesis (Muth, 1961) and was able to demonstrate rigorously how a short-run trade-off would result if inflation was unanticipated due to incomplete information. However, in the Lucas (1972) model 'there is no usable trade-off between inflation and real output'. In a world where economic agents have imperfect information unanticipated money has temporary real effects (Blanchard, 1990).

Combining the rational expectations doctrine with the natural rate hypothesis, as Lucas did in his seminal paper, produces an economy where Friedman's *k* per cent monetary growth rate rule is optimal. In Thomas Sargent's view, Lucas's contribution, more than anything else in the scientific literature 'did in for Keynesian countercyclical policy' (see Jordan et al., 1993). Robert Hall (1996) has gone so far as to describe Lucas's 1972 paper as 'probably the most significant paper in theoretical macroeconomics since Keynes'. Building on that paper Lucas revived economists' research interests into business cycle phenomena, an area which had been well established before Keynes redirected effort towards explaining the level of output at a point in time in disequilibrium (Lucas, 1980b; Cooley and Prescott, 1995; Hodrick and Prescott, 1997). It was one of Lucas's notable achievements that he took up the Hicks–Hayek challenge to demonstrate that it was possible to develop an 'equilibrium theory of the business cycle' (Lucas, 1975, 1981c).

Lucas's seminal contributions (Lucas, 1972, 1973, 1975, 1976), together with those of other prominent rational 'expectationists', such as Thomas Sargent and Neil Wallace (1975, 1976), Robert Barro (1974, 1976) and Finn Kydland and Edward Prescott (1977) helped produce what John Taylor (1989) has called a 'rational expectations revolution' which 'swept macroeconomics in the 1970s' (Fischer, 1996). In 1995 Robert Lucas was awarded the Nobel Prize in Economics 'For having developed and applied the hypothesis of rational expectations, and thereby having transformed macroeconomic analysis and deepened our understanding of economic policy.' Lucas's work, and that of other leading new classicists, has not only led to the widespread practice of applying equilibrium modelling to macroeconomic analysis, but it has also accelerated the movement towards the now widely accepted view that any satisfactory macroeconomic analysis needs to be based on firm microfoundations (Hoover, 1988). Their contributions to deepening our understanding of economic policy can be seen in three main directions. First, they served to further undermine the belief that the authorities can influence output and employment in the short run by pursuing a systematic monetary policy. The so-called policy ineffectiveness proposition (Sargent and Wallace, 1975, 1976) implies that only random or arbitrary monetary policy actions undertaken by the authorities can have short-run real effects because they cannot be anticipated by rational economic agents. Given that such actions would only increase the variation of output and employment around their natural levels, increasing uncertainty in the economy, the proposition provides an argument against discretionary policy activism in favour of rules. Second, they served to shift the emphasis away from viewing specific monetary (and fiscal) policy actions as a control theory problem, towards a discussion of rules set within a game-theoretic framework. Most notably the influential work of Kydland and Prescott (1977) on the issue of dynamic time inconsistency has provided another argument in the case for monetary policy being conducted by rules rather than discretion (Fischer, 1990). Their analysis, exemplified by reference to the Phillips curve trade-off between inflation and unemployment, illustrates how the authorities having announced a policy of monetary contraction to reduce inflation will – if the policy is believed and agents reduce their inflation expectations – have an incentive to renege, or cheat on their previously announced policy and implement expansionary monetary policy in order to temporarily reduce unemployment. In circumstances where the authorities have discretion to vary the strength of monetary policy, and have in consequence an incentive to cheat, the credibility of announced policy will be significantly weakened. The analysis implies that economic performance could be improved if discretionary powers are taken away from the authorities and has highlighted the importance of establishing the credibility and reputation of policy and the policymakers (Taylor, 1982; Alesina and Tabellini, 1987). In reality the possibility of devising fully contingent rules runs into the problem that unforeseen situations which require discretion are inevitable. As Colander and Daane (1994) argue 'To tie one's hands in the hope of taking advantage of rules over discretion is to tie one's hands in cases where discretion is called for'. Third, following the 'Lucas critique' of econometric policy evaluation Lucas (1976) undermined confidence that traditional Keynesian-style macroeconometric models could be used to accurately predict the consequences of various policy changes on key macroeconomic variables. As an example take the role of rational expectations in determining the output/employment costs of reducing inflation. New classicists claim that traditional estimates of these costs are unreliable because they do not take into account how economic agents adjust their expectations and behaviour in response to a policy change. According to the new classical view, provided an announced monetary contraction is believed to be credible, rational economic agents will immediately revise their expectations of inflation downwards in line with the anticipated effects of monetary contraction on the rate of inflation. In such circumstances the output/employment costs of monetary disinflation will be non-existent or negligible. The essence of the Lucas critique is that conventional macroeconometric models are likely to perform poorly when confronted with a change in policy regime. However, in an examination of the performance of the Eckstein–DRI Phillips curve during the Volcker deflation (1979–83) Blanchard (1984) finds 'no evidence of a major shift in the Phillips curve'.

Earlier we drew attention to the speed of success of the Keynesian revolution and how, according to Colander and Landreth (1996) an important factor in that success was that Keynesian thinking can be reduced to 'simple textbook models'. While the pedagogical revolution in the case of new classical economics has been small by comparison, there is no doubt that new classical economics is having an increasing impact on textbooks at all levels (Snowdon and Vane, 1998). A cursory examination of the textbooks written by some of our interviewees confirms the fact that, while the extent and style of coverage of new classical ideas varies from author to author, issues such as rational expectations, time inconsistency, credibility, reputation, equilibrium business cycles (both real and monetary) and Ricardian equivalence can now be found in all the most recent editions of intermediate macroeconomic textbooks (see Blanchard, 1997a; Hall and Taylor, 1997; Mankiw 1997a). Even at the Principles level the 'invisible hand' of Robert Lucas is clearly present (Mankiw, 1997b; Taylor, 1998a).

The new classical contributions were so influential in the 1970s that by 1978 Lucas and Sargent felt confident enough to provocatively claim that the predictions of Keynesian economics

> were wildly incorrect and that the doctrine on which they were based is fundamentally flawed, are now simple matters of fact, involving no novelties in economic theory. The task which faces contemporary students of the business cycle is that of sorting through the wreckage, determining which features of that remarkable intellectual event called the Keynesian Revolution can be salvaged and put to good use, and which others must be discarded.

The Lucas and Sargent (1978) paper is a brilliant exercise in the use of rhetoric (Backhouse, 1997a). While many economists did not accept the case against Keynesian economics had been made conclusively Lucas and Sargent argued that the flaws in Keynesian thinking were 'fatal'. In 1980 Lucas announced the 'death' of Keynesian economics (Lucas, 1980a).

Ironically, while the new classical contributions have had an enormous methodological influence on the development of modern macroeconomics, the early 1980s witnessed the demise of the 'monetary surprise' equilibrium explanation of the business cycle. This was due in large part to the problem of reconciling the magnitude and length of business cycles – supposedly caused by incomplete information – with the fact that aggregate price level and money supply data is readily available to economic agents at a relatively low cost (Tobin, 1980a). In addition, contrary to the policy ineffectiveness proposition, a number of studies, most notably those by Frederic Mishkin (1982) and Gordon (1982), found evidence suggesting that both unanticipated *and* anticipated monetary policy affects output and employment. The events of the early 1980s also provided ammunition to critics of the new classical approach who pointed to the depth of the recessions in both the US (1981–82) and UK (1980–81) economies associated with the Volcker/Reagan and Thatcher 'announced' monetary disinflations. The response of new classical economists to the latter experiences is to remind critics that announced disinflationary policies must have credibility if a negligible sacrifice ratio is to be expected. Sargent (1993), for example, blames the high sacrifice ratio resulting from the Thatcher disinflation on her initial political weakness and lack of credibility when the policy was first announced in 1979. As it turned out Thatcher proved to be a 'hard-nosed' wolf in sheep's clothing. The new classical framework predicts a relatively high sacrifice ratio in the case of a new government, without an established reputation, announcing a hard-nosed disinflationary policy. In such cases the private sector takes time to learn the true intentions of the policy maker (Backus and Driffill, 1985). Many new Keynesians place less emphasis on credibility issues and stress the inertia arising from nominal wage and price rigidities as a cause of the observed output and employment costs of disinflation. The work of Taylor (1979, 1983) and Blanchard (1983, 1986a) shows how the staggering of price and wage adjustment can generate real effects even in the case of credible monetary disinflations. The Taylor–Blanchard approach suggests that overlapping price and wage decisions create an inflationary momentum that only a recession can break (Blanchard and Summers, 1988). This implies that a gradualist approach to disinflation, as suggested by Friedman, will be less costly than a Hayekian inspired policy of rapid disinflation ('cold turkey') supported by Sargent. Recent work by Laurence Ball (1994) suggests that 'the sacrifice ratio is lower when disinflation is quick, and when wage setting is more flexible'.

While the events of the early 1970s seriously undermined the then-prevailing Keynesian views, by the mid-1970s Keynesian models were being modified to take into account both the influence of inflationary expectations and the impact of supply shocks. In the former case by the mid to late 1970s, at least as far as the US was concerned, the majority of mainstream Keynesians had come to accept that the Phillips curve was vertical in the long run (see for example Gordon, 1975; Blinder, 1988a). In response to events in the 1970s Gordon produced his 'triangle model' where the rate of inflation depends on the combined influence of three variables, namely, inertia, demand and supply. Gordon claims that this model, which was in existence before the Lucas and Sargent (1978) remarks, resurrected the Phillips curve from the 'wreckage' of the 1970s (Gordon, 1997). The new breed of post-1975 'Keynesian' models not only incorporated a vertical long-run Phillips curve but also included supply-shock variables. This latter development was very important because it allows for the possibility of a positive relationship between inflation and unemployment ('stagflation') in the short run (Gordon, 1998). Keynesians continue to justify their advocacy of the use of discretionary aggregate demand policies to stabilize the economy, in the short run, on the grounds that it takes a long time for the economy to return to the natural rate of unemployment. The potential to identify and respond to major economic disturbances both from the demand and supply side of the economy remains a central feature of mainstream Keynesian analysis. While the undisputed reign of Keynesian economics ended in the mid-1970s, it has proved to be far from defunct (Shaw, 1997).

MAINSTREAM DEVELOPMENTS IN MACROECONOMICS SINCE THE EARLY 1980s

Leaving aside for the time being the renaissance of economic growth analysis (see the next section below) three important developments within macroeconomics have taken place since the early 1980s, namely, (i) the real business cycle approach to economic fluctuations; (ii) the development of new Keynesian macroeconomics; and (iii) the development of the 'new' political macroeconomics. Interestingly all of these approaches arose out of the 'rational expectations revolution' of the 1970s and the methodological implications for macroeconomic analysis which followed from that development.

Real Business Cycle Theory

As we have noted earlier the 1970s vintage of new classical models, which incorporated the assumptions that markets continuously clear and agents form 'rational' expectations, explained fluctuations in output and employment as the result of unanticipated monetary shocks. In the 1980s a second phase of equilibrium theorizing was initiated by the seminal contribution of Kydland and Prescott (1982) which, following Long and Plosser (1983), has come to be referred to as real business cycle theory. Modern equilibrium business cycle theory starts with the view that 'growth and fluctuations are not distinct phenomena to be studied with separate data and analytical tools' (Cooley and Prescott, 1995). Proponents of this approach view economic fluctuations as being predominantly caused by persistent real (supply-side) shocks, rather than unanticipated monetary (demand-side) shocks, to the economy. The focus of these real shocks involves large random fluctuations in the rate of technological progress that result in fluctuations in relative prices to which rational economic agents optimally respond by altering their supply of labour and consumption. For example, Kydland and Prescott (1991b) estimate that 'if the only impulses were technology shocks, the US economy would have been 70 per cent as volatile as it has been over the past period'. Perhaps the most controversial feature of this approach is the claim that fluctuations in output and employment are Pareto efficient responses to real technology shocks to the aggregate production function. This implies that observed fluctuations in output are viewed as fluctuations in the natural rate of output, not deviations of output from a smooth deterministic trend. As such the government should not attempt to reduce these fluctuations through stabilization policy, not only because such attempts are unlikely to achieve their desired objective but also because reducing instability would reduce welfare (Prescott, 1986). In conventional Keynesian analysis equilibrium is identified with a full employment growth path. Departures from full employment are viewed as disequilibrium situations where societal welfare is below potential and government has a role to correct this macroeconomic market failure using fiscal and monetary policy. In sharp contrast the 'bold conjecture' of real business cycle theorists is that each stage of the business cycle, boom and slump, is an equilibrium. 'Slumps represent an undesired, undesirable, and unavoidable shift in the constraints that people face; but, given these constraints, markets react efficiently and people succeed in achieving the best outcomes that circumstances permit ... every stage of the business cycle is a Pareto efficient equilibrium' (Hartley et al., 1998).

Needless to say the real business cycle approach has proved to be highly controversial and has been subjected to a number of criticisms (see for example Summers, 1986; Mankiw, 1989; Ryan and Mullineux, 1997; Hartley et al., 1997, 1998). One important criticism relates to the nature of the deterioration of a country's production capabilities in a recession, that is, what are the negative technological shocks that cause recessions? (Mankiw, 1989). In response to this line of criticism Gary Hansen and Edward Prescott (1993) define technological shocks as any change in 'the production possibility sets of the profit centres'. Viewed this way, changes in the legal and regulatory system are capable of inducing negative or positive changes in technology due to the impact they have on the incentives facing profit centres.

Despite the numerous criticisms, real business cycle theorists have made several important and lasting contributions to modern macroeconomics (Williamson, 1996; Danthine, 1997). First, real business cycle theory has challenged the conventional approach in which growth and fluctuations are studied separately using different analytical tools. Until the early 1980s the conventional wisdom, accepted by Keynesian, monetarist and new classical economists alike, was to interpret fluctuations in output as being short-run fluctuations, around a rising long-term trend, primarily caused by aggregate demand shocks. In effect Kydland and Prescott derive the implications for the growth path of equilibrium aggregate output when an economy is subject to a continuous series of technological shocks. Thus both trend and cycle have the same origin, namely, shocks to technology (productivity). By integrating the theory of economic growth and fluctuations the real business cycle approach has irreversibly changed the direction of modern business cycle research and helped to further refocus macroeconomists' attention to the supply side of the economy.

A second, important influence of the real business cycle research programme has been to highlight the intertemporal and dynamic characteristics of macroeconomics. Any analysis of key macroeconomic variables such as consumption, saving, labour supply and investment all have an intertemporal dimension. Modern equilibrium theorists therefore regard the mainstream IS–LM model as a completely deficient framework for dynamic analysis. To real business cycle economists, progress in macroeconomics will involve further development of the 'Dynamic Stochastic General Equilibrium Theory' but where other important features of the real economy such as monetary factors and price rigidities are integrated into the model to produce a 'New Neoclassical Synthesis' (Danthine, 1997; Farmer, 1997). However in order to satisfy Colander's (1988) 'teachability' criteria a compromise between sophistication and simplicity will have to be found.

A third influence has been methodological in character. Rather than attempting to provide models capable of conventional econometric testing, real business cycle theorists, inspired by the work of Kydland and Prescott (1982), have developed the calibration method in which the simulated results of their specific models (when hit by random shocks) in terms of key macroeconomic variables are compared with the actual behaviour of the economy. In doing so real business cycle theorists have provided a new research methodology for macroeconomics involving quantitative 'general equilibrium' dynamic models.

In a review of business cycle methodology Lucas (1980b) argues that a major objective of theoretical economics is to 'provide fully articulated economic systems that can serve as laboratories in which policies that would be prohibitively expensive to experiment with in actual economies can be tested at much lower costs'. In effect a major task for theorists is to build a 'mechanical imitation economy'. Given economists' inability to test policies directly on the *actual* economy Lucas argues that progress in economic analysis ultimately depends on technical developments within the discipline which enable progress towards the construction of an analogue system where simulations can be carried out. Lucas's (1980b) paper is the reference point for the modern era of equilibrium theorizing. As Stephen Williamson (1996) points out 'In Lucas one finds a projection for future research methodology which is remarkably close to the real business cycle program'. Following these guidelines Kydland and Prescott (1982) proceeded to take 'macroeconomic modelling into new territory' (Lucas, 1987) by operationalizing the methodological approach outlined by Lucas. The new research method, with its emphasis on the stylized facts of the business cycle to be explained, and the construction of general equilibrium models which replicate such stylized facts, has refocused attention on, and stimulated renewed interest into, empirical knowledge of business cycle phenomena. Their methodology, known as 'calibration' or 'computational experiments' consists of the following steps (Kydland and Prescott, 1996; Backhouse, 1997b).

(i)   Pose a question relating to a specific issue of concern, for example an important policy issue such as 'What is the quantitative nature of fluctuations caused by technology shocks?'

(ii)   Use a 'well tested' theory, where 'theory' is interpreted as a specific set of instructions about how to build the imitation economy.

(iii)   Construct a model economy and select functional forms. Kydland and Prescott (1982) utilize the basic stochastic neoclassical growth model as the cornerstone of their model.

(iv)   Calibrate the model economy using data from pre-existing microeconomic studies and knowledge of the 'stylized facts'. Where no information exists select values for parameters so that the model is capable of mimicking the real world behaviour of variables.

(v)   Run the experiment and compare the equilibrium path of the model economy with the behaviour of the actual economy. Use these types of simulations to answer questions relating to the important issues initially identified under (i).

In their seminal 1982 paper Kydland and Prescott use the neoclassical growth model and follow the calibration/simulation procedure to see if the model can explain aggregate fluctuations when the model economy is subject to technological shocks. As Prescott (1986) recalls 'the finding that when uncertainty in the rate of technological change is incorporated into the growth model it displays business cycle phenomena was both dramatic and unanticipated'. Whereas conventional Keynesian, monetarist and early new classical models regard the business cycle as a problem to be solved by either discretionary or rules-based policies, real business cycle theorists conclude from their research that fluctuations 'are what standard economic theory predicts' (Prescott, 1986).

On the negative side one of the problems with calibration is that it currently does not provide a method that allows one to judge between the performance of real and other (for example, Keynesian) business cycle models. As Hoover (1995a) notes 'the calibration methodology, to date, lacks any discipline as stern as that imposed by econometric methods ... Above all, it is not clear on what standards competing, but contradictory, models are to be compared and adjudicated.' Nevertheless calibration has provided an important new contribution to the methodology of empirical macroeconomic research – for more detailed discussions of calibration see Quah (1995); Hoover (1995a); Hansen and Heckman (1996); Sims (1996); Kydland and Prescott (1991a, 1996); Cooley (1997), Hartley et al. (1998).

Before proceeding to outline some of the key features associated with new Keynesian macroeconomics, and the 'new' political macroeconomics, it is worth commenting on two, more traditional, alternative approaches to empirical macroeconomic research. The first of these involves what can be referred to as the narrative approach. Earlier we highlighted the key role played by Friedman and Schwartz's (1963) *A Monetary History* in changing economists' views on the cause of the Great Depression and the real effects of monetary disturbances. You will recall that their research involved a detailed documentation of data and historical circumstances surrounding events (see Lucas, 1994b; Miron, 1994; and Smith, 1994, for reviews of *A Monetary History* 30 years after its publication, and Hammond, 1996, for a discussion of Friedman's research methodology, and debate with his critics, over the causal role of money in business cycles). Clower (1964), in his review of *A Monetary History*, was one of the first economists to understand that the Marshallian approach of Friedman and Schwartz was an important methodological contribution. To Clower, Friedman and Schwartz's careful historical analysis of modern historical events such as the Great Depression was superior to the neo-Walrasian research programme which had yielded 'no novel empirical results' (Hammond, 1996). It is somewhat ironic that while this particular approach has not been widely favoured by economists, Lawrence Summers (1991) has argued that careful historical discussions of specific events, as exemplified by the National Bureau narrative approach used by Friedman and Schwartz (1963), have been far more successful in persuading economists of the importance of monetary factors, than more sophisticated econometric methods. More recently Christina Romer and David Romer (1989) have undertaken research, in the spirit of Friedman and Schwartz, on the question of whether monetary policy matters. Using the historical records of the Federal Reserve System they identified six occasions in the postwar period when the Federal Reserve expressed its intentions to move towards contractionary monetary policy in an attempt to deliberately engineer a recession to reduce inflation. They found that on all six occasions following the intended shift to anti-inflationary monetary policy there was a substantial, and highly significant, fall in output below what would have been expected. They interpreted these results as 'decisive' evidence that negative monetary policy shocks have large effects on real economic activity.

While acknowledging the importance of the so-called narrative approach Kevin Hoover and Stephen Perez (1994) have challenged the Romers' methodology on three independent fronts namely that they: (i) cannot discriminate between monetary and non-monetary shocks (for example oil shocks) as the cause of recessions; (ii) cannot distinguish between cases where tighter monetary policy is causally efficacious and cases where the Federal Reserve failed to act in line with its announced intentions to tighten monetary policy; and (iii) provide an inappropriate and misleading guide to the quantitative effects of monetary policy shocks. Given such criticisms they argue that the Romers' methodology fails to sustain causal inference and instead falls foul of the fallacy of *post hoc ergo propter hoc* (see Tobin, 1970). Discussion of this more recent research utilizing Friedman and Schwartz's 'narrative approach' acts to illustrate the longstanding problem of trying to establish the extent to which, in this case, money plays an independent causal role in producing fluctuations in real and nominal output.

The second approach to empirical macroeconomic research, which has been the one principally favoured by economists since the 1940s, is the Cowles Commission approach to econometrics. This research method has traditionally involved the formal integration of statistical and economic theory leading to the estimation of economic parameters, and the testing of economic theories, using a range of statistical techniques, most notably regression analysis. In response to the fierce debates that have taken place within econometrics concerning the use of the 'traditional research strategy', over recent years econometricians have developed a range of more sophisticated statistical techniques such as vector autoregressions and cointegration. The problem that currently faces the economist undertaking empirical macroeconomic research is that of deciding which is the appropriate technique to adopt, not least because different techniques can give contradictory results. Accessible discussions of new research strategies within macroeconometrics can be found in Hylleberg and Paldam (1991); Kydland and Prescott (1991a, 1996); Gerrard (1995); Hoover (1995c); and Wickens (1995).

New Keynesian Economics

The announcement by Lucas (1980a) of the 'death' of Keynesian economics turned out at best to be premature. A second major development within macroeconomics arising out of the rational expectations critiques of the new classical economists of the 1970s is new Keynesian macroeconomics. By combining rational expectations with the natural rate hypothesis and the assumption of continuous market clearing new classical models imply that anticipated monetary policy changes have no effect on output and employment even in the short run. This highly controversial policy ineffectiveness proposition critically depends upon the assumption that prices are perfectly and instantaneously flexible so that markets continuously clear, rather than the rational expectations hypothesis *per se*. Stanley Fischer (1977) and Edmund Phelps and John Taylor (1977) were able to show that nominal demand disturbances are capable of producing real effects in models incorporating rational expectations, providing the new classical assumption of continuous market clearing is abandoned; and that in such models systematic monetary policy can help stabilize the economy. Following these embryonic new Keynesian contributions macroeconomists realized that the rational expectations hypothesis was a necessary but not a sufficient condition for policy ineffectiveness.

Since the late 1970s a considerable amount of effort has been directed into exploring a variety of reasons for wage and price stickiness that prevent market clearing (Snowdon and Vane, 1997a). This has involved research into the causes and consequences of: (i) nominal wage stickiness (see Fischer, 1977; Taylor, 1979; Laing, 1993); (ii) nominal price stickiness (see Mankiw, 1985; Akerlof and Yellen, 1985; D. Romer, 1993); (iii) real rigidities (see Solow, 1979; Yellen, 1984; Shapiro and Stiglitz, 1984; Lindbeck and Snower, 1986; Phelps, 1994); and (iv) co-ordination failures (see Diamond, 1982; Cooper and John, 1988; Ball and Romer, 1991).

In explaining business cycle fluctuations new Keynesians have chosen to emphasize nominal price rigidities over nominal wage rigidity. This is in sharp contrast to Keynes, the orthodox Keynesianism of Modigliani and the neoclassical synthesis, which emphasize nominal wage rigidities. In orthodox Keynesian models a combination of price-taking firms, neoclassical production technology and sticky nominal wages imply that aggregate demand contractions will be associated with a rise in real wages during a recession, that is real wages move *countercyclically*. By 1980 Gregory Mankiw had concluded that such models made little sense even if modified to allow for rational expectations (for example, Fischer, 1977) since they imply that 'recessions must be quite popular. Sure a few people get laid off. But most people get to enjoy the higher real wages that result when prices fall and their nominal wages do not. ... If high real wages accompanied low employment as the *General Theory* and my Professors had taught me, then most households should welcome economic downturns' (Mankiw, 1991; see also Snowdon and Vane, 1995). Furthermore the weight of evidence does not support the countercyclical real wage prediction as an undisputed statistical regularity of the business cycle (Abraham and Haltiwanger, 1995; Brandolini, 1995; Millard et al., 1997). Thinking about this real wage puzzle led Mankiw and others to redirect their attention to the pricing behaviour of firms operating in imperfectly competitive product markets, where 'menu costs' and 'near rational behaviour' are important elements (Mankiw, 1985; Akerlof and Yellen, 1985). To Mankiw (1992) new Keynesianism is Keynes reincarnated rather than resurrected!

Critics of new Keynesian menu cost models doubt that such frictions can be used to explain aggregate fluctuations in output and employment of the magnitude experienced in the real world (Barro, 1989; Tobin, 1993). In a recent review of new Keynesianism, Assar Lindbeck (1998) questions the assumption in menu cost models that somehow individual firms find it cheaper to reduce employment rather than prices in response to a decline in product demand. Given the significant hiring and firing costs confronting the modern firm, particularly in Europe, this seems implausible. However, Lindbeck agrees that the main contribution of the new Keynesian literature has been to 'strengthen the microeconomic foundations for the existence and persistence of aggregate excess supply of labour, and for various transmission mechanisms of aggregate product-demand shocks to output and employment'.

Building on this theme Huw Dixon (1997) argues persuasively that the 'fundamental new idea behind new Keynesian models is that of *imperfect competition*'. This is the crucial innovation which differentiates new Keynesians from Keynes, orthodox Keynesians, monetarists and new classicals. Yet it is here that we encounter one of the great puzzles in the history of economic thought. Why did Keynes show such little interest in the imperfect competition revolution taking place on his own doorstep in Cambridge? Richard Kahn, author of the famous 1931 multiplier article and colleague of Keynes, was fully conversant with the theory of imperfect competition well before Joan Robinson's famous book was published on the subject in 1933. Given that Keynes, Kahn and Robinson shared the same Cambridge academic environment during the period when the *General Theory* was being written, it is remarkable that Keynes adopted the classical/neoclassical assumption of a perfectly competitive product market which Kahn (1929) had already argued was unsound for short-period analysis! (Marris, 1991). As Dixon (1997) notes 'Had Kahn and Keynes been able to work together, or Keynes and Robinson, the *General Theory* might have been very different'. Inspired by the work of Michal Kalecki, post Keynesians have always stressed the importance of price fixing firms in their models (Arestis, 1997).

One of the most important contributions of new Keynesian macroeconomics has been to develop models with coherent microfoundations, in which prices and wages adjust only gradually. By combining these elements with the idea of rational expectations and the natural rate hypothesis (or NAIRU) new Keynesians have shown how fluctuations in aggregate nominal demand can have significant real effects. Olivier Blanchard and Nobuhiro Kiyotaki (1987) in their interpretation of the menu cost insight show that the macroeconomic effects of nominal price rigidity generates what they call an *aggregate demand externality*. In the case of a decline in aggregate demand society would be considerably better off if all firms cut their prices, but the private incentives to do so are absent (Gordon, 1981, 1990). Because aggregate fluctuations in an imperfectly competitive world are inherently non-Pareto optimal, a policy-induced increase in output and employment can increase societal welfare. Therefore, new Keynesians have been able to re-establish a case for policy effectiveness and justify interventionist policies to stabilize the economy. For example, the gradual adjustment of prices and wages in new Keynesian models implies that a policy of monetary expansion, even if anticipated by rational economic agents, will lead to an increase in output and employment. This is in sharp contrast to new classical models where anticipated monetary policy is neutral in the short run. Furthermore in some new Keynesian analysis the equilibrium rate of unemployment is affected by the path taken by the actual rate of unemployment so that in circumstances where unemployment remains above the natural rate for a prolonged period the natural rate will tend to increase due to so-called hysteresis effects. In models where hysteresis effects are important the natural rate of unemployment or NAIRU is not independent of aggregate demand. In his 1968 paper Friedman argued that the natural rate of unemployment was determined by supply-side factors only (Blanchard and Summers, 1986, 1987; Cross, 1995, 1996; Blanchard and Katz, 1997). Such hysteresis or path-dependency effects imply that the sacrifice ratio involved in the wake of a severe deflation is likely to be much greater than is implied by orthodox monetarist and new classical models. In such a situation the natural and actual rates of unemployment can be reduced by a combination of supply and demand side policies.

The 'New' Political Macroeconomics

During the past decade or so research into the various forms of interaction between politics and macroeconomics has become a major growth area giving rise to a field known as the 'new political macroeconomics' (Alesina, 1995; Alt and Alesina, 1996; Alesina and Rosenthal, 1995). This research area has developed at the interface of macroeconomics, social choice theory and game theory. Of particular interest to macroeconomists is the influence that political factors have on such issues as business cycles, inflation, unemployment, growth, budget deficits and the conduct and implementation of stabilization policies (Snowdon and Vane, 1999).

Politico-economic models, initially developed in the 1970s by William Nordhaus (1975), Douglas Hibbs (1977) and Bruno Frey and Friedrich Schneider (1978), view the government as an *endogenous* component of the political and economic system. The conventional *normative* approach, in sharp contrast, regards the policymaker as a 'benevolent social planner' whose only objective is to maximize social welfare. The normative approach is concerned with how the policymaker *should* act rather than how they *do* act.

Alberto Alesina (1994) has highlighted two general political forces which are always likely to play a crucial distorting role in the economy. The first factor is the incumbent policymaker's desire to retain power, which acts as an incentive to *'opportunistic'* behaviour. Second, society is polarized and this inevitably gives rise to some degree of social conflict. As a result *ideological* considerations will manifest themselves in the form of *'partisan'* behaviour and actions.

Prior to the rational expectations revolution taking hold of economists' research agendas, the politico-economic literature was dominated by the Nordhaus (1975) opportunistic model, the Hibbs (1977) 'strong' partisan model, and the Frey and Schneider (1978) 'weak' partisan model (Garratt, 1995). Nordhaus's model predicts self-interested opportunistic behaviour, irrespective of party allegiance, prior to an election. When these political motivations are mixed with myopic non-rational behaviour of voters and non-rational expectations of economic agents, a political business cycle is generated which ultimately leads to a higher rate of inflation in a democracy than is optimal. In the Hibbs (1977) model 'left' inclined politicians have a greater aversion to unemployment than inflation and 'right' inclined politicians have the opposite preference. The Hibbs model therefore predicts a systematic difference in policy choices and outcomes in line with the partisan preferences of the incumbent politicians.

Both of these models were undermined by the rational expectations revolution. By the mid-1970s models which continued to use adaptive expectations or were reliant on a long-run Phillips curve were coming in for heavy criticism. The scope for opportunistic or ideological behaviour seemed to be extremely limited in a world dominated by rational 'forward looking' voters and economic agents who could not be systematically fooled. However, after a period of relative neglect a second phase of politico-economic models emerged in the mid-1980s. These models capture the insights emanating from including the rational expectations hypothesis in macroeconomic models. Economists such as Kenneth Rogoff and Anne Sibert (1988) have developed *rational opportunistic* models, and Alesina has been prominent in developing the *rational partisan* theory of aggregate instability (Alesina, 1987, 1988; Alesina and Sachs, 1988; Snowdon and Vane, 1997c). These models show that while the scope for opportunistic or ideological behaviour is more limited in a rational expectations setting, the impact of political distortions on macroeconomic policymaking are still present given the presence of imperfect information and uncertainty over the outcome of elections (Alesina and Roubini, 1992). As such their work points towards the need for greater transparency in the conduct of fiscal policy and the introduction of central bank independence for the conduct of monetary policy (Alesina and Summers, 1993; Alesina and Gatti, 1995; Alesina and Perotti 1996a; Snowdon, 1997).

In introducing 'The New Monetary Policy Framework' for the UK economy on 6 May 1997, which established 'operational independence' for the Bank of England, Chancellor Gordon Brown, in an official statement, provided the following rationale for the government's strategy:

> We will only build a fully credible framework for monetary policy if the long-term needs of the economy, not short-term political considerations guide monetary decision-making. We must remove the suspicion that short-term party political considerations are influencing the setting of interest rates.

Chancellor Brown's decision to grant much greater independence to the Bank of England had its origins in a 1992 Fabian Society paper entitled 'Euro Monetarism', written by Ed Balls. As a former student of Larry Summers at Harvard, Balls was familiar with the empirical work on central bank independence produced by Alesina and Summers (1993). In a visit to the US in March 1997 Shadow Chancellor Brown and his economic adviser met both Alan Greenspan and Larry Summers. And so was born the strategy to go for immediate greater independence if elected (see Smith, 1997).

More recently Alesina has extended the reach of the new political macroeconomics and has been involved in joint research looking into the origin and persistence of rising fiscal deficits and debt ratios, the political economy of growth, the optimal size of nations and the economic and political risk in fiscal unions (Alesina and Perotti, 1996b, 1997a; Alesina et al., 1996; Alesina and Spolare, 1997; Alesina and Perotti, 1998). With respect to achieving a reduction in the fiscal deficit/GDP ratio Alesina's research has indicated that successful fiscal adjustment is highly correlated with the composition of spending cuts. Unsuccessful adjustments are associated with cuts in public investment expenditures whereas in successful cases more than half the expenditure cuts are in government wages and transfer payments (Alesina et al., 1998). In addition, because fiscal policy is increasingly about redistribution in the OECD countries, increases in labour taxation to finance an increase in transfers is likely to induce wage pressure, raise labour costs and reduce competitiveness (Alesina and Perotti, 1997b). Research into the optimal size of nations has indicated an important link between trade liberalization and political separatism. In a world dominated by trade restrictions large political units make sense because the size of a market is determined by political boundaries. If free trade prevails relatively small homogeneous political jurisdictions can prosper and benefit from the global marketplace (Alesina and Spolare, 1997). Work on the implications of fiscal unions has also indicated the potential disadvantages of larger units. While larger jurisdictions can achieve benefits in the form of a centralized redistribution system, 'these benefits may be offset (partially or completely) by the increase in the diversity and, thus, in potential conflicts of interests among the citizens of larger jurisdictions' (Alesina and Perotti, 1998).

The developments within modern macroeconomics that have taken place since the late 1960s, outlined above, have refocused the attention of macroeconomists towards the analysis of inflation, the role of monetary policy, the influence of political distortions on macro outcomes, the importance of institutional design for successful policy implementation and the relevance of supply-side considerations when modelling the economy (Taylor, 1995). Given the experience of the Great Inflation this is hardly surprising. In some ways we can almost think of the Great Depression as having caused the Great Inflation in that the constraints on monetary policy were loosened during the post World War Two period in response to fear of the possible return of 1930s-style unemployment. Whatever other problems it caused, the gold standard acted as an effective nominal anchor against inflation. The emphasis of economists on price stability during the last 20 years 'is something of a throwback to the pre-depression gold standard' (Calomiris and Wheelock, 1998). In trying to understand the causes of the Great Inflation the work related to time inconsistency, credibility, reputation and political distortions has led to an increasing number of economists supporting central bank independence in the conduct of monetary policy. In addition, an increasing number of countries have chosen to adopt an inflation target to act as a 'nominal anchor'.

CENTRAL BANK INDEPENDENCE AND INFLATION TARGETING

The general debate on the relative merits of rules v discretion in the conduct of fiscal and monetary policy was given a tremendous stimulus by the introduction of the rational expectations hypothesis. The new classical contributions of Kydland and Prescott (1977) and Barro and Gordon (1983), which highlighted issues relating to time inconsistency, credibility and reputation, provided extra weight to the case for monetary rules associated with Friedman. The politico-economic literature has also shown how political distortions arising from strong opportunistic or partisan behaviour can generate a non-optimal outcome for aggregate variables.

If inflation has significant real costs then institutions and policy regimes need to be developed which can create long-run price stability. But what is meant by 'price stability' and how significant are the costs of inflation? In August 1996 the Federal Reserve Bank of Kansas City sponsored a symposium entitled 'Achieving Price Stability' attended by a distinguished group of Central Bankers and economists including Alan Greenspan, Mervyn King, Stanley Fischer, John Taylor, Lawrence Summers and Martin Feldstein (see Greenspan et al., 1996). In his opening remarks to the conference the Chairman of the US Federal Reserve provided the following operating definition of price stability: 'Price stability obtains when economic agents no longer take account of the prospective change in the general price level in their economic decision making' (Greenspan et al., 1996). However, participants at the conference, while advocating price stability as the primary goal of monetary policy, disagreed about the appropriate definition of price stability. Fischer suggested a range of 1–3 per cent; Taylor defined price stability as 1 or 2 per cent measured inflation taking into account the upward bias in official calculations, while Feldstein made a strong case for a target of zero inflation. Those economists who prefer a low but positive target rate of inflation do so because of reasons relating to measurement error, the employment/output costs of disinflationary policies implemented to achieve the zero inflation goal, and the need to lubricate the labour market and conduct monetary policy. The lower the target rate of inflation the more difficult it becomes for the monetary authorities to engineer reductions in the real wage rate and the real interest rate (Akerlof et al., 1996). Fischer argues that a negative real interest rate is often needed during recessions in order to engineer a recovery. With a zero inflation target and a floor of zero for the nominal interest rate then it becomes impossible to generate a negative real interest rate. The difficulties encountered with the operation of monetary policy in a zero inflation/deflationary environment have been most evident in Japan in recent years. Hence a majority of economists seem to favour an inflation target of around 2 per cent.

What are the costs of inflation? Here it is important to distinguish between the costs of *anticipated* inflation and the costs of *unanticipated* inflation. The costs of a fully anticipated inflation relate to (i) the costs of operating a tax system which is imperfectly indexed; (ii) the 'shoe leather' effects of economizing on real money balances; (iii) the 'menu' costs of revising price lists; and (iv) the cost of adapting less than fully indexed financial contracts.

The costs of unanticipated inflation relate to (i) the impact of unplanned redistributions of income (for example from creditors to debtors); (ii) the costs imposed by additional uncertainty about future prices on decisions relating to consumption, saving and borrowing and investing; and (iii) the distorting impact of inflation on relative price signals which damages the process of efficient resource allocation in market economies guided by *relative* prices (Briault, 1995). Since there is evidence that inflation uncertainty is positively correlated with the rate of inflation, the costs of inflation are likely to rise the higher the rate of inflation (Joyce, 1997). Lower inflation can therefore have benefits on both the *level* of output and the *growth rate* of output. So even if there are significant short-run costs of reducing inflation the long-run discounted net benefits of a permanently higher level of output are likely to be positive for plausible discount rates (Bakhshi et al., 1997).

The relationship between inflation and growth has recently been the subject of numerous empirical studies. Fischer (1993) argues that a stable macroeconomic environment is 'necessary though not sufficient for sustainable economic growth' and finds that evidence from 80 countries supports the view that inflation is negatively correlated with growth. In an empirical study of over 100 countries Barro (1995) finds clear evidence of adverse effects from inflation on growth where inflation exceeds 10–20 per cent per year. Although these effects are not large, over time even small changes in growth rates have dramatic effects on living standards (see Table 2). For this reason Barro concludes that the Bank of England's interest in price stability is justified. Hence the balance of opinion among economists is that inflation above moderate rates is harmful to economic efficiency and long-run growth.

For these reasons many economists in recent years have argued in favour of institutional reform involving Central Bank Independence (CBI) as a means of achieving a low and stable rate of inflation. The assumption underlying this argument is that such an institution (at least in principle) should be capable of conducting monetary policy in a manner free from opportunistic and partisan influences. Alberto Alesina and Roberta Gatti (1995) distinguish between two types of variability which can contribute to aggregate instability. The first is *economic variability* resulting from different forms of exogenous shocks to aggregate demand and supply. The second type is *political variability* or policy-induced disturbances. It is this second type of variability that CBI is best designed to combat.

Because a majority of economists emphasize excessive monetary growth as the underlying cause of *sustained* inflation it follows that prolonged differences in countries' rates of inflation result from variations in their rates of monetary growth (Lucas, 1996; Romer, 1996). Any plausible explanation of these 'stylized facts' must therefore include an understanding of central bank behaviour (Walsh, 1993). In particular we need to identify the reasons why monetary policy is conducted in a way that creates a positive average rate of inflation which exceeds that regarded as desirable. The main reasons identified by economists as to why the monetary authorities may generate inflation include (i) opportunistic and/or partisan political pressure to lower unemployment as discussed in the politico-economics literature; (ii) dynamic consistency influences as emphasized by Kydland and Prescott (1977); and (iii) the need to finance fiscal deficits through seigniorage, that is the raising of revenue by printing money. By creating inflation the government imposes an inflation tax on the holders of money. This form of financing of fiscal deficits by monetary expansion is particularly important in economies with inefficient or underdeveloped fiscal systems (Cukierman, 1994).

The *theoretical* case for CBI relates to the general acceptance of the natural rate hypothesis that in the long run the rate of inflation is independent of the level of unemployment. Hence with no long-run exploitable trade-off, far-sighted monetary authorities ought to select a position on the long-run Phillips curve consistent with a low sustainable rate of inflation. In addition, an independent central bank will benefit from a 'credibility bonus', whereby disinflationary policies can be accomplished at a low 'sacrifice ratio' (Cukierman, 1992; Goodhart, 1994a, 1994b).

The *empirical* case for CBI is linked to cross-country evidence which shows that for advanced industrial countries there is a negative relationship between CBI and inflation (Alesina and Summers, 1993; Bleaney, 1996). In a recent empirical investigation of 18 OECD countries Kaddour Hadri, Ben Lockwood and John Maloney (1998) find evidence of a negative relationship between central bank independence and inflation. It should be noted, however, that the negative correlation between inflation and CBI does not prove causation and the evidence is much less robust for larger samples of data, especially those including developing countries (Cukierman, 1992; Eijffinger and Keulen, 1995; Jenkins, 1996; Minford, 1997). Poor countries with shallow financial markets and unsustainable budget deficits are unlikely to solve their inflation problems by relying on the creation of an independent central bank (Mas, 1995). However, at least as far as the advanced industrial democracies are concerned, the theoretical and empirical work *suggests* that monetary constitutions should be designed to ensure some degree of central bank autonomy.

Although the success of the independent German Bundesbank in delivering low inflation over a long time period has inspired other countries to follow that example, it is also clear that some important problems emerge with the measurement, form and consequences of CBI. The whole question of independence is one of degree (Eijffinger and Keulen, 1995). Although the Federal Reserve and the Bank of England are 'independent', it is clear that legal independence does not, and cannot, completely remove the influence of 'monetary politics' (Mayer, 1990b; Havrilesky, 1993; Woolley, 1994). For example, Henry Chappell, Thomas Havrilesky and Rob McGregor (1993) show how partisan influences on the conduct of monetary policy can arise through Presidential appointments to the Board of Governors of the Federal Reserve. Through these 'political' appointments and other forms of moral suasion and signalling, the Fed's policy making can never be totally independent of political pressures. During early October 1998, on the eve of the monthly meeting of the Bank of England's Monetary Policy Committee, both the UK Prime Minister, Tony Blair, and UK Chancellor of the Exchequer, Gordon Brown, made speeches (in China and the US respectively) which highlighted the dangers of recession and unemployment. With UK manufacturing industry clamouring for an interest rate cut it is difficult not to interpret such speeches as an attempt to 'bounce' the 'independent' Bank of England into toeing the political line!

In discussing the form of CBI, Fischer (1995a, 1995b) makes the important distinction between '*goal independence*' and '*instrument independence*'. The former implies that the central bank sets its own objectives (that is, political independence) while the latter refers to independence with respect to the various levers of monetary policy (that is, economic independence). The recently created 'independent' Bank of England has instrument independence only. An inflation target of 2.5 per cent, which is the Bank's explicitly stated monetary policy objective, is set by government and therefore the decisions relating to goals remain in the political sphere (Bean, 1998; Budd, 1998).

The distinction between goal and instrument independence can also be used to illustrate the difference between the two main models of CBI which have been developed in the theoretical literature. Both types of model evolved in response to the widely held view that discretionary policy making is subject to an inflation bias. The first model is based on Rogoffs (1985) '*conservative central banker*'. In this model an inflation-averse conservative central banker is appointed who places a higher relative weight on the control of inflation than does society in general (for example President Jimmy Carter's appointment of Paul Volcker as Chairman of the Fed in 1979). This is meant to ensure that the excessive inflation associated with the time inconsistency problem is kept low in circumstances where it would otherwise be difficult to establish a pre-commitment to low inflation. Overall, lower average inflation and higher output variability is predicted from this model (Waller and Walsh, 1996). However, the research of Alesina and Summers (1993) shows only the first of these two predictions appear in cross-sectional data. In contrast, Michael Hutchison and Carl Walsh (1998), in a recent study of the experience of New Zealand find that central bank reform appears to have increased the short-run output inflation trade-off. Rogoff's conservative central banker has both goal and instrument independence and is best represented by the German Bundesbank, which in 1997 remained the most independent central bank in Europe (Tavelli et al., 1998). In Rogoff's model the conservative central banker reacts less to supply shocks than someone who shared society's preferences indicating a potential trade-off between flexibility and commitment. In response to this problem Susanne Lohmann (1992) suggests that the design of the central bank institution should involve the granting of partial independence to a conservative central banker who places more weight on inflation than the policy maker, but 'the policymaker retains the option to over-ride the central bank's decisions at some strictly positive but finite cost'. Such a clause has been built into the Bank of England Act where the following reserve power is set out: 'The Treasury, after consultation with the Governor of the Bank, may by order give the Bank directions with respect to monetary policy if they are satisfied that the directions are required in the public interest and by extreme economic circumstances.' It remains to be seen if such powers are ever used.

The second alternative model, associated with Walsh (1993, 1995a, 1998), utilizes a principal–agent framework and emphasizes the *accountability* of the central bank. In Walsh's contracting approach the central bank has instrument independence but no goal independence. The central bank's rewards and penalties are based on its achievements with respect to inflation control. The Reserve Bank of New Zealand resembles this principal–agent type model. An important issue in the contracting approach is the optimal length of contract for a central banker (Muscatelli, 1998). Long terms of appointment will reduce the role of electoral surprises as explained in the Alesina model. But terms of office which are too long may be costly if societal preferences are subject to frequent shifts. Chris Waller and Carl Walsh (1996) argue that the optimal term length 'must balance the advantages in reducing election effects with the need to ensure that the preferences reflected in monetary policy are those of the voting public'.

In recent years many countries have set about reforming their institutions of monetary policy, including the former communist transition economies, countries in the developing world and OECD economies, and the UK where CBI was introduced in May 1997 by the newly elected Labour Party administration. Of crucial importance to the successful operation of EMU will be the effectiveness of the new 'independent' European Central Bank (ECB) which will have the responsibility of conducting monetary policy for an economy comparable in size to the US, and populated by almost 300 million people. Although the new ECB has constitutional independence in accordance with the Maastricht Treaty, in reality it cannot operate in a political vacuum. Of obvious concern to members of the EMU is the democratic accountability of the ECB. This is of crucial importance given the recognized potential for political conflict within the EU (Feldstein, 1997a, 1997b; Obstfeld, 1997; Smaghi, 1998). This potential for conflict between a 'Conservative' ECB and individual country governments has recently been enhanced by the coming to power in Europe of 'Centre Left' politicians combined with the establishment of the ECB whose objective is to achieve low inflation in the range 0–2 per cent. The newly elected (September 1998) German administration is generally recognized as neo-Keynesian in spirit and as early as November 1998, Oskar Lafontaine, Germany's Minister of Finance was in verbal conflict with the EU's leading central bankers over the future conduct of monetary policy, with Lafontaine urging a more activist monetary policy geared more to employment and output. Such early conflict between governments and central bankers over the conduct of monetary policy does not bode well for the success of EMU.

Most reforms have adopted some variant of the principal–agent framework whereby the central bank is 'contracted' to achieve clearly defined goals, provided with instrument independence and held accountable for deviating from the politically chosen objectives (Bernanke and Mishkin, 1992; Walsh, 1995b). In New Zealand, Canada, Israel, Austria, Sweden, Finland, Spain and the UK, emphasis in recent years has been placed on the central bank achieving an *inflation target*. In an inflation targeting regime monetary policy decisions are guided by forecasts of future inflation compared to the announced target range and failure to meet the inflation target involves a loss of reputation for the Central Bank (Green, 1996; Friedman and Kuttner, 1996; Bernanke and Mishkin, 1997; Svensson, 1997a; Artis et al., 1998; Haldane, 1998; Vickers, 1998).

Figure 5 traces the path of inflation in the UK over a 50-year period. This inflation record is poor relative to the other major OECD economies, particularly in the 1970s and especially when compared with the record of the former West Germany. The graph also indicates the variety of *monetary regimes* or *nominal anchors* which have been adopted in the UK over this 50-year period. As Mervyn King (1997) notes, the data indicate that large increases in the rate of inflation during the 1970s and, to a lesser extent in the late 1980s, both occurred in periods when the framework for monetary policy was, at best, 'opaque'. Conversely, 'the introduction of clear and transparent monetary regimes, be it monetary targeting, the ERM or direct inflation targeting, have often coincided with sustained falls in inflation'. An inflation targeting regime was introduced in the UK in November 1992 following departure from the ERM. While the UK record of inflation in the period since the introduction of this regime has been relatively good the jury is still out on the effectiveness of this form of nominal anchor in the longer term. However, Lars Svensson (1997b) argues that an inflation targeting regime is far superior to monetary growth or exchange rate targeting regimes as an effective nominal anchor.

One of the most important theoretical objections to CBI is the potential for conflict that it generates between the monetary and fiscal authorities (Doyle and Weale, 1994; Nordhaus, 1994). In countries where this has led to conflict (such as the US in the period 1979–82) large fiscal deficits and high real interest rates have resulted. This monetary/fiscal mix is not conducive to growth and, during the early period of Reaganomics in the US, came in for severe criticism from many economists – see Blanchard (1986b), Modigliani

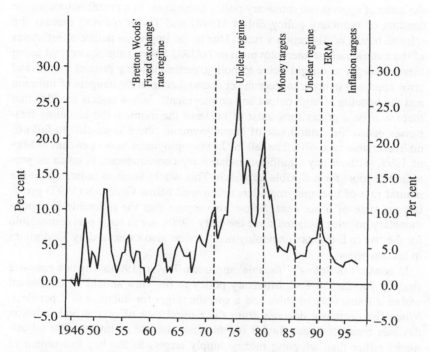

Note: *Inflation is measured as the annual increase in the retail price index from 1946–74, and in the retail price index *excluding* mortgage interest payments from 1974–97

Source: Adapted from *The Bank of England Quarterly Bulletin*, November 1997

*Figure 5 Forms of 'nominal anchor' and annual UK inflation, 1946–1997**

(1988b) and Tobin (1987). The tight monetary easy fiscal mix is hardly a surprising combination given the predominant motivations that drive the Fed and the US Treasury. Whereas independent central banks tend to emphasize monetary austerity and low inflation, the fiscal authorities (politicians) know that increased government expenditure and reduced taxes are the 'meat, potatoes and gravy of politics' (Nordhaus, 1994). To the critics CBI is no panacea. In particular to say that inflation should be the primary goal of the central bank is very different from making inflation the sole goal of monetary policy in all circumstances (Akhtar, 1995; Carvalho, 1995/96; Minford, 1997; Forder, 1998; Posen, 1998).

The steady growth, low unemployment, low inflation performance of the US ('Goldilocks') economy during the period 1992–99 has once more raised the issue of appropriate monetary policy guidelines. In a recent debate on the conduct of monetary policy Solow (1998) and Taylor (1998b) discuss the relative merits of discretion v rules. Due to the imprecise nature of estimates of the natural rate of unemployment or NAIRU Solow cautions against using these concepts as a rigid guide to policy, recommending instead a 'trial and error approach in order to steer the economy between the dangers of inflation and the benefits of high output and employment'. Solow rejects the idea that there will be a precipitous burst of inflation the moment the economy trespasses below the natural rate of unemployment, 'there is no cliff to fall off, no irreversible take-off'. The fall in US unemployment to 4.3 per cent in May of 1998, without any significant inflationary consequences, is taken as providing support for a flexible approach. This would seem to indicate that the natural rate of unemployment has fallen well below Gordon's (1997) previous estimate of 6 per cent. Solow also argues that the inflexible European monetary policies, pursued since the early 1980s, are in large part responsible for the rise in European unemployment (a view also expressed by Modigliani in his interview).

In contrast to Solow's 'flexible' approach, Taylor (1998b) urges a cautious strategy for the US Fed. Monetary policy in his view should be conducted within a framework of rules and a specific target for inflation of 2 per cent. When the economy deviates from the natural rate of output and inflation deviates from its target, Taylor recommends the use of interest rate adjustments rather than adopting money supply targets as the key instrument of policy and restates the case in favour of a specific formula for policy, first recommended at the 1992 Carnegie Rochester Conference. This policy formula, known as 'Taylor's rule' is given by (3):

$$i = \dot{P} + g(y) + h(\dot{P} - \dot{P}^*) + r^* \tag{3}$$

where y = real GDP measured as the percentage deviation from potential GDP, i = the short-term nominal rate of interest in percentage points, $\dot{P}$ is the rate of inflation and $\dot{P}^*$ the target rate of inflation, r^* is the 'implicit real interest rate in the central bank's reaction function' and the parameters g, h, $\dot{P}^*$ and r^* all have a positive value. With this rule short-term nominal interest rates will rise if output and/or inflation are above their target values and nominal rates will fall when either is below their target value. In Taylor's view this flexible rule is superior to the pure discretion advocated by Solow since 'a monetary policy which risks a rise in inflation also risks another recession'. According to Mankiw (1997a) Taylor's rule is not only simple but 'also resembles actual Fed behaviour in recent years'. Given that in the autumn of 1998 the US Fed cut the Federal Funds rate on three occasions (29 September, 15 October and 17 November) in a short period of seven weeks suggests that the US Fed is concerned about a sharp downturn in economic activity. In Solow's view the Taylor rule comes close to 'mimicking the discretionary behaviour of the central bank' and the Fed's recent reaction to growing concerns about 'global deflation and recession' is in keeping with this assessment. Thus Taylor's rule 'may be the rule that Alan Greenspan and his colleagues are (perhaps unconsciously) following' (Mankiw, 1997a).

The issue of European monetary policy following monetary union is a matter of great importance given the high rates of European unemployment experienced since the early 1980s. To some economists the unemployment problem in Europe is not fundamentally a monetary policy issue but a supply-side problem, often referred to as 'Eurosclerosis'. During the 1950s and 1960s the European 'welfare state' OECD economies experienced lower unemployment on average than that experienced in the US. Since around 1980 this experience has been reversed. Many economists have attributed the poor labour market performance in Europe to various institutional changes which have adversely affected the flexibility of the labour market, in particular measures relating to the amount and duration of unemployment benefit, housing policies which limit mobility, minimum wage legislation, job protection legislation which increases hiring and firing costs, the 'tax wedge' between the cost of labour to firms (production wage) and the net income to workers (consumption wage), and 'insider' power (Siebert, 1997; Nickell, 1997). In the face of an increasingly turbulent economic environment economies require ongoing restructuring. Lars Ljungqvist and Thomas Sargent (1998) argue that the generous entitlement programmes in the European OECD welfare states have generated 'a virtual time bomb waiting to explode'. That explosion arrives when large economic shocks occur more frequently. The welfare state programmes hinder the necessary restructuring of the economy and this shows up as high and prolonged rates of unemployment.

An alternative Keynesian view has recently been put forward in a 'Manifesto' by Modigliani, Solow and others (Modigliani et al., 1998). These economists accuse Europe's policymakers of adhering to a 'pernicious orthodoxy' whereby 'a limited number of supply-side policies are to be devoted to fighting unemployment, and that demand management (and particularly monetary policy) is to be devoted to fighting inflation'. They also express the view that an important cause of the high rates of European unemployment experienced since the early 1980s has been due to 'policy errors'. In particular, the push towards the euro in recent years has led to very restrictive aggregate demand policies being followed. The solution to the unemployment problem in Europe therefore requires micro-oriented supply-side policies *combined with more expansionary aggregate demand policies*. It is crucial that these policies work in tandem. As the article points out, this broad view of the European unemployment problem is held by many economists including Alan Blinder, Olivier Blanchard, Paul Samuelson and James Tobin.

While accepting some of the supply-side arguments Solow (1998) and Modigliani (1996) see a significant part of the rise in European unemployment as having its origin in the tight anti-inflationary monetary policies which have been a characteristic of the past two decades. Blanchard (1997a) also points out that the Eurosclerosis view does not explain why unemployment has increased during a period 'when most of these rigidities have actually decreased'. Hysteresis effects may also be an important contributing factor in the case of Europe (Blanchard and Summers, 1986, 1987; Blanchard, 1997c; Blanchard and Katz, 1997). During the 1990s UK unemployment has followed the US unemployment path reasonably closely. However, controversy exists as to how much this decline in unemployment in the 1993–98 period is due to greater labour market flexibility induced by the 1980s labour market reforms, and how much is due to the relaxation of monetary policy after the UK was liberated from the straightjacket imposed by membership of the ERM in the 1990–92 period. As we noted above, a predominantly 'Conservative' ECB will have to face some tough decisions after January 1999 if European unemployment remains stubbornly high. This will be especially the case if left of centre governments in Europe constantly push for an easing of monetary policy.

THE RENAISSANCE OF ECONOMIC GROWTH RESEARCH: SOLOW, LUCAS AND ROMER

There is no doubt that one very important consequence arising from the work of Keynes was that it led to a shift of emphasis from the classical long-run issue of economic growth to the shorter-run issue of aggregate instability. As Tobin (1997) emphasizes Keynesian economics does not pretend to apply to the long-run issues of growth and development. This is in sharp contrast to the work of Adam Smith, David Ricardo and the other classical economists who sought to understand the nature and causes of the 'Wealth of Nations' rather than focus on the issue of short-run instability. This should hardly surprise us given the rapid self-equilibrating properties of the classical macroeconomic model.

The importance of economic growth as a basis for improvements in human welfare cannot be overstated. The impact of even small differentials in growth rates, when compounded over time, are striking. Table 2 shows the compounding effect of sustained growth on the *absolute* living standards of six hypothetical countries, labelled A–F, each of which starts out with an income per capita of £100. The table also shows how, over a period of 50 years, *variations* in growth

Table 2   The cumulative impact of growth

Period in years	A 1%	B 2%	C 3%	D 4%	E 5%	F 10%
0	£100	£100	£100	£100	£100	£100
10	110	122	134	148	163	259
20	122	149	180	219	265	673
30	135	181	243	324	432	1 745
40	149	221	326	480	704	4 526
50	164	269	438	711	1 147	11 739

rates between countries A–F, cause a substantial divergence of *relative* living standards. In the case of country F the impact of a 10 per cent growth rate on income per capita over 50 years almost defies comprehension. David Romer (1996) has expressed this point succinctly as follows 'the welfare implications of long-run growth swamp any possible effects of the short-run fluctuations that macroeconomics traditionally focuses on'. In reviewing the differential growth performances of countries such as India, Egypt, the 'Asian Tigers', Japan and the US, and the consequences of these differentials for living standards, Lucas (1988) comments that 'the consequences for human welfare involved in questions like these are simply staggering. Once one starts to think about them, it is hard to think about anything else'. Robert Barro and Xavier Sala-i-Martin (1995) also argue that 'Economic growth ... is the part of macroeconomics that really matters', a view in large part endorsed by Mankiw (1995a) who writes that 'long-run growth is as important – perhaps more important – than short-run fluctuations'.

Implicit in these views is the assumption that economists now know enough about the causes of recessions that a recurrence of an event such as the Great Depression will not be repeated. Lucas (1994b), for example, argues that the disastrous events following the Wall Street crash of October 1929 were a 'preventable disaster' and that economists now have sufficient understanding of such events to be able to avoid a repeat of the inter-war policy mistakes. Given the international financial and economic crisis which has been gathering pace during 1997–98 it is to be hoped that the optimism of Lucas is justified.

The new empirical growth literature indicates that across the world's economies income per capita disparities are large and in many cases have grown since 1870. The data also reveals that growth rate differences between countries across time and space are significant (Pritchett, 1997; Jones, 1998; Temple, 1999). Table 3 illustrates the comparative experience of heavily

Table 3 GDP relative to the US, selected countries, 1960 and 1990

	Population (millions)	Proportion of US GDP per capita (at current prices)	
	1990	1960	1990
Zaire	36	0.05	0.02
Nigeria	96	0.05	0.05
India	850	0.07	0.07
China	1134	0.05	0.07
Bangladesh	108	0.09	0.08
Pakistan	112	0.07	0.08
The Philippines	61	0.12	0.10
Indonesia	178	0.06	0.11
Iran	56	0.23	0.16
South Africa	38	0.21	0.18
Thailand	56	0.10	0.20
Brazil	149	0.18	0.22
Argentina	32	0.44	0.25
Mexico	81	0.28	0.32
Korea	43	0.09	0.38
Japan	124	0.30	0.81

Note: Most recent figures for Zaire from 1989

Source: Temple (1999)

populated countries which in 1960 might have been considered 'developing'. That there are 'enormous disparities in living standards' is self-evident. Table 4 also indicates that the world has also witnessed a significant number of growth 'miracles', heavily concentrated in East Asia, and 'disasters', heavily concentrated in Sub-Saharan Africa. In 1960 African countries were regarded by many economists as having more growth potential than East Asian countries. But as William Easterly and Ross Levine (1997) note, on average, 'real per capita GDP did not grow in Africa over the 1965–90 period while, in East Asia and the Pacific, per capita GDP growth was over 5 per cent'. There seems little doubt that a significant factor contributing to 'Africa's growth tragedy' has been the frequent adoption of economic policies detrimental to long-term sustainable growth and development (Parente and Prescott, 1992; Woglin, 1997). Many development disasters in Africa and elsewhere have also often been associated with prolonged military and political conflict.

Table 4   Growth miracles and disasters, 1960–1990 (Annual growth rates of output per worker)

Miracles	Growth	Disasters	Growth
Korea	6.1	Ghana	−0.3
Botswana	5.9	Venezuela	−0.5
Hong Kong	5.8	Mozambique	−0.7
Taiwan	5.8	Nicaragua	−0.7
Singapore	5.4	Mauritania	−0.8
Japan	5.2	Zambia	−0.8
Malta	4.8	Mali	−1.0
Cyprus	4.4	Madagascar	−1.3
Seychelles	4.4	Chad	−1.7
Lesotho	4.4	Guyana	−2.1

Note: Figures for Botswana and Malta based on 1960–89

Source: Temple (1999)

Stephen Parente and Edward Prescott (1993), in an examination of a large sample of countries over a long time period, find four 'economic development facts' namely that: (i) there are great disparities of wealth among countries; (ii) wealth disparity has not increased or decreased; (iii) the wealth distribution has shifted up, that is, there is no absolute poverty trap and most countries, rich and poor, have become richer; (iv) there have been development miracles and development disasters. The progress of some countries has been nothing short of spectacular. Given these 'facts', Parente and Prescott argue that any development theory which fails to account for them 'is simply not a development theory'.

One important source of divergence in per capita incomes has arisen because of political developments which have influenced the choice of economic system and policies. Those countries which attempted to 'develop' behind the 'Iron Curtain' now have much lower income per capita than countries which had a comparable income per capita in 1950 and followed the capitalist path. 'The fact that a large part of the globe fell under communist rule in the twentieth century is a major factor making for enormous disparities in the world's distribution of income and wealth across nations' (De Long, 1999). The most obvious examples involve the comparative development experiences of East and West Germany, North and South Korea, and China with Taiwan/Singapore/Hong Kong. But comparisons between other neighbouring countries seem reasonable, for example comparisons between Russia and

Finland, Hungary and Austria, Slovenia and Italy, Cambodia and Thailand, reveal significant differences in living standards. These 'natural experiments' show that where national borders also mark the boundaries of public policies and institutions, easily observable differentials in economic performance emerge (Olson, 1996). It seems that the most significant reason for the ultimate failure of the Soviet economy 'was the death, by slow torture, of Soviet economic growth' (Weitzman, 1996). The wide variety of growth and development experiences is illustrated in Table 5 which provides data relating to a number of countries including the G7 economies, some communist and former communist countries, three 'Asian Tigers', and a selection of countries from Africa, Latin America and Asia. In addition to information on GNP per capita and GDP growth, figures for life expectancy are included because 'life expectancy is a kind of weighted composite of progress in meeting physiological needs' (Hicks and Streeten, 1979). Basic needs such as nutrition, education, clean water, medical care, sanitation and housing are all inputs into the health production function which largely determine life expectancy. In the words of the 1998 Nobel Laureate, 'mortality data are informationally rich' (Sen, 1998).

The majority of former 'Iron Curtain' centrally planned economies, with different degrees of commitment and success, have now embarked on a 'transition' path towards becoming capitalist market economies. While successful transition will undoubtedly improve economic performance in the long term, in the short run almost all transition economies have experienced dramatic declines in GDP before growth recovers. This 'U shaped' pattern of output decline and recovery appears to be a stylized fact of the experience of transition in the former communist European countries. Blanchard has explained this evolution of output as a product of the 'disorganization' which results from a movement from plan to market (Blanchard, 1996; Blanchard and Kremer, 1997). However, providing reformers complete the agenda of fiscal and monetary stabilization, privatization programmes, a stable framework of law and order and political stability, the transition economies have enormous growth potential. Unfortunately, most of the countries of the former USSR have made unsatisfactory progress on all of these institutional prerequisites and are also 'still mired in stabilization crises' (Sachs and Warner, 1995; Blanchard, 1997b). In the case of China the economic reform process began following the death in 1976 of Mao Zedong. Economic development rather than revolutionary politics and class struggle became the number one goal (Perkins, 1988). While Deng Xiaoping and the new leadership were well aware of the spectacular growth performance of some of their capitalist neighbours and the damaging effect on the economy of Mao's 'messianic missions', they had no blueprint for reform. China therefore 'stumbled' on a gradualist and eclectic reform strategy that has 'proved remarkably success-

Table 5   Development indicators

Country	Population (millions) 1997	GNP per capita 1997 $	GNP per capita 1997 PPP	Growth of GDP % p.a. 1990–97	Life expectancy Male	Female
Japan	126	37 850	23 400	1.4	77	83
Singapore	3	32 940	29 000	8.5	74	79
USA	268	28 740	28 740	2.5	74	80
Germany	82	28 260	21 300	na	73	80
Austria	8	27 980	21 980	1.6	74	80
France	59	26 050	21 860	1.3	74	82
Hong Kong	7	25 280	24 540	5.3	76	81
Finland	5	24 080	18 980	1.1	73	81
UK	59	20 710	20 520	1.9	74	80
Italy	57	20 120	20 060	1.1	75	81
Canada	30	19 290	21 860	2.1	76	82
Greece	11	12 010	13 080	1.8	75	81
S. Korea	46	10 550	13 500	7.2	69	76
Argentina	36	8 570	9 950	4.5	69	77
Brazil	164	4 720	6 240	3.1	63	71
Hungary	10	4 430	7 000	−0.4	65	75
Poland	39	3 590	6 380	3.9	68	77
Thailand	61	2 800	6 590	7.5	67	72
Russia	147	2 740	4 190	−9.0	60	73
Peru	25	2 460	4 390	6.0	66	71
Belarus	10	2 150	4 840	−6.5	63	74
Egypt	60	1 180	2 940	3.9	64	67
Bulgaria	8	1 140	3 860	−3.5	67	75
Ukraine	50	1 040	2 170	−13.6	62	73
China	1 227	860	3 570	11.9	68	71
Pakistan	137	490	1 590	4.4	62	65
India	961	390	1 650	5.9	62	63
Kenya	28	330	1 110	2.0	57	60
Vietnam	77	320	1 670	8.6	66	70
Cambodia	11	300	na	6.2	52	55
Bangladesh	124	270	1 050	4.5	57	59
Nigeria	118	260	880	2.7	51	55
Ethiopia	60	110	510	4.5	48	51
World	5 829 t	5 130 w	6 330 w	2.3 w	65 w	69 w
Low income (63)	2 048 t	350	1 400	4.2	58	60
High income (52)	926 t	25 700	22 700	2.1	74	81
Sub-Saharan Africa (49)	614 t	500	1 470	2.1	51	54

Key: t = totals; w = weighted average; na = not available

Source: *World Development Report*, World Bank, 1998/99

ful in moving the economy from a Soviet-style command system to what by the early 1990s was an economy governed in large part by market forces' (Perkins, 1994). China's experience is unique in that it has experienced spectacular growth in its transition from a rigid centrally planned economy to an increasingly open and market based economy (Borensztein and Ostry, 1996; Hu and Khan, 1997).

Towards Neoclassical Growth Theory

Given the significant adverse impact that poor growth performance has on economic welfare and the resultant importance attached to growth by economists, it is perhaps surprising that the research effort in this field has been cyclical. As we have already noted, growth issues were a major concern of the classical economists. However, during the period 1870–1945 economists' research was heavily influenced by the 'marginalist revolution' and was therefore predominantly micro-oriented, being directed towards issues relating to the efficient allocation of given resources (Blaug, 1997b). For a quarter of a century after 1929–33, issues relating to the Great Depression and Keynes's response to that event dominated discussion in macroeconomics.

During the period following the Second World War the contemporary literature on problems of economic development grew rapidly (Hunt, 1989). This was in large measure a response to the perceived sense of political urgency which arose as the newly independent former colonies sought to jump on the escalator of economic growth. Since the corpus of existing orthodox theory *appeared* inadequate to the needs of low income countries a burgeoning research effort in this area sought to identify a basic theoretical structure from which economists could deduce useful policy recommendations. In the development enthusiasm of the 1950s there was widespread acceptance of the view that poor countries were plagued by pervasive market failures. Since it was assumed that all governments aimed to maximize social welfare and were in possession of full information on which decisions could be made it seemed obvious, indeed almost self-evident, that a *dirigiste* strategy was the best way of achieving the desired objective of rapid economic growth and the elimination of poverty (Meier, 1994). In contrast to the economic disasters experienced by the capitalist democracies during the 1930s, the Soviet Union appeared to offer an alternative style of growth and development which seemed to avoid the costly instability associated with capitalism. With distrust of the market mechanism, widespread export pessimism and a rose- coloured view of Soviet economic performance distorted by a lack of reliable data, many developing countries opted for an inward-looking strategy of import substitution supported by an enthusiasm for economic planning which, with the benefit of hindsight, is hard to comprehend (Krueger, 1994,

1997). In sum, the 'view that a more or less free market would not solve the development problem was widely accepted' (Bruton, 1998). To many development theorists neoclassical economics seemed most suited to static issues of resource allocation, but of limited relevance when it came to dynamic issues of economic growth and development. This fracture between development economics and growth theory also had methodological origins.

During the period from the early 1930s until the 1950s economic analysis was undergoing a dramatic methodological transformation involving the formalization and mathematization of the discipline. These developments in economics were led in the twentieth century by economists, mainly of European origin, who frequently came from backgrounds where mathematics, the sciences and/or engineering had formed a significant part of their schooling and university education. Among others, major contributions were made by Jacob Marshack (engineering), John von Neumann (mathematics and physics), Ragnar Frisch* (mathematical statistics), Jan Tinbergen* (physics), Maurice Allais* (engineering), Leonid Kantorovich* (mathematics), Tjalling Koopmans* (physics and mathematics), Trygve Haavelmo*, Kenneth Arrow* (mathematics), John Hicks* (mathematics), Lawrence Klein* (mathematics), Gerard Debreu* (mathematics), Paul Samuelson* (mathematics) and Wassily Leontief* (see Beaud and Dostaler, 1995; Blaug, 1998. *Indicates the award of a Nobel prize in economics). Despite Keynes's mathematical background (a first class honours degree in mathematics from Cambridge) his hostility to the mathematization of economic analysis is well known and echoes that of his teacher and mentor Alfred Marshall, also a first class mathematics graduate from Cambridge (Krugman, 1998). But within months of the publication of the *General Theory* the book was being translated into determinate simultaneous equations by John Hicks, Roy Harrod and James Meade (Skidelsky, 1992). To the technically minded younger generation of economists such as Samuelson, Modigliani, Solow and Tobin the emergence of quantitative Keynesian macroeconomics was a form of language with great appeal. However, this formalistic revolution in economics tended to create a gulf between those economists who were focused on the immediate concerns of practical policy making and those who emphasized the importance of model building using new tools. As Paul Romer argues in his interview the practical benefits of model building tend to be long term, 'there is an inter-temporal trade-off between results and tool building' with the latter enabling economists to 'give better policy advice in the future'. This tension undoubtedly contributed to the separate evolution of development economics and growth theory during the 1950–70 era. Growth theory was *par excellence* a prime candidate for the model builders.

In the post 1945 period there have been three waves of interest in growth theory (Solow, 1994). The first wave of interest focussed on the neo-Keynesian work of Roy Harrod (1939, 1948) and Evsey Domar (1947). In the mid-1950s the development of the neoclassical growth model by Robert Solow (1956) and Trevor Swan (1956) stimulated a second more lasting and substantial wave of interest, which, after a period of relative neglect between 1970 and 1986, has been reignited (Mankiw et al., 1992). The third wave, initiated by the research of Paul Romer (1986) and Robert Lucas (1988) led to the development of *endogenous growth theory* which emerged in response to theoretical and empirical deficiencies in the neoclassical model.

The Harrod–Domar model 'sanctioned the overriding importance of capital accumulation in the quest for enhanced growth' (Shaw, 1992). As a result development economists during the 1950s concentrated their research effort into understanding how to raise savings ratios so as to enable less developed economies to 'take-off' into 'self sustained growth' (Lewis, 1954; Rostow, 1960). However, a major weakness of the Harrod–Domar approach was the assumptions of a fixed capital-output ratio and zero substitutability between capital and labour (that is, fixed factor proportions). These are 'crucial' but inappropriate assumptions for a model concerned with long-run growth. These assumptions also lead to the renowned instability property that 'even for the long run an economic system is at best balanced on a knife-edge equilibrium growth' (Solow, 1956). This property does not fit well with the actual experience of growth (Jones, 1975). Following the seminal contributions of Solow and Swan the neoclassical model, which better fits growth experience, became the dominant approach to the analysis of growth (see also Tobin, 1955).

The 'Old' Neoclassical Growth Theory

Between 1956 and 1970 economists refined what Lionel McKenzie (1998) calls the 'old growth theory' better known as the Solow neoclassical model of economic growth (Solow, 1970; Mankiw, 1997a; Blanchard, 1997a; Hall and Taylor, 1997). This model remains the essential starting point to any discussion of economic growth. 'Whenever practical macroeconomists have to answer questions about long-run growth they usually begin with a simple neoclassical growth model' (Mankiw, 1995b).

The Solow growth model is built around the neoclassical production function (4):

$$Y = F(K, AL) \tag{4}$$

Where Y is real output, K is capital, L is the labour input and A is a measure of technology, that is, the way that inputs to the production function can be transformed into output. The term AL is the labour input measured in efficiency units, and captures both the quantity of labour and the productivity of labour which is determined by available technology. It is assumed that technological progress is *labour augmenting*. If workers acquire new knowledge their productivity increases augmenting the effective labour supply.

Building on this basic framework the Solow model highlights the impact on growth of saving, population growth and technological progress in a closed economy setting without a government sector. Since the model is concerned with long-run growth all p´...ces are fully flexible, there is a positive elasticity of substitution between capital and labour and full employment equilibrium prevails (actual output always equals potential output). The unstable equilibrium of the Harrod–Domar model is avoided, there are no Keynesian demand deficiency crises and monetary influences can be ignored in accordance with the classical long-run neutrality proposition. Only one type of good is produced which can either be consumed or invested so there are no problems associated with a discrepancy between *ex ante* saving and investment. In the Solow model saving *is* investment (Jones, 1975). Saving (S) is assumed to be a fixed proportion (s) of current income (Y). Income by definition consists of consumption (C) plus investment (I). We can therefore write equation (5):

$$Y - C = S = sY = sF(K, AL) \tag{5}$$

Assuming constant returns to scale the production function (4) can be written down in intensive form as (6):

$$y = f(k) \tag{6}$$

where $y = Y/AL$ is output per unit of effective labour, that is, labour measured in efficiency units; $k = K/AL$ is the amount of capital per unit of effective labour. Equation (6) shows that output per unit of effective labour is a positive function of the amount of capital per unit of effective labour. The production function (6) is 'well-behaved' and therefore satisfies the conditions shown by (7) and (8):

$$f'(k) > 0, \quad \text{for all } k \tag{7}$$
$$f''(k) < 0, \quad \text{for all } k \tag{8}$$

that is, the marginal product of capital is positive for all levels of k and diminishes as k increases.

From (5) and (6) we can write the savings function in intensive form as (9):

$$sy = sf(k) \tag{9}$$

The accumulation of capital evolves according to (10) which is the fundamental differential equation of the Solow model:

$$\dot{k} = sf(k) - (n + g + \delta)k \tag{10}$$

where $\dot{k}$ is the rate of change of the capital stock per unit of effective labour, s is the saving rate, n is the rate of population (labour force) growth, g is the rate of *labour augmenting technical progress*, and δ is the rate of depreciation of the capital stock. Solow's model assumes that s, n, g, and δ are determined exogenously.

We can think of the expression $(n + g + \delta)k$ as the 'required' or 'break even' investment necessary to keep the capital stock per unit of effective labour (k) constant (Romer, 1996; Blanchard, 1997a; Mankiw, 1997a). In order to prevent k from falling some investment is required to offset depreciation. This is the $(\delta)k$ term in (10). Some investment is also required because the quantity of effective labour is growing at a rate $(n + g)$. Hence the capital stock must grow at rate $(n + g)$ just to hold k steady. This is the $(n + g)k$ term in (10). When investment per unit of effective labour is greater than required or break even investment then k will be rising and in this case the economy is experiencing *capital deepening*. Given the structure of the Solow model the economy will, in time, approach a *steady state* where actual investment, $sf(k)$, equals break even investment, $(n + g + \delta)k$. In the steady state the change in capital per worker $\dot{k} = 0$ although the economy continues to experience *capital widening*, the extension of existing capital per worker to additional workers.

Using * to indicate steady state values we can define the steady state as (11):

$$sf(k^*) = (n + g + \delta)k^* \tag{11}$$

Figure 6 captures the essential features of the Solow model outlined by equations (4) to (11). In Figure 6a the curve $f(k)$ graphs a well-behaved intensive production function; $sf(k)$ shows the level of savings per worker at different levels of the capital labour ratio (k); the linear relationship $(n + g + \delta)k$ shows that break even investment is proportional to k. At the capital labour ratio k_1, savings (investment) per worker (B) exceeds required investment (C) and so the economy experiences *capital deepening* and k rises. At k_1 consumption per worker is indicated by D–B and output per worker is y_1. At k_2, because $(n + g + \delta)k > sf(k)$ the capital–labour ratio falls, capital becomes *'shallower'* (Jones, 1975). The steady state balanced growth path occurs at k^* where investment per worker equals break even investment. Output per worker is y^* and consumption per worker is E–A. In Figure 6b the relationship

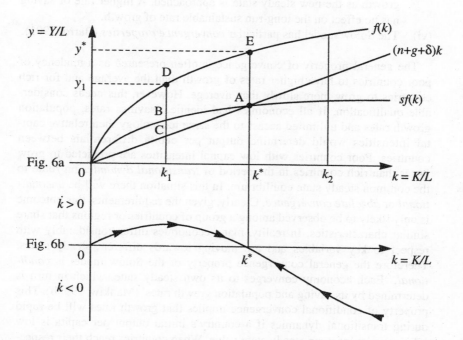

Figure 6   The Solow growth model

between $\dot{k}$ (the rate of change of the capital labour ratio) and k is shown. When $\dot{k} > 0$, k is rising, when $\dot{k} < 0$, k is falling.

The Solow model outlined above allows us to make several predictions about the growth process.

(i)   In the long run an economy will gradually approach a *steady state equilibrium* (y^*, k^*) which is independent of the initial conditions.

(ii)   The steady state balanced rate of growth of *aggregate output* (Y) depends on the rate of population growth (n) and the rate of technological progress (g).

(iii)   In the steady state balanced growth path the rate of growth of *output per capita* (y) depends solely on the rate of technological progress (g).

(iv)   For a given depreciation rate the *level* of output per capita depends on the savings rate (s) and the population growth rate (n). A higher rate of saving will increase y^*, a higher population growth rate will reduce y^*.

(v)   The impact of an increase in the savings rate on the *growth* of per capita output is temporary. An economy experiences a period of higher growth as the new steady state is approached. A higher rate of saving has no effect on the long-run sustainable rate of growth.

(vi)   The Solow model has particular *convergence properties* (Barro, 1991).

The general property of convergence is often presented as a tendency of poor countries to have higher rates of growth than the average and for rich countries to grow more slowly than average. However, this needs considerable qualification. If all economies had identical savings rates, population growth rates and unlimited access to the same technology then relative capital intensities would determine output per capita differentials between countries. Poor countries with low capital intensities are predicted to grow faster than rich countries in the period of *transitional dynamics* on route to the common steady state equilibrium. In this situation there will be *unconditional* or *absolute convergence*. Clearly, given the requirements, this outcome is only likely to be observed among a group of countries or regions that share similar characteristics. In reality, many economies differ considerably with respect to key variables and are moving towards different steady states. Therefore the general convergence property of the Solow model is *conditional*. 'Each economy converges to its own steady state, which in turn is determined by its saving and population growth rates' (Mankiw, 1995b). This property of conditional convergence implies that growth rates will be rapid during transitional dynamics if a country's initial output per capita is low relative to its long-run steady state value. When countries reach their respective steady states, growth rates will then equalize in line with the rate of technological progress. Clearly if rich countries have higher steady state values of $k*$ than poor countries, there will be no possibility of convergence in an absolute sense. As Barro (1997) notes, 'a poor country that also has a low long-term position, possibly because its public policies are harmful or its saving rate is low, would not tend to grow rapidly'. Conditional convergence therefore allows for the possibility that rich countries may grow faster than poor countries.

In a second very influential paper on growth accounting Solow (1957) showed how researchers can use a Cobb–Douglas production function (12) in order to identify the sources of growth (Mankiw, 1997a; Hall and Taylor, 1997).

$$Y = A\ K^{\alpha}L^{\beta}, \text{ where } \alpha + \beta = 1 \text{ and } 1 > \alpha > 0 \qquad (12)$$

In equation (12) A is an index of total factor productivity, that is the amount that output would increase as a consequence of improvements in the methods of production with the capital labour ratio held constant. The exponent on the capital stock (α) measures the elasticity of output with respect to capital and the exponent on the labour input (β) measures the elasticity of output with respect to labour. The weights α and β reflect the income shares of capital and labour respectively and given a constant returns to scale production function sum to unity. In the US capital receives about a third of gross national income and labour receives about two-thirds. Therefore $\alpha = 1/3$ and $\beta = 2/3$.

Since the growth rate of Y will be the weighted sum of the growth rates of A, K and L, (12) can be written down as (13).

$$\Delta Y/Y = \Delta A/A + \alpha \Delta K/K + \beta \Delta L/L \qquad (13)$$

By rearranging (13) Solow was able to estimate the contribution of technical progress as a residual:

$$\Delta A/A = \Delta Y/Y - (\alpha \Delta K/K + \beta \Delta L/L) \qquad (14)$$

In (14) the '*Solow residual*' is $\Delta A/A$. In his 1957 paper Solow estimated US GDP for the period 1909–49 and found that of the average annual growth rate of 2.9 per cent, 0.32 percentage points were attributable to capital accumulation, 1.09 per cent resulted from an increase in the labour input and 1.49 per cent could be attributed to technical progress. Over the same period per capita output grew by 1.81 per cent of which 1.49 percentage points could be attributed to technical progress. From this research it appeared that the bulk of growth in per capita income is due to growth of total factor productivity. But in the Solow model technological progress is exogenous, that is, not explained by the model (Fagerberg, 1994). The Solow residual turned out to be 'a measure of our ignorance' (Abramovitz, 1956; see also Harberger, 1998). As Barro and Sala-i-Martin (1995) conclude, this was 'an obviously unsatisfactory situation' and David Romer (1996) comments that the Solow model 'takes as given the behaviour of the variable that it identifies as the main driving force of growth'.

Although the lack of a theory of technological change is a clear weakness of the basic neoclassical growth model many general predictions from the theory are 'broadly consistent with experience' (Mankiw, 1995b). For example, cross-country data indicates a strong negative correlation between population growth and income per capita and a strong positive correlation between income per capita and savings rates. As predicted by the model, rates of growth in the rich OECD economies are relatively low while spectacular growth rates have been observed in countries moving from an initial position of relatively low income per capita and low capital intensity. There is also strong evidence of absolute convergence among relatively homogeneous economies such as the OECD and between regions and states within the US,

Europe and Japan (Baumol, 1986; Barro and Sala-i-Martin, 1991, 1995). In larger, more diverse data sets there is little evidence of the expected negative relationship between growth rates and some initial (for example 1960) level of income per capita, that is, absolute convergence (Romer, 1986, 1989; De Long, 1988). However, 'the central idea of conditional convergence receives strong support from the data' (Barro, 1997). The growth accounting research of Alwyn Young (1992, 1995) has shown that the rapid growth of the Asian Tiger economies is easily explicable and can be attributed mainly to rapid accumulation of factor inputs rather than unusually high total factor productivity growth. As Paul Krugman (1996) indicates, an implication of this research is that this rapid growth can therefore be expected to slow down considerably in the future as it has done already in Japan. The Solow model can also provide a plausible account of the 'miracles' of Japanese and German post 1945 growth in terms of the transitional dynamics towards a high income per capita steady state (Mankiw, 1997a).

However there are a number of puzzles which the Solow model finds difficult to explain. First, income per capita differentials across the world are much greater than predicted by the model. 'Although the model correctly predicts the directions of the effects of saving and population growth, it does not correctly predict the magnitudes. In the data the effects of saving and population growth on income are too large' (Mankiw et al., 1992). Second, given the common production function the marginal product of capital should be much higher in poor countries than in rich countries. But the rate of return to capital in poor countries is less than expected and the anticipated massive flows of capital from rich to poor countries have not been observed across poor countries as a whole (Lucas, 1990). Third, the rate of convergence is only about half that predicted by the model and the economy's initial conditions influence the outcome for much longer than the model says it should (Mankiw, 1995b).

Towards Endogenous Growth

Between 1970 and 1985 macroeconomic research was dominated by theoretical issues relating to the degeneration of the orthodox Keynesian model, new equilibrium theories of the business cycle, supply shocks, stagflation, and the impact of rational expectations on macroeconomic modelling and policy formulation. Although empirical growth-accounting research continued (for example Denison, 1974) on the theoretical front work ground to a halt because economists had run out of ideas.

During the 1960s David Cass (1965) and Tjalling Koopmans (1965) made improvements to the basic Solow model by endogenizing savings behaviour. However, the introduction of optimizing behaviour into the model did not change the conclusion that in the long run per capita income growth depends on exogenous technological progress. The lack of theoretical developments in the 1970s led Solow (1982) to comment that 'I think there are definite signs that growth theory is just about played out ... an unpromising pond for an enterprising theorist to fish in'.

During the 1980s several factors led to a reawakening of theoretical research into the growth process and new directions in empirical work also began to develop. On the theoretical front Paul Romer (1986) began to publish material relating to his 1983 University of Chicago PhD thesis. In the same year, 1986, William Baumol and Moses Abramovitz each published highly influential papers relating to the issue of 'catch-up and convergence'. These contributions were soon followed by the publication of Lucas's 1985 Marshall lectures given at the University of Cambridge (Lucas, 1988). This work inspired the development of a 'new' breed of *endogenous growth models* and generated renewed interest in empirical and theoretical questions relating to long-run development (Romer, 1994a; Barro, 1997; Jones, 1998; Aghion and Howitt, 1998). Another important influence was the growing awareness that the data suggested that there had been a slowdown in productivity growth in the post 1973 period in the major OECD economies (Romer, 1987b). Stanley Fischer described this slowdown as 'the most significant macroeconomic development of the last two decades' (see Fischer et al., 1988). In 1996 the first issue of a new *Journal of Economic Growth* was launched. Furthermore many authors of popular economics textbooks began to present their discussion of economic growth towards the beginning rather than at the end of the text (see D. Romer, 1996; Hall and Taylor, 1997; Mankiw, 1997a, 1997b). Economic growth has once more become an active and vibrant research area and is central to contemporary macroeconomics (Klenow and Rodriguez-Clare, 1997).

An Augmented Neoclassical Model

Recently Solow (1997d) has provided an impressive defence of the 'old' growth theory which, despite its limitations, he believes is reasonably consistent with the evidence from new data sets. In his view the empirical evidence does not suggest the wholesale abandonment of the neoclassical model. In response to the recognized limitations of the Solow model some economists have sought to extend the basic neoclassical framework by adopting a 'new view' of capital. Gregory Mankiw, David Romer and David Weil (1992) 'augment' the Solow model by including the accumulation of human capital as well as physical capital. With this modification Mankiw et al. claim that much of the cross-country income differentials can be explained without abandoning the convergence properties of the Solow model. By adding human capital to the model the production function becomes (15):

$$Y = K^{\alpha}H^{\beta}(AL)^{1-\alpha-\beta} \quad \text{and} \quad \alpha + \beta < 1 \quad\quad (15)$$

Where H is the stock of human capital. With $\alpha + \beta < 1$ there are diminishing returns to 'broad capital'. With a larger capital share ($\alpha + \beta = 2/3$) the average product of labour declines more slowly as accumulation takes place since the size of the capital share determines the curvature of the production function and hence the speed at which diminishing returns set in. As a result of this augmentation of the model the transition to the steady state is much slower and 'most international differences in living standards can be explained by differences in the accumulation of both human and physical capital' (Mankiw, 1995b). However, because the exponents on K and H sum to less than one, this is not a model of endogenous growth. Per capita income will eventually settle down in a steady state and grow at the exogenously determined rate of technological progress. While the augmented model better explains international differences in living standards it cannot account for the *persistence* of economic growth. Endogenous growth theory shows how persistent growth may take place without having to resort to exogenous technological progress.

Endogenous Growth Theory

By the 1980s dissatisfaction with the neoclassical model of growth existed on both theoretical and empirical grounds. In attempting to account for the huge income per capita differentials that exist between countries the neoclassical growth model requires differences in capital per worker which are far too large. The data indicate that differences in capital per worker are too small to explain the observed income per capita differentials. While the Solow model can explain differentials of an order of magnitude slightly in excess of two, actual differentials vary by a multiple in excess of ten (Mankiw, 1995b). Because the original Solow model does not provide satisfactory answers to some of the central questions about economic growth, some economists, since the mid-1980s, have sought to construct alternative models of growth where the long-run growth of income per capita depends on 'investment' decisions rather than unexplained technological progress. But as Nick Crafts (1996b) notes, the term investment in the context of these new models refers to a broader concept than the physical capital accumulation reported in the national accounts, research and development (R&D) expenditures and human capital formation may also be included. 'The key to endogenous steady state growth is that there should be constant returns to broad capital accumulation' (Crafts, 1996b). Hence in order to construct a simple theory of endogenous growth the long-run tendency for capital to run into diminishing returns needs to be modified.

In 1986 Romer's seminal paper 'Increasing Returns and Long-Run Growth' was published, effectively launching the new growth theory. Romer's 1986 model is a variant of the earlier 'learning by doing' model of Kenneth Arrow (1962) and also returns to a theme first highlighted in 1890 by Alfred Marshall and extended in 1928 in a famous paper by Allyn Young (Blitch, 1995). In Romer's model 'per capita income in different countries can grow without bound. ... The level of per capita output in different countries need not converge; growth may be persistently slower in less developed countries and may often fail to take place at all' (Romer, 1986). The key insight was to show how the creation of new knowledge by individual firms 'produces a positive external effect on the production possibilities of other firms because knowledge cannot be perfectly patented or kept secret' (Romer, 1986). While each firm in the economy operates with a constant returns to scale production technology, the act of investing by firms creates new knowledge as a byproduct which has spillover effects. An increase in any individual firm's capital stock generates an increase in its stock of knowledge. However, because each firm's knowledge has public good characteristics all other firms have access to any new ideas which originate with an act of investment by any individual firm. These 'externalities' raise the level of knowledge throughout the economy as a whole. Following Barro and Sala-i-Martin (1995) let the production function for an individual firm *j* be shown by (16):

$$Y_j = F(K_j, A_j L_j) \qquad (16)$$

where A_j is an index of knowledge available to the individual firm. Given the spillover effects discussed above, the change in each firm's technology, A_j, will match the economy's overall learning, and will therefore move proportionately with changes in the aggregate capital stock, K. By replacing A_j with K in equation (16) we can write the firm's (*j*) production function as (17):

$$Y_j = F(K_j, K L_j) \qquad (17)$$

If each firm expands K_j, then K will also rise, providing spillover benefits which have positive effects on the productivity of all firms. For a given aggregate labour force, L, there are constant returns to capital accumulation 'at the social level' when K and K_j expand together. If we drop the assumption of a fixed labour force, then the doubling of inputs L and K will more than double output because knowledge is a factor in the production function (Shaw, 1992). The economy as a whole therefore operates under conditions of increasing returns to scale and knowledge displays increasing marginal productivity (in an alternative endogenous growth model developed by Lucas, 1988, the main engine of growth is the accumulation of human capital and the main source of disparities in living standards among nations arises from differences in human capital).

The simplest model of endogenous growth is the so-called AK model (Romer, 1987a; Lucas, 1988; Rebelo, 1991). Assuming a constant positive level of technology, A, zero population growth and 'broad capital' as the only factor of production, output is proportional to the broad capital stock. In this model the marginal product of capital is constant and broad capital should be viewed as a fixed proportions composite of human and physical capital.

$$Y = AK \qquad (18)$$

In (18) the marginal product of capital is the constant, A.

Equation (19) shows how capital is accumulated assuming all saving is invested.

$$\dot{K} = sY - \delta K = sAK - \delta K \qquad (19)$$

This can be rewritten as (20):

$$\dot{K} / K = sA - \delta \qquad (20)$$

Since from (18) output is proportional to capital we can write the growth rate (g) of output as (21):

$$g = \dot{Y} / Y = sA - \delta \qquad (21)$$

This shows the rate of growth as an increasing function of the rate of investment. As long as $sA > \delta$ continuous growth of income occurs even without assuming exogenous technological progress. Given a constant population, equation (21) implies that per capita income is also an increasing function of investment (Jones, 1998). Therefore government policies that can successfully increase the investment rate have the potential to permanently increase the rate of growth of the economy. In addition policies which raise the baseline technology, A, can also influence the long-run per capita growth rate (for example improvements in the economy's infrastructure). The AK model is illustrated in Figure 7. If initially the economy is at point G and has a capital stock of K_1 and an aggregate level of output of Y_1, it is easy to see that because total investment at point B is greater than total depreciation, shown at point C, the capital stock will continuously accumulate and, unlike the Solow model, income will continue to grow even though technology is constant. In effect the transitional dynamics of the Solow model last indefinitely!

In Romer's 1986 model the growth of knowledge results from learning externalities among firms. Dissatisfied with that approach Romer (1987a,

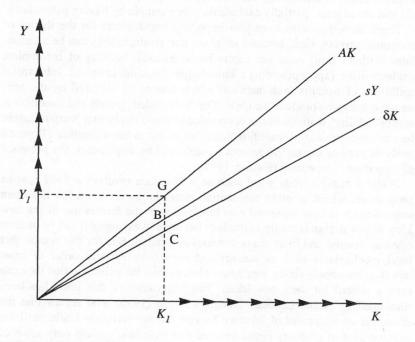

Figure 7   Endogenous growth

1990) went on to develop a neo-Schumpeterian model of endogenous technological change based on three premises. First, as in the Solow model, the
basic driving force behind economic growth is technological change, that is
improvements in knowledge about how we transform inputs into outputs in
the production process. Second, technological change is *endogenous*, being
determined by the deliberate activities of economic agents acting largely in
response to financial incentives (Grossman and Helpman, 1994; Aghion and
Howitt, 1998). Third, the defining characteristic of ideas/knowledge is that
'once the cost of creating a new set of instructions has been incurred, the
instructions can be used over and over again at no additional cost' (Romer,
1990). Therefore ideas are *non-rivalrous* goods, their use by one firm or
person does not in any way reduce their availability to other firms or persons.
Ideas are also *partially excludable*, where excludability is defined as the
ability of the owners of a good to prevent other economic agents from using it
without payment. As Romer notes 'excludability is a function of the technology and the legal system'. Given Romer's second premise that technological
change results from the purposeful actions of self-interested economic agents,

improvements in technology (new ideas) must generate benefits to individuals that are at least 'partially excludable', for example by having patent laws.

These three premises have two important implications for the theory of economic growth. First, because ideas are non-rivalrous they can be accumulated without limit on a per capita basis. Second, because of incomplete excludability (appropriability) knowledge creation involves substantial spillovers of benefits (externalities) which cannot be captured by the economic agents who produce the ideas. The 'unbounded' growth and 'incomplete appropriability' features of the economics of ideas imply that 'output cannot be a constant-returns-to-scale function of all its inputs taken together'. Romer's analysis implies increasing returns to scale and by implication the presence of imperfect competition (Romer, 1994a).

While a non-rivalrous good such as a new idea involves a *fixed cost* of production, which is often substantial, once the new knowledge has been created there is zero *marginal cost* involved with the further use of the new idea. A new design is costly to produce but once in existence it can be used as often as desired and in as many contexts as desired. It is for this reason that legal mechanisms such as *patents* and *copyrights* exist in order to grant investors monopoly rights over a new idea, at least for a time, so that they can earn a reward for their new ideas. The importance of this issue has been illustrated by Nobel Laureate Douglass North (1990) who argues that the economic development of Western Europe did not seriously begin until the development of property rights ensured that individuals could reap some of the benefits of their 'ideas' and helped to speed up the pace of technological change (Crafts, 1995). The era of modern economic growth, beginning with the industrial revolution in Britain, 'occurred when the institutions protecting intellectual property rights were sufficiently well developed that entrepreneurs could capture as a private return some of the enormous social returns their innovations would create ... history suggests that it is only when the market incentives were sufficient that widespread innovation and growth took hold' (Jones, 1998).

By developing an endogenous theory of technological change Romer has challenged the traditional and augmented versions of the Solow neoclassical growth model. In the neoclassical model technology is assumed to be exogenous and hence available without limitation everywhere across the globe. Romer (1995) rejects this assumption on the basis of 'overwhelming evidence' that technology is not a pure public good. The neoclassical model emphasizes 'object gaps', differences in physical and human capital, in explaining income per capita differentials across nations. In contrast, P. Romer (1993) emphasizes 'idea gaps', productivity differences resulting from technology gaps, as the main source of divergent living standards. If Romer is correct and the poor countries do suffer from idea gaps then a significant part of worldwide poverty can be eliminated 'at relatively low cost' via techno-logical 'catch-up'. A clear implication of this analysis is that nations that isolate themselves from the free flow of ideas will suffer relative stagnation since trade policies affect innovation and growth (Romer, 1994b; Proudman and Redding, 1997).

Some Policy Implications

Reflecting Romer's emphasis on the importance of 'ideas' the 1998/99 *World Development Report* looks at the problems of economic development from the perspective of knowledge. The Report identifies two types of knowledge which are critical for the developing world. First, poor countries lack knowl-edge about technology. This 'knowledge gap' can be narrowed by acquiring ideas through an open trading regime, encouraging inward investment, pro-moting local R&D initiatives, expanding education and using modern communications technology to spread knowledge more widely. Second, poor countries suffer from information deficiencies relating to the *attributes* of many economic activities, for example inadequate information relating to the financial sector in East Asia (Radelet and Sachs, 1998). Both of these influ-ences affect the pace of economic progress. In order for developing countries to take advantage of the opportunities for catch up they 'must be open to new ideas and capture the benefits of technological progress by closing the gaps in knowledge' (World Bank, 1998/99).

The importance of knowledge for economic development can be illustrated by the respective development experiences of Ghana and the Republic of Korea. Figure 8 shows the evolution of income per capita for the two coun-tries over a 30-year period. In 1960 there was no discernible income per capita differential between the two countries but by 1990 Korea's income per capita was six times higher than Ghana's. The World Bank economists at-tribute half of that differential to Korea's greater success in organizing and using knowledge.

As Table 2 demonstrates small differences in growth rates result in large differences in the level of income per capita within a relatively short histori-cal time period. Given that capital and technology can migrate across political boundaries the persistence of significant differences in the level of output per worker suggests the presence of persistent barriers to factor mobility. An obvious deterrent to the free flow of capital from rich to poor countries arises from the greater risk involved in investing in countries characterized by macroeconomic instability, inadequate infrastructure, poor education, ethnic diversity, widespread corruption, political instability and frequent policy re-versals. While the presence of technological backwardness and income per capita gaps creates the potential for catch up and convergence, Moses

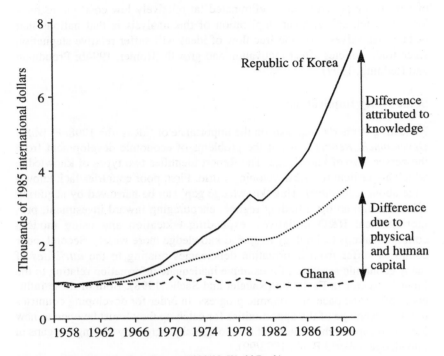

Source: *World Development Report* (1998/99, World Bank)

Figure 8   The importance of knowledge

Abramovitz (1986) has highlighted the importance of 'social capability' without which countries will not be able to realize their potential. Social capability refers to the various institutional arrangements which set the framework for the conduct of productive economic activities and without which market economies cannot function efficiently. Building on that idea (inherited from Adam Smith) Robert Hall and Charles Jones (1997) explain the large differentials in output per worker across nations as a result of differences in social infrastructure, 'the collection of laws, institutions and government policies that make up the economic environment'.

Social Infrastructure →→ (Inputs, Productivity) →→ Output per Worker

Countries with perverse infrastructure, such as a corrupt bureaucracy, generate rent-seeking activities devoted to the *diversion* of resources rather than productive activities. In an environment of weak law and contract enforcement, poor protection of property rights, confiscatory taxation and widespread corruption, rent-seeking activities will become endemic and cause immense damage to innovation and other growth-enhancing activities. There is abundant evidence that economic incentives can influence the productivity and interests of talented individuals who potentially can make a huge contribution to the accumulation of wealth. For individuals or groups of individuals to have an incentive to adopt more advanced technology or engage in the creation of new ideas requires an institutional framework which allows for an adequate rate of return. The reason why income per capita is so high in the US compared to India 'must be that India has been less successful than the US in setting up economic institutions conducive to development' (Hansen and Prescott, 1993). The major observed income differentials we observe around the world have a lot to do with differences in the quality of countries' institutions and economic policies (Olson, 1996; Woglin, 1997). This explains the rapid growth witnessed in a subset of East Asian developing countries since around 1960 and the relative stagnation of most of Sub-Saharan Africa over that same period (North, 1990; Murphy et al., 1991, 1993; Parente and Prescott, 1992; Shleifer and Vishny, 1993; Mauro, 1995, 1998; Ades and Di Tella, 1997; Hall and Jones, 1999).

The relatively (to other similar economies) poor performance of the UK economy in the 1950–80 period is well documented (Crafts and Toniolo, 1996) and recent research in growth analysis provides some useful insights into that record. The new growth economics implies that policy and institutions have potentially strong effects on the growth rate and give emphasis to broad capital accumulation and policies to encourage more rapid technical change such as R&D expenditures. Foreign direct investment can benefit the economy by reducing the 'ideas gap' and the endogenous innovation literature draws attention to the importance of incentives and the need to enhance the appropriability of returns in order to encourage the development of new goods and production processes. Viewed in this light Crafts (1996a, 1996b) argues that 'British supply-side policy during the years of rapid relative decline from the 1950s through to the 1970s appears most unfortunate' (Crafts, 1996b). It is in this context that the Autumn 1994 speech by the then Shadow Chancellor, Gordon Brown, should be viewed. In referring to 'post-neoclassical endogenous growth theory' Brown was hopefully drawing attention to the need for new thinking on the form and style of supply-side policies from Labour Party politicians!

Of great concern to many contemporary observers of the US economy has been the erosion of *technological leadership* (measured by productivity performance) experienced during the past quarter century. This leadership has existed for over a century after the US overtook the UK in terms of average labour productivity around 1890. The major factors contributing to US leadership were resource abundance combined with the scale advantages from a large single market (Nelson and Wright, 1992; Rosenberg, 1994; Romer, 1996). The consolidation and preservation of leadership by the US up until the mid-1950s owed a great deal to 'massive private and public investment in R&D and scientific and technical knowledge'. The erosion of US leadership by those major OECD economies possessing the requisite 'social capabilities' was inevitable as these economies followed the US example of investing in human capital and developing their own R&D sectors. In absolute terms the US remains the world's biggest spender on R&D but, as Figure 9 indicates, is slightly behind Japan when R&D expenditures are measured as a percentage of GDP. Table 6 shows that this situation with respect to Japan has prevailed since 1988 and that Germany also had a greater ratio of R&D expenditure to GDP in the period 1986–90. When it comes to non-defence-related R&D both Japan and Germany are ahead of the US in terms of R&D expenditures measured as a percentage of GDP.

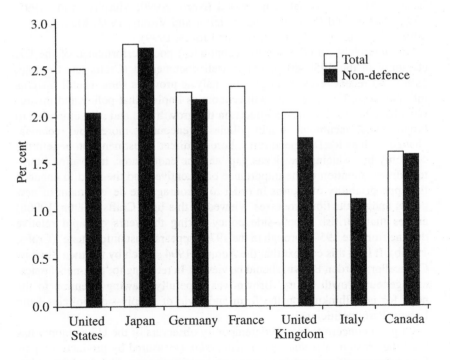

Source: National Science Foundation – National Patterns of R&D Resources, 1997

Figure 9   R&D expenditures as a percentage of GDP (1995)

Table 6 International R&D expenditures (total and non-defence) as a percentage of GDP, 1981–1997

| | Total R&D expenditures | | | | | | | Total non-defence R&D expenditures | | | | |
Year	United States	Japan	Germany*	France*	United Kingdom	Italy	Canada	United States	Japan	Germany*	France	United Kingdom
1981	2.32	2.13	2.43	1.97	2.37	0.88	1.25	1.73	2.12	2.34	1.57	1.84
1982	2.49	2.22	2.52	2.06	NA	0.91	1.40	1.79	2.21	2.44	1.66	NA
1983	2.55	2.35	2.52	2.11	2.19	0.95	1.37	1.80	2.34	2.43	1.74	1.69
1984	2.61	2.43	2.51	2.21	NA	1.01	1.41	1.83	2.41	2.42	1.82	NA
1985	2.74	2.58	2.72	2.25	2.23	1.13	1.45	1.89	2.56	2.60	1.87	1.76
1986	2.71	2.55	2.73	2.23	2.25	1.13	1.49	1.86	2.53	2.61	1.84	1.82
1987	2.68	2.62	2.88	2.27	2.19	1.19	1.44	1.83	2.60	2.75	1.85	1.79
1988	2.64	2.66	2.86	2.28	2.14	1.22	1.39	1.84	2.63	2.74	1.85	1.80
1989	2.60	2.77	2.87	2.33	2.15	1.24	1.39	1.88	2.75	2.75	1.92	1.81
1990	2.64	2.85	2.75	2.41	2.18	1.30	1.47	1.97	2.83	2.62	1.95	1.84
1991	2.71	2.82	2.61	2.41	2.11	1.32	1.52	2.10	2.79	2.51	1.98	1.79
1992	2.64	2.76	2.48	2.42	2.13	1.31	1.57	2.07	2.73	2.39	2.04	1.83
1993	2.52	2.68	2.43	2.45	2.15	1.26	1.63	1.98	2.65	2.35	2.10	1.85
1994	2.43	2.64	2.33	2.38	2.11	1.16	1.62	1.95	2.60	2.25	2.05	1.84
1995	2.52	2.78	2.28	2.34	2.05	1.14	1.61	2.05	2.74	2.20	NA	1.78
1996 prelim.	2.55	NA	2.26	NA	NA	1.13	1.59	2.10	NA	NA	NA	NA
1997 prelim.	2.59	NA	NA	NA	NA	NA	NA	2.15	NA	NA	NA	NA

Notes:
*   German data before 1991 are for West Germany only
Key: GDP = Gross Domestic Product; NA = not available

Source: National Science Foundation – National Patterns of R&D Resources, 1997

A clear implication of Romer's research is that for the US to maintain its leadership position, government policies must continue to support a high level of R&D activities in both private and public institutions. Given the well-documented large divergence between social and private rates of return from R&D expenditures the government has a vital role to play in preventing underinvestment in this activity. Neo-Schumpeterian analysis points towards the creation and preservation of institutions that foster invention and innovation (Oakley, 1990).

Future Directions of Research

What will be the likely future direction of research in the area of growth analysis? In recent years the burgeoning literature on the new growth empirics has extended research into a number of important areas. In particular there has been an outpouring of research examining the influence on growth of demographic factors, financial sector performance, government spending, income distribution, the macroeconomic environment and political and social influences. Jonathan Temple (1999) suggests that research using cross-country regressions should now be complemented with historical analysis of individual country experience to try and identify some interesting 'natural experiments'. Jeffrey Sachs and Andrew Warner (1997) argue in favour of more research into the impact of geography, resource endowments and climate on long-term growth and David Landes (1990, 1998) has emphasized the importance of geography and culture as a stimulus to Europe's industrial revolution. Howard Pack (1994) has drawn attention to the empirical short-comings of endogenous growth theory and urges testing the insights of the new theories against the economic evolution of individual countries. Solow's (1994) vision of the research agenda is to recommend the extraction of 'a few workable hypotheses' from the available case studies so as to throw light on good ways 'to model the flow of productivity increasing innovations and improvements'. The neo-Schumpeterian work of Phillipe Aghion and Peter Howitt (1998) clearly points to the need for further research into 'how organizations, institutions, market structure, market imperfections, trade, government policy and the legal framework' affect long-run growth via their influence on economic agents' incentives to innovate. While Zvi Griliches (1994) doubts that economists can ever produce a fully endogenous theory of economic growth given the inherent uncertainties associated with innovative activity, Romer is more ambitious and optimistic. Reflecting on the origins of endogenous growth Romer (1994a) expresses hopes that the new breed of endogenous innovation models holds out the prospect that in the future economists will be able to offer policy makers something more useful than the policy silent neoclassical framework where long-run growth is driven by unexplained technological progress. In particular the new growth theories provide insights into the impact of trade on growth, the role of multinationals, the impact of taxes and subsidies in promoting R&D expenditures, the importance of intellectual property rights, and the design of public policy towards the creation of institutions that can foster the production and accumulation of knowledge (Nelson and Romer, 1996).

MACROECONOMICS AT THE MILLENNIUM: IS THERE A CONSENSUS?

Our discussion has highlighted *some* of the major developments in the evolution of modern macroeconomics and inevitably has focused on areas of controversy and disagreement. However it would be wrong to conclude that there is no consensus on a number of key macroeconomics issues. Here we summarize six main areas on which there now appears to be widespread though by no means unanimous agreement, noting that in some instances this agreement has only been reached after intense debate and controversy in the past. The present consensus view among macroeconomists can be characterized as follows:

1. The trend movement of real GDP is *primarily* driven by supply-side factors. As such, in the long run, the growth of real GDP depends upon increases in the supply of factor inputs and improvements in the state of technology (Solow, 1997b). While there are various policies governments can adopt to influence economic growth – including encouraging education and training, capital formation, and research and development – there is continuing debate over what is the best way to increase the economy's productive capacity and what role the government can and should play in encouraging growth.
2. Real GDP fluctuates around a rising long-term trend and short-run fluctuations in real GDP are *primarily* caused by aggregate demand shocks (as we have seen real business cycle theorists such as Prescott challenge this view). The reason why movements in aggregate demand can influence real output is linked to the presence of nominal rigidities. Macroeconomists also debate whether governments cause instability and what policies they can and should pursue to reduce short-run fluctuations in economic activity. In attempting to identify the main cause of cycles emphasis is placed on various sources of aggregate demand shocks, including: changes in autonomous expenditures (Keynesians); changes in the rate of monetary growth (monetarists); unanticipated monetary shocks (new classicals). Interestingly, compared with the experience of

the Great Depression fluctuations in real GDP in the post-Second World War period have been relatively minor – the main exceptions being the periods following the two adverse OPEC oil price (supply) shocks and the period of disinflation in the early 1980s in the US and Europe. As Solow (1997b) puts it, 'fluctuations around trend are contained in a moderately narrow corridor'.

3.   While the authorities face a short-run trade-off between inflation and unemployment, in the long run the trade-off disappears. As Blinder (1997) argues, the expectations-augmented Phillips curve 'has worked very well' and along with 'Okun's Law' represents a 'sturdy empirical relationship'. In the short run it is widely accepted that the authorities can reduce unemployment below the natural rate by engaging in expansionary aggregate demand policies. Reducing unemployment involves a short-run trade-off as inflation increases. Alternatively enacting contractionary aggregate demand policies which reduce inflation involves a short-run trade-off as unemployment increases. In the long run, however, there is no trade-off between inflation and unemployment. A corollary is that in the long run the authorities can achieve a lower rate of inflation with no change in the natural rate of unemployment, and that to reduce the natural rate, which is held to be independent of the level of aggregate demand, requires microeconomic (aggregate supply management) policies which improve the structure and functioning of the labour market. Some new Keynesians would add one important qualification to this consensus view, namely that in circumstances where the actual rate of unemployment remains above the natural rate for a prolonged period, the natural rate (or what Keynesians would prefer to refer to as NAIRU) will tend to increase due to hysteresis effects. In other words, some new Keynesians argue that the natural rate (or NAIRU) can be affected by the level of aggregate demand (Blanchard, 1997c).

4.   In the long run the rate of growth of the money supply determines the rate of inflation. Friedman has convinced the majority of the profession and policy makers that *sustained* inflation is a monetary phenomenon and that the main aim of monetary policy should be the pursuit of a low and stable rate of inflation. Indeed many countries now have a long-run inflation target with monetary policy directed to keep the growth of aggregate demand stable in order to create macroeconomic stability.

5.   In contrast to the dominant Keynesian view held in the 1950s and early 1960s it is now widely accepted that governments should not attempt to 'fine tune' their economies in order to keep output and employment close to, or at, their full employment or natural levels using discretionary aggregate demand policies. Most economists now accept that the stabi-

lizing potential of activist discretionary fiscal policy is at best limited and that the stabilizing role of fiscal policy lies embedded in automatic stabilizers. Furthermore there has been a marked change of focus away from fiscal policy towards monetary policy as the main tool of stabilization policy. The modern discussion over rules versus discretion involves that between advocates of flexible Taylor-type rules versus those who favour rough tuning. With respect to monetary policy there are few remaining advocates of Friedman's hard core monetarist prescription for a k per cent rule for money growth. The empirical evidence also indicates that in the short run monetary policy has real effects so both the 'classic Keynesian' and 'vintage RBC' views have been 'buried' (Eichenbaum, 1997).

6. Again, in contrast to the 1950s and 1960s when stabilization was regarded as a control-theory problem, it is now viewed as a game-theoretic problem. The insight that the policy regime adopted by the authorities affects people's expectations and behaviour is now widely accepted. So too is the importance given to establishing the credibility of policy and the design of institutions to conduct credible policy, as evidenced by the increasing attention given to the issue of central bank independence. Furthermore, most economists agree that the short-run output/employment costs of disinflation will be less if policy is credible. While Taylor (1997) includes the rational expectations hypothesis in his core of practical macroeconomics, Solow (1997b) remains a sceptic.

To sum up, 'the good news for policymakers is that there is indeed a core of usable macroeconomics; the good news for macroeconomic researchers is that there is a lot of work still to be done' (Blanchard, 1997c).

As to the future course of macroeconomics two main pathways immediately stand out. First, real business cycle models are likely to be integrated more into the mainstream (Danthine, 1997). Certainly over recent years a number of real business cycle models have introduced nominal rigidities which allow for the short-run effects of money on output and employment. Second, there is likely to be continuing interest shown in the new growth theory and the new growth empirics (Temple, 1999). By providing a better understanding of the growth process, new growth theory holds out the prospect of providing insights which may prove invaluable in helping design policies which could make a significant difference to long-term growth rates and living standards. However, in 1998, with the world economy in a state of uncertainty and fears of widespread deflation, the ghost of John Maynard Keynes is with us once more. Those who ignore the lessons of economic and political history do so at their peril!

We began this chapter with a quotation from Mark Blaug. It therefore seems fitting to close this opening chapter with another of his views which we find most appealing.

> I have never been able to grasp how one can understand any idea without knowing where it came from, how it evolved out of previous ideas. ... Great theories, in economics as in other subjects, are path dependent ... that is, it is not possible to explain their occurrence without considering the corpus of received ideas which led to the development of that particular new theory; had the body of received ideas been different we would have arrived at a different theory at the culmination of that development. In other words, without the history of economics, economic theories just drop from the sky; you have to take them on faith. The moment you wish to judge a theory, you have to ask how they came to be produced in the first place and that is a question that can only be answered by the history of ideas. (Blaug, 1994c)

James Tobin
(b. 1912)

James Tobin is currently Sterling Professor Emeritus of Economics at Yale University. As one of America's most prominent and distinguished Keynesian economists he has been a longstanding advocate of Keynesian stabilization policies and a leading critic of monetarism and the new classical equilibrium approach. He has made fundamental contributions to monetary and macroeconomic theory as well as important contributions to the links between cyclical fluctuations and economic growth. In 1981 he was awarded the Nobel Prize in Economics: 'For his analysis of financial markets and their relations to expenditure decisions, employment, production and prices.'

We interviewed Professor Tobin in his office on 17 February 1993 and subsequently corresponded in January/February 1998.

KEYNES AND KEYNESIAN ECONOMICS

You began your study of economics at Harvard the very year that the General Theory *was published. What attracted you to economics?*
It was an unbelievably happy combination of a subject that promised to save the world and was fascinating from an intellectual puzzle-solving point of view. I was also very much worried about the Great Depression and had every

reason to think that the massive failure of our economies was the key to many other of the world's ills, political as well as economic.

The General Theory *is a very difficult book and reflects Keynes's 'long struggle to escape' previous ideas. What were your first impressions of the* General Theory?
I didn't know enough to know it was a difficult book which I had no business reading. I was 19 years old. My tutor at Harvard, who had been in England for a year, just said at our first one on one tutorial meeting 'Why don't you and I read this new book I've heard about for our tutorial this year?' I didn't know any better so I read it, and I didn't feel it was that difficult. One of the exciting things, of course, for a 19-year-old was the sense of intellectual revolution, overturning the obsolete wisdom encrusted in the past, especially when the new theory was on the side of promising to do something constructive about the main problems that concerned me and people of my generation.

Skidelsky (1992) in his biography of Keynes (Volume II) has argued that 'Keynes's inspiration was radical but his purpose conservative'. How did Keynes reconcile these two opposing forces?
I think that what Skidelsky says is essentially right. Compare Keynes's remedies for the problems of the world at the time to those of Marxians and Spengler's *Decline of the West* – all those apocalyptic warnings of the death of capitalism, because capitalism can't ever succeed. Keynes comes along and says that the basic problem is not really the organization of the economy but rather the way that aggregate demand is controlled. Keynes had no great complaint about the way the economy allocates the resources that it does employ, just that it doesn't employ them all.

It only took about twelve years for the General Theory *to capture the hearts and minds of the vast majority of the economics profession. Why did Keynes's ideas spread so quickly?*
Well, because it did look as if they would work to remedy the problems of the Great Depression. There was a lot of anxiety in all countries that after the Second World War we would revert to the depression conditions of the pre-war period. Keynes's ideas looked like a pretty good way to avoid that possibility. In the United States, consider the spending for mobilization even before we got in the war, and what it did to GNP and employment. That was a dramatic living vindication of Keynes's ideas.

You are widely recognized as being America's most distinguished Keynesian economist. Are you happy with the label Keynesian and what does being a Keynesian mean to you?

If you'd asked me that, let's say 25 years ago, I would have said that I don't like any label and that I'm just an economist working on problems that I happen to be interested in; macroeconomic problems, monetary–fiscal policy and all those things. There appeared to be a considerable practical consensus about these matters. A lot of my work had been fixing up Keynes in various ways where I found theoretical problems or a lack of 'micro foundations'. In fact the first thing I wrote and got published (in 1941) was a piece of anti-Keynesian theory on his problem of the relation of money wage and employment. So at that time I would have said let's not label people, let's just do our work. After the counter-revolutions, when all these schools and labels arose, I certainly would be proud to be regarded as a Keynesian, considering the alternatives (*laughter*).

What are the fundamental propositions which Keynesians adhere to?
One way to put it is to say that there is a two-régime model of the economy. Sometimes the economy is in a classical situation where markets are clearing (demand equals supply) and the economy's ability to produce output is supply constrained. You can't produce any more because there are essentially no idle resources (I exaggerate to simplify). Therefore the constraint on output is *capacity*. That capacity constraints results in a price and income structure that equalizes demand and supply at those prices. At other times the economy is in a Keynesian situation in which the constraint on actual output is *demand* – aggregate spending. Extra output would be produced if there were extra aggregate real demand, and the inputs to make it are available at real returns which won't exceed what the factors of production could earn by their productivity if they were employed. That situation obtains lots of the time, not always, and there are then demand-increasing policies that will eliminate the social waste involved. That I think is the distinction. Whereas for the real business cycle theorists (like Ed Prescott) and new classical guys (like Robert Barro) you are always supply-constrained. There is just one régime, and the observed cyclical fluctuations are fluctuations in voluntary willingness to be employed.

Some interpretations of the neoclassical synthesis which emerged in the late 1950s and early 1960s suggest that the General Theory *represents a special case of a more general classical model. What is your view on that particular interpretation?*
I wouldn't interpret it that way. Rather there was a consensus on the two-régime model just mentioned. I thought there was also a normative consensus, in the sense that you shouldn't regard any output that you get from putting unemployed resources to work as free, because you have alternative ways of putting unemployed resources at work. The same classical opportunity cost

considerations that determine allocation of resources in a classical equilibrium determine the allocation of resources as among different ways of returning to that supply-constrained régime. So I think in that sense there is no excuse for wasteful projects to increase employment, like digging holes in the ground, because you can arrange to employ people by investments or other projects that are socially beneficial. In that sense the classical opportunity cost considerations apply in either regime. But that's only if you're prepared to do something to get out of the wasteful situation that you're in.

Has too much been made of the Pigou effect as a way of diminishing Keynes's contribution to economic theory?
Of course. I've said that all the time in print. It's a very slender reed on which to assert the efficacy of self-adjusting mechanisms. For one thing the accounting aggregation of credits and debts doesn't necessarily imply behavioural netting out of credits and debts. I believe that the effects of deflation on aggregate demand can be perverse if debtors have a bigger propensity to spend from wealth than creditors do – a reasonable expectation. Then there's the whole issue how you get to the lower price level from where you are. The immaculate conception effect of getting there suggests there's no real time involved – it's just the static comparison of one price level to another price level. As Keynes himself observed, although he didn't make of it a point of theoretical principle, the process of deflation – or disinflation for that matter – involves an increase in the real interest rate and certainly produces perverse effects.

Do you think that if Keynes had still been alive in 1969 (aged 86) he would have been awarded the first Nobel Prize in economics?
Very likely. He would have got my vote. As for Keynes versus Tinbergen and Frisch, the actual recipients, I don't know. The prize says for economic *science*. In some senses they might have been considered to have made identifiable innovations more similar to those of Nobel-winning natural scientists. But JMK would have been an early award-winner.

How do you feel about your award of the Nobel Prize in 1981? What do you consider to be your most important contributions to macroeconomics?
I never thought I was going to get it. I was interested in straightening out macroeconomics and the neoclassical synthesis as I understood them, in generalizing monetary models to take account of the variety of assets, in portfolio theory and its macroeconomic implications – that's what I was trying to do.

Why do you think there are so many conflicting interpretations of the General Theory?

Well, I suppose one reason is that the book is ambiguous in many ways and has a number of strands that could be cited to support different messages. They allow people a variety of different views about the world, in particular, on the one hand, since people interpret the *General Theory* as a kind of general equilibrium model of the determination of output, employment, interest rates that could be used in both of the two régimes I referred to above. That's what J.R. Hicks was doing in his famous article. On the other hand you have Chapters 12 on long-run expectations, which suggests that maybe there is not an investment function at all. In the Hicks general equilibrium model you have got to have an investment function. The second approach, stressing the conventionality of expectations and animal spirits, may be seen as opening the way to a different kind of model. This would be supported by Keynes's own tentative advocacy of the socialization of investment, his suspicion that maybe investment wouldn't be adequately stabilized by monetary and fiscal policy, his feeling that you need some central planning to get it right. I guess those ambiguities allow us to interpret it one way or the other. Of course, some people hoped to extract from Keynes a much more radical position with regard to the social and political institutions than he had explicitly expressed. I have in mind Mrs Robinson and others who claim to be the true heirs of Keynes. I never could get that excited about this kind of battle over Keynes's mantle so to speak. The central part of the book, the central core of the modelling, is on the other side, Hick's side, in my opinion. Certainly that's in practice the model that has been taught and has influenced policy making and macroeconomic theorizing for more than 50 years.

Do you think teaching the IS–LM model is still an important part of an undergraduates' understanding of the macro economy given the criticisms of the IS–LM model by people like Robinson, Clower and Leijonhufvud?
Yes I think the IS–LM model is the tool of first resort. If you're faced with a problem of interpretation of the economy – policy or events – probably the most useful first thing you can do is to try to see how to look at it in these terms. Since students are in that position, yes they need to know it. It's not the end of the matter by any means. I don't say that it's enough. I doubt if Keynes or Hicks would have thought it enough. But it's a start and lots of times it's exactly right.

CRITIQUES OF KEYNESIANISM

Would you accept that many of the theoretical changes made in the 1970s, and inspired by people like Lucas, were the inevitable consequence of defects in the Keynesian model?

No I wouldn't accept that. I do think the idea of model consistent expectations is a good idea. It would be a bad feature of any equilibrium model that people chronically perpetuate mistaken expectations about variables, mistaken in the sense that they are different from those that the model persistently creates itself. But I think that applying that idea to dynamic situations where learning is going on and people can have a lot of different opinions about the world is carrying it too far.

How important do you think it is for macroeconomics to have neoclassical choice-theoretic foundations?

Well, I think it's important for the behavioural equations of a macroeconomic model not to contradict choice-theoretic considerations, to be in principle consistent with them. But I think the stronger version of 'microfoundations' is a methodological mistake, one that has produced a tremendous amount of mischief. I refer to the now orthodox requirement of postulating representative agents whose optimizations generate 'macroeconomic' behavioural equations. That is a considerable sacrifice of the essence of much of macroeconomics. Suppose you have a lot of different types of agents, who are all maximizing. Then it's their aggregation into a behavioural equation that you want for a macro model. That aggregation won't necessarily be the solution for any single agent. To insist that it must be seems to be me very wrongheaded. It has put us on the wrong track in macroeconomics or what passes for macroeconomics.

In the late 1960s you had a considerable debate with Friedman who at one stage argued that the main differences between macroeconomists were over empirical matters. Surely the 1970s demonstrated that there were some fundamental theoretical differences between macroeconomists?

What Friedman was saying was disingenuous. He had a theory of the demand for money which put a lot of variables in the demand function including various interest rates, and yet his monetary policy propositions were based on the assumption that interest rates were not in the function. He asserted empirical results that he was unique in finding – that the interest elasticity of the demand for money was negligible. When he was really stuck by the weight of evidence, he then wrote that the question of the size of interest elasticity of the demand for money had nothing to do with anything. The only way one could make sense of that particular proposition was that you were going to be at full employment anyway, no matter what the stock of money was, and so the interest rate would have to be what was consistent with the demand and supply of savings at full employment. But that was a complete evasion of the original issues of our debate. He had never before said that monetary policy would have *no* effects on real variables. He said they have a lot of effects on real variables. He had some kind of Phillips curve (although he didn't call it that) in his mind, and even when he invented the natural rate he still did. He didn't deny that monetary policy would have some effects on real output during cyclical fluctuations – so he was caught between being a true new classical economist, in which case he was going to have to say that money doesn't ever matter, or being a pragmatic monetarist where he didn't have a good theoretical or empirical basis for what he had been saying.

What exactly is the difference between Friedman's concept of the natural rate of unemployment and NAIRU – the non-accelerating inflation rate of unemployment? Is there some important difference between these two concepts?
I don't think there is a big practical difference. Maybe what was in the mind of Modigliani when he started that acronym, was that Friedman said that the natural rate was the amount of unemployment that was the solution to Walrasian general equilibrium equations – a proposition that neither he nor anybody else ever proved as far as I know – complete speculation. I mean, why would Walrasian equations have any unemployment at all in their solution? (*laughter*). That identification of the natural rate doesn't make any sense, and it's certainly not true. When Modigliani and others started talking about NAIRU, they were talking more about a pragmatic empirical idea.

At the end of the day politicians make economic policy. The public choice school, as well as the work of your colleague William Nordhaus on political business cycles, suggests that politicians may actually use economic policy for their own gain. Do you think that Keynes was perhaps naive in thinking that we could hand over policy making to politicians and they would follow the advice of economists?
I won't quote the last paragraph of the *General Theory*, which says that in the long run ideas matter. I think that's true, but I think my point would be a little different. If we are advising government officials, politicians, voters, it's not for us economists to play games with them. It's not for Keynes to say, I am not going to suppress the *General Theory* and not tell the House of Commons, the Labour Party, the Tories, whomever, that it would be possible to reduce unemployment by public works expenditure. If I am giving advice to them about war finance – or whatever else my advice will be not to do bad things – I am not going to decide myself that they are so evil and irresponsible that I don't give them advice about what actions will do what. I don't think that Jim Buchanan has, or I have, the right to withhold advice from Presidents of the United States or Members of Congress or the electorate on the grounds that if they knew what we know, they would misuse it. I don't think that is for us to decide.

You have said that good papers in economics contain surprises and stimulate further work. On this criteria the 1970s contributions of people like Lucas, Sargent, Wallace and Barro were good. Do you feel that new classical macroeconomics has changed macroeconomics for the better?

In some respects I think Lucas's ideas about policies being anticipated by actors, so you can't be sure that behaviour will stay put when you change policy, is an important idea, one we have to worry about. I don't think it is as important an idea as he seemed to think it was. I thought his ingenious explanation of how you can have observations that look like Phillips curves yet have none of the operational policy implications of the curve – that was neat. However, I think it turned out not to be a good idea. It didn't survive because of the implausible notion that people are confused about what the money supply is. If they're confused, why don't we publish the money supply data every Friday afternoon – which in the US we do of course and have been doing for a long time. I observe that the new classicals no longer pay any attention to this misperception story. They have become much more extreme. Barro's (1974) paper was provocative and stimulated a lot of theoretical and empirical work. I had a paper in my Jahnsson lectures (Tobin, 1980b) that gave, I don't know, say 15 reasons why Barro's neutrality proposition doesn't work, and I think there have been numerous articles since on each of them.

We have seen a lot of contributions recently from what are called new Keynesian economists. What is the central difference between your view of Keynesian economics and the new Keynesian contributions? Is it that they accept rational expectations and a lot of monetarist ideas?

Yes, they accept rational expectations. Moreover they accept the methodology of choice-theoretic foundations and representative agents, much more than I would. They accept market-clearing, except as it is modified by imperfect competition, much more than I would. They regard their task as to give a rationale for the alleged rigidity of money wages and money prices, a rationale that allows nominal shocks to create real consequences. I think that was *not* Keynes's idea. Keynes was primarily concerned not with nominal demand shocks but real demand shocks, which would create problems even if prices were flexible. They have said that all they are going to do is show how it is rational for nominal prices to be inflexible and derive unemployment results from that. I don't find it extremely convincing – and I'm sure Keynes would have not – that the whole effective demand problem is that there are real costs of changing nominal prices on the menu at the restaurant. I think Keynes would have laughed at the idea that menu costs are a big enough resource-using problem to cause the Great Depression or any other substantial losses of economic activity. It's not credible. If I had a copyright on who could use the term Keynesian I wouldn't allow them to use it (*laughter*).

What do you think of the real business cycle approach?
That's really the enemy at the other extreme of macroeconomics. Real business cycle theory suggests that society is a moving equilibrium responding continuously to technological–productivity–supply shocks all the time, and that the economy is doing the best job possible in responding to them. It's those benign responses that generate the fluctuations we call business cycles. There isn't any unemployment in the Keynesian sense. There are simply intertemporal substitutions of employment now and employment later, which are rational responses to the stochastic environment in which people live. I don't see any credibility to the idea that people are doing a lot of intertemporal substitution as to how much they want to work. To interpret the rise in unemployment in this country from 5.7 per cent in 1978 to 11 per cent in 1982 as a desire on the part of workers to take leisure in preparation for working when real wages will be higher – that is ridiculous (*laughter*).

Should we take Lucas's (1978a) advice and abandon the concept of involuntary unemployment?
Certainly not. Any time that you don't have supply and demand equal at existing prices then there is involuntary something. Some people would like to supply more, or some people might like to demand more, at those prices but are not able to do so. The only way you can say that everything must be voluntary is to assume market clearing all the time – that at every moment in time the economy is in market clearing equilibrium.

In new classical models full employment is equated with actual unemployment. How should we define full employment?
I would define it, as Keynes did, in a classical way at the point where people are on the supply curve for labour, getting all the work they are willing to accept at real wages that employers can and will pay for them. Keynes himself allows for intersectoral flux and frictional unemployment, but essentially I wouldn't define equilibrium full employment any differently from a classical model.

There seems to be more consensus amongst economists on microeconomic issues than macroeconomic issues. Why do you think this is the case?
Let's go back to what Keynes said. He didn't have any big reservations about the way the market economy allocates the resources it does employ. I think myself, and many microeconomists and economists in general would say, that Keynes gave away too much. He should have recognized more externalities in the ordinary market allocation of resources, and he should have worried more about the possible social wastes of monopolistic competition, than he did. In many areas of microeconomics like rent control and minimum wages,

choice-theoretic opportunity-cost methodology is being used the way we are trained to use it. That's the secret that we know, and sociologists and other social scientists don't know. We are a more scientific discipline, but I don't think that all is well in those respects. What rational expectations has done to macroeconomics is what game theory has been doing to microeconomics. Game theory has the problem that it leads to multiple solutions all the time, so it doesn't seem to get results. It's got the same fascination for people looking for ways to use their mathematical and puzzle-solving prowess as rational expectations has, and that comes at the expense of more pragmatic, and empirical, and institutional industrial organization studies. So, I am not so sure that all is well in microeconomics either. A lot of good policy work continues in more applied areas.

Do you see any signs of an emerging consensus in macroeconomics?
It may be coming, but I don't see it. There is still great conflict.

ECONOMIC POLICY

When in office Mrs. Thatcher repeatedly stated that in her view inflation was the most important target for macroeconomic policy. How do you react to this view?
Well, that's substituting a subordinate target for a real target. To the extent that inflation is damaging to real standards of living now or in the future, then inflation is something to worry about. But you could easily make greater sacrifices of real output and real consumption in the name of inflation than the benefits of reducing inflation are worth.

Structural budget deficits have been a feature of the US economy in the 1980s and indeed at the moment there is a lot of talk of the problem of growing budget deficits. Are budget deficits damaging? Do you think that the structural budget deficit of the US economy is a real problem, and what should be done about it?
Well, again you have to keep your eye on the ball and not confuse ends and means. When you think about the objectives to which fiscal policy may be relevant, it is the growth of our capacity to provide higher standards of living to people in the future. For the United States we are talking about a deficit that is in dollars, a debt that is in the currency that we print. It's not a debt in sterling, in yen, or anything else. It's largely an internally held debt and when you think about international wealth balance sheets it's not important whether foreigners hold our federal public debt, or hold other assets. There is a burden, however, in that the public debt diverts some private wealth that

could be placed in privately owned productive capital to holding government paper that was generated to finance private or collective consumption. In that sense deficits which increase the debt have been using savings that could have been used for productive investments in capital that would have raised real wages that our grandchildren would earn. But that doesn't mean we need a deficit reduction this year, when the economy is in a slump. Today GDP is not supply constrained; the amount of investment in the economy is not constrained by the supply of saving. In fact deficit reduction in a weak economy would be counterproductive, reduce GDP, reduce investment. We would be doing not as well for our children and their children as we would if we did some spending on public investment or cut taxes in ways that stimulate private investment. All this is terribly mixed up in the political discussion about deficits. I have been one of the principal opponents of the kind of fiscal policy that the Reagan and Bush administrations ran for 12 years. And at the same time, to rush in to a blind policy of deficit reduction that begins too soon, before we are out of the slump – I wouldn't do that either. It all gets back to trying to suit the medicine to the circumstances of the patient.

Are you still an advocate of incomes policies? Some Keynesians like Alan Blinder have little enthusiasm for such policies, whereas you seem to think that incomes policy has a role to play in addition to demand management.
Well I thought income policy did have a role in the 1970s, and especially in the disinflation that was going to take place beginning in 1979. I think we could have done that disinflation with less loss in output and employment if we'd used some kind of incomes policy then. Right now, I'm not very excited about incomes policy. One thing that has come out well in the 1980s, partly a matter of good fortune, is that we haven't had any more oil shocks. Wage pressures are also very moderate. In 1979/80 there were very few economists who would have said it was possible to get unemployment down to almost 5 per cent in 1988 and have virtually no inflationary consequences. I wouldn't have said that 10 years earlier – yet it happened. We don't have an inflation problem right now. If it comes back, then incomes policy may be a possible thing to do, but I wouldn't muddy the waters and get excited about it right now.

Why has Keynesian economics experienced something of a restoration in the last decade?
Well, it's because you have had Keynesian problems for the last five years. Keynesian economics got a bum rap in the 1970s. I see it all the time. People say 'Why do you want to go back to the failed policies of the 1970s and the late 1960s'. Keynesian policies were thought to be responsible for inflation and stagflation – people never mention, or erase from the memory, the oil

shocks and the Vietnam War. Now we are back to a more normal environment and the new classical ideas are not so appealing to a new generation of economists, who have grown up subsequent to the high tides of the counter-revolutions.

If you were advising Clinton about the economic strategy to be pursued over the next four years what are the important things you think he should do?
Well, that's a tricky thing for reasons we already discussed. The problem he has right now is to pep up the economy and the recovery. The economy is doing a little better than it was six months ago, but it is still not doing great. At the same time there is all this pressure to do something about the federal deficit. He is trying to do both. Since one really requires more deficit while the other requires less deficit, it's rather difficult. I'm afraid the stimulus he is going to give is not very big, and it's not going to last long enough. There is going to be a deficit-increasing phase of his programme this year and maybe next year (1994) his budget is going to be deficit neutral. Thereafter tax increases and cuts in entitlements and other outlays are going to be phased in, so eventually for the fiscal year 1997 he will be able to say that he will have done what he said. He is asking for both these things at once. It's sort of like saying we're going to have to perform some surgery on this patient but right now the patient is a little weak, so we'll have to build the patient up first. There are two difficulties. One is that the dual approach is a rather subtle point to explain – why we do one thing now when we are going to do the opposite later. In fact, he hasn't even explained it yet.

Maybe he doesn't understand it.
Oh he does, this is a smart guy. This is as smart a politician as I have ever met – he understands it.

ADDITIONAL QUESTIONS ANSWERED BY CORRESPONDENCE: JANUARY/FEBRUARY 1998

In your 1995 paper 'The Natural Rate as New Classical Economics' you suggested that Friedman's 1968 paper 'The Role of Monetary Policy' is 'very likely the most influential paper ever published in an economics journal'. In what important ways did that paper change macroeconomics and do you regard the natural rate hypothesis as part of the 'core' of mainstream macroeconomics?
Perhaps that was hyperbole, but the article was certainly very influential in the profession and, in its implications for policy all over the world, far beyond. If, as I argued in my 1995 paper, the article was a giant step towards

New Classical Macro and Real Business Cycle Theory, then the initial impact of the Friedman paper was greatly multiplied. If those doctrines are now the core of mainstream macroeconomics, then the natural rate idea is likewise. While this may be true of academic macro theory, I think it is not true of practical macro as used in government policy and business practice. There the NAIRU is the preferred concept, and as I have argued in the 1995 paper and elsewhere it is not the same as the natural rate. Both concepts have suffered from the empirical surprises of the last few years, when previous estimates of the NAIRU turned out to be wrong. Moreover, the idea that there is a vertical Phillips curve in the long run has lost ground relative to my own idea that a trade-off persists at low rates of inflation, a proposition recently supported by Akerlof, Dickens and Perry (1996) in *Brookings Papers*.

The US economy currently (January 1998) has an unemployment rate of 4.7 per cent and an inflation rate of just over 2 per cent. Given that most estimates of the natural rate of unemployment for the US economy are around 6 per cent, how would you account for this current situation?
Indicators of labour market tightness other than the unemployment rate suggest that labour markets are considerably less tight than the unemployment rate itself would suggest, given the experience since the mid-1970s. Vacancies (proxied in US by help-wanted indexes) are more plentiful, quitting jobs less frequent relative to losing jobs, and persons counted as out of labour force more available for work. The Beveridge curve seems to have shifted back to its location in the 1950s and 1960s. Other factors include the decline in trade union membership and power *vis-à-vis* private business employers, the increased acceptability of downsizing employment to improve the bottom line and stock prices, even at the expense of long-time employees, import competition, yes, but especially domestic competition, and of course the absence of supply shocks, which has more to do with the stagflation of the 1970s than New Classicals want to remember. It very well may be possible to reduce unemployment to 4 per cent, the target of the Kennedy administration in the 1960s, while keeping inflation below 3.5 per cent.

Although unemployment in the US and UK economies is relatively low at the moment, the average rate of unemployment in the European Union economies is relatively high. How can we explain the considerable unemployment differentials that exist at the moment between the US and countries such as France and Germany? Do you think that EMU is likely to exacerbate the unemployment problem in Europe?
I am incorrigible. I still believe that wilfully bad macro policy is responsible for much of the excess unemployment in Europe. It can't be that the natural rate keeps rising along with the actual rate, from single to double digits. The

Europeans conclude that if they don't see significant deflation at whatever actual U-rate, then that rate must be equal to or less than the natural rate, so that any expansionary monetary or fiscal policy will cause inflation to increase. But it may be that the short-run Phillips curve is pretty flat, so that this inference is not justified. Anyway they never try the experiment of expansionary policy. I can believe that there are more structural obstacles to reducing unemployment in continental Europe than in America and Britain. I can believe that Thatcher's bashing of labour unions helped, although I didn't see UK wages and prices tumbling when sterling was pegged to the DM. I think some of the structural problems on the continent reflect hysteresis. The governments and central banks never tried to recover from the 1979–82 recessions, unlike the US, so the cyclical unemployment achieved by those recessions became 'structural'. Whatever the nature and cause, European unemployment is a disgrace and should be within the power of European governments to correct in some way, rather than complain about, as if it has been imposed on them by the US.

I don't expect EMU to change the unemployment situation much either way. If anything, it will get worse. EU members haven't done much under the EMS to improve their own macro outcomes. But to the extent they have done anything individually, they won't have any macro policy tools once they are in EMU. Nor will the new central bank act differently from the Bundesbank, and the Union has no fisc with which to conduct fiscal policy.

Do you feel that there has been any move towards greater consensus in macroeconomics since we last talked to you in 1993?
Maybe there's more consensus in macro theory, in the sense that Keynesian theory is just ignored and graduate students don't learn anything about it. Maybe there's more consensus in practical macroeconomics, because it can't help having large Keynesian elements and because mechanical monetarism is dead.

Many prominent macroeconomists (for example Barro and Sala-i-Martin, 1995; Lucas, 1987) have argued that the part of macroeconomics that really matters is growth. Do you agree with this view and have the endogenous growth theories of the past decade improved our understanding of growth processes?
Yes, without doubt increasing the productivity, health and life expectancy of billions of people in poor and underdeveloped countries throughout the world adds more utility than reducing the unemployment in Western Europe by three or four points. I don't think the macroeconomists studying growth have answers on how to do that. Aggregate demand problems are a luxury available to advanced industrial capitalist countries. The basic problem of poor

countries is poverty of supply. It's possible that aggregate demand shortage – the social disorganization of unnecessary poverty in the midst of potential plenty in the Great Depression – is no longer a high-priority problem because macroeconomics solved it, not because it never was a problem and the macro theory and policy it evoked was wrong. The fact that there are few auto accidents at intersections doesn't suggest that traffic lights are unnecessary. Barro and Lucas, it seems to me, trashed demand-oriented macroeconomics and then left the field, saying it's not interesting anyway. The endogenous growth theories, which interestingly enough rely on externalities of one kind or another to overcome diminishing returns, are intriguing but not as yet convincing to me.

N. Gregory Mankiw
(b. 1958)

Gregory Mankiw is currently Professor of Economics at Harvard University. Best known for his work on such issues as price adjustment, financial markets, monetary and fiscal policy, and economic growth he is widely acknowledged as being a leading exponent of the new Keynesian school of macroeconomics.

We interviewed Professor Mankiw in his office at Harvard University on 18 February 1993 and subsequently corresponded in February/March 1998.

GENERAL ISSUES

Why do you think we have so much controversy in macroeconomics compared to microeconomics?
That is a hard question. It is certainly true that there is more agreement among microeconomists as to how they approach things. That is, most microeconomists start off with utility and profit maximization as the underlying motives and go from there. Macroeconomics is in some ways harder since you are dealing with the whole economy; the field therefore requires more simplifying assumptions to make anything manageable, to make the problem simpler than it really is in the world. I think there is disagreement as to which simplifying assumptions are the most natural or the most useful.

How important do you think it is for macroeconomics to have neoclassical choice theoretic foundations?

Well it is certainly true that all macro phenomena are the aggregate of many micro phenomena; in that sense macroeconomics is inevitably founded on microeconomics. Yet I am not sure that all macroeconomics necessarily has to start off with microeconomic building blocks. To give an analogy, all of biology is in some sense the aggregate of particle physics, because all biological creatures are made up of particles. That doesn't mean that the natural place to start in building biology is to start with particle physics and aggregate up. Instead I would probably start with theory at the level of the organism or the cell, not the level of the sub-atomic particle. We have a lot of models like the IS–LM model in macroeconomics that are very useful for studying the macroeconomy, even though those models don't start off with the individual unit and build up from there.

Which papers or books do you feel have had the biggest impact on the development of macroeconomics over the last 25 years?

The biggest impact has undoubtedly come from Lucas. He put the cracks into the Keynesian consensus that existed in the 1960s. He really pulled macroeconomics apart by proposing new and intriguing ideas. The disagreements today among macroeconomists have largely arisen from the critiques of Lucas and of his followers. As you know, I don't agree with Lucas's solutions, but I take the problems that he pointed out very seriously. A lot of the work that I and other new Keynesians have done are a response to the problems that he pointed out in the old Keynesian ideas.

To some extent you've answered our next question. Where did you draw inspiration for your own work?

It's been a combination of influences. Part comes from the older generation of macroeconomists. I view a lot of the work I do as building on the work of Tobin, Modigliani and Friedman. I see a lot of truth in the views they were pushing. I also take the problems that Lucas pointed out very seriously. A lot of new Keynesian work is trying to reformulate the 1960s Friedman–Tobin view of the world. What is now called the neoclassical synthesis had a large element of truth in it. On the other hand, it had problems, and Lucas pointed out those problems very forcefully. We need to fix those problems and address the concerns that Lucas had while still maintaining the element of truth in the neoclassical synthesis.

KEYNES AND THE *GENERAL THEORY*

One interpretation of the neoclassical synthesis which emerged at the end of the 1950s suggested that the General Theory *was a special case of a more general classical model. Would you agree with that interpretation?*
I would say that the classical model and the Keynesian model make different assumptions about adjustment of prices. I think of the classical model as being the model that assumes complete price flexibility, and therefore describes a horizon over which it is plausible to make such an assumption. Probably a period of years, rather than a period of months. The Keynesian model applies over a horizon where wages and prices are relatively inflexible or sluggish. Both models are special cases of a more general model which allows a varying degree of flexibility and sluggishness in prices depending on the horizon we want to study. When we study the effect of policies over a quarter or a decade, we want to make a different assumption about the degree of flexibility of prices.

Why do you think there are so many conflicting interpretations of the General Theory?
There are a lot of conflicting interpretations because Keynes had a lot of different ideas. The ideas don't necessarily have to be packaged all together, so some people grab on to one set of ideas and say that this is really what is central to what Keynes was saying and other people grab onto other sets of ideas. The question is, when we look at the market imperfection that we call the business cycle, which set of general ideas from the *General Theory* are the most important? There is so much in the *General Theory* that it is hard to comprehend it all at once. Some is very important, but some is not particularly important. Disagreements come by choosing different pieces of Keynes's world view and emphasizing those.

Do you think that if Keynes had still been living in 1969 he would have received the first Nobel Prize in Economics?
Oh undoubtedly. I think there are a few very very important economists of the century, and there is no question that Keynes has got to be on anybody's shortlist.

NEW CLASSICAL MACROECONOMICS

Do you regard new classical macroeconomics as a separate school of thought from monetarism?
I think so. My impression is that monetarism is a school of thought that says fluctuations in the money supply are the primary cause of fluctuations in

aggregate demand and income, whereas new classicism is a particular theory as to why fluctuations in aggregate demand might matter through an unanticipated price surprise. This price surprise view proposed by Lucas is, I think, the next step after monetarism. More recently, new classical economists have turned their attention to real business cycle theory, which is the antithesis of monetarism.

Do you think that overall the new classical contributions have had a beneficial effect on the development of macroeconomics?
Debate is healthy, and the new Keynesian school arose largely in response to the new classical school. In that sense it is a debate leading to greater truths, and it has been helpful. A lot of the specific contributions, especially real business cycle theory, are probably not going to survive the test of time. The literature on the time inconsistency of policy is a contribution that will survive and has probably been one of the most important contributions to policy analysis in the past two decades.

How important is the rational expectations hypothesis?
It is important in the sense that it has now become the working hypothesis of all practising macroeconomists. Economists routinely assume that people are rational when they make decisions: they maximize utility, they rationally maximize profits, and so on. It would be peculiar for us to assume that people are rational except when they come to form expectations and then they act irrationally. I don't think the rational expectations hypothesis is important in the sense of having all the sweeping implications as was at first believed. At first people thought that it had all sorts of properties about policy being ineffective.

Isn't that more to do with the market clearing assumption?
Exactly. People have come to realize that it is other assumptions, like the market clearing assumption, that are really important and that rational expectations in itself doesn't have implications as sweeping as was once thought.

You have questioned the argument that the disinflation experience of the early 1980s both here and in Britain has provided decisive evidence against the new classical claim of painless disinflation. Is this because the deflation was unanticipated?
There are two new classical views. The first is the price surprise theory of Lucas. The second is real business cycle theory. This second view says that money anticipated or unanticipated doesn't matter. My view of that is that it is completely at variance with the evidence. Larry Ball has a paper that shows systematically for a large number of countries that whenever you have a

major disinflation it is associated with a period of low output and high unemployment (see Ball, 1994). So I think that the evidence is completely clear on that. The evidence is more favourable to early new classical theory. You're right that to a large extent the disinflation was unanticipated even in the United States where Volcker said he was going to disinflate. I don't think people believed he was going to disinflate as fast as he did. Most measures of expectations of inflation did not come down until after the recession was well under way. I am sympathetic to the view that credibility is one determinant of how costly a disinflation will be.

KEYNESIANISM AND THE NEW KEYNESIANS

Do you regard yourself as a Keynesian?
I do but I'm always nervous about the term because the term Keynesian can mean different things to different people, just as different people will read the *General Theory* and pull out different elements as being important. People use the word Keynesian in so many different ways that recently I have actually tried to avoid using the term at all on the grounds that it is more confusing than illuminating. I think of myself as a Keynesian in the sense of believing that the business cycle represents some sort of market imperfection on a grand scale. In that sense I think of myself as a Keynesian. Milton Friedman was also a Keynesian in that sense. My own views emerged as much from Milton Friedman as they have from John Maynard Keynes. Some people take the word Keynesian as meaning a belief in fine tuning the economy so that the government controls every wiggle of ups and downs. Other people take it as a belief that deficit spending is not a bad thing. I don't subscribe to either of those views. I think that the broad theme of the *General Theory* is that the business cycle is something that we really need to worry about because it is a sign of a market imperfection. In that way I am a Keynesian, but as I said so is Milton Friedman.

Was the breakdown of the Phillips curve fatal for orthodox Keynesianism?
It highlighted the absence of a good theory of aggregate supply. What orthodox Keynesians had was a pretty good theory of aggregate demand. The IS–LM model has held up pretty well as a general structure for think-ing about how aggregate demand is determined. The problem is once you've got aggregate demand – a downward sloping curve in P–Y space – you still need a good story for the aggregate supply curve. The Phillips curve came out of nowhere. It is really just an empirical description of what was true in the data without any particularly good theories as to why it should look that way, how it would change in response to policy, and what might make it

unstable. So we never had a good theory of that, and the breakdown of the Phillips curve made that very apparent and provided room for the more general critique that Lucas put forward. The deficiency on the supply side was always a weakness, but it wasn't given attention until the Phillips curve broke down.

What would you summarize as being the central propositions of new Keynesian macroeconomics?
The central propositions are largely theoretical rather than policy oriented. New Keynesians accept the view of the world summarized by the neoclassical synthesis: the economy can deviate in the short term from its equilibrium level, and monetary and fiscal policy have important influences on real economic activity. New Keynesians are saying that the neoclassical synthesis is not as flawed as Lucas and others have argued. The purpose of the new Keynesian school has been largely to try to fix those theoretical problems raised by Lucas and also accept Lucas's argument that we need models supported by better microeconomic foundations.

So you wouldn't subscribe to arguments in favour of incomes policies advocated by post Keynesians?
No, not at all. When the government gets in the business of setting wages and prices it is not very good at it. The setting of wages and prices should be left to free markets.

So you are no Galbraithian?
Absolutely not (*laughter*).

How important is the theory of imperfect competition to new Keynesian macroeconomics?
A large part of new Keynesian economics is trying to explain why firms set and adjust prices over time in the way they do. Firms in a perfectly competitive environment don't have any choice over what their prices are going to be. Competitive firms are price takers. If you want to even talk about firms setting prices you have to talk about firms that have some ability to do so, and those are firms that have some market power: they are imperfectly competitive. So I think imperfect competition is central to thinking about price setting and therefore central to new Keynesian economics.

This is strange, because if you think of the 1930s, you had Keynes and Joan Robinson at Cambridge. Joan Robinson developed the theory of imperfect competition and Keynes developed his General Theory. *Why did it take so long to bring these two ideas together?*

I don't think that Keynes was as worried about building his model based on micro foundations as we are today. Joan Robinson was building the microeconomics that would later prove to be very useful for addressing the macroeconomics of Keynes, but Keynes, not having read Robert Lucas yet, wasn't worried about building the microeconomics of aggregate supply (*laughter*).

In a sense haven't the post Keynesians been ahead of you here? People like Paul Davidson have for years taken imperfect competition as their micro foundation. So are the new Keynesians simply catching up on what the post Keynesians did quite a while ago?
They have a broad theme of imperfect competition, but the details are not very similar. My impression is that the new Keynesian economics is much more in line with the neoclassical synthesis than with the post Keynesians.

You will obviously be very familiar with Alan Blinder's recent surveys. Are they supporting the new Keynesian views? (See Blinder, 1991.)
Alan is providing a way of judging a variety of different new Keynesian views. There are a lot of new theories about wage and price rigidities. He is trying to sort out which is right and wrong using a fairly novel perspective of asking firms how they set wages and prices. This is terrific work, but what we are going to learn in the end is still unclear. He is still producing the papers and we haven't seen all the results yet. The goal is to provide one way of deciding which theories we like and which we don't . It's a very exciting project.

An important distinction seems to be made by new Keynesians between real rigidities and nominal rigidities. Why is it important to make this distinction?
The reason is that a real rigidity, which is a rigidity in a relative price, is not a reason for monetary non-neutrality. Unions, for example, could set rigid real wages away from equilibrium. A rigid real wage is not going to provide any reason to believe that money is not neutral, since it does not create any nominal lever for money to work on. It would cause unemployment but not monetary non-neutrality. To get monetary non-neutrality, which is a central challenge for macro theorists, you need some nominal rigidity such as sticky prices. Having said that, there does seem to be a variety of real rigidities in the world; unions setting wages way above equilibrium levels for example. The question is whether nominal and real rigidities interact. One of the big themes of this literature, mainly due to Larry Ball and David Romer, is that real and nominal rigidities seem to reinforce each other. The real rigidity is actually going to make the nominal rigidity a lot more important than it would be otherwise.

Critics of the menu cost literature, Robert Barro for example, have suggested that this is a small peg on which to hang an explanation of the business cycle. How can small menu costs have such large real effects on the macro economy? (See Barro, 1989.)

It is clear that menu costs are quite small. Firms don't bear huge costs when they change their prices. Yet it is also clear that recessions are very costly events. The question is whether these relatively small menu costs can be a key part of understanding this relatively costly business cycle. This literature shows that price adjustments by firms have external effects. When a firm decides to keep prices sticky, this could well be costly for the economy in a way that is not costly for the firm who is making the decision.

How do efficiency wage and insider/outsider theories fit into new Keynesian thinking?

Both of those theories provide a particular explanation for real rigidities, such as why real wages don't move to the equilibrium level in labour markets. As I said before, real rigidities and nominal rigidities can complement each other. That is, the insider/outsider and efficiency wage explanations for rigid real wages in some senses complement the menu cost story of rigid prices.

Is the idea of hysteresis crucial to new Keynesian macroeconomics?

Actually I don't think of it as being crucial. It is an interesting idea, that a recession can have long-lived effects on the economy and leave permanent scars after the initial cause of the recession has gone. For example, the high unemployment in Europe in the 1980s persisted far longer than anyone could explain with standard models. But if this idea turned out to be wrong it would not bring down the rest of our theories. This has been an interesting, but relatively separate, question.

Do you see the concept of NAIRU, and Friedman's natural rate, as being the same idea or are they different?

I have always thought of them as being basically the same. Most new Keynesian models involve some sort of natural rate; in that sense Milton Friedman has won the debate. Most new Keynesians believe in the natural rate hypothesis except for a small group of people working with hysteresis. The natural rate hypothesis is pretty well entrenched.

What about the concept of full employment? It was difficult to think of doing macroeconomics 15–20 years ago without the concept of full employment being central. What do we do about issues like involuntary unemployment? Lucas suggests that we should abandon this concept, what are your views on this? (See Lucas, 1978a.)

I think there is involuntary unemployment. Part of the new Keynesian literature has come up with models of the labour market to explain why involuntary
unemployment exists, why real wages don't adjust to equilibrate labour markets. There is a lot of truth to the efficiency wage theories and the insider/
outsider theories, for example.

Do new Keynesians think of full employment as the natural rate?
I avoid the term full employment because it suggests that the natural rate is in
some sense desirable. I think there is some natural rate which is the long-run
unemployment rate that the economy tends to, that can't be influenced by
monetary policy in the long run. That doesn't mean that it is immutable in
response to any policy intervention. There are things that have been done to
the labour market that either increase or decrease the natural rate, things like
the minimum wage, unemployment insurance laws, labour training policies.
There are all sorts of things that the government can do to change the natural
rate. I don't like calling it full employment because good labour market
policies might well raise employment beyond that level.

*How important do you think it is to take into account fairness when looking
at the labour market? We are thinking here of the work of George Akerlof,
Janet Yellen and Robert Solow who have stressed the idea of fairness. Doesn't
this work suggest that perhaps new Keynesians should start looking more
closely at the psychology and sociology literature? (See Akerlof and Yellen,
1990; Solow, 1990.)*
Some of the papers that they have written have been extremely interesting. I
don't think there is a lot of compelling evidence yet that we need to abandon
neoclassical assumptions. I'm not doing so yet in my work, but I'm certainly
happy to read the work of others who are doing so (*laughter*).

*In your recent edited volumes of collected papers on new Keynesian econom-
ics you say that 'new Keynesian macroeconomics could just as easily be
labelled new monetarist economics'. What exactly did you mean? (See Mankiw
and Romer, 1991.)*
The challenge raised by the real business cycle school is the question of
whether money is neutral and, if not, why not? Twenty years ago, when
Friedman and Tobin were debating, there were some things they agreed on.
They agreed on the proposition that the Federal Reserve was an important
player in the economy, that what it did really mattered. The real business
cycle school has challenged that by writing down models without any real
effects of monetary policy. What the new Keynesian models have tried to do
is establish why money is not neutral, what microeconomic imperfections are
necessary to explain monetary neutrality at the macro level. In this sense,

these models are trying to support both traditional Keynesian and monetarist views.

Would you agree with Stanley Fischer that the views of Friedman, Brunner and Meltzer are closer to those of Keynesians than they are to equilibrium business cycle theorists? (See Fischer, 1988.)
Oh yes absolutely. The essence of real business cycle models is the absence of any role for the Federal Reserve, whereas I think Brunner, Meltzer and Friedman would agree with Tobin that the Fed is very important. None of them would ever argue that money is neutral in the way that real business cycle theorists have.

James Tobin has suggested that good papers in economics contain surprises. What surprises have new Keynesian papers uncovered? (See Tobin, 1988.)
One of the big surprises is that one can go a lot further with menu cost models than people once thought. A lot of people used to see these models as a silly way of thinking about price rigidity. What the new literature is trying to do is to say no, maybe we should take menu cost models seriously. I think the complementarity between real and nominal rigidities is a surprise. As I mentioned earlier one of the disappointing features so far of the new Keynesian literature is that it hasn't been as empirical as I would have liked. That is a problem being remedied right now in some research. Ultimately that is where the literature should go. More empirical work is needed.

Peter Howitt has talked about a Keynesian recovery, Alan Blinder about a Keynesian restoration, you seem to prefer the term reincarnation. Is there something important in the different terms used? (See Howitt, 1990; Blinder, 1992a and Mankiw, 1992.)
I chose the term reincarnation because it means rebirth into another body. While there are many similarities between new and old Keynesian economics, there are also a lot of differences as well, and I wanted to emphasize that. In some senses the spirit of Keynes has been brought back, but it doesn't look like the old Keynes. In fact Keynes might not recognize the new Keynesians as Keynesians at all. In general, people might not recognize themselves after they have been reincarnated. So that is why I used the term reincarnation (*laughter*).

Would you say that your work is, with respect to Keynes, faithful in spirit, but critical in detail?
I think that is fair. It tries to go beyond Keynes in a sense of taking microfoundations more seriously. Alan Blinder wrote a paper 'Keynes after Lucas' and I think that title pretty much describes new Keynesians. It takes

some of Keynes's ideas seriously, and it also takes some of the critiques of Lucas seriously as well. (See Blinder, 1986.)

Do you think Keynes would have been a new Keynesian?
I don't know, I think Keynes was a very unpredictable fellow. I guess he would see some things in it he would like, and some things in it he wouldn't.

REAL BUSINESS CYCLE THEORY

You've recently argued that real business cycle theory has served an important function in stimulating and provoking scientific debate, but you predict that the approach will eventually be discarded. What are your main objections to real business cycle theory? What are the weaknesses, theoretical, empirical or both?
My objections are mainly empirical. Theoretically they are very elegant models and that is a large part of their appeal. They are very parsimonious models. But when I look at the real world I see the same things that Milton Friedman and James Tobin do, which is a very powerful Federal Reserve board in the United States or the Bank of England in the UK. There is a lot of evidence across countries that periods of disinflation are periods of low output and high unemployment. Those effects are completely absent in real business cycle models. I think the central driving forces for the business cycle that those models highlight – technology shocks – aren't very important.

Isn't the procyclical behaviour of the real wage a strong feature of these theories? How do new Keynesians explain the movement of real wages over the business cycle?
The theories do predict procyclical wages. Although I've not looked at the models carefully on this question, my understanding is that they predict very procyclical, real wages. While it is true that real wages are procyclical, my reading of the evidence is that they are only mildly procyclical. Therefore, the fact that these theories predict very procyclical real wages, and the data shows that they are only mildly procyclical, makes it hard to reconcile this model with the evidence. I think the real wage evidence is not that hard to explain. If you believe in a world where wages and prices are sluggish over time, the cyclical behaviour of the real wage is really a question of whether wages or prices are more sluggish. The fact that real wages are roughly acyclical, maybe slightly procyclical, is some indication to me that wages and prices are simply equally sticky. This is consistent with Alan Blinder's evidence which says that prices change on average once a year, and we know a lot of wages change on average once a year. So I think that explanation is consistent with a lot of the evidence.

How do we explain procyclical productivity? Some Keynesians seem to suggest that it is due to labour hoarding.
The procyclical behaviour of productivity is a puzzle for people who don't believe in technology shocks. The traditional explanation for why productivity is procyclical is labour hoarding. In recessions firms keep on workers they don't really need so that they can have the workers still available when the next boom comes, and that tends to give the appearance of procyclical productivity. These theories make a lot of sense to me. I know I work my secretary harder when I have more work to be done; therefore her productivity is procyclical. I know I work harder when there is more work to be done (*laughter*). I think there is a lot of casual evidence that labour hoarding and procyclical effort are important.

MACROECONOMIC POLICY

One of the central ideas of Keynesian economics is that an increase in aggregate demand will stimulate the economy. Under what circumstances do you think a government should actually stimulate demand?
There are a couple of questions. First, when should it act? Second, how should it act? That is, should it use monetary or fiscal policy? On the first question, one should stimulate aggregate demand when it is too low to maintain full employment – that is when you observe very high unemployment or when there is reason to believe that unemployment is going to rise. The policy implications of a lot of new Keynesian theories really go back to a lot of the policy implications of the neoclassical synthesis of the 1960s. Some of the limitations on policy that were then debated are still relevant today. Even if you accept everything that new Keynesians say about prices being sluggish and so on, there is still the question of how good the government is at responding in a timely fashion to the shocks? In that debate, I side to a large extent with Milton Friedman. The government is very bad at recognizing shocks in a timely fashion, and when they do respond to shocks they often do so quite late and often counterproductively. So while I see the business cycle as a sign of market failure I also think it is a kind of market failure that a government is very limited in its ability to fix. If we have a very deep persistent recession, certainly something on the lines of the Great Depression, there is room for the government to do something. For the relatively minor wiggles that we have experienced in the postwar economy, it is not clear that the government can do a lot better than it has.

Do you think Keynes was politically naive in thinking that politicians would be advised by technocrats and take the correct action? We are thinking here of the public choice literature and the political business cycle literature. Can we actually trust politicians once they have their hands on the fiscal and monetary levers to use them in the right way?

I think that is a serious concern but there are a lot of ways of fixing that problem. For example, there is a large literature showing that countries with more independent central banks have a lower inflation on average. With less independence in the central bank, there is more political pressure and therefore a greater possibility of following a policy of inflating too much. There are ways around the political problem, like making independent central banks, which to some extent are staffed by technocrats. For that reason an independent central bank would be better at fine tuning the economy, to the extent we fine tune it at all, compared to fiscal policy which is always run by politicians.

You've said that the literature on time inconsistency has provided a persuasive case for a commitment to some sort of rule for monetary policy; do you also support fiscal rules?

Fiscal rules have to be well crafted. A balanced budget amendment that is too strict could be a disaster. At certain times, like recessions and wars, it is appropriate to run budget deficits. So any fiscal rule has to take into account those special situations where budget deficits are the appropriate policy response. A fiscal rule by itself wouldn't be a bad idea, but it has to be well crafted and so far I haven't seen one that is.

Isn't one of the problems with devising rules that if the economy is hit by an unforeseen shock then the government really has to renege on that rule and take some discretionary action? It is difficult to think of a rule which really would be binding.

There are two parts to the question. First, how might you make the rule binding? Second, do you want to make the rule binding? One way to make the rule binding is reputational. Many rules are rules just because long tradition has established them as rules and people don't want to break tradition. Another more legalistic way of imposing rules is by writing them into the constitution. I think the harder question you raise is do you want to make rules binding? The question is whether you can write a rule that works well even in response to unforeseen events. If it becomes too costly to be tied by the rule people will stop abiding by it. What we want to do is write down a rule that will be good in response to normal kinds of shocks. That is, you don't know what the shocks are going to be, but you know what kind of shocks are possible. You've got oil shocks, monetary demand shocks and so on. You write down a rule that is good in response to the kinds of shocks you expect the economy to experience, based on the shocks experienced in the past. Therefore, unless something completely unforeseeable happens, you stick by the rule.

Leijonhufvud once argued that the economy can be thought of as travelling along a corridor, as long as it stays in the corridor leave it alone, but if it gets out of this corridor into a severe recession that is the time for intervention. Is that what you are saying? (See Leijonhufvud, 1981.)
Well no, because recessions are reasonably foreseeable. Although you don't necessarily know when a recession is going to occur, you know that one will occur eventually. A recession is one of the contingencies that you want your rule to deal with. So I don't think a recession *per se* is one of those extraordinary events that make you want to break the rule. A recession is something you can plan for in advance. I'm talking about an event that not only can you not predict when it is going to happen, but you have never even thought that it might happen. For example, before 1973 people never imagined an OPEC supply shock. The whole idea of OPEC never even crossed anybody's mind. That is the type of situation where you might want to rethink the rule. Now that we know what OPEC is capable of, we can write down a rule that takes oil shocks into account.

What is the role of fiscal policy in new Keynesian macroeconomics?
To a large extent new Keynesian economics has been about the theory of aggregate supply and why it is that prices adjust slowly. It has been relatively neutral on the question of what determines aggregate demand, in particular whether monetary or fiscal policy levers are most useful. As I mentioned a moment ago, I am sceptical personally about the usefulness of fiscal policy in fine tuning the economy because, at least in the United States, the Congress acts very slowly. Even as we are doing this interview (18 February 1993) the Congress is debating a fiscal stimulus, even though the recovery has been going on for about a year now. By the time this fiscal stimulus actually has an effect on the economy, my guess is that we will be pretty close to the natural rate again. This is the perfect example of how the lags can be very long in fiscal policy. Monetary policy is a more useful tool for stabilizing aggregate demand.

Do budget deficits matter?
I think they matter a lot. The main way they matter is not for short-run macroeconomic reasons but for long-run reasons – reasons that are best described not by Keynesian models but by growth models. The evidence as I see it is that large budget deficits reduce national saving. And the lesson from growth theory and growth experience across countries is that low saving leads to low growth. This is a big problem for the United States today.

If you were advising President Clinton about macroeconomic policy for the next three or four years what would be the kinds of policies you feel are necessary?

My reaction to President Clinton's speech (17 February 1993) is that I don't think we need the fiscal stimulus that he is proposing. Recovery is already on its way. It wasn't a very deep recession to start off with, so I'm not terribly shocked that there is a mild recovery. It will take the fiscal stimulus a while to get people employed. I am happy that he is worried about the budget deficit, as low national saving is an important macro problem in the long term in the United States. Yet I am disappointed that he is putting so much emphasis on tax increases rather than spending cuts. That is really a view not so much about macroeconomics as about the size of government. I am also disappointed that he is giving no attention to the low rate of private saving in the United States. I would recommend tax reforms to remove the present disincentives toward saving. So I give him a mixed review.

CURRENT AND FUTURE PROGRESS IN MACROECONOMICS

Much research in the 1980s, your own included, was directed at providing more rigorous microeconomic foundations for the central elements of Keynesian economics. Taking an overview of the last decade how successful do you think that research has been in providing a more substantial microfoundation for Keynesian economics?

It has been successful at the theoretical level in the sense that one can now say that Keynesian economics, the economics of wage and price rigidities, is well founded on microeconomic models. There are now several microeconomic models that people can pull off the shelf. The theoretical challenge of Lucas and his followers has been met. It is less clear whether this line of research is going to be successful as an empirical matter. That is, to what extent does it yield new insights to help us understand actual economic fluctuations? Does it give us new ways to look at data and policies? The jury is still out on that one. There is a small empirical literature, but I can probably count the number of empirical papers on the fingers of two hands. I hope it is a growth area, but so far the literature has not been as empirically oriented as I would like.

Do you think there is some truth to the view that at the moment we have too many theories?

Yes, I have a lot of sympathy with that view. There is too big a premium for coming up with clever new theories in the profession. Yet I don't know of any way to solve this problem. Obviously I believe the things I believe, and I can't tell people that they should believe what I believe, just because there are too many theories (*laughter*). It would be nice if macroeconomists reached a consensus and they could do more work on details and less work on creating brand new theories of the business cycle. Until we do naturally reach a consensus, there is no way to enforce that by fiat.

Do you see any signs of an emerging consensus in macroeconomics?
That is a good question. I change my mind on that a lot depending on what conference I go to (*laughter*). I think there are certainly groups within the profession that are agreeing with each other. There is much agreement among new Keynesian people like Olivier Blanchard, Larry Ball, David Romer, George Akerlof, Alan Blinder and so on. Whether we as a group are coming to agreement with some of the real business cycle group is hard to say. I'm delighted that some of the people who previously worked closely with the real business cycle models are now trying to incorporate monetary effects into those models. That provides a hope that somewhere down the line the new Keynesian models and the real business cycle models are going to merge to some grand synthesis that incorporates the strengths of both approaches. That hasn't happened yet; that is just a hope.

ADDITIONAL QUESTIONS ANSWERED BY CORRESPONDENCE: FEBRUARY/MARCH 1998

When we last talked with you in February 1993 you were somewhat hopeful that 'somewhere down the line the new Keynesian models and real business cycle models are going to merge to some grand synthesis that incorporates the strengths of both approaches'. Have developments in macroeconomic research during the last five years moved in the direction of more consensus as you had hoped?
To some extent, yes. Increasingly, there are economists (such as Bob King, Julio Rotemberg, and Mike Woodford) trying to integrate the insights of the new Keynesian and real business cycle literatures. Not surprisingly, this raises a host of difficult technical issues. We have long known that dynamic sticky-price models are hard to solve except in some special cases. But some progress has been made.

Your new Principles of Economics *textbook (Mankiw, 1997b) has generated a great deal of interest and comment. For example, in his* Wall Street Journal *review of your book (9 October 1997), Mark Skousen interprets your overall message to be that 'classical economics is now the "general theory" and*

Keynesian economics to be the "special" case'. Skousen also writes that 'virtually the entire book is devoted to classical economics leaving the Keynesian model as an afterthought in the end chapters'. Is this an accurate view of the balance of the book and your own current position?

I have been delighted about the response to my new textbook. Some of the commentary, such as the Skousen op-ed piece in the *Wall Street Journal*, exaggerated what my book does, and the *Journal* published a letter I wrote responding to that article. In the book, I try to present a balance between Keynesian and classical ideas. The Keynesian analysis is developed over three full chapters, which explain and apply the model of aggregate demand and aggregate supply. That is perhaps less coverage than in many traditional texts, but in no sense is Keynesian economics treated as a mere 'after-thought'. I begin with classical ideas – including long-run growth, the quantity theory of money, and so on – but by the end of the book the student is fully acquainted with the importance and role of Keynesian theory.

In our previous interview you commented that the 'natural rate hypothesis is pretty well entrenched' and that 'most new Keynesians believe in the natural rate hypothesis'. How do you account for the remarkably low combination of inflation and unemployment currently being experienced in the US economy?

It seems increasingly clear that the natural rate of unemployment has fallen in the United States. At one level, that is not terribly shocking, since in principle there is no reason to think the natural rate must be constant. Various changes in the labour market can alter the natural rate. But I have not yet seen a good explanation of the decline, which is somewhat troubling. Some people might react by rejecting the whole natural-rate framework, but I am not ready to do so. In part, I remain committed to the natural-rate model because I have not seen a good alternative to it.

Your research interests in recent years have been more focused on economic growth than the short-run issues of aggregate fluctuations. Unlike Paul Romer and other endogenous growth theorists you provide a spirited defence of a modified Solow model in your (1995b) 'Growth of Nations' paper. What is your assessment of the progress which has been made in this burgeoning research area since 1986?

The growth literature has been a very positive development for the economics profession. After all, long-run growth is at least as important for human welfare as the business cycle, so it's great that the issue is being studied seriously again. In my new principles textbook, as well as in my intermediate macro text, I introduce the topic of long-run growth quite early. This is, in large part, a reflection of the research trend started by Paul Romer and others.

On the question of what progress has been made, I remain somewhat ambivalent. There are now many theoretical models of growth and more empirical studies than we have data points. Yet it is hard to find important questions that we can now answer with confidence that we couldn't answer before. Adam Smith once said, that 'little else is requisite to carry a state to the highest degree of opulence from the lowest barbarism, but peace, easy taxes, and tolerable administration of justice'. That still seems like the best policy advice. In that sense, we haven't made much progress in 200 years. On the other hand, perhaps we better understand why Smith's instincts were right ones, and that is progress.

What are the main differences between your view of technological progress and Paul Romer's?

I don't disagree with Paul Romer about technological progress. It comes mainly from the creation of ideas that are largely but not completely public goods. Both of us would agree that this explains why most nations are richer that they were a century ago.

Where Romer and I seem to disagree is whether this old insight is important for understanding cross-country differences. I have argued that much of the international variation in living standards can be explained by differences in the quantities of human and physical capital. As I understand Paul Romer's view, he is sceptical of this possibility. He argues that differences in knowledge across countries are important; in essence, he claims that different countries have access to different sets of blueprints. One problem in testing these two views is that physical capital and human capital (schooling) can be measured and evaluated, which is what I tried to do in my (1992) *Quarterly Journal of Economics* paper with David Romer and David Weil, while the 'ideas' that Paul Romer emphasizes are harder to measure. I am sure that there is some truth in both the 'capital view' and the 'ideas view' and that other things – trade policy, property rights, and so on – matter as well. The relative importance of these different factors is ultimately an empirical question that is very hard to answer conclusively.

Milton Friedman
(b. 1912)

Milton Friedman is currently Senior Research Fellow at the Hoover Institution, Stanford University. Along with John Maynard Keynes he is arguably the most famous economist of the twentieth century. Professor Friedman is widely recognized as the founding father of monetarism and an untiring advocate of free markets in a wide variety of contexts. He has made major contributions to such areas as methodology; the consumption function; international economics; monetary theory, history and policy; business cycles and inflation. In 1976 he was awarded the Nobel Prize in Economics: 'For his achievements in the fields of consumption analysis, monetary history and theory and for his demonstration of the complexity of stabilization policy'.

We interviewed Professor Friedman in his study at his apartment in San Francisco on 8 January 1996, while attending the annual conference of the American Economic Association.

BACKGROUND INFORMATION

What first attracted you to study economics and become an economist?
I graduated from college in 1932. As a college student I had majored jointly in economics and mathematics and when I graduated I was offered two postgraduate scholarships. At that time there weren't any such things as our

current generous fellowships, graduate scholarships consisted of somebody offering to pay for your tuition, period. I was offered one in mathematics at Brown and one in economics at Chicago. Now put yourself in 1932 with a quarter of the population unemployed. What was the important urgent problem? It was obviously economics and so there was never any hesitation on my part to study economics. When I first started in college I was very ignorant about these matters because I grew up in a rather low income family which had no particular understanding of the broader world. I was very much interested in and pretty good at mathematics. So I looked around to see if there was any way I could earn a living by mathematics. The only way I could find before I went to college was to become an actuary and so my original ambition when entering college was to become an actuary. I did take some of the actuarial exams in my first two years at college, but I never continued after that.

KEYNES'S *GENERAL THEORY* AND KEYNESIAN ECONOMICS

At Chicago as a graduate student what interpretation did your teachers put forward to explain the Great Depression?
Well that's a very interesting question because I have believed for a long time that the fundamental difference between my approach to Keynes and Abba Lerner's approach to Keynes, to take a particular example, is due to what our professors taught us. I started graduate school in the fall of 1932 when the Depression wasn't over by any means. My teachers, who were Jacob Viner, Frank Knight and Lloyd Mints, taught us that what was going on was a disastrous mistake by the Federal Reserve in reducing the money supply. It was not a natural catastrophe, it was not something that had to happen, it was not something which had to be allowed to run its course. There were things which should be done. Jacob Viner, from whom I took my first course in pure economic theory as a graduate, had given a talk in Minnesota in which he very specifically called for expansive policy on the part of the Federal Reserve and the government. Therefore the Keynesian revolution didn't come as a sudden light from the dark showing what you could do about a situation that nobody else seemed to know how to do anything about.

Can you recall when you first read the General Theory *(1936) and what your impressions were of the book?*
I can't really answer that, I don't recall. I may be able to tell you if I look in my original copy of the *General Theory* as I sometimes had a habit of marking in my books the date when I bought them and how much money I paid for

them. Yes here it is. I bought it in 1938 and paid $1.80 cents for it (*laughter*). That's probably when I first read it but I can't remember my impressions, it's a long long time ago, but I do remember that in the early 1940s I wrote a book review in which I was very critical of the Keynesian analysis contained in the book that I reviewed.

Why do you think Keynes's General Theory *captured the minds of such a large percentage of the economics profession in such a relatively short period of around a decade following its publication in 1936?*
I don't think there is any problem in explaining that at all. If you took the economics profession as a whole what I have described as the teaching at Chicago was very much an exception. The bulk of the teaching in schools of economics went more nearly along the lines of a Mises–Hayek view. If you take the London School of Economics that's where the contrast with Abba Lerner was most obvious because he, and most of the people who were studying economics, were taught that the Depression was a necessary purgative through which the economy had to go in order to cure the ills that had been produced by the prior expansion. That's a terribly dismal approach. Then all of a sudden out of the blue comes this attractive doctrine from Cambridge, Keynes's *General Theory*, by a man who already has an enormous reputation primarily because of *The Economic Consequences of the Peace* (1919). He says, look we know how to solve these problems and there is a very simple way. Given a hypothesis which tells you why we got into this trouble you would surely grasp at that when the only alternative you had was the dismal Austrian view (*laughter*).

How important was Paul Samuelson's (1948) introductory textbook and Alvin Hansen's (1953) intermediate textbook in contributing to the spread of Keynesian economics?
They were very important. I think Hansen was really important in the United States, I can't say about the rest of the world, partly because he had undergone such a sharp conversion. If you look at his early work before Keynes, it was strictly along the Mises–Hayek line. Hansen was very much a believer that this was a necessary purgative but then he suddenly saw the light and he became a convinced exponent of Keynesianism. He was at Harvard at the time whereas he had been at Minneapolis when he expressed the earlier view. He was a very good teacher, a very nice human being. He had a great deal of influence, I don't have any doubt at all. Samuelson's influence comes later. Unless I'm mistaken Hansen converted by 1938 or 1939 but Samuelson's elementary text only came after the war so he was a much later influence. Hansen was extremely important because of his effect on the people at Harvard. There were a very good group of economists at Harvard who played

a significant role at the Federal Reserve, the Treasury and in Washington who were recruited during the war. So I think Hansen played a very important influence.

A prominent real business cycle theorist Charles Plosser (1994) has suggested that in the absence of John Hicks's IS–LM framework Keynes's General Theory *would have been much less influential. Do you agree with this view?*
I believe that there is a great deal to that because later Samuelson was able to use his cross diagram that came entirely out of Hicks's IS–LM framework. I think that's a correct observation.

If Keynes had lived to have been awarded the Nobel Prize in Economics, what do you think the citation would have been?
It depends on when it would have been awarded. If it had been awarded at the beginning in 1969 the citation would undoubtedly have been 'the man who showed us how to get out of depressions and how to pursue a policy that would lead to reasonably full and stable employment'. But if the citation had been in 1989, let's say, I think it would have been written differently. It would have said 'an economist whose continued work beginning with his *Treatise on Probability* (1921), and right on through, has had a major influence on the course of the economics profession'. But you know that's just conjecture, who knows what it would have been (*laughter*). Let me make clear my own view about Keynes. I believe that he was a great economist, one of the great economists of our time and that the *General Theory* is a remarkable intellectual achievement. We had a phenomenon that needed an explanation. How could you have widespread unemployment in the midst of an economy with such large productive capacity? That was a phenomenon in search of an explanation and he produced an explanation for it which, in my opinion, was the right kind of an explanation. What you need to do is to have a very simple theory that gets at the fundamentals. No theory is successful if it's extremely complicated and difficult because most phenomena are driven by a very few central forces. What a good theory does is to simplify, it pulls out the central forces and gets rid of the rest. So Keynes's *General Theory* was the right kind of theory. Science in general advances primarily by unsuccessful experiments that clear the ground and I regard the *General Theory* as having been an unsuccessful experiment. It was the right kind of a theory; it had content because it enabled you to make predictions, but when you made those predictions they were not confirmed and as a result I regard it as an unsuccessful experiment.

What do you think has been the main contribution that the new Keynesian literature has made to the development of macroeconomics?

Well I'm not going to comment on that because I really haven't followed it carefully enough. Since our *Monetary Trends* (Friedman and Schwartz, 1982) came out and particularly since my book on *Money Mischief* (1992) came out I really haven't been doing any work on issues like that. In the past three or four years I have rather been working on my wife's and my memoirs.

MONETARISM

Do you regard your (1956) restatement of the quantity theory of money as a more sophisticated elaboration of the Keynesian theory of liquidity preference?
Not at all. I regarded it, as I said then, as a continuation of the general monetary theory that I had been taught as a student before Keynes's theory came out. One component of it is consistent with liquidity preference analysis. But if you are asking me whether at the time that was my motivation, or my understanding of it, I have to say no.

Do you view your restatement then as a distinct break with Keynesian analysis?
No. I didn't look at it in that way at all. I was just trying to set down what I thought was a reformulation of the quantity theory of money. Remember Keynes was a quantity theorist. Look at his *Monetary Reform* (1923) for example, which I believe is one of his best books, a much under-appreciated and more useful book than the *General Theory*. Unlike the *General Theory* it was not an attempt to construct a new theory. It involved an application of the existing theory to a set of interesting phenomena, the immediate postwar inflations. It's a very good piece of work which is straight quantity theory and I was a quantity theorist. So if you ask in what way was Keynes's liquidity preference theory different from the quantity theory that he had adopted in his *Monetary Reform* (1923), it was different only in the idea of having a liquidity trap. That was the only essential different idea. In my reformulation I don't have a liquidity trap, a liquidity trap is possible but that's not a part of the analysis.

Although the belief in a stable demand for money function was well supported by empirical evidence up to the early 1970s since then a number of studies have found evidence of apparent instability. Does this undermine the case for a fixed monetary growth rule?
Yes and no. If you have a stable money demand function that's not the same as saying that it's never going to shift, never going to be affected by anything else. Let's take the case of the United States which I know best. If you take the period after the Second World War to let's say 1980, you have a very stable money demand function and it doesn't matter whether you use the base,

M1, M2 or M3, you'll get essentially the same result. In the early 1980s there were a series of structural changes in the system, in particular the payment of interest on demand deposits which had the effect of changing the money demand function, particularly for the base and M1. There's a period of about five years where it is very hard to know what's going on because of these structural shifts. Then from about 1985 on the earlier demand function with M2 is re-established, but not with M1 or the base, they are very unstable. If you plot, as I have done, the rate of change of these various aggregates year over year against year over year changes in inflation two years later, up to 1980 it doesn't matter, they are all pretty good. After 1980 M1 and the base go haywire completely. On the other hand the relationship with M2 stays pretty much the same. So there is a real problem there because if, as many people were (I was not), you were thinking in terms of M1 as the major monetary aggregate it would have been a mistake to have continued this steady rate of growth. But if you had continued a steady rate of growth of M2 you would have been all right.

How do you react to Robert Lucas's (1994b) suggestion that the 1970s were a time of prosperity for the Friedman and Schwartz (1963) volume The Monetary History of the United States, *while the 1980s must be viewed as a time of mild recession. Has this been due to the influence of real business cycle theorists?*

I'm not sure how to answer that. I really have never looked at the history of the volume itself in terms of prosperity or recession (*laughter*). There were three reviews in all on what was the thirtieth anniversary of the volume. I must say that the review I like best is the one by Jeffrey Miron because it emphasized what I think is really important and is relevant, not merely to monetary issues but to the economics profession as a whole, namely the importance of testing your theories on historical and empirical material. It seems to me that in many ways one of the contributions of the *Monetary History* was methodological. I don't mean it didn't make a substantive contribution but there was also a methodological contribution and Miron emphasized that, if I remember rightly, in his review. But now to your question. There is the problem of keeping science distinct from politics. The 1980s was the Reagan period. I was known as a close adviser to Reagan. The academic community was almost wholly anti-Reagan, although that was probably less true of economics than it was of any other academic discipline you can name. I'm talking here about the social sciences and the humanities, not the natural sciences. I may be entirely wrong on this, I hope I am, but I believe that the fact that I was connected with the Reagan administration had something to do with the desire on the part of the economics profession to separate themselves from my work. There's one other thing that has to be said. The interesting thing in any science, whether it's economics or mathematics or anything else, is not repeating the past but going ahead to new things. Every science every 10 or 20 years has to have a new fad or it goes dead. I think that the emphasis on real business cycle theory did provide a new fad for a while which has had a great deal of influence on the work that economists have done.

Would you agree that your (1968) paper on 'The Role of Monetary Policy' has perhaps turned out to be your most influential paper?
As to that I don't doubt that it had a great deal of influence. But when you talk about comparisons it is hard for me to decide between that and 'The Methodology of Positive Economics' (1953a) which had as much influence in a different direction, not on the substance but on the methodology.

How far do you think that the influence of your (1968) paper was greatly enhanced because it anticipated the events of the 1970s and in particular predicted accelerating inflation?
On that I don't think there is any doubt whatsoever. It was a major reason for the shift in attitude. As I said earlier the right kind of a theory is one that makes predictions that are capable of being contradicted. The Keynesian theory made a prediction that was capable of being contradicted and it was contradicted. The theory I was describing also made predictions; in this case it made predictions that we would experience accelerating inflation and it was not contradicted.

In the same year as your Presidential Address to the American Economic Association Edmund Phelps in his (1967) Economica article also denied the existence of a long-run trade-off between inflation and unemployment. Are there are significant differences between your Phillips curve analysis and that of Edmund Phelps?
There are enormous similarities and tremendous overlaps. The main difference is that I was looking at it from the monetary side whereas Edmund Phelps was looking at it from the labour market side. But the theories are the same, the statements are the same, there is no difference there.

Is there any significant difference between your definition of the natural rate of unemployment and Keynes's definition of full employment?
That's a tough one. His definition of full employment is simply a situation in which there is no unsatisfied employee, in which anybody who is willing to work for the current wage has a job. I think I'm quoting it reasonably correctly. My definition of the natural rate of unemployment is that rate at which demand and supply are equal so there is no excess supply or demand

and in which people's expectations are satisfied. I think both of these are related to Wicksell's natural rate of interest. I don't think there is much difference between us.

In your (1968) paper you highlighted the implications of introducing inflationary expectations into the Phillips curve. Since then adaptive expectations has gone out of fashion following what could be described as a rational expectations revolution. Which hypothesis do you favour as a way of modelling how economic agents form such expectations?

I'm not sure how to answer that. The theoretical principle has always been the same, that what matters is what the expectations are and that they play a very important role. That's an old idea, that's not anything new. I'm sure you can find it in Marshall. I know you can find it in Schumpeter. In fact you can find it everywhere. The adaptive expectations approach was simply a way to try to make that empirically observable and in many cases it seemed to work. The most obvious case was Phillip Cagan's (1956) study of hyperinflation in Germany and other European countries and there adaptive expectations worked up to the point at which you had reform. Then it didn't work at all. The best studies along that line were Tom Sargent's (1982) later studies about the effect of the monetary reforms.

Rational expectations, Bob Lucas's approach, in a way is obvious and well known. Everybody knew in the past that a rational man would not base his expectations simply on what had happened in the past if there was a major change or any significant changes in public policy, he would also look at what he knew about that. The contribution of Lucas was partly to give that notion a name and I don't think you want to underestimate the importance of naming things. You know nobody can take everything into their head at one time as Marshall used to say, you can't do it. You have to have ways of simplifying things and showing how things fit together. Bob Lucas's real contribution was showing how you might be able to mathematize and empirically design studies that would give you some way to get an empirical counterpart of the hypothetical and unmeasurable rational expectation. That was his real contribution.

I have always had great difficulties with the basic notion that there is some sense in which you can say expectations are correct or not correct. Let me explain what I mean. At the moment it is perfectly rational to suppose that there will be a major inflation some time in the next 20 years. There have been lots of major inflations. Suppose I have an expectation that there is a 10 per cent chance of there being a major inflation and no major inflation occurs. All along I have been betting that there might be a major inflation and I have been buying real assets, rather than nominal assets, in order to protect myself. If a major inflation doesn't occur in what sense can you say I was wrong?

There was always a chance. In a way the probability of anything happening *ex post* is always one. How do I judge whether someone's so-called rational expectations were correct? You might say that you have to get a distribution of what happened. Do I have to take 1000 years, 100 years, 50 years? What is the right basis? Moreover every rational expectation notion recognizes that in advance what you have is a probability distribution, not a single point, and that gets to the question of whether there is such a thing as objective probability? The only probability notion I can make sense of is personal probability in the spirit of Savage and others. Keynes's degree of belief is in the same family. In fact I believe that Keynes's contribution in his *Probability* book has been underrated and overlooked. The whole Bayesian movement today in statistics, which has had a great deal of influence on statistical methods, is based on the idea of personal probability, of degree of belief. It is based on the kind of idea that Keynes was putting forward in his (1921) *Treatise on Probability* volume.

Should we worry about moderate rates of inflation when the evidence seems to suggest that they don't have strong effects on real variables?
No, we should not worry about moderate inflation except as a breeder of larger inflation and that's a big exception (*laughter*). My summary of the evidence on that, and I really can't pretend this is authoritative because I haven't followed the research in that area for the past few years, is that there is a short-term relation between unexpected inflation and unemployment. But there is no long-term relation and even the short-term relation is very weak. The main case that I cite on the long-term relation is the United States from 1879–96 and from 1896–1913. From 1879–96 prices fell at about 3 per cent per year, not regularly of course but on the average, and from 1896–1913 they rose at about 3 per cent per year. Yet the rate of real growth is roughly the same in the two periods.

Over the years monetarism has often been associated with conservative politics. Is this alleged association inevitable?
The alleged association is not inevitable. Karl Marx was a quantity theorist. The Bank of China (communist China) is monetarist. Moreover, I am not myself a conservative. I am a liberal in the classical sense or, in the terminology that has become common in the United States, a libertarian in philosophy. In any event, monetarism properly interpreted is an objective set of propositions about the relation between monetary magnitudes and other economic variables. Conservative, radical, communist, socialist, any ruling authorities can only achieve their objectives if they can predict what the consequences of their actions will be. A correct body of monetarist propositions is as necessary to authorities of one stripe as of another.

NEW CLASSICAL MACROECONOMICS

It can be argued that one of the most difficult things in economics is to create a new vision. Is this one of the most important features of Robert Lucas's impact?

No because I think that vision was present in a way before. Everybody knew that you ought to be forward looking. What he did was to develop a method whereby you could make that vision operational. Once I got together some quotations on expectations. One particularly good one from Schumpeter just stated out and out the notion of rational expectations in the sense of the vision, but it wasn't operational. I think Lucas's big contribution was to make it operational. Everybody understood that people behaved on the basis of what they anticipated in the future and the question is how do you approximate that. Of course the real start of rational expectations was John Muth's (1961) piece in *Econometrica*.

Why do you think new classical macroeconomics proved to be so attractive to the younger generation of economists in the United States?

The policy ineffectiveness proposition was very popular for a while but it's another one of those theories which is the right kind of a theory but is contradicted by its predictions. Nobody in the face of the experience of the early 1980s can believe the policy ineffectiveness proposition is a valid prediction of what will happen in the short term. The 1980–82 recession really completely contradicted it. I really don't know how popular the approach was. It was popular with a small group. The beauty of it is that it brings you back to a pure theoretical analysis. It's not sort of besmirched by any complexities, any complications, any friction, anything else (*laughter*). It hangs together as a theoretical matter if people correctly anticipate the future, but the situation will be wholly different if they don't.

Kevin Hoover (1984) has drawn a methodological distinction between your work as a Marshallian and that of Robert Lucas as a Walrasian. Is that distinction valid?

There is a great deal to that. On the whole I believe that is probably true. I have always distinguished between the Marshallian approach and the Walrasian approach. I have always been personally a Marshallian. That doesn't mean that the Walrasian approach is not a useful or appropriate approach. People's temperaments and attitudes are different I guess. I yield to no one in my admiration for Marshall as an economist, but he had real flaws as an individual. The way he treated his wife was disgraceful. We found out about it way back in the 1950s when we spent a year at Cambridge in 1952–53. We spent a lot of time at the Marshall library and read a good deal of the

Marshall documents. It seemed that Mary Paley his wife was a very able, competent woman. I won't go into that story it will take us too long.

How important has the Kydland–Prescott time inconsistency argument been in the rules v discretion debate?
That has been quite influential in the debate and is a very nice and entirely valid point.

Since the demise of the monetary-surprise version of new classical macroeconomics in the early 1980s the new classical approach has been revitalized by real business cycle theory. Has this, in your opinion, been a fruitful line of research?
I have some hesitancy in answering that question because I have not followed or investigated that literature as much as I should in order to give a considered answer. I really don't believe that there is a business cycle, it is a misleading concept. The notion of a business cycle is something of a regularly recurring phenomenon that is internally driven by the mechanics of the system. I don't believe there is a business cycle in that sense. I believe that there is a system that has certain response mechanisms and that system is subject over time to external random forces (some large, some small) that play on it and it adapts to those forces. The adaptation process has certain regularities that in a way is going back to the basic Slutsky idea of an accumulation of random forces. Some of those forces are unquestionably real and in so far as the real business cycle people emphasize that the disturbances come from outside, that's all to the good. On the other hand the mechanism that reacts to the real disturbances is largely monetary, and by underplaying the monetary role in the process the so-called real business cycle theory has not been very helpful. You probably know my own little piece on what I call the 'plucking model' in *Economic Inquiry* (1993). It was written many years earlier in an annual report of the National Bureau of Economic Research and it's also in the collection of papers contained in *The Optimum Quantity of Money* (1969) though I modified it a little for the *Inquiry* version, but not much. To quote: 'consider an elastic string stretched taut between two points on the underside of a rigid horizontal board and glued lightly to the board. Let the string be plucked at a number of points chosen more or less at random with a force that varies at random, and then held down at the lowest point reached. The result will be to produce a succession of apparent cycles in the string whose amplitudes depend on the force used in plucking the string' and so on. For me personally I find that a much more useful model than the model of a self-generating cycle.

With the growth in the popularity of real business cycle models in the 1980s many new classical macroeconomists have turned to the calibration method

rather than conventional econometric techniques to test the performance of their models. How do you view the calibration method?
I believe that it is evading the issue. It isn't enough to show that the characteristics of the time series can be duplicated in a model. If the model has any meaning it is going to make predictions about things that can be observed and contradicted. You can match any set of data precisely with a least squares regression if you have enough variables in it.

METHODOLOGICAL AND GENERAL ISSUES

You commented earlier that your (1953a) essay on the 'Methodology of Positive Economics' has been one of your most influential papers. Did you in any way anticipate the controversy that your paper would subsequently generate?
No.

Is the philosophy of science and formal methodology an area that still interests you?
It was an area that interested me at the time but after I wrote that paper I decided I really would rather do economics than tell people how to do economics. I found out that my views were very similar to Karl Popper's and I followed his writings in a sort of a vague way, but not very seriously. One of the major reasons why that article led to so much controversy is that I decided early on that I wasn't going to answer attacks on it (*laughter*). I am serious. If you want to get controversy about one of your articles write something which will be attacked and then don't answer the attackers because it opens a field day.

Why do you think there is more consensus among economists over microeconomic issues compared to macroeconomic issues?
Primarily because there has not been in the microeconomic area anything comparable to the Keynesian revolution in the macroeconomic area. For a time it looked as if the imperfect competition developments of Chamberlin and Robinson would play the same role in the microeconomic area, but they turned out to be more readily absorbed in the traditional classical body of microeconomic theory as presented in Marshall's *Principles*. A second reason, indeed the one that gave rise to the Keynesian revolution, was that the issues of employment/unemployment and business cycles became major political issues.

How important do you think it is for macroeconomic models to have choice-theoretic micro foundations?

It is less important for macroeconomic models to have choice-theoretic micro-foundations than it is for them to have empirical implications that can be subjected to refutation. Choice-theoretic microfoundations may provide hypotheses for improving macroeconomic models, but the key macroeconomic models have been of long standing and have had a great deal of success without the more recent emphasis on choice-theoretic microfoundations.

Do you think that attempts to try to understand the reasons for wage and price rigidities is a fruitful line of research?
I don't believe that you can tell people what is a fruitful line for research. Everything is a fruitful line of research. I remember very well when I was advising doctoral students about their theses, they would come in and say well a lot's been done on that subject. There is no subject on which there isn't more to be done, building on what's gone before. I don't have any doubt that there are wage rigidities because obviously there are, it's a fact of life, it's hard to deny it. The question is whether they are important or not, in what ways they are important and in what kind of phenomena are they important. As I said before the essence of a successful theory is that it extracts the key elements from the whole host of attendant circumstances. So I wouldn't want to discourage anybody from doing research in that area. Moreover I wouldn't want to discourage anybody from doing research in any area. What people have to do is to do things that interest them, follow up their own insights and their own ideas.

Robert Lucas (1994a) has argued that 'professional economists are primarily scholars ... whose responsibility is to create new knowledge by pushing research into new and hence necessarily controversial territory'. Where do you see macroeconomic research heading?
Economists are scholars but they are going to be influenced by developments in the world around them. There is no doubt that the great interest in business cycles was partly a consequence of the phenomenon of the Great Depression. We have in the world today the most striking phenomena: on the one hand there is the worldwide technological revolution, and on the other hand there is the political revolution – the collapse of the Soviet Union and the independence of its satellites. Both influences have had one common effect – what has been called the globalization of the economy, a term I hate. Both revolutions have led to a situation in which a producer can produce a product anywhere in the world, sell it anywhere in the world, use resources located anywhere in the world and be himself located anywhere in the world. So it is no longer meaningful to talk about the domestic content of things. Is a car made in America when parts of it come from Japan and parts come from another country? That's always been true, but it's a much more important phenomenon today. In addition there are also issues relating to the so-called

underdeveloped or backward countries which are now coming into the modern stream for the first time. Those are phenomena of major importance and they need to be discussed and analysed. It is appropriate that economists should move to see how they can understand those phenomena and what can contribute to those phenomena. I have no doubt that this will be a major focus of research over the coming years.

In your (1991) Economic Journal *paper you drew attention to major improvements in the 'engine of analysis' but seemed to suggest that the quality of much economic research had declined. Can you elaborate on this view?*
I don't believe I was saying that. What I would say is that economics has become increasingly an arcane branch of mathematics rather than dealing with real economic problems. There is no doubt that that has happened. I believe that economics has gone much too far in that direction, but there is a correction on the way. Take the *Economic Journal.* It has introduced a section on current controversies which is a real departure from the kind of thing it had before. There is no doubt that it's become harder for anybody to keep up with the literature, except in his or her own special field and I believe that's a very bad feature of the developments in economics. In that sense, what you said about the decline and deterioration in economic research is true. But the engine of analysis as a technical, theoretical structure has certainly improved over the period a great deal.

Why do you think the leadership in macroeconomic research passed from the UK to the US after the Second World War?
The answer is simple. If you have too strong an orthodoxy you are not going to have any leadership. What happened was that Britain was a leader in the 1930s, no question. But that became solidified into a rock of orthodox opinion which was not going to be a breeding ground for leading the future. Of course this is a complicated question because it is all tied up with the change in the role of Britain as a whole in the world as a result of the Second World War. The First World War reduced the influence of Britain a great deal as a world leader and the Second went further. But I really do think fundamentally the problem was that the leadership in economics at Cambridge, England became hardened into an orthodoxy, which is not a good breeding ground for revolutionary or innovative work.

ECONOMIC POLICY

Some economists, perhaps most, would argue that the fundamental difference between monetarists and Keynesians is not so much their respective views on the influence of the money supply but their differing views on the equilibrating powers of the market mechanism. Whereas monetarists have faith in the equilibrating tendencies of market forces Keynesians argue that there is substantial market failure requiring some sort of activist intervention at the macro level. Would you agree with this view?

I do not agree with this view. There are monetarists of all kinds, some who stress market failure and some who do not. All economists – monetarists, Keynesians, or what-not – recognize that there is such a thing as market failure. I believe that what really distinguishes economists is not whether they recognize market failure, but how much importance they attach to government failure, especially when government seeks to remedy what are said to be market failures. That difference in turn is related to the time perspective that economists bring to various issues. Speaking for myself, I do not believe that I have more faith in the equilibrating tendencies of market forces than most Keynesians, but I have far less faith than most economists, whether Keynesians or monetarists, in the ability of government to offset market failure without making matters worse.

*You have argued (*American Economic Review, *1968) that most disagreements appear not to be concerned with the major goals of economic policy but rather are over the choice of appropriate instruments to achieve the goals. In the light of your work on the consumption function and monetary economics in general, what role do you see for fiscal policy in a macroeconomic context?*

None. I believe that fiscal policy will contribute most if it doesn't try to offset short-term movements in the economy. I'm expressing a minority view here but it's my belief that fiscal policy is not an effective instrument for controlling short-term movements in the economy. One of the things I have tried to do over the years is to find cases where fiscal policy is going in one direction and monetary policy is going in the opposite. In every case the actual course of events follows monetary policy. I have never found a case in which fiscal policy dominated monetary policy and I suggest to you as a test to find a counter example. There are two possible explanations for that. One which I really believe to be true is that the Keynesian view that a government deficit is stimulating is simply wrong. A deficit is not stimulating because it has to be financed and the negative effects of financing it counterbalance the positive effects, if there are any, on spending. But that may not be the reason because there is the other reason that it is much harder to adjust fiscal policy in a sensitive short-term way than it is to adjust monetary policy. So I don't really believe that there is any role for fiscal policy in the short term. There is an enormous role for fiscal policy in terms of the long-term allocation of resources among different uses and that is where the argument really needs to be.

Are you saying that even in the case of the 1930s you would not have advocated expansionary fiscal policy?
It wasn't fiscal policy it was monetary policy that dominated. There was nothing you could do with fiscal policy that was going to offset a decline of a third in the quantity of money. Let me show you a current example. Take Japan right now. They are wasting their time and money in trying to have an expansive fiscal policy without an expansive monetary policy. I'm exaggerating a little about Japan because in the last year or so, mostly since the appointment of the new Head of the Bank of Japan, they have been starting to follow an expansive monetary policy. I believe that Japan is going to show a considerable degree of improvement and that they will start to come back up. It's a very interesting phenomenon because the behaviour of the Japanese central bank in the past five years duplicates the behaviour of the Federal Reserve after 1929.

Persistent high unemployment has been a feature of European economies since the early 1980s. A variety of explanations have been put forward including hysteresis theories. How do you explain such persistent unemployment?
I believe it is a consequence of the extensive welfare state and rigidities in the system. I have just read a very interesting working paper of the Federal Reserve Bank of Chicago co-written by Lars Ljungqvist and Tom Sargent (1998). I agree with their conclusion. They start out by saying one obvious explanation is the welfare state arrangements and the change in the incentives that people have. But then an obvious answer to that is why didn't that have the same effect on unemployment earlier. Their explanation is that the earlier period was a more nearly stationary period in which it was not necessary to make rapid and extensive dynamic adjustments to the changes in circumstances. But in the last 10 or 20 years, what with the technological revolution and the political revolution, it has been necessary to make major changes and the European system is rigid. It's okay if everything goes along smoothly but it's not very good at adapting to major dynamic change. It seems to me that that makes a great deal of sense. You might ask the question why is it that the United States hasn't had the same experience. I'm not sure that my answer now will be true in the future because we have been going in the same direction although we haven't gone nearly as far. We have a much more flexible wage system. It's much easier to fire people although it is getting harder and harder to hire people. There are more and more disincentives to employers to hire people because of affirmative action and all the rules and regulations involved. But still we are better off than the European economies.

In another highly influential paper published in 1953(b), only nine years after the establishment of the Bretton Woods fixed exchange rates system, you presented the case for flexible exchange rates. In the light of experience since the breakdown of the system in the early 1970s how do you respond to the issue of variability or instability, which critics of flexible exchange rates have highlighted?

The variability has been much larger than I would have expected. I don't have any doubt about that, but there are two propositions. Number one, the reason for the high variability has been because of the highly variable forces that have been playing upon the international market which derive in my opinion from the fact that beginning in 1971 the world had a monetary system that had no prior predecessor, no precedent whatsoever. For the first time in the history of the world no current major, or minor currency for that matter, in the world was linked to a commodity however indirectly. To begin with everybody was sailing on an uncharted sea and on that uncharted sea some went one way and some went another. So you had a much wider variability in the rates of inflation in different countries than you were accustomed to and that led to a greater variability in exchange rates. The second proposition is that the variability in exchange rates was a good thing. If you had tried to maintain fixed exchange rates under those conditions it would have required major interferences in the freedom of trade among various countries. So that while the variability of exchange rates was much greater than I would have anticipated I believe it was a necessary reaction, maybe over-reaction, to what was going on and that if you look at the experience over that time it did not have any serious negative effects. I don't doubt that any exchange rate adjustment is going to be overdone. If you need a large change it's going to be too large and then it's going to come back again because of the influence of (a) expectations and (b) speculation. But I don't believe you have any examples of destabilizing speculation. The speculators have on the whole performed a positive function. The European Exchange Rate Mechanism was fundamentally unstable and in so far as the speculators broke it in September 1992, earlier than otherwise, it was a desirable thing. Britain made a great mistake by linking its currency to the Exchange Rate Mechanism, it should never have done that and it paid dearly for doing so.

What are your views on the desirability of forming a single currency in Europe?

There are two different questions, the desirability and the possibility. I believe that it is an impossible thing to do and this is something that I have been saying over and over again everywhere. It seems to me that you must distinguish between a unified currency and currencies linked by a fixed exchange rate. You can only have a unified currency if you have only one central bank, one locus of authority. I cannot believe that you are going to be willing to close down the Bank of England, that France is going to be willing to close down the Bank of France and so on. So it seems to me political unification has to come first. How many times do we have to see the same phenomenon repeat itself? After the war there was the Bretton Woods system and it broke down, in the 1970s the 'Snake' broke down and so on. How many times do you have to repeat an experience before you realize that there must be some real problem in having fixed exchange rates among countries that are independent. The period of the nineteenth century, which is always pointed to, can be distinguished from the current period in a very simple way. Government spending of the major countries in the pre-1913 period was around 10 per cent of the national income. A system that could operate when governments were spending 10 per cent of the national income cannot operate when governments are spending 50 per cent of the national income. There is a sense in which a single currency is desirable, but what does it mean to say something unachievable is desirable?

It is interesting that you say you need political unification before economic union as many critics in Britain suspect that monetary union is being used as a way of moving towards political union.
I don't doubt that. I don't doubt that the Germans and the French are trying to do that, but I don't believe that they will succeed.

Macroeconomics is not a laboratory science, we learn from events. What did we learn from the so-called 'monetarist experiments' in the US and UK at the start of the 1980s?
You have got to distinguish between two different things. The so-called monetarist experiment was in 1979 when Volcker announced that he was going to take the quantity of money and not the interest rate as his guide. But he didn't do it! If you look at the monetary aggregates they were more variable during the Volcker period than at any previous time in history. So he did not follow a monetarist course. On the other hand if you eliminate the perturbations and you look at the general direction over the period from 1980–95 in every country in the world aggregate monetary growth has come way down and with it has come inflation. So I think that the experiment in all of the countries of the world has been enormously confirmatory of the proposition that inflation is a monetary phenomenon.

Why do governments create inflation?
They create inflation in order to get the revenue from it and the reason it has come down is not because governments have become more noble but because you can't get much revenue out of it. I gave a talk at the Bank of Japan in 1985, on which I based the last chapter of my book *Money Mischief* (1992). I entitled it 'Monetary policy in a fiat world'. To quote 'inflation has become

less attractive as a political option. Given that the voting public is very sensitive to inflation it may currently be politically profitable to establish monetary arrangements that will make the present irredeemable paper standard an exception to Fisher's generalization'. In Fisher's *Purchasing Power of Money* (1911) he says that every attempt at a paper money standard has been a disaster. How do governments get money from inflation? Number one, there is the direct value of the high-powered money base. That's a very small source, it's trivial. Much more important are two other sources. One is that if your tax system is expressed in nominal terms, inflation raises taxes without anyone having to vote for higher taxes. The second is that if you have been able to issue securities at an interest rate that is lower than the rate of inflation you can expropriate those securities. The expropriation of past debt plus the automatic increases in taxes were undoubtedly the major source of revenue for the United States from the inflations of the 1970s. There is no doubt about that. I remember having breakfast on some occasion with the then Senator Long from Louisiana who was on the Finance Committee. He said you know we never could have passed these rates of tax on current incomes if it hadn't been that they were automatically brought up there by inflation. It would have been politically impossible. The adjustment of tax rates for inflation, indexing the tax rates, has eliminated one source of revenue. The fact that bond markets have become so much more sensitive to inflation has eliminated the second. So how much revenue can you now get out of inflation? It isn't worth inflating. If you have inflation in the future my prediction is that it will only be as an attempt for full employment purposes and not as a way to raise revenue. That's why I'm pretty confident that you are not going to have a major inflation in the future.

Do you think that disinflation can ever be achieved without significant real output/employment costs?
I doubt it very much. That's why you don't want to let inflation get started because it's so hard to bring it down.

PERSONAL INFORMATION

What importance do you personally attach to being awarded the Nobel Prize in Economics?
Obviously it is extremely rewarding. However, when I first learned of the award from a reporter in a parking lot in Detroit who stuck a microphone in my face and asked, 'Do you regard this as the high point of your career?', I answered, 'I care more what my successors fifty years from now will think about my professional work than I do about the judgement of seven people

from Sweden who happen to be serving on the Nobel Committee'. I do not mean to denigrate the Nobel Committee. They have been doing a very conscientious and good job on the whole, but at the same time what really matters to a scientist is the long-run effect of his work on his science.

The number of books and refereed articles you have had published is prodigious.
I don't know what it is. It is very large, yes.

How have you found the time to write so much and has this impinged on your family and social life?
(*Laughter*) No. For much of our married life and the first part when we were at Chicago in particular, we typically spent three solid months in the country at our second home in New Hampshire to begin with and later on in Vermont. Then later on I split my life 50–50, we spent six months a year in Chicago and six months a year in Vermont. Almost all of my writing was done in Vermont or in New Hampshire, relatively little during the actual school year. I managed pretty much to keep down outside activities. I didn't go away from Vermont or New Hampshire to make speeches or to address committee meetings or hearings. There were occasional exceptions but for the most part I made it an absolute rule. When I look at my remaining diaries from that period I am shocked by how full the pages are when I am in Chicago and how empty they are when I'm up in Vermont or New Hampshire (*laughter*). So that's the only reason I was able to write as much as I did.

Do you find it ironic that many of your views, once the subject of intense debate and controversy, are now firmly embedded as part of the established mainstream orthodoxy in macroeconomics?
I find it very satisfying but not ironic at all. Why should it be ironic? New ideas have to fight a battle to get accepted. If you are against the conventional wisdom the course of reaction from your critics is very simple. The first reaction is that it's all a bunch of nonsense, it's just so extreme it can't possibly be right. The second reaction is, well you know there is something to it. The third reaction is it gets embedded in the theory and nobody talks about it any more.

Don't you need to be thick skinned and have great strength of conviction in your views in such circumstances?
I don't think the question is one of having a thick skin. I think the question is one of belief in what you are doing. Conviction is strong. I have never been bothered by intellectual attacks, that hasn't been a problem. I've always had very good personal relations with people whose views are different from

mine. With very very rare exceptions, I never had any personal problems. Paul Samuelson and I, for example, are good personal friends.

Have you any, as yet, unfulfilled academic ambitions?
No I don't think so. My main ambition now is to get our memoirs finished. We've been working on them too long. Over the last year and a half I've had health problems which has slowed down our progress on our memoirs.

One final question. John Burton (1981) has described you as the Adam Smith of the twentieth century. Is that a description you would be happy to have?
(*Laughter*). Sure I'd be happy to have that. Adam Smith was the great father of modern economics, there's no question. I'd regard it as a great compliment to be regarded in that way. But I believe that view is based not on my scientific work but on my outside activities propagandizing for free markets.

Robert E. Lucas Jr
(b. 1937)

Robert Lucas is currently John Dewey Distinguished Service Professor at the University of Chicago. Best known for his equilibrium approach to macroeconomic analysis, and his application of rational expectations to the analysis of macroeconomic policy, he is widely acknowledged as being the leading figure in the development of new classical macroeconomics. In addition to his highly influential work on macroeconomic modelling and policy evaluation he has made a number of important contributions to other research fields including, more recently, economic growth. In 1995 he was awarded the Nobel Prize in Economics: 'For having developed and applied the hypothesis of rational expectations, and thereby having transformed macroeconomic analysis and deepened our understanding of economic policy'.

We interviewed Professor Lucas in New Orleans, in his hotel room, on 3 January 1997 while attending the annual conference of the American Economic Association.

BACKGROUND INFORMATION

As an undergraduate you studied history at the University of Chicago and you also started graduate school as a student of history at Berkeley. Why did you decide to switch to study economics as a postgraduate student back at Chicago?

I was getting more interested in economics and economic history as a history student. The work of Henri Pirenne, the Belgian historian, who stressed economic forces influenced me. When I was at Berkeley I started taking some economic history classes and even attended an economics course. That is when I first learned what a technical field economics is and how impossible it would be to pick it up as an amateur. I decided then that I wanted to switch to economics. I didn't have any hope of financial support at Berkeley to study economics so that was what led me back to Chicago.

Did you find the techniques and tools used by economists difficult to master when you did make the switch?

Sure, but it was exciting for me. I had no idea that people were using mathematics for social science questions before I got into economics. Once I became aware of that I enjoyed it enormously.

Was mathematics a strong subject for you when you were in high school?

In high school it was and in college I took a little bit, but dropped out. I was not interested in hard science. I wasn't really motivated to keep going in maths, but when I learned how maths was being used in economics it rekindled my interest in the field.

Which economists have had the most influence on your own work?

Dozens and dozens of people. Samuelson's *Foundations* was a big influence when I started graduate school. His book was just a bible for my generation of economists. Friedman was a great teacher, really an unusual teacher. Anyone from Chicago will tell you that.

In what respect? Was it his ability to communicate complex ideas?

That's a hard question to answer. I think it was the breadth of problems he showed that you could address with economic reasoning. That's what Friedman emphasized. No single problem was analysed all that deeply but the range of problems included everything. So we got the impression, and rightly so, that we were getting a powerful piece of equipment for dealing with any problem that came up in human affairs.

To what extent did the work of the Austrians (Hayek and so on) influence your ideas?

I once thought of myself as a kind of Austrian, but Kevin Hoover's book persuaded me that this was just a result of my misreading of Hayek and others.

David Laidler (1992) has drawn attention to what he described as 'the appalling low standards of historical scholarship amongst economists'. Is it important for an economist to be a competent historian?

No. It is important that some economists be competent historians, just as it is important that some economists be competent mathematicians, competent sociologists, and so on. But there is neither a need nor a possibility for everyone to be good at everything. Like Stephen Dedalus, none of us will ever be more than a shy guest at the feast of the world's culture.

KEYNES'S *GENERAL THEORY* AND KEYNESIAN ECONOMICS

You were born in 1937. The Great Depression was a huge influence on economists such as Friedman, Samuelson and Tobin in stimulating their interest in economics in the first place. Do you regard the Great Depression as the premier macroeconomic event of the twentieth century?

I think that economic growth, and particularly the diffusion of economic growth to what we used to call the Third World, is *the* major macroeconomic event of the twentieth century. But the Great Depression is a good second. I was too young to know what was going on at the time, but the Depression was the main influence on my parents. They became politically aware during the 1930s. Politics and economics were issues that were always talked about in my house when I was growing up.

How important do you think historical events are for theoretical developments? For example it is generally recognized that the Great Depression led to the General Theory.

Absolutely.

Do you think they are crucial?

Yes, I like that example.

What about the influence of increasing inflation in the 1970s? Do you think that event played the same kind of role in the move away from Keynesian economics, just as the Great Depression led to the development of Keynesian economics?

The main ideas that are associated with rational expectations were developed by the early 1970s so the importance of the inflation that occurred was that it confirmed some of these theoretical ideas. In a way the timing couldn't have been better. We were arguing that there was no stable Phillips curve relating unemployment and inflation. You could go either way on that question given the available postwar data up to the early 1970s, but by the end of the 1970s it was all over.

How do you view Keynes as a macroeconomist?
I suppose Keynes, via Hicks, Modigliani and Samuelson, was the founder of macroeconomics, so one has to view him as a leading figure in the field!

Robert Solow (1986) has described the General Theory *as 'the most influential work of economics of the twentieth century, and Keynes as the most important economist'. Yet the impression one gets from your various comments on Keynes is that you find the* General Theory *almost incomprehensible. You certainly don't seem to regard it in the same light as Solow.*
If you look through Solow's collected writings for evidence of intellectual indebtedness, evidence that scholars look for – citations and transfer of ideas – you would find almost no influence of Keynes. So I think such comments are somewhat disingenuous, unless he is thinking simply of ideology. Of course Keynes is an extremely important figure in twentieth century history, but I think his major influence was ideological. The Depression followed soon after the Russian revolution, and there was a lot of idealism about socialism as a way of resolving economic problems, especially as the Soviet Union had no depression. Keynes went to great lengths to disassociate himself from the rest of the economics profession in the *General Theory* making almost no references to mainstream economists in the entire book, compared to the *Treatise on Money* which is full of references to mainstream economists. The message of the *General Theory*, in which he emphasized the seriousness of depressions, is that they can be solved within the context of a liberal democracy without having to resort to centralized planning. That was a highly important message which certainly sustained defenders of democracy in countries like yours and mine that maintained it. It helped to organize the entire world after the war and was the flag around which liberal democracies rallied. The *General Theory* was an unusually important book in that sense. Maybe more important than economic theory. But that seems to be a different question from that of the influence of Keynes's theoretical ideas on the way we practise economics, which I think is now very slight.

Should students of macroeconomics still read the General Theory?
No.

Had Keynes still been living in 1969 do you think he would have been awarded the first Nobel Prize in Economics? Would he have received your vote?
I thought Joan Robinson would get the first one, so my credentials as a Nobel forecaster have been dubious from the start. But certainly Keynes would have

got one early on. Since I am not a member of the Swedish Academy, I do not have a vote to cast.

Do you find it puzzling that both Keynes and Marshall started off as mathematicians and yet both of them in terms of their methodology seemed to downplay the use of mathematics in economics, not regarding it as an important way of setting down economic ideas? Why do you think they turned away from what was becoming a major trend in economic science?
When Marshall was educated, and even when Keynes was educated, England was a mathematical backwater. If they had been educated in France, Germany or Russia, working with people like Kolmogorov, Borel or Cantor, they would have thought differently. Walras, Pareto and Slutzky thought differently. The people who were giving birth to mathematical economics were mainly on the continent at that time.

Is it your view that the traditional approach of distinguishing between short-run and long-run forces in macroeconomics has been misconceived and counterproductive? Did Keynes send everyone off down the wrong track?
The short-run–long-run distinction is Marshall's, not Keynes's. Indeed, Keynes is quite explicit in the *General Theory* that he thinks that permanent stagnation can result from demand deficiencies. Samuelson's neoclassical synthesis reclaimed the long run for neoclassical analysis, at least here in the States. Now Samuelson's students – my whole generation – are trying to get the short run back, too! It's hard going, I know, but Samuelson already did the easy part, and we have to make a living somehow.

The 1930s sent all of us off on the wrong track, starting with Keynes. Even today, 50 years after the Depression ended, public figures talk about every little wiggle in the GNP figures as though it were the end of capitalism. If Keynes were alive today, he would take pride in his role in setting up the system that permitted the recovery of Europe and the Japanese miracle, and he would be excited about the prospects for integrating the second and third worlds into the world economy. I think he would be as impatient with the overemphasis on short-term fine tuning as I am.

MONETARISM

What were the major factors which contributed to the rise of monetarism both in academia and policy circles during the 1970s?
It is hard for me to say because I was raised as a monetarist in the 1960s (*laughter*).

Well in the UK circumstances were very different, monetarist ideas came as much more of a shock to many British economists who were steeped in what Coddington (1976) has labelled 'hydraulic Keynesianism' and Samuelson (1983) has referred to as the 'Model T' version of Keynes's system.
Our leading Keynesian theorists, people like Tobin and Modigliani, always had a role for money in their models and the models that I learnt as a graduate student. Isn't it true that in England monetarism is used as a much broader label for the whole Thatcher programme?

The UK media has certainly tended to think of supply-side economics and monetarism as being the same. Sometimes any belief in the market mechanism and laissez-faire *philosophy is also classified as being a part of monetarism.*
You can take the various elements separately and mix them any way you like.

Do you see Friedman as almost single-handedly having engineering a monetarist counter-revolution?
Friedman has been an enormous influence. It is hard to say what would have happened without him.

We know from our own experience as undergraduate students of economics in the late 1960s in Britain that Friedman was often portrayed as some sort of strange crank in Chicago.
Well that was the way people tried to deal with him here too in a way, but not successfully.

Moving on to Friedman's 1968 AER *article. In 1981 Robert Gordon described it as probably the most influential article written in macroeconomics in the previous twenty years, while more recently James Tobin (1995) has gone much further when he described it as 'very likely the most influential article ever published in an economics journal'. What importance do you attach to that particular article?*
It had a huge influence on me. Leonard Rapping and I were doing econometric work on Phillips curves in those days and that paper hit us right when we were trying to formulate our ideas. Our models were inconsistent with Friedman's reasoning and yet we couldn't see anything wrong with his reasoning. It was a real scientific tension of trying to take two incompatible points of view and see what adjustments you can make to end up in a coherent position. Edmund Phelps was pursuing similar ideas. Phelps spelled out the theory a little more clearly than Friedman did and he had an enormous influence on me as well.

Was this with respect to the need for micro foundations?
Yes. I always think of the proposition that there is no long-run Phillips trade-off as the Friedman–Phelps proposition.

What do you feel remains of the monetarist counter-revolution today?
It has gone in so many different directions. Rational expectations macroeconomics has gone in many different directions. There is real business cycle theory which assigns no importance to monetary forces. This work has been hugely influential, on me as well as on others, although I still think of myself as a monetarist. Then there are those whom Sargent calls fiscalists, people who think that government deficits are crucial events for the determination of inflation and whether they are financed by bond issues or money issues is secondary, or maybe not relevant at all. Then there are old-fashioned monetarists, which is where I would class myself, with people like Friedman and Allan Meltzer. One of the things that people are coming to agree on, although not too many come right out and say it, is that econometrically it seems to be hard to account for more than a quarter to a third of US real variability in the postwar period to monetary forces, no matter how you look at the data. People from very different points of view have come up with that as a kind of upper bound. I used to think that monetary shocks were 90 per cent of the story in real variability and I still think they are the central story in the 1930s. But there is no way to get monetary shocks to account for more than about a quarter of real variability in the postwar era. At least, no one has found a way of doing it.

One of the consensus propositions now is that monetary forces cause inflation, certainly in the long term. That still leaves open the question, if we know what causes inflation, why do governments insist on increasing the money supply too rapidly? What are the forces which lie behind monetary expansions?
Well, to be fair, since the 1970s the advanced capitalist countries have what I would regard as a fantastic record on inflation. Every central bank has shifted its focus exclusively, or almost exclusively, on price stability. They have done a great job. I like the idea of going from 3 per cent to 0, but the big thing is going from 13 per cent to 3. Everyone would agree with that. So the record in the advanced countries has just been tremendous, although there are still a few outliers in some Latin America countries where inflation is still a persistent problem. Chile though has dealt with inflation forcefully and they have had a solid record for 10 years. Country after country is coming around to deal with inflation by restricting money growth. But there is still ignorance and there is always going to be a temptation to generate surprise inflation in order to default on obligations.

Do you think that Democratic governments will tend to generate in the long term more inflation than Republican governments because of their greater announced commitment to employment targets?
Easy money and tight money have been an issue in the United States since the nineteenth century. I guess it is a pretty good generalization that the Republicans on the whole have been a tight money party.

According to Alberto Alesina's (1989) rational partisan model it should generally be better.
I think of Nixon and Ford as having been fairly inept at monetary policy (*laughter*).

Alan Blinder (1986, 1988a, 1992b) has argued that during the 1970s American Keynesianism absorbed the Friedman–Phelps proposition and that after allowing for the effects of the OPEC supply shock, a modified Keynesian model was quite capable of explaining the 1970s macroeconomic phenomena. Do you think he is wrong?
The direct effect of the OPEC shock was minor in my opinion. I like to be more explicit about which models are being discussed and what properties are being boasted about. I don't know what 'modified Keynesian model' Alan is referring to.

In his view the expectations-augmented Phillips curve had become part of mainstream macroeconomics by the mid-1970s and by then Keynesianism had become 'less crude' having absorbed some of Friedman's monetarist arguments. However rational expectations models remained controversial.
I don't know how you would separate those two. But again I don't know whether Alan is referring to some body of research, or whether he just means to say that he thinks he is pretty much on top of things (*laughter*).

NEW CLASSICAL MACROECONOMICS

Did you regard your work and that of your associates in developing new classical macroeconomics as having created a separate school of thought from monetarism?
I don't like the collective, me and my associates (*laughter*). I am responsible for my work just as Sargent, Barro and Prescott are responsible for their own work. When you are in the middle of doing research, it's a paper-by-paper, problem-by-problem kind of thing. You don't say 'I am a school and here is what my school is going to do'. These labels get pasted on after the fact, they don't play much of a role. My most influential paper on 'Expectations and the

Neutrality of Money' (1972) came out of a conference that Phelps organized where Rapping and I were invited to talk about our Phillips curve work. Phelps convinced us that we needed some kind of general equilibrium setting. Rapping and I were just focusing on labour supply decisions. Phelps kept on insisting that these labour suppliers are situated in some economy, and that you have to consider what the whole general equilibrium looks like, not just what the labour supply decision looks like. That's what motivated me. I didn't think of it as being monetarist but I didn't think of it as a new school either.

Do you regard the new classical approach as having resulted in a revolution in macroeconomic thought?
Sargent once wrote that you can interpret any scientific development as continuous evolution or discontinuous revolution, at your pleasure. For myself, I do not have any romantic associations with the term 'revolution'. To me, it connotes lying, theft, and murder, so I would prefer not to be known as a revolutionary.

One of the policy implications of new classical analysis is that there will be no trade-off between inflation and unemployment even in the short run following announced anticipated monetary expansion. How do you now view this policy ineffectiveness proposition in the light of the disinflationary experience of both the UK and the USA economies in the early 1980s?
It is nearly impossible to tell what was and was not anticipated in any particular episode, so the 1980s did not offer a crucial test of anything. Sargent's two essays on disinflation in his book *Rational Expectations and Inflation* (1993) provide the best analysis of this issue, and a serious discussion of what is meant by an 'anticipated' policy change.

The early 1980s witnessed the demise of your monetary surprise version of the new classical model. On reflection how do you view this work and what do you think remains of that first phase of the new classical revolution?
I discuss this in my Nobel lecture (1996). My models stress the distinction between anticipated and unanticipated inflation and I arrived at that distinction through an information processing model. But other people have arrived at the same distinction by thinking about contracts. There are many ways to motivate that distinction. At the time I guess I thought my way of looking at it was just a lot better than other people's ways of looking at it (*laughter*). Now they all seem pretty similar to me. I think this distinction between anticipated and unanticipated money, and how different their effects are, is the key idea in postwar macro. I would like to see it embodied in better theoretical models. I hope it doesn't get forgotten or lost.

What do you regard as being the most serious criticisms that have been raised in the literature against new classical equilibrium models?
To me the most interesting debates are not about classes of models but about particular models. For example, Mehra and Prescott's (1985) paper on 'The Equity Premium' highlighted the failure of any neoclassical model that we know about to account for the enormous differential between the return on equity and the return on bonds. Now they certainly didn't view this fact as a failure of neoclassical economics as a body of thought, but on the other hand it is undeniably a failure of a *particular* neoclassical model. I think that is a much more fruitful way to proceed. I think general discussions, especially by non-economists, of whether the system is in equilibrium or not are almost entirely nonsense. You can't look out of this window and ask whether New Orleans is in equilibrium. What does that mean? (*laughter*). Equilibrium is just a property of the way we look at things, not a property of reality.

Many critics of new classical macroeconomics have argued that there is a lack of available supporting evidence of strong intertemporal labour substitution effects. How do you react to this line of criticism?
I'm not at all sympathetic to it. I don't know what you mean by the 'available evidence'. The degree of intertemporal substitution of labour assumed in real business cycle models is *selected* to generate employment fluctuations of the magnitude we observe, which is to say, to be consistent with some of the 'available evidence'. Economists who have used survey data on individuals have been unsuccessful in explaining employment fluctuations at the individual level – we just haven't learned anything about preferences from their work. This is a disappointment, but no good purpose is served by re-interpreting this failure as though it were a successful attempt to estimate something.

Do you consider your 1972 Journal of Economic Theory *paper on 'Expectations and the Neutrality of Money' to be your most influential paper?*
It seems to be, or maybe the paper on policy evaluation (1976).

How important do you think the 'Lucas critique' has been?
I think it has been tremendously important, but it is fading. It used to be that you could hold that up, like a cross to a vampire, and defeat people simply by saying 'Lucas critique'. People have gotten tired of that and I think that is fair enough. If you want to criticize work effectively you have to get into it and criticize its details. But I think it is basic that you can't get economic conclusions without putting in some economic theories, some economic structure.

Your 1978 paper with Thomas Sargent 'After Keynesian Macroeconomics' seemed to be pronouncing the death of Keynesian macroeconomics. Do you now think that this was perhaps premature given its revival in the form of new Keynesian economics?

Well, the label 'Keynesian' is a flag a lot of people salute, so it's not going to lie around unused. Of course Sargent and I were talking about a particular set of models which we were completely clear about.

You were talking about 1960s-style Keynesian models?

The Wharton model, the Michigan model, the MPS model, models which existed and were in some sense Keynesian. If a completely different class of models comes up which people like to call Keynesian, of course our criticisms can't apply. You can't write a paper in 1978 criticizing work done in 1988 (*laughter*).

That (1978) paper contains a lot of powerful rhetorical statements. Were you conscious of this at the time of writing?

Yes. We were invited to a conference sponsored by the Boston Fed. In a way it was like being in the enemy camp and we were trying to make a statement that we weren't going to be assimilated.

REAL BUSINESS CYCLE THEORY

In your 1980 paper 'Methods and Problems in Business Cycle Theory' you seem to be anticipating in some respects the next decade's work. You appear to be asking for the kind of methodological approach which Kydland and Prescott were about to take up. Were you aware of what they were doing at the time?

Yes. But I wasn't anticipating their work.

But your statements in that paper seem to be calling for the kind of methodology that they have used.

Well Prescott and I have been very close for years and we talk about everything. But if you're asking whether at the time I wrote that paper I had an idea that you could get some sort of satisfactory performance out of a macroeconomic model in which the only disturbances were productivity shocks, then the answer is no. I was as surprised as everybody else when Kydland and Prescott showed that was possible (*laughter*).

Is it fair to say that you, Friedman, Tobin and other leading macroeconomists up until 1980 tended to think of a long-run smooth trend around which there are fluctuations?

Yes.

Basically differences of opinion concerned what caused these fluctuations and what you could do about them. Then Kydland and Prescott (1982) came along and changed that way of thinking.
Well, they talk about business cycles in terms of deviations from trend as well. The difference is that Friedman, Tobin and I would think of the sources of the trend as being entirely from the supply side and the fluctuations about trend as being induced by monetary shocks. Of course we would think of very different kinds of theoretical models to deal with the long-run and the short-run issues. Kydland and Prescott took the sources that we think of as long term to see how well they would do for these short-term movements. The surprising thing was how well it worked. I am still mostly on the side of Friedman and Tobin, but there is no question that our thinking has changed a lot on the basis of this work.

In an article in Oxford Economic Papers *Kevin Hoover (1995a) has suggested that 'the calibration methodology, to date, lacks any discipline as stern as that imposed by econometric methods ... and above all, it is not clear on what standards competing, but contradictory models are to be compared and adjudicated'. Does this pose a problem?*
Yes, but it is not a problem that's resolved by Neyman–Pearson statistics. There the whole formalism is for testing models that are nested. It has always been a philosophical issue to compare non-nested models. It's not something that Kydland and Prescott introduced. I think Kydland and Prescott are in part responding to the sterility of Neyman–Pearson statistical methods. These methods just don't answer the questions that we want to answer. Maybe they do for studying the results of agricultural experiments, or something like that, but not for dealing with economics.

Would you agree with the view that a major contribution of the real business cycle approach has been to raise fundamental questions about the meaning, significance and characteristics of economic fluctuations?
I think that is true of any influential macroeconomics. I don't think that statement isolates a unique contribution of real business cycle theory.

In commenting on recent developments in new classical economics Gregory Mankiw (1989) has argued that although real business cycle theory has 'served the important function of stimulating and provoking scientific debate, it will (he predicts) ultimately be discarded as an explanation of observed fluctuations'. What are your predictions for the future development of macroeconomics?
I agree with Mankiw, but I don't think he understands the implication of his observation. We are now seeing models in the style of Kydland and Prescott

with nominal rigidities, imperfect credit markets, and many other features that people thinking of themselves as Keynesians have emphasized. The difference is that within an explicit equilibrium framework we can begin to work out the quantitative implications of these features, not just illustrate them with textbook diagrams.

NEW KEYNESIAN ECONOMICS

When we interviewed Gregory Mankiw in 1993 (see Snowdon and Vane, 1995) he suggested that 'the theoretical challenge of Lucas and his followers has been met' and that Keynesian economics is now 'well founded on microeconomic models'. Do you think that new Keynesians such as Mankiw have created firm microeconomic foundations for Keynesian models?
There are some interesting theoretical models by people who call themselves 'new Keynesians'. I don't know who first threw out this challenge but I would think it was Patinkin. When I was a student this idea of micro-foundations for Keynesian models was already on everyone's agenda and I thought of Patinkin as the leading exponent of that idea.

Keynesian models in the 1960s, and this is what excited people like Sargent and me, were operational in the sense that you could quantify the effects of various policy changes by simulating these models. You could find out what would happen if you balanced the budget every year, or if you increased the money supply, or changed fiscal policy. That was what was exciting. They were operational, quantitative models that addressed important policy questions. Now in that sense new Keynesian models are not quantitative, are not fitted to data, there are no realistic dynamics in them. They are not used to address any policy conclusions. What are the principal policy conclusions of 'new Keynesian economics'? Ask Greg Mankiw that question the next time you interview him (*laughter*). I don't even ask that they prove interesting policy conclusions, just that they attempt some. Everyone knows that Friedman said we ought to expand the money supply by 4 per cent per year. Old Keynesians had similar ideas about what we ought to do with the budget deficit, and what they thought the effects of it would be. New Keynesian economics doesn't seem to make contact with the questions that got us interested in macroeconomics in the first place.

In Europe, where currently unemployment is a much bigger problem compared to the United States, some new Keynesian work has tried to explain this phenomenon in terms of hysteresis effects. This work implies that Friedman (1968) was wrong when he argued that aggregate demand disturbances cannot affect the natural rate. So in that sense some new Keynesian econo-

mists are trying to address the problem of unemployment, suggesting that aggregate demand management still has a role to play.

When Friedman wrote his 1968 article the average rate of unemployment in the US was something like 4.8 per cent and the system always seemed to return to about that level. Since then the natural rate has drifted all over the place. It looked much more like a constant of nature back in those days than it does now. Everyone would have to agree with that. That is not a theory but an observation about what has happened. Now in Europe the drift upwards has been much more striking. Unemployment is a hugely important problem. But I don't want to call anyone who notes that that is a problem a Keynesian. Ljungqvist and Sargent (1998) have done some very exciting work on this trying to make the connections between the European welfare state and unemployment rates. I don't know whether they have got it right or not.

That has also been a theme of Patrick Minford's (1985) work in the UK.
It is a tough theme to defend though, because the welfare state has been in place for 30 years more or less in its present form in most European countries.

Perhaps the best way is to identify changes within the incentive structure rather than the level of benefits.
Yes, that is what you have got to do. Ljungqvist and Sargent try to address that issue as well.

GENERAL AND METHODOLOGICAL ISSUES

Do you think it is healthy to subject students to a breadth of perspectives at the undergraduate level?
I don't know. I teach introductory macro and I want my students to see specific, necessarily pretty simple, models and to compare their predictions to US data. I want them to see for themselves rather than be just told about it. Now that does give a narrowness to their training. But the alternative of giving them a catalogue of schools and noting what each says without giving students any sense of how economic reasoning is used to try to account for the facts, is not very attractive either. Maybe there is a better way to do it.

Have you ever thought of writing a basic introductory textbook?
I have thought a lot about it, but it would be hard to do. I sat down once with my course notes, to see how far the notes I had been using over the years were from a textbook, and it was a long long way (*laughter*). So I have never done it.

Is the philosophy of science and formal methodology an area that interests you?
Yes. I don't read very much in the area but I like to think about it.

You acknowledge that Friedman has had a great influence on you, yet his methodological approach is completely different to your own approach to macroeconomics. Why did his methodological approach not appeal to you?
I like mathematics and general equilibrium theory. Friedman didn't. I think that he missed the boat (*laughter*).

His methodological approach seems more in keeping with Keynes and Marshall.
He describes himself as a Marshallian, although I don't know quite what that means. Whatever it is, it's not what I think of myself as.

Would you agree that the appropriate criterion for establishing the fruitfulness of a theory is the degree of empirical corroboration attained by its predictions?
Something like that. Yes.

You are Friedmanite on that issue of methodology?
I am certainly a Friedmanite. The problem with that statement is that not all empirical corroborations are equal. There are some crucial things that a theory has to account for and if it doesn't we don't care how well it does on other dimensions.

Do you think that it is crucial for macroeconomic models to have neoclassical choice theoretic microfoundations?
No. It depends on the purposes you want the model to serve. For short-term forecasting, for example, the Wharton model does very well with little in the way of theoretical foundations, and Sims, Litterman, and others have had pretty good success with purely statistical extrapolation methods that involve no economics at all. But if one wants to know how behaviour is likely to change under some change in policy, it is necessary to model the way people make choices. If you see me driving north on Clark Street, you will have good (though not perfect) predictive success by guessing that I will still be going north on the same street a few minutes later. But if you want to predict how I will respond if Clark Street is closed off, you have to have some idea of where I am going and what my alternative routes are – of the nature of my decision problem.

Why do you think there is more consensus among economists over micro-economic issues compared to macroeconomic issues?

What is the microeconomic consensus you are referring to? Does it just mean that microeconomists agree on the Slutsky equation, or other purely mathematical propositions? Macroeconomists all take derivatives in the same way, too. On matters of application and policy, microeconomists disagree as vehemently as macroeconomists – neither side in an antitrust action has any difficulty finding expert witnesses.

I think there is a tremendous amount of consensus on macroeconomic issues today. But there is much that we don't know, and so – necessarily – a lot to argue about.

Do you see any signs of an emerging consensus in macroeconomics, and if so what form will it take?
When a macroeconomic consensus is reached on an issue (as it has been, say, on the monetary sources of inflation) the issue passes off the stage of professional debate, and we argue about something else. Professional economists are primarily scholars, not policy managers. Our responsibility is to create new knowledge by pushing research into new, and hence necessarily controversial, territory. Consensus can be reached on specific issues, but consensus for a research area as a whole is equivalent to stagnation, irrelevance, and death.

In what areas, other than the monetary sources of inflation, do you think there is now a consensus in macro? Do you think, for example, that there is a majority of economists who are now anti fine tuning?
Yes. Fine tuning certainly has come down a few pegs. Paul Krugman has been doing a lot of very effective writing attacking non-economists writing about economic matters. Paul is speaking for the whole profession in a very effective way and addressing the most important questions in social science. Economists have a lot of areas of agreement, partly due to the fact that we look at numbers. If somebody says the world is breeding itself into starvation, we look at numbers and see that per capita incomes are rising in the world. It seems to be that on a lot of questions there is a huge amount of consensus among economists. More and more we are focusing on technology, supply-side, long-run issues. Those are the big issues for us now, not on depression-prevention.

ECONOMIC GROWTH

In their recent book on economic growth Robert Barro and Xavier Sala-i-Martin (1995) express the view that 'economic growth is the part of macroeconomics that really matters'. In your Yrjo Jahnsson lectures (1987) you seem to be saying something similar, that macroeconomists have spent too much time on stabilization and neglected growth which is a far more important issue for macroeconomics to look at.

Yes. That is becoming the consensus view. David Romer's new textbook which we use in our first-year graduate macro course at Chicago, begins with growth. Romer would call himself a new Keynesian and he is perfectly entitled to call himself that. But his book shows a shift in emphasis towards long-run growth questions. Quite rightly I think.

So it's back to the classics and the grand issues of the long run?
Yes. Okay (*laughter*).

What in your view was the stimulus to the new endogenous growth economics? Was it the lack of convergence which people were observing empirically between rich and poor countries, apart from maybe a 'convergence club'?
No. What is new about the new growth theory is the idea that what we ought to be trying to do is get a single neoclassical model that can account for rich and poor countries alike in the same terms. This contrasts with the view which we had in the 1960s that there was one theory for the advanced countries and some other model was needed for the third world. The whole presumption in the 1960s was that some explicit policy, perhaps based on the Russian model, was needed to promote development in poor countries. We didn't think of economic growth as something that just happened through market forces.

What do you see as being the important policy implications of the work that has been done so far on endogenous growth? Some economists have interpreted the work as suggesting that there is a more positive role for government than, say, was the case with the Solow model.
Yes. An implication of the Solow model was that the long-term growth rate of an economy was dictated by technological change and there wasn't anything we could do about it. Some of the endogenous growth models have the property that the long-term growth rate is endogenously determined and that changes in the tax structure, for example, can influence what that growth rate is. We can now use these new models to analyse the growth effects of changes in tax policy. That is something we couldn't do before. But these effects I think are pretty small. Even where you have a model where growth rates can be changed by policy the effects seem to be pretty modest.

What in your view is the reason why the 'Tiger' economies of South East Asia have been so successful? While the Tiger economies have been catching up with the West with 8 or 9 per cent growth rates, in Africa the 1980s was almost a completely lost decade as far as economic growth was concerned.

Well, you know Africa has had awful politics.

Do you think African countries generally lack the necessary institutional framework required for successful development?
No. There has been much too much socialist influence. The common feature of countries like Taiwan, Korea, Japan is that they have had some kind of conservative, pro-market, pro-business, economic policies. I mean I wouldn't exactly call them free trade because Japan and Korea at least are very Mercantilist in their trade policies, which I don't approve of. But it is better than socialism and import substitution by a long, long way.

While they have been outward-looking some development economists would argue that within a lot of the South East Asian Tiger economies there has been quite a lot of government intervention. As such they see it as being an example of successful government intervention.
Right. That is how everybody in Japan and Korea sees it (*laughter*).

You don't see it that way?
Even Chicago Korean students think that the Korean growth rates have been engineered by government manipulation. I don't agree with that view. I don't see any evidence for that at all. But it is hard to refute. There is no question that governments have been extremely active in doing things that they think promote economic growth.

ECONOMIC POLICY

In your 1978 AER *paper on 'Unemployment Policy' you suggested that macroeconomic analysis would make better progress if the concept of involuntary unemployment was abandoned. Many economists, for example Kevin Hoover (1988, 1995b), have criticized you for this and question whether you can regard unemployment as simply voluntary.*
There is both an involuntary and a voluntary element in any kind of unemployment. Take anybody who is looking for a job. At the end of the day if they haven't found one, they are unhappy about it. They did not choose to find one in some sense. Everyone wishes he has better options than he does. But there is also obviously a voluntary element in unemployment when there are all these jobs around. When we are unemployed it is because we think we can do better.

I suppose this is something that bothers Europeans more because aggregate unemployment is much more of an issue in Europe. It doesn't seem to be as much of an issue in the United States.

It should be.

Many European economies including Germany, France and Italy are currently experiencing unemployment rates in excess of 10 per cent.
Well if you go into the neighbourhoods within a mile of my university you will find 50 per cent unemployment rates. So it is an issue here too.

The Bank of England is less independent than the German Bundesbank. Do you see that as a possible reason why Britain's inflation performance has been less successful than that of Germany?
I don't know, it could be. I don't feel I have much understanding of the political sources of differences in monetary policy across countries.

Economic policy doesn't seem to have been guided by new classical theoretical developments in the same way as it has by Keynesianism and monetarism. Why has its impact been less influential in economic policy making?
Why do you say that? We have talked about the increasing focus of central bankers on inflation and the de-emphasis of everybody on fine tuning. That is an important trend in the last 20 years in the US and Europe, and to my mind a very healthy one.

Would this not have come about in any case as a result of Friedman's influence, without rational expectations and equilibrium theorizing?
Maybe.

Have you ever been invited to be an economic adviser in Washington? Is that a role you see for yourself?
No.

You once made a comment (Lucas, 1981a) that 'as an advice-giving profession we are in way over our heads'. Is that the reason you haven't considered such a role more seriously?
No. No not at all. I believe economists ought to run everything (*laughter*).

So did Keynes.
I know. I don't think I personally have any particular talent or liking for that kind of role. But I am glad that other people like John Taylor or Larry Summers do. For example, I think that the whole reason the Clinton health insurance reform fell on its face was that not enough economists were involved. I like economics and I think economics is hugely relevant on almost any issue of national policy. The more good economists are involved the happier I am. But I don't personally feel drawn to doing it.

What are your views on European Monetary Union?
Again I don't know enough about the politics, which has to be central.

Does it make economic sense to you?
Well it's an issue in inventory theory. The cost of dealing with multiple currencies is that if you are doing business in Europe you, or people you hire to help you, have to have stocks of inventories of a lot of different currencies because payments are coming due in a lot of different currencies. The inventory cost of holding money is the interest foregone you could have earned by holding interest-bearing assets. If you have a common currency you can consolidate your cash inventories so that there is a saving involved. That is a very modest saving, but it is positive. But obviously multiple currencies are not inconsistent with a huge amount of prosperity. If you can consolidate all the better, but those purely economic gains are pretty modest. If you don't trust somebody else to run your monetary policy maybe you want to oppose monetary union. For myself, I would be happy to turn my monetary policy over to the Germans any day (*laughter*).

PERSONAL INFORMATION

When we interviewed Milton Friedman (see Snowdon and Vane, 1997b) he commented that he had experienced three reactions to many of his views, to quote: 'the first reaction is that it's all a bunch of nonsense, the second reaction is that there is something to it and the third reaction is that it gets embedded in the theory and nobody talks about it anymore'. How well does this parallel with new and controversial ideas you have fought to get accepted?
A little bit. But you know Milton is like Keynes. He goes directly to the public, to the voters, with ideas. The reactions he is talking about are the reactions of non-economists, of politicians, of a huge range of people, to the changes in policies he is advocating. My career hasn't really taken that form. My influence has been very much more inside the profession and for that matter on a technical subset of the profession. Insofar as I have had any influence on the larger world you can't really identify it because my influence is contained with the influence of many others. How do you tell my influence from Tom Sargent's influence? Nobody other than professional economists would even have heard of me. No one in the US Congress is going to say 'I favour Lucas's policy'. The reply would be, 'who is Lucas?'! (*laughter*).

Turning to the award of the Nobel Prize. When we interviewed James Tobin in 1993 (see Snowdon et al. 1994) and asked him how he felt about being awarded the Prize his reaction was somewhat defensive along the lines that he didn't ask for it, the Swedish Academy gave it to him. In correspondence we asked Milton Friedman a similar question and he acknowledged that it was extremely rewarding. He also told us that he first learned of the award from a reporter who stuck a microphone in his face when he was in a parking lot in Detroit (see Snowdon et al. 1994). We were wondering what importance do you attach to having been awarded the Nobel prize?

Oh it was a tremendous thing for me. I don't know what else I can say. I don't know what Jim could have possibly have had in mind. He was certainly pleased when it happened and he certainly merited the award. Reporters will ask you, and this annoys me too after a while, 'what did you do to deserve this prize?'. They should look up what the Swedish Academy said on the internet. I don't want to have to defend it. If that is what Jim meant then I have been through the same thing and I am just as irritated by it as he is.

What issues or areas are you currently working on?

I'm thinking about monetary policy again actually. In particular all central banks now want to talk about the interest rate as being the immediate variable they manipulate. I don't get it and yet their record on controlling inflation is pretty good. Talking in terms of interest rate targets as opposed to monetary targets seems to me just the wrong way to think about it, but if so, why does it work so well?

Finally is there any question that you would have liked to have been asked in this interview?

I don't know (*laughter*). Your questions are interesting to me. You guys are economists and it's a lot more fun being interviewed by an economist than being interviewed by a journalist who is completely ignorant of economics (*laughter*).

Alberto Alesina
(b. 1957)

Alberto Alesina is currently Professor of Economics and Government at Harvard University. Known for his major contributions, both in terms of theoretical analysis and empirical investigation, into the various forms of interaction between politics and macroeconomics; his work on politico-economic cycles, the origin and implications of fiscal deficits, and the relationship between political stability and economic growth has been particularly influential.

We corresponded with Professor Alesina in March/April 1997.

BACKGROUND INFORMATION

How did you become interested in economics and where did you study as an undergraduate and postgraduate student?
In high school I was very interested in socio-political problems. I thought that economics was the most rigorous of the social sciences. As an undergraduate I studied at Università Bocconi in Milan, Italy (1976–81) and took both my Masters degree and PhD at Harvard University (1982–86).

Which papers and/or books have influenced your research interests?
I have been much more influenced by 'facts' rather than by specific papers or books and have always been very interested in the policy-making process.

The basic fact which has always impressed me is how different actual policy making is from the predictions of models which assume social planners and a representative consumer. I always noted how in politics discourse is about redistributive conflicts while in most macroeconomic models distributive issues are absent.

Is there any aspect of the Italian economy and/or political system that stimulated your interest in the link between economics and politics?
Yes: the inability of government after government in Italy to address serious fiscal problems has been an important influence. More generally, thinking about Italy made me wonder about the relationship between political fragmentation and economic performance.

Do you regard yourself as belonging to any identifiable school of thought in macroeconomics?
No.

KEYNES AND KEYNESIANISM

Was Keynes naive in assuming that economic policy should be, and would be, carried out in the public interest?
If we can characterize Keynes's view as such, I would say *yes*, although I think that your question oversimplifies his view.

In Roy Harrod's 1951 biography of Keynes he argued that Keynes tended to think of important decisions being taken by 'intelligent people' and gave little consideration to the political constraints placed on this vision by 'interfering democracy'.
If one reads beyond the *General Theory*, for instance the pamphlet *How To Pay For The War*, I think that one can see that Keynes was aware of the subtleties of policy making. I agree that in his main scientific work he did not consider the effects of political distortions on policy making. You can't expect everything from the same economist. He did quite a lot as it is!

Do you think that Keynesian economics, with its emphasis on discretionary fiscal policy, has fundamentally weakened the fiscal constitutions of Western industrial democracies?
No. In my opinion this point has been overemphasized. Italy, for instance, has accumulated a very large debt for several reasons. The adoption of Keynesian policies is not one of them.

Have Italy's fiscal problems stemmed from its political system?
Yes, from its fragmented political system, over powerful unions, lack of a strong party committed to fiscal discipline and an overextended and entrenched bureaucracy.

Why are some countries more prone to budget deficits than others? Why is deficit reduction such an intractable problem?
In my paper with Roberto Perotti (1995a) we conclude that it is difficult to explain these large cross-country differences using economic arguments alone. Politico-institutional factors are crucial to understanding budget deficits in particular, and fiscal policy in general. While the economies of the OECD countries are relatively similar, their institutions, such as electoral laws, party structure, budget laws, central banks, degree of centralization, political stability and social polarization, are quite different. In a companion paper examining fiscal adjustments in OECD countries (Alesina and Perotti, 1995b) we find that coalition governments are almost always unsuccessful in their adjustment attempts, being unable to maintain a tough fiscal stance because of conflicts among coalition members. We also find that a successful fiscal adjustment is best started during a period of relatively high growth, does not raise taxes, but rather cuts transfer programme and government wages and employment. Politicians and their advisers must stop thinking of just about everything on the expenditure side of the government budget as untouchable.

What do you regard as being the most important contribution made by Keynes to our understanding of macroeconomic phenomena?
The idea that aggregate demand policy matters because of lack of complete price flexibility.

THE POLITICAL BUSINESS CYCLE

Prior to Michal Kalecki (1943) were there other economists who anticipated the possibility of a political business cycle?
Not that I know of.

To what extent could the deep UK recession of 1979–82 be viewed as being politically induced? For example it can be argued that the then Prime Minister, Margaret Thatcher, used high unemployment in order to restore the health of British capitalism, a development consistent with Kalecki's model.
Thatcher's recession was the result of the need for disinflation. I am not sure that unemployment is needed 'in order to restore the health of capitalism'. Unemployment is in part a cyclical phenomenon, in part the result of supply-

side rigidities. This latter influence is particularly strong in the European economies.

How important are macroeconomic variables for voting behaviour?
In the United States, the rate of GNP growth is extremely important, inflation and unemployment somewhat less so. In other countries the evidence is less clear cut, in part due to differences in the electoral systems. In general, the state of the economy is very important for elections but how this effect manifests itself may vary dramatically from one country to another.

Nordhaus's (1975) model is intuitively very appealing. What do you regard to be its main strengths and weaknesses?
Its main strength is that it makes a simple powerful point which is easily testable. Its main weaknesses are that it is based on the assumption of extremely naive behaviour, and also has very weak empirical support.

How can voters (principals) ensure that their agents (the politicians) refrain from opportunistic behaviour which creates economic inefficiencies?
Mainly with the threat of voting them out of office.

NON-RATIONAL PARTISAN THEORY

What do you regard to be the important contributions of Hibbs (1977) to the development of politico-economic models?
Hibbs played an important role by introducing ideological-partisan differences and moved attention away from models in which it was assumed that all politicians have identical motivations.

How strong is the evidence that inflation is more harmful to higher income than lower income groups?
The evidence on this is not very strong. How harmful inflation is depends on the level of inflation and various institutional arrangements, such as indexation.

For the postwar period as a whole is the empirical evidence supportive of the partisan view that left of centre governments favour and achieve lower unemployment than right of centre governments? Have left of centre administrations also been associated with higher inflation than right of centre administrations?
To some extent yes. However, the success of left-wing governments in reducing unemployment has only been temporary. After taking into account structural breaks such as the break in exchange rate regime in the early

1970s, the oil shocks, and so on, it is true that left of centre governments have been associated with higher inflation than those right of centre.

RATIONAL EXPECTATIONS AND BUSINESS CYCLE MODELS

Do you attribute the decline of interest in politico-economic explanations of the business cycle between the late 1970s and mid-1980s to theoretical developments associated with Robert Lucas and the rational expectations revolution or was empirical failure a more important factor?
I think that the 'rational expectations revolution' was a much more important contributing factor to the decline of interest in such models. Furthermore, empirical 'failures' have not stopped economists investigating this matter further in the 1990s.

An important criticism of democratic markets is that voters are, in most cases, uninformed. For each voter the benefits of gaining more information will be outweighed by the costs. In this world of imperfect information is it not inevitable that politicians will engage in opportunistic fiscal behaviour prior to elections?
To some extent this is the case, but I would not overemphasize this point for several reasons. First, if this were the main explanation for budget deficits, it should apply (more or less) to every democracy. Thus one should not observe such large differences in fiscal policies in OECD democracies. Second, large deviations from efficient policies, such as huge deficits in election years, are easily observable, if not by the individual voter, then certainly by the press. Third, I do not know of any conclusive evidence which shows that larger deficits favour the re-election of an incumbent. I think that in practice what happens all the time is that in election years fiscal favours may not be very large, and may therefore be hard to detect. Nevertheless, the political benefits may be quite significant. Let me add on this point that I am not a great fan of models of politics where imperfect information is the critical factor. I personally think that conflict of interest is much more important than asymmetric information.

In 1988 George Bush told the American electorate: 'Read my lips, no new taxes'. Each year in the UK the Chancellor of the Exchequer in his budget speech emphasizes the competence of the administration in managing fiscal affairs. Do you regard these examples as typical of the kind of political behaviour predicted by the Rogoff–Sibert (1988) class of rational opportunistic models?

With the caveats discussed in the previous answer, I think that Rogoff and Sibert have a good point. Their model is also much more consistent with the empirical evidence than the original Nordhaus model. My empirical research on the subject is quite supportive of their model. This research is included in Alesina and Roubini, with Cohen (1997): *Political Cycles and the Macroeconomy*, MIT Press.

What role does 'fiscal illusion' play in politico-economic models?
I think that this concept is oversold. Explanations of excessive fiscal deficits based on fiscal illusion are not totally convincing because they imply a systematic bias in the errors made by the electorate concerning their estimation of the costs and benefits of taxes and spending. Fiscal illusion is also unable to explain the timing of the deficit problem in OECD economies or the cross-country differences in budget deficits. I prefer models based on rational behaviour and expectations.

RATIONAL PARTISAN THEORIES

How strong is the evidence against the median voter theorem?
It depends. For large elections I would not use it: in fact, its key implication is that when in office all the parties do the same thing. This is clearly inconsistent with the evidence even of predominantly two-party systems that exist in countries such as the UK and the US. In multi-party systems the median voter theorem proves to be even less applicable. Therefore, for macroeconomic and macropolitical research I would not use it. On the other hand, if I want to study voting behaviour on one issue in a committee of five people, then the median voter theorem is a good start!

In the UK Tony Blair's 'New Labour Party' has been moving closer to the position adopted by the Conservative Party on many economic issues. For example, on 20 January, 1997 the Shadow Chancellor of the Exchequer, Gordon Brown, promised the electorate that 'New Labour' would not increase tax rates if elected. On 21 January 1997 Tony Blair promised not to reverse the Conservative Party's industrial relations legislation of the 1980s. Does this imply that polarization is less important than it used to be?
In the case of the UK we shall have to wait and see! However, on the more general issue of increasing party convergence, in *Political Cycles and the Macroeconomy* (1997) we conclude that 'the idea that political parties are becoming more alike when it comes to macroeconomic management is somewhat exaggerated'. Our view is that while the macroeconomic problems of the 1970s and early 1980s 'have probably made politicians on both sides of

the political spectrum more cautious in terms of macroeconomic management, they have not completely eliminated ideological differences'. Furthermore, we also point out that 'both left-wing and right-wing governments in the next decade will have to face issues of fiscal retrenchment' and that 'partisan conflicts are very likely to explode on how to achieve this goal'.

In your rational partisan models (1987, 1989) you appear to adopt an eclectic approach to your theoretical framework based on a variant of the 'monetary surprise' rational expectations model associated with Fischer (1977). Lucas and other new classical theorists now appear to attach more importance to real shocks as an explanation of postwar macroeconomic fluctuations. Does this not undermine the basis of models based on monetary shocks?
I do not like the view that macroeconomic fluctuations are due to either supply or demand shocks. First, an economy can be subjected to both types of shock. Second, real business cycle models have certainly not been an empirical success. The rational partisan theory does not imply that real shocks do not exist. In fact in empirical testing one may want to control for supply shocks.

What are the essential predictions of the rational partisan theory and have they been supported by empirical work?
The basic idea of the model is that, given the sluggishness in wage adjustments, changes in the inflation rate associated with changes in government create temporary deviations of real economic activity from its natural level. At the beginning of a right-wing government output growth is below its natural level and unemployment is above its natural level. The opposite is predicted for left-wing governments. After expectations, prices and wages adjust, output and employment return to their natural level and the level of economic activity should be independent of the party in office. However, the rate of inflation should remain higher throughout the term of a left-wing government. These implications of rational partisan theory are consistent with the empirical evidence particularly for a subset of countries with bipartisan systems or with clearly identifiable movements from left to right and vice versa. The rational partisan theory is less applicable, and in fact tends to fail in countries with large coalition governments with frequent government collapses.

In the UK the Conservative Party gained power in the four elections between 1979 and 1992. President Clinton has also been re-elected. What does the rational partisan theory predict will be the effect of the repeated re-election of a particular party?
Strictly speaking, it depends on how unexpected is the re-election. If the Conservative Party had been sure to win in the previous four elections, not

much should have happened to the economy. Inflation should have continued to remain low and growth (*ceteris paribus*) should have been stable. President Clinton was probably less sure of being re-elected. In this case the model predicts that growth should slightly increase in the US.

What is likely to happen according to your model if a left-of-centre party gains office at the peak of an economic expansion?
According to the model, the left-of-centre party will do as much as possible to avoid a recession, including increasing inflation. If we speak of the UK in 1997, one has to consider other issues which may influence the outcome, such as European Monetary Union. This kind of issue is clearly not considered in the model.

What are the main policy implications of your models for the conduct of macroeconomic policy and the design of political institutions?
The model in its stripped down version is 'positive' rather than 'normative', thus it does not have any direct policy implications. However, the model can be used in a normative direction. Let me give a couple of examples to illustrate the point. First, the model suggests that independent Central Banks, by insulating monetary policy from partisan influences, can reduce the extent of both monetary and real variability. This point is formally derived in my paper with Roberta Gatti (1995). Second, as for political institutions, the model points towards a trade-off. Proportional electoral systems which result in coaliton governments lead to 'compromise' and policy moderation. This reduces partisan fluctuations and polarization, but may induce deadlocks in policy making, particularly with respect to fiscal issues. Majoritarian systems leading to two-party systems have the opposite feature, namely more policy polarization but no policy deadlocks. Extreme versions of the two systems are unlikely to be optimal although I regard the risk of excessive 'governing by coalition' to be a particularly significant problem in the European context.

Which is likely to create the most instability: exogenous or endogenous timing of elections?
Endogenous elections undoubtedly generate more frequent elections. Whether that creates more or less instability is less obvious. Italy is a perfect example. One may argue that in the postwar period Italy has been very unstable because it has had numerous government changes and many early elections. On the other hand, one may argue that at least until the early 1990s nothing much ever changed, because the same parties and individuals were always in office.

What are the main weaknesses of the rational partisan theory?

I guess I am not the right person to ask that particular question, but elsewhere (1995) I have pointed out that the Achilles' heel of the rational partisan theory is that the mechanism of wage formation is postulated exogenously rather than derived from optimal individual behaviour.

Would you agree that rational voters will make their voting decision based on information relating to both the past performance of a political party as well as expected future performance?
Past information has to be used to form expectations about the future. Even voters who are forward looking have to look backward to form expectations. The question: are voters backward or forward looking is very misleading. Furthermore, I find the research on this point often both confused and confusing. A different, more useful, question is whether the voters use 'efficiently' the past information that they have to form expectations about the future. In other words, the question is whether voters use 'rationally' their past information. This is a difficult but well posed question, which is similar to questions raised in finance.

To what extent does opportunistic behaviour and partisan behaviour depend on the confidence of an incumbent administration that it will be re-elected? Is it the case that the more confident an administration is of re-election, the more likely it is to behave ideologically?
Possibly, perhaps likely. I have not seen a 'rational' model making this point. Bruno Frey and Freidrich Schneider back in 1978 made this point in their 'non rational' models.

GENERAL MACROECONOMIC ISSUES

How influential has the literature relating to time inconsistency, credibility and reputation been to the development of politico-economic models?
In my case these contributions have been very influential. I think that this literature has been an important driving force behind the new wave of politico-economic models in the 1990s although it is fair to say that now this literature has a life of its own.

Why do governments create inflation?
One important reason is to try to reduce unemployment. A second reason relates to the financing of budget deficits. Also, when inflation gets entrenched in the system it is costly to reduce it. These reasons may apply differently to different countries, and at different points in time.

What is the relationship between political and economic instability? How has the UK managed to combine political stability with a relatively poor economic performance in the postwar period? How does this compare to the Italian experience?

The UK has been 'stable' but very polarized. Conservative and Labour governments have had very different programmes. On the other hand Italy has had the opposite problem, namely frequent government changes but with always the same people ending up in office. The result for Italy has been a lack of fiscal discipline. However, concepts such as political stability and polarization are difficult to measure in practice.

Should Central Banks have goal independence as well as instrument independence? What is your view of the contracting approach suggested by Carl Walsh?

Legislatures should set once and for all, price stability (defined as low inflation, between 0 and 3 per cent) as the sole goal of monetary policy. Central Banks should do whatever they want to achieve that goal. I do not know whether you want to call this instrument or goal independence. Carl Walsh (1995a) has produced a good paper but I would like to see further work in a more political direction. For example, how does Walsh's contracting approach deal with the fact that in the real world we have partisan and opportunistic politicians, rather than benevolent social planners?

Are you in favour of monetary and fiscal rules?

My answer to the previous question covers my views on monetary rules. Personally I am against balanced budget rules for national governments but in favour of such rules for subnational governments.

Does reducing inflation from moderate rates, say from 10 per cent to 5 per cent, bring any significant real economic benefits in the form of improved performance with respect to employment and economic growth?

If inflation remained stable forever at say 10 per cent, with perfect certainty and everything adjusted, it wouldn't matter very much. But higher inflation results in more variable and less predictable inflation, which is costly. Thus, on balance I believe that there are benefits in reducing inflation.

Where do you stand on the issue of European Monetary Union? For countries like Italy and the UK do the costs of Monetary Union not outweigh the benefits?

The benefits of Monetary Union have been oversold. There are clearly both pros and cons to such an arrangement. Italy has benefited from the Maastricht target, otherwise it would have done even less to put its 'house in order'.

However, this is not sufficient reason to join a Monetary Union. Although a full answer to this question would require a whole article, my feeling is that the economic arguments in favour of European Monetary Union are quite weak.

In your view what are the most important lessons and policy implications to arise from recent research into the interaction of politics and the macro-economy?
First procedures, namely how policies are determined. This matters for the outcome. Second, when thinking about 'optimal institution building' one should not ignore conflicts of interests. Third, models based on 'social planners' cannot completely explain the empirical evidence and may be misleading or useless if used for policy prescriptives.

What kind of political system is most conducive to macroeconomic stability?
For an OECD economy I would choose an electoral system with a majoritarian emphasis. The American system of Presidential–legislative checks and balances has also worked quite well. Different electoral systems imply different choices in the trade-off between moderation and gridlock. An English system is probably at the extreme of the 'no moderation but no gridlock' scale. The current Italian system is at the opposite end. Perhaps the US system is a happy medium.

At the moment what research are you currently engaged in and what in your opinion are the important areas of research which macroeconomists should concentrate on in the future?
I am working on three main areas. The first area is the issue of the political economy of major fiscal adjustments where I have already published several papers with Roberto Perotti. I am also interested in what determines the number and shapes of countries, that is, economic theories of secessions and mergers and their relationship with factors such as geography and trade and so on. For example, see my paper with Enrico Spolare (1997). Third, I am also researching into the effect of socio-ethnic fragmentation on the choice of fiscal policy in US cities and localities. Personally, I find issues relating to fiscal policy more intriguing than those associated with monetary policy especially as we know less about the former than the latter. I think that the political economy of social security reforms and, more generally, reforms of the welfare state will be the number one item in the policy agenda of OECD countries during the next decade. The research of economists needs to keep up with important events.

Robert W. Clower
(b. 1926)

Copyright Dorothy Hahn

Robert Clower is currently Professor Emeritus of Economics at UCLA and Hugh C. Lane Distinguished Professor of Economic Theory at the University of South Carolina. He is best known for his influential contributions to monetary theory and macroeconomics, and in particular for his seminal contribution to the disequilibrium approach in Keynesian macroeconomics.

We interviewed Professor Clower in Charleston, in a hotel lobby, on 20 June 1997 while attending the annual conference of the History of Economics Society.

BACKGROUND INFORMATION

What attracted you to study economics?
Pure accident. When my father, who taught economics, was taken ill in 1948, my college (Washington State College) was so crowded with veterans (GI Bill students – of which I was one) it was impossible to find a qualified substitute for him, even for a week. My father was expected to recover. At the time I was taking some final electives in my second year, which I guess would be regarded as soft options in England. I was also in three of my father's classes: Labour Economics; European Economic History; and History of Thought. I had been reading intensively in all these areas for nearly

two years in preparation for Law School. As the college couldn't get anyone to substitute for my father they asked me if I would take over his classes. When I took them over the kids loved it and I enjoyed teaching them. Then when my father died the college appointed me Associate Professor and paid me his salary. I was demoted to instructor in the Fall (*laughter*). That's the way it happened and it never occurred to me to change jobs afterwards.

Do you ever wish that you had become a lawyer?
No. In fact I have done a lot of Constitutional Law along the way. I was a highly paid consultant in a number of anti-trust cases in the 1970s and early 1980s. The one thing I told myself when I went into the army in 1943 was that I would never become a teacher or economist; my father was both. Then when my father fell ill I suddenly found myself teaching economics! I enjoyed teaching, although at first I treated it as an activist platform for preaching against the Republicans and so forth. Then I went to Britain on a Rhodes Scholarship. You know I nearly gave economics up in my second year at Oxford; I couldn't think of anything that seemed worth writing about. My wife and I had been married five years and wanted to start a family and as I couldn't see any way of completing my dissertation I thought about going to law school after all. After we had our baby I had only two months to write my dissertation from start to finish. Alan Walters helped me on the research side, although I didn't acknowledge that at the time. Both his part and mine were brilliant but they didn't go together so my dissertation was not accepted for the Oxford D.Phil. After that I had two papers published in the *Review of Economic Studies* in 1952. One paper was on 'Professor Duesenberry and Traditional Theory', the other on 'Graaff's Producer–Consumer Theory'. By then I knew I would stay in economics for the rest of my life.

You received your BA in 1948 and MA in 1949, both from Washington State College, and a Bachelor of Letters (B.Litt.) from Oxford University in 1952.
Well, I actually went to Oxford University to do a D.Phil. but I flunked. So I earned a Bachelor of Letters (converted into a Master of Letters degree in 1978). I was at Oxford in the first B.Phil. group (1949–52) but I was actually reading for a D.Phil. Later (1978), however, I was awarded a Doctor of Letters degree by Oxford (Frank Hahn was my external examiner; I don't know if he's ever forgiven himself!).

As a student, either at Washington State College or Oxford University, did any of your lecturers stand out as being particularly influential or inspirational?
At Oxford no, it was atrocious. I was mainly in workshops. I went to a maths lecture in 1949 (on complex variables), just to see what the lecture style was

like. I lasted about five minutes; it was an undergraduate lecture and it struck me as boring; the lecturer had no passion. I also tried out a series of lecturers on monetary theory by Hicks in 1951. He started with around 100 students. The next day he had six, the day after he was left with one, and the day after that I left (*laughter*). These people would just read their lecture notes. Why sit and listen to people stutter for an hour when you can read their work? I have never wasted my time with lectures. All my education (at least since 1948) has been through reading.

Now Washington State was another matter. At that time it was just a good Liberal Arts college. We had some great scholars who were also dedicated teachers. Many were Europeans who had found a place to live during the Depression and stayed there during and after the Second World War. While at WSC after leaving Oxford in 1952, I came to know Galbraith (newly elected chairman of economics at Harvard), and he arranged to have them offer me a fellowship. I was supposed to spend a year there, submit my Oxford (failed) thesis to them, and get a Harvard PhD. The thesis was flunked at Oxford as 'not in a form fit for publication'. My Oxford examiners thought it would take six months to put it in a form fit for publication – but thought it would be unkind to make 'an American' hang around Oxford for another half year, so they awarded me a B.Litt. , as a kind of consolation prize. My examiners were very bright (one was Ian Little), but neither was terribly sensible. Had I gone on, the thesis would still have been unfit for publication in six years (*laughter*).

Which economists have had the most influence on your own work?
Keynes and Marshall. Both were great economists. But now I've gone back from them. Mill and Smith are more important and Walras was no slouch; but it seems that the best part of Walras (Lessons 5–11) are ignored by most modern economists.

KEYNES'S (1936) *GENERAL THEORY* AND KEYNESIAN ECONOMICS

Why do you think there are so many different interpretations of Keynes's (1936) General Theory?
Mainly because there is very little analytic content in the book. The polemics are what win people over and what draw you in. You know I think Keynes was, in his way, an incredible conman. As far as I can see his message is simply classical economics, an aggregated version of Marshall and I continue to feel that the more I read of him. I admire Keynes not only as an economist and a thinker but also as a politician and an expositor. Look at the gift he

displayed in the last two-thirds of Chapter 3 on 'The Principle of Effective Demand' which is completely fraudulent from an analytical point of view. I read that in 1946, and being ignorant of any other writing on economic theory I had no trouble in understanding Keynes. That's the kind of writing style he employed. The only work of Keynes I read before the *General Theory* was the *Economic Consequences of the Peace* (1919). In those days I was interested in politics, not economics. I read Marshall first and then went to Keynes. In fact I went to Keynes before I had even finished half of Marshall and I thought at first that he was an under-consumptionist like all the rest. But when I got to Chapter 3 I thought this guy has got the right message and I have been on his bandwagon ever since. You know I was asked once, in the Rhodes Scholarship Competition around 1948, who were my favourite literary figures. I mentioned Thomas Wolfe, for *Look Homeward Angel* and *Of Time and the River*, William Shakespeare and John Maynard Keynes. They were all masters of the English language and that has always affected me, although I don't know why.

While both Marshall and Keynes were mathematics graduates they didn't think it important to use maths in their work.
No, neither do I.

So you sympathize with them then on this issue?
Well, I don't think one should ever ignore mathematics when it can be useful. I certainly don't agree with Marshall that you should throw it away. But I think that if you are going to use maths you must bear in mind that you are in economics. There are very few serious mathematicians who study economics. If you are a serious mathematician then you do serious mathematics and that I believe in. I also believe in serious applied mathematics. What I see in economics is mainly second-rate mathematicians who couldn't make it in maths. That's what troubles me. I think there is just an endless array of problems where a clear understanding of maths is potentially useful. I'm doubtful about highly technical mathematics and I don't think there is much use for advanced calculus even though economists use it extensively. But simulation techniques, computer programming and so forth are valuable. I think we are getting more and more use these days out of simulation. When I first started with simulation in 1958 it was too much hard work, but now it is possible to do incredible things with a lap-top which we couldn't do before.

Do you regard the central message of the General Theory *to be that capitalism doesn't work very effectively?*
No, certainly not that. In the first place the basic presumption in Keynes is the same as in Marshall and Walras, that we live in a world where markets

generally work rather well and only occasionally will the system break down. I think Keynes completely missed the point. After all, in Chapter 3 he talked about aggregate demand and aggregate supply, the intersection of which gives you the point of effective demand. Well that would be irrelevant unless the economy as a whole operated almost perfectly, almost all of the time, which of course it has ever since we have known it. Returning to the political theme, I think he was an activist who thought something ought to be done in Britain. In my opinion he completely misconstrued the situation in Britain. The problem in Britain at that time was too much government intervention in the economy. Yet Keynes wanted more, which was insane. Petur Jonsson (1997) has an interesting conference paper here in which he points out that the influence of John Hobson on Keynes is much more important than most people realize, and that Keynes went out of his way, having corresponded with Hobson, almost to dismiss and disown him. Keynes didn't have a single message that wasn't already in Hobson's writings. I don't think Keynes added a darn thing except polemics. As a result he developed a following amongst people who were activists, including left-wing liberals like Lawrence Klein and Paul Samuelson. Many others were card-carrying communists at that time. I was also a very left-wing activist and Chairman of my local American Veterans Committee. After being there for two years I discovered that half of the members of my group were card-carrying communists. If you wanted to see a real knee-jerk liberal it was me (*laughter*). Therefore I know exactly why Keynes was so attractive. I thought he was a godsend to those of us who wanted to ruin those Republicans (*laughter*).

You describe yourself as being a left-wing activist when you were young. Were you ever attracted to the contributions of Marx?
No. I thought he was silly and also religious, which I am not. I don't believe in God or anything connected with any kind of religion. I liked the good writing in Marx and Engels's *Communist Manifesto* and I was fascinated by Marx's letters to the *New York Herald Tribune* during the Civil War. They were brilliant. I also read the first volume of *Das Kapital* and was amused by all the purple language in it.

Which parts of the General Theory *do you think are still valid?*
Well, I would recommend that everyone read the first three chapters, but read them critically. Alternatively read my revision of Chapter 3 in Harcourt and Riach (1997). You can't distinguish my revision from Keynes because it reads just like it was Keynes. In fact I didn't change the last two-thirds, I left the polemics in, but I corrected the mathematical mistakes in the first third of the chapter. I don't recommend that students read the whole book but I have always told my undergraduate students that they should read Chapters 1–3

and 18. They will get confused with all the other stuff. I sometimes recommend that they read the last chapter, Chapter 24 on 'Social Philosophy', because of his nice comments. However, I don't care much for the final paragraph of the book where he argued that in the long run it is ideas, not vested interests, which have the greatest influence. I think that is crap. In any case Keynes borrowed it from Lionel Robbins's (1934) *The Great Depression*. The same phrase can be found there. Funny place to borrow it from (*laughter*).

Aside from the General Theory *which other contributions from Keynes do you admire?*
Well, I was absolutely delighted with his *Economic Consequences of the Peace* (1919) and *A Tract on Monetary Reform* (1923). The *Treatise on Money* (1930) is too tough, but chapter by chapter there are parts that are wonderful. But you must ignore all the fundamental equation garbage. I generally steer people away from the *Treatise on Money* except for the 'Gold Standard' chapter. *Essays in Biography* (1933b) is also important, especially Keynes's appreciation of Marshall. Everyone should read that. Among scientists Marshall was one of the greatest in his century, in any country, in any subject. I concur with Keynes's assessment, Marshall was just incredible.

When he describes Marshall's qualities in that essay, do you not think he is describing himself in the context of what it takes to make a good economist?
No, I don't think so. Keynes had talents that Marshall lacked completely. But he never had Marshall's dedication to real inductive science. An odd thing is that you can see a hint of Marshall in *Indian Currency and Finance* (1912) and also a hint of the early mathematical Marshall in the *Treatise on Probability* (1921), which is a classic in statistics too. Keynes didn't like hard work and sometimes just wanted to get through things rapidly, in a somewhat facile manner. Now in contrast Marshall did everything thoroughly. If you compare the eight editions of Marshall's *Principles of Economics* it is remarkable to see the change from one edition to another. I have just been re-reading the first and eighth editions and there are some remarkable differences. I find going back and re-reading the original papers and books of the great economists a fantastic experience. Every time you learn something new.

Given that some people do not regard Keynes to have been a great theoretician do you think he would have been awarded the first Nobel Prize in economics if he had still been living in 1969?
It wouldn't have made any difference. He might have got the Nobel Peace Prize (*laughter*). I wrote an (unpublished) essay on that subject in the late 1960s when it was first announced that the Bank of Sweden was going to

endow a so- called Nobel Prize in Economics. It is not a Nobel Prize in any normal sense. To think of an economist being a Nobel Laureate in any scientific sense is about as easy as thinking of the President of the US being a chimpanzee or making a chimpanzee the President of the US (*laughter*).

If you had ever had the chance to talk with Keynes what would you have liked to discuss with him?
Champagne. His sex life (*laughter*). My father met Keynes and argued with him when he was in Chicago in 1931. After Keynes had completed the *Treatise on Money* he went to give the Harris Foundation Lectures at Chicago where he met with graduate students. My father was in that group. Later on when Patinkin was working in Chicago in the Archives he came across this guy, F. W. Clower, who had given Keynes a hard time about the theory of savings. It turned out it was my father. Dad never mentioned that, but he did tell me how exciting it was to just watch Keynes lecture. You know my father was the only person at Washington State College who had a copy of the *General Theory*. He gave it to me to read in 1946 when I came back from the army.

How important was Hicks's (1937) Econometrica *article 'Mr Keynes and the Classics: A Suggested Interpretation' to the development of Keynesian economics?*
I suspect it was terribly important but not because of analytical content, which Hicks never really understood and got wrong, by and large. If you compare that paper with his *Economic Journal* review of the *General Theory* you will see that he was trying to figure out a way to encapsulate the central message of the *General Theory* within the framework of *Value and Capital* (1939), which he had just about completed at that time. If you follow through the mathematics in Hicks's (1937) paper there are reasons to wonder exactly what he was doing. He has got only two price variables, a price of capital goods and a price of consumption goods, both determined by supply and demand. The quantity of money determines income, and income is a function of the two prices. So he has got three equations and only two prices. That is when the interest rate got thrown in, as he needed a third variable. It just appears magically. There is no bond or credit market. Suddenly r just appears, pulled right out of thin air. This was Hicks's way of doing mathematical economics. He never thought of it as serious mathematics and of course he wasn't a serious mathematician. But it is the verbal part of the SI–LL paper that is really important.

Charles Plosser (1994) has suggested that in the absence of John Hicks's IS–LM framework Keynes's General Theory *would have been much less influential. Do you agree with this view?*

No, I think that is silly given the influence of Samuelson and Klein, who was Samuelson's first PhD student. The Keynesian revolution was just a repetition of what Samuelson had been talking about. Samuelson was the most influential writer and thinker of the entire period. Everyone was talking about Samuelson when I was an undergraduate in 1946. We all knew that his book was coming out. Now, if you can imagine, the most popular textbook in 1946, and the only one available in the US after the war, was by John Ise, and this had only one or two paragraphs about Keynes. It was a beautiful book, pure Marshall. When Samuelson's first edition came out in 1948 that was the end of it. It completely took over the market. Samuelson was charged with being a fellow traveller and communist, given the activist tone and approach of the book. The Republicans hated him, especially Senator McCarthy. He got into the mainstream by introducing into the 1951 edition the paragraph that was later turned into the neoclassical synthesis. His sales had started to fall even before this. To bring his sales up he created the neoclassical synthesis. I think that was done explicitly in the third edition, probably in 1955. Kerry Pearce and Kevin Hoover (1995) have recently followed this through and it is very interesting. I actually discussed with Samuelson how his textbook suddenly became more middle of the road, but he says he doesn't remember the conversation. However I wrote it down at the time and sent a copy to Axel Leijonhufvud. Bob Solow's comment to me was 'I have known this man all my life and he wouldn't do that'. When Solow asked him, Samuelson's response was that he didn't recall the conversation he had with me in 1967. But he also didn't deny it (*laughter*). Samuelson has said that it is amazing how much you learn from writing a textbook and how important it is to find a way to teach people so they don't get distracted with side issues. But at the time he told me I was very upset because I was excessively principled about that kind of thing. His attitude was – if it causes trouble, add a new word. It was never called the neoclassical synthesis until 1955, but the same paragraph is there, without that phrase, in the second edition.

You are known mainly for your work in monetary theory and macroeconomics.
That is so funny given that all my work is in micro. Even my Keynesian Counter-Revolution paper is a piece of micro.

Which paper do you consider to have been your most influential?
Well, I am not the best judge of that. I can tell you what I think ought to be my most influential paper, but that is different.

Which paper is that?
Well the 1965 and 1967 papers are fine because they set the stage. But the really important paper was my (1964) review of Friedman and Schwartz's

Monetary History in the *Journal of Economic History*. I also have an important paper on the 'Theoretical Foundations of Monetary Policy' (1971) which I presented in 1970 when Friedman was in the audience. Another paper which I think is very important and may have been more influential than any of the others is the one on the 'Keynesian Perplex' in *Zeitschrift für Nationalökonomie* (1975).

Did you in any way anticipate the interest that your 1965 paper subsequently generated?
Yes. It first appeared in 1963 when it was translated by Niehans for *Schweizerische Zeitschrift*. Brechling, Niehans, Negishi, Klein, Hahn were all at the 1962 Conference of the International Economic Association where I presented the paper. Patinkin was my discussant. I was a replacement for Modigliani and I only had about three weeks to write the paper. I wrote another paper first and threw it away before writing the Keynesian Counter-Revolution. I don't know how it came out so well, but I remember I was working nearly 20 hours a day on it while in Liberia.

What do you regard to be the main strengths and weaknesses of that paper?
Well, the main strength is in the paragraph at the end of the paper that no-one bothers to look at. In that paragraph I point out that when you introduce transactions into these models you lose all help from linear dynamic systems. When you introduce transactions you have non-linearity and create a terrible problem for the logistics of exchange that is never looked at. That was completely missed by Negishi, Hahn and Patinkin. The only people who saw the importance of my paper were Niehans and Brechling. The dual decision hypothesis was frankly a bit of Keynesiana. I threw it in so that it looked like I was saying something new. I got closer to the truth in my 1967 paper on 'A Reconsideration of the Micro Foundations of Monetary Theory'. I didn't realize at the time that the technique I used in that paper, a dichotomized budget equation, is actually in Lange's 1942 paper on Say's Law. I always thought Lange had it completely wrong, but I realized later on that if you apply mathematics to Lange you come out with my entire paper. Walras also had a dichotomized process where you have a constraint on expenditure. You need cash on hand to have a demand and if you offer goods for sale you are demanding money. That essential idea is obvious enough. But the cash-in-advance constraint was misconstrued by Lucas, who named it after me. Lucas and others seem to think that I had a cash-in-advance constraint in that model with credit. Yet I was very explicit that my model applied only to a pure cash economy with absolutely no credit. My paper starts out with an axiomatic treatment of these issues that should have been absolutely clear, including an exchange matrix and the like. So that paper should have been

much more important than it was seen to be at the time. Now one person, Peter Howitt, finally got it right but not in the first version. He was asked to write a piece on Money and Finance for the Palgrave Dictionary. At first he read my paper like everyone else. I got so upset that I wrote him a four-page revision. In the final version he got it right and nailed it on Lucas where it belongs. So you see the things you get credit for are often the things you don't want to be known for, like the dual decision hypothesis.

Was Axel Leijonhufvud one of your PhD students?
Well Axel is basically self-taught. I met him for the first time in 1963 after I had come back from Liberia. Although we only spent an hour or two together we became instant and lifelong friends. He was leaving almost immediately for the Brookings Institution on a fellowship there. I knew that he was going to do a dissertation at Northwestern and that I would be on his committee. I think they made me his supervisor, but Axel didn't need a supervisor. One of our colleagues at the time said that if we appointed this graduate student Associate Professor it would raise the standard of the university. That was about right. He was 32-years-old and he had a wisdom then that was just unbelievable. So when you ask whether he was once one of my students the answer is no, but I did supervise his thesis. My main contribution was to get him to stop writing and publish the introduction. His actual dissertation was on the Debt–Inflation Theory of Great Depressions. I argued with him that it was too big a subject and that he should narrow it down. So he started writing the introduction which became *Keynesian Economics and the Economics of Keynes* (1968). Strotz, Eisner and I were on the committee that passed Axel's thesis at the AEA meetings in 1967. By that time the thesis was already published in mimeograph form by UCLA. I believe they raised Axel from an Assistant to an Associate Professor on the strength of that book before he was even awarded his PhD.

What do you think of the subsequent work by Barro and Grossman, and Malinvaud?
Well I commissioned the Barro and Grossman book for Basic Books. Grossman came to Essex for six months and we had many long conversations before he started working on his papers. He always seemed to have his feet on the ground and was very quick. Barro's background was in physics so he had a very inductive approach to economics. I think they collaborated very well but somehow or other the book became too mechanical. It was turned down by Basic Books and had to be published by Cambridge. Although it did well its main contribution seems to have been its influence on the work of Malinvaud.

What is your opinion of the new Keynesian literature?

Are you talking about new Keynesian, post Keynesian, post-post Keynesian? (*laughter*). Efficiency wage theory and stuff like that is all Marshall converted into general equilibrium analysis. I don't know what to think of it. Some people will try to do anything to convert Keynes into a mathematical framework they can understand instead of taking the time to learn some real economics. I swear there are more sects now in Keynesian economics than there are in the Christian religion and they all hate each other (*laughter*).

MONETARISM

Friedman seems to think that Keynes was at his best during his monetarist phase. Do you agree?
Well, in his early work Keynes was a monetarist. Friedman likes the *Tract on Monetary Reform* (1923) because Keynes recommended that we control economic activity by varying the stock of money. That is why he was so shaken up when he went back and read Keynes's early work. When I was at Northwestern and Friedman was at Chicago I saw him almost every week. Milton, Harry Johnson and I often got together. I think I was invited so that Milton and Harry wouldn't fight too much. I was a calming influence, if you can believe that. Harry and I were always good friends and he would make his snide remarks through me, directed at Milton.

Do you think that Milton Friedman has been the most influential economist since Keynes?
Yes. Even more influential in this century than Keynes in his way. It is now Friedman's ideas that are winning the battle all over the world, even in Britain.

Are you referring to Friedman's views on markets or monetarism?
Friedman is a Marshallian. Marshall and Friedman go together. By the way Hicks, who never read Marshall until after he left Cambridge, became a Marshallian in his later years.

You have commented (Clower, 1984 p. 264 'Afterword' in Donald Walker, ed., Money and Markets, Cambridge University Press) that the essential art of economics … is to tell a good story in a persuasive way'. Do you think that is one reason why Friedman has been so influential? Is rhetoric important?
No doubt. But in Milton's case it isn't rhetoric. If you read his *Newsweek* articles you will find that he always makes a coherent argument after first marshalling all the facts. He doesn't have throw-away lines. I think Friedman is like Stigler, the other really great economist of this century, who has been

influential in every direction. Friedman does serious economics and doesn't indulge in wishful thinking. The real curse of economics is when people jump to conclusions because they want to.

Do you think that Friedman's 1967 Presidential Address to the AEA, which was subsequently published in the AER *(1968), has been his most influential piece of work?*
No. While the 1967 address impressed a lot of people it only received a lot of attention afterwards because it was taken up by the rational expectations people. Lucas (1972) some ten years or so later on made a mess out of Muth's (1961) original hypothesis. But by God it did a lot for people who were second-rate mathematicians and those in econometrics who didn't want to do any serious empirical work. It is wonderful as a substitute for thinking.

Do you think that monetarism is an important force anymore?
I don't even know what it is. I think the problem is that monetarism came to the fore right after the period when we still had a basically money economy. At that time you could figure out what the monetary base was. Now, when you talk about money, you are talking about currency, demand deposits and so forth. These days the velocity in all insured banks in the US is something like twice a day for the average account and ten times a day in New York. You have 365 trillion dollars worth of transactions being carried out with less than half a trillion dollars in so-called money. So what would monetarism be now? What we have is an idiotic Federal Reserve System where they think they control something. All they do is mess up the money market.

NEW CLASSICAL MACROECONOMICS

What factors contributed to the rise of new classical macroeconomics in academia in the 1970s?
At the time I think it appealed to people who weren't really interested in doing any serious work in economics. Kevin Hoover's (1988) book is probably the best analysis of the subject of new classical macroeconomics. There is really nothing very new or classical about most aspects of it. The whole notion of rational expectations has always struck me as being completely absurd.

Why do you think it proved so attractive to the younger generation of economists in the United States?
Haven't you noticed that it is dead now?

It has reappeared in the form of real business cycle theory.
Well that is even dumber and is now moribund. You will never hear about this junk later on. It made no sense in the beginning and will not make any in 20 years. The amazing thing is that some people have taken it seriously.

To what extent can the popularity of new classical macroeconomics be attributed to the fact that it proved to be article laden, opening up a rich vein of topics to mine and publish?
Well you have to be a pretty good technician to write the stuff, but I don't think that is the main reason. The point you might not be aware of is that the entire profession changed very significantly around 1970 when the universities in this country were expanding in some areas. In mathematics and engineering the jobs weren't available. In particular there were no openings in maths. A lot of second-rate people in these areas came flooding into economics. By that time economics was becoming a subject where you could use calculus. Economics is the easiest subject to teach with two equation systems and a little calculus. You can spend 40 hours lecturing and never have to open a book or know any economics at all. I think that is why it became very popular. It looked ideal to someone who just does arithmetic and requires no serious work.

GENERAL

You have commented that during your five-year period as managing editor of the American Economic Review *you received 'close to a thousand manuscripts a year' and that 'the profession would be better off ... if most of them hadn't been published'. How did your experience as managing editor of the* AER *compare with that as managing editor of* Economic Inquiry?
I had a very different experience with the *Economy Inquiry*. I got interesting papers there, about 300 a year. I had no trouble in finding papers that had original ideas although they weren't crafted as well as the papers submitted to the *AER*. At the *AER* it took me roughly three minutes to figure out if a paper was worthless. Typically I was rejecting 60 per cent or more within ten minutes. So we had a real good turnaround and yet people complained about that. Would they have preferred to wait 18 months to get the same answer? (*laughter*).

When you are teaching economics, how important do you think it is for students to study the history of economic thought?
It is hopeless unless they have some feel for economics to try to get them into the history of economic thought. I have always taught the history of thought

throughout my career. I occasionally give my students selections from Hume's essays, especially 'Of Money' and 'Of Interest', and occasionally Chapter 7 of Smith's *Wealth of Nations*. I usually let them know about the invisible hand section of *Moral Sentiments* and parts of his *History of Astronomy*. I try to make them aware that Smith was quite a scientist and knew a lot about Newton.

Do you still teach macroeconomics?
No. I am a disaster when teaching either macro or micro. I can't go in with a straight face and teach much of the material expected. Yet if I was to start tearing the stuff up you can imagine how confused they would get. Students have to have a textbook that they can get answers from. So I have asked to be taken off teaching macro and micro. I teach only Economic Issues now. I talk about current events and try to give my students some feel for market competition, the struggle of entrepreneurs to find space in the modern world with marketing techniques actually being the only form that price competition has taken for 100 years. I never mention elasticity of demand, or garbage like that. I never deal with utility maximization which is even worse nonsense. Economics can get along fine without it and if students never learned it they would be better off. When you get to the stage where Friedman has to pretend to be using that in his work on the consumption function you know that things have gone too far (*laughter*).

Do you think studying economics today is more difficult than it was say 20 or 30 years ago?
Well it is like asking me whether I think becoming a Catholic and going through the catechism is more difficult than it was 50 years ago. The answer is no. The students are being bamboozled by their instructors into believing that they are learning something about the real world. What they are really learning is a catechism. You've seen the textbook test banks. If you learn the book you can answer the test banks. That is all many of these guys are doing. I like Samuelson's (1997) comment that the only way we are going to improve the subject is to have a lot of textbook writers die off.

What value do you place on this type of interview for students studying economics?
I guess it all depends on who you are interviewing (*laughter*). What I can tell you is that my honours students at South Carolina were fascinated by the interviews in your book (see Snowdon et al., 1994). After reading the interviews they went back and did some reading in economics.

When we interviewed Milton Friedman in January 1996 he suggested that 'economics has become increasingly an arcane branch of mathematics rather than dealing with real economic problems'. Would you agree with this view?
Yes, of course. That is the same theme he pursued in his 1946 paper 'Lange on Price Flexibility and Employment' which is reprinted in *Essays in Positive Economics* (1953). If you think Friedman's comments are strong you should read me on this subject! (See Clower, 1995.)

So in your view economic theory should be driven by empirical problems?
Obviously. We are supposed to be a science, not a branch of mathematics. A lot of people treat economics as if it were a branch of mathematics and then translate it into words. One of the few candid people who was awarded the Nobel Prize before 1990 was Debreu. When asked by the press how he felt about being awarded the prize he said he didn't know anything about economics and that he was a mathematical economist.

What do you think of the recent emphasis given by macroeconomists to the issue of economic growth?
(*Laughter.*) Most economists don't know anything about economic growth. You can't model growth processes when you are dealing with a complex of institutions. If you want to see an intelligent treatment of growth you must read my book *Growth Without Development* published by Northwestern University Press in 1966. I co-authored the book with Dalton, Harwitz and Walters. You know Alan Walters is probably the world's greatest applied economist. He understands the world. We were fellow students at Nuffield in the 1950s and have been close friends ever since.

How far do you think that most economic issues revolve around problems concerning information and co-ordination?
Well clearly without information and co-ordination this hotel wouldn't work and I wouldn't get my supper when I went home (*laughter*). I like the view expressed by Simon Newcomb (1885) in his *Principles of Political Economy* that there is nothing more exciting in the chemical or physical world, or anywhere else, than the social organism. What is really interesting is the scientific problem of how a very complex system operates. It is like studying the brain. We have no real understanding of how any modern economy operates. For instance when you deal with general equilibrium theory you don't even realize that the economy isn't simply a monolith, a single cluster of transactors. If you take unemployment in South Carolina at the present time, it ranges from about 2 per cent in some counties up to 18 per cent in others. Why is that? How can we talk about the economy as if it were a single entity, as we do in macroeconomics, if there isn't something holding all the

bits together. At present the average rate of unemployment in the US is around 5.6 per cent and that is the case in all of the states. How in God's name can 50 states so far separated have so similar an experience. Now if you go back to colonial times you wouldn't find that kind of connection between say Boston and New Orleans. You do now though. What is the explanation?

What are you currently working on?
A book on *Monetary Economics* with Peter Howitt, among other things. I am afraid I have rather a full plate at present.

In your paper with Peter Howitt in the David Colander (1996) volume you seem to be directing your emphasis to how markets actually work.
Yes. But we are much further on than that. That paper is at least three to four years old. I have a paper in the *Brock University Review* (1994) called 'The Fingers of the Invisible Hand' which in part goes back to my 1972 Monash Lecture on 'The Ideas of Economists'. It is also a development of my introduction to readings in *Monetary Theory* (1969). It also ties in with work undertaken by Ostroy and Starr (1974) on 'Money and the Decentralization of Exchange'. Ask yourself, what do you get in general equilibrium? You get the proof of the existence of consistency of plans. In Hicks and Patinkin trade starts when you are in equilibrium. But you are never in equilibrium. All you know is that an equilibrium exists somewhere. It is not possible to find it, it is not computable. If you could figure it out it would have to be either exact or you would have rounding errors. Ross Starr pointed out these problems in his 1971 dissertation for Arrow. That is what Peter and I are trying to deal with. You know Joan Robinson quoted a letter from me one time. I sent her a letter and said that she should stop worrying about production all the time. Production takes place whenever a firm sets up a market and starts taking in goods and putting them out on the other side in a more convenient form. It is a bundling of inputs into an output. She thought that I was being silly. I remember that I wrote that I hoped my letter would not annoy her too much. In a typical response she said 'how much annoyance would be just enough?' (*laughter*).

John B. Taylor
(b. 1946)

John Taylor is currently Mary and Robert Raymond Professor of Economics at Stanford University. He is best known for his work on the development of rational expectations models with staggered wage setting, the design of monetary policy rules for the conduct of economic policy and international policy co-ordination.

We interviewed Professor Taylor in a common room in Grey College, University of Durham on 11 September 1997 while attending the annual conference of the Money, Macro and Finance Research Group.

BACKGROUND INFORMATION

What attracted you to study economics?
I originally became interested in economics as an undergraduate in college. I was fascinated by the way structured mathematical quantitative techniques could be used to address real world problems. I really found that fascinating. As I had a particular interest in the quantitative side I took quite a few courses in statistics and mathematics in college. I was an undergraduate at Princeton and was lucky to be given good advice and be taught by people like Dick Quandt and Burt Malkiel, who were themselves very excited about what they were doing. My senior thesis at Princeton was actually very close to what I

193

am working on now: monetary policy rules. I wrote it with the help of Phil Howrey, who is now at Michigan. After that I decided to go to graduate school to study economics.

Have you always had a keener interest in macro, as opposed to micro, issues?
Yes. Right from the start macro issues fascinated me, although I am not sure why. In part I think it is because when I first started studying economics I was more aware of macro issues and problems. I graduated from college in 1968 at a time when people were still talking about the success of what was then the New Economics. Thereafter when so much controversy and debate arose I decided to stick with macro. When I went to graduate school at Stanford I changed my focus towards econometrics but always with the intention of using those econometric skills for the study of macro. Partly because of the tremendous amount of controversy building up in macro at that time, and partly because I got very interested in the problem of joint estimation and control, I decided to focus my studies and dissertation more on the technical side of things: on time series econometrics and dynamic optimization theory. My thesis adviser Ted Anderson is a statistician. In fact I wrote a very technical paper on optimal control theory for my PhD thesis. That turned out to be really fortuitous because at that point in time all the work on introducing new ideas in macro, including rational expectations, was using time series econometrics and stochastic modelling. So I was fortuitous to have had that technical training and at the same time not have really received a macro training that was in any one particular school. That allowed me to be more open to new ideas.

DEVELOPMENT OF MACROECONOMICS

Which papers and/or books would you identify as having had a major impact on the development of macroeconomics since the publication of the General Theory?
Well, the classic works on consumption by Friedman and Modigliani and on financial markets by Tobin are very important. The works by Phelps and Friedman on the Phillips curve are even more important in the way they changed the discipline. The Lucas papers published in the early 1970s were also very influential. Then there is a collection of papers that Lucas and Sargent put together on *Rational Expectations and Econometric Practice* (1981) which contains material on consumption theory, investment, monetary theory, time inconsistency and so on. I view that collection of papers as the modern equivalent of the *General Theory*, not only in the context of being highly technical but also being representative of a new way of thinking.

What do you think was Keynes's major legacy to economics?
Well I think that Keynes showed the importance of aggregate demand in a more general way than had been known earlier. The notion of aggregate demand shocks as a source of the business cycle has had a lasting effect. Of course Keynes's followers put much less emphasis on the supply side and inflation which meant that Keynesian theory was bound to run into problems at some stage. I don't think the notion of sticky wages and prices so much comes from Keynes. If you look at earlier work before Keynes it contains all kinds of descriptions of rigidities. Even David Hume in his essays talked about the slow adjustment of prices.

Do you regard Friedman and Lucas to have been the most influential macroeconomists since Keynes?
Yes. Both Friedman and Lucas have had a major impact on the discipline, but in different ways. Friedman, very early on, questioned certain aspects of Keynesian modelling and policy. If you go back it is remarkable to see how far Friedman once was from the mainstream. Today a lot of Friedman's views are mainstream, especially in the way people think about the unemployment–inflation trade-off, consumption, and money's impact on the economy. His influence has been longer and broader than Lucas's. Lucas has focused his attention more on the technical modelling side of macroeconomics. His main influence has therefore been in terms of the way he has changed how macroeconomists construct and use models in their work. On a personal level, his demonstration of the importance of rational expectations and his 1976 paper on 'Econometric Policy Evaluation: A Critique' has had a great influence on my work.

Do you view the development of macroeconomics in terms of an evolutionary process or in terms of a series of revolutions and counter-revolutions?
I view it more in terms of an evolutionary process that takes a while to occur. However when you look back over a period of say 20 or 25 years the changes look revolutionary. If you look at macroeconomic papers written now versus 25 years ago they are completely different. In that way it looks more like a revolution has taken place in macroeconomics. Over one or two years you don't notice developments, because they evolve slowly over time. The rational expectations revolution that began in the early 1970s resulted in as big a change as did the Keynesian revolution. I think of them analogously. In both cases they involved highly technical pieces of work, only readable by professional economists. Then the ideas seeped into textbooks, econometric models and finally into policy.

Would you agree with James Tobin (1996), who has argued along the lines that the field of macroeconomics is split into schools which differ in their theories and hence in their policy recommendations.

I understand his viewpoint, but I don't see it that way personally. I enjoy, and have learned from, talking with Jim Tobin. But I also learn a lot from talking with people from other schools. If you look at things more from a scientific perspective there is considerable similarity between the schools. Sometimes the differences are stylistic or involve a particular type of policy orientation that people start off with. My feeling is that, by thinking about things more on a scientific basis, you can appreciate the work done in different schools. I also think that there could be more communication between the schools. Jim Tobin is correct in the sense that schools have not communicated much with each other in the past, but that is changing. I sense that certain schools, like the real business cycle school and schools that focus more on sticky wages and prices, are coming together very rapidly right now.

Thinking back to the impact that new classical macroeconomics had on the development of macroeconomics in the 1970s, why was the policy ineffectiveness proposition taken so seriously at that time?

Well I think there are two main reasons. First, the main application of it was to the breakdown of the Phillips curve, *the* most significant macroeconomic event at that time. Lucas illustrated the policy evaluation critique with three examples, one was the breakdown of the Phillips curve, one was the consumption function and one was investment. The policy ineffectiveness proposition showed you even more dramatically how wrong you could be by not dealing with expectations properly. Second, because there was a way of dealing with the Lucas critique by adopting the rational expectations assumption, the policy ineffectiveness proposition generated a lot of interest in policy evaluation. I had very little interest in the policy ineffectiveness proposition *per se*. My interest was in doing policy evaluation, by developing new models with rational expectations and sticky prices and then using those models for policy.

The paper you co-wrote with Phelps, as well as Fischer's paper, which were both published in the Journal of Political Economy *in 1977, incorporated rational expectations into a model with sticky wages. That type of model now forms part of the mainstream textbook approach. Looking back how important was this work?*

I thought it was very important at the time and was surprised it didn't move more rapidly into the mainstream. I had a pragmatic view – perhaps because I had not been trained in any particular school – that you had this technique of rational expectations and also an enormous number of interesting policy problems which had yet to be addressed with this method. You also had some early models – the ones that Lucas and Sargent worked with which assumed flexible prices – which didn't seem to make a great deal of sense. They had some applications, but for the most part they didn't seem nearly accurate enough to be used in practice. While I was surprised that sticky wage or price rational expectations models didn't catch on more quickly, what surprised me even more was the way that models with money and monetary policy in them (both sticky and flexible price rational expectations models) were abandoned for real business cycle models which excluded money entirely.

When we interviewed Robert Lucas he suggested that 'the distinction between anticipated and unanticipated money is the key idea in post-war macro'. Do you agree? If not, what do you regard as being the key idea?
Well the key idea is rational expectations and in a sense that means being able to distinguish between anticipated and unanticipated changes. So I think that there is some agreement between us there. But it is not just the distinction between anticipated and unanticipated *money* that matters. Other examples include the distinction between anticipated and unanticipated changes in interest rates, or in taxes or government spending. Also other kinds of policy changes are important. For example, in my work I place greater emphasis on changes in the *systematic* part of monetary policy – how money or interest rates react to shocks – than on the shocks to money.

In your view what impact has unit root econometrics and real business cycle research had on macroeconomics?
The unit root literature had an impact in telling people that some of the fluctuations in the economy – perhaps a significant fraction – were not just temporary demand shocks but could actually affect the long-term trend in the economy. It helped people see that the fluctuations could be due to real factors, and that the growth trend could change and you could be on a new growth trend fairly randomly. If instead the economy returned to the original trend path, then there would be more of a demand interpretation of the fluctuations. Real business cycle research had a similar kind of impact in that it helped people see that fluctuations could be coming from the supply side – not from a theoretical, rather from an empirical, perspective. That is useful when describing reality because not all fluctuations are from the demand side. While a big fraction of business cycle fluctuations is from the demand side, longer-term fluctuations are most likely from the supply side. The other main contribution from real business cycle research is purely technical. The people who work on those models have developed a methodology and skills which enable them to extend the models in many ways, perhaps to introduce rigidities, sticky prices and contracts and utilize the models in ways that

wouldn't have been possible if they hadn't invested in the methodology. Thus, real business cycle research has been a good influence on modelling techniques, although a lot of the benefits have yet to be seen. I guess that in ten years time we will see an even greater influence of their work on macro modelling, but in a different and more general context than at present.

How do you view the work of new Keynesian economists on the micro founda-tions of sticky prices and wages?
Well I think that work on menu costs or other costs of adjusting prices is still somewhat disappointing in terms of what they have been able to deliver. It has been very interesting and I have been fascinated by it, but what has disappointed me is that in very few cases have those models been able to make a difference for policy. Such work on the microfoundations of stag-gered price and wage setting models hasn't helped us learn much more about how policy works or how interventions might make a quantitative difference.

Ben Bernanke (1995) has suggested that finding a coherent explanation of the Great Depression is the 'Holy Grail' of macroeconomics. Which explanation do you favour?
Well the most significant factor is monetary policy. I think that is true in the broadest sense. Ben Bernanke focuses more on banking failures and the credit side, which I regard as part of monetary failure. For me the most convincing explanation is the failure of monetary policy to keep what we would now call aggregate demand stable. If that had been done we could have avoided the Great Depression or at least had a much smaller downturn. Recovery from the Great Depression also appears to have been largely monetary-induced. Christina Romer (1990, 1992, 1993) has some nice work on that subject. Of course there were adverse dynamic effects which went beyond the influence of monetary policy. For example, the reduction in training for workers, people who were removed from the labour force for long periods of time, international effects and the trade wars came about because of the Great Depression. In this century we have learned from two big events in terms of policy, the Great Depression and the Great Inflation. That we have learned so much from those two events is one of the main reasons why we seem to be doing better now in stabilizing inflation and real output.

ECONOMIC POLICY

What do you regard to be the proper fiscal role of government?
The most important thing is to make sure that the automatic stabilizers are working and not get in their way. Discretionary policy on the fiscal side is

almost useless at this point in time, due to lags and the distrust people have of government fiscal policy due to deficits. In the 1991 US recession President Bush proposed a discretionary fiscal package and it didn't go anywhere. President Clinton came in and proposed one and that didn't go anywhere. In the meantime changes in taxes and spending through automatic stabilizers dominated. On the longer-term side fiscal policy should promote economic growth through low marginal rates of taxation so as to encourage saving and investment. Keeping things as simple and credible as possible is important. Also we shouldn't be involved with changing things all the time, which is disruptive.

What other factors caused the move away from fiscal policy towards monetary policy as the main tool of stabilization policy?
The realization that so many of the factors in the business cycle were monetary. Also the fact that our experience with discretionary fiscal policy has been so disappointing. We saw how important monetary policy was in the 1960s, 1970s, 1980s and still is today. Finally the ability of monetary policy to operate more quickly is a big advantage.

What is your view of the Ricardo–Barro debt equivalence theorem?
In the context of long-run fiscal policy it is useful in that it focuses your attention on the amount of resources absorbed by government spending. A major effect of government on the economy is measured through government purchases as a share of GDP. It seems to me that the way purchases are financed is less important. What I like about the Ricardian equivalence view, although it is too extreme, is that it emphasizes the spending side as the way the government affects the economy. There are, however, a lot of examples such as Martin Feldstein's studies of social security where empirically it doesn't hold.

How do you view the supply-side approach to fiscal policy which was prominent in the early 1980s?
Well, the approach was useful in that it focused our attention on the supply side of the economy and on incentives. This effect was similar to the impact of real business cycle research. However the notion that you can cut tax rates and raise more revenue is wrong in many cases, and has not held up with respect to broad changes in taxes. It is wrong and irresponsible to tell government to cut any tax rate and their revenue will go up. This would occur when tax rates are very high or when elasticities are very high, which is not always the case.

What do you regard as being the most important role for monetary policy?

To keep inflation steady and low, as a long-term goal. That is best for the real side of the economy and generates a more satisfactory growth rate. It also ensures a better short-run macroeconomic performance by keeping the business cycle smaller. For example, over the last 15 years we have had the first and second longest periods of peacetime expansion in US history, with a fairly short recession in between. The reason is that we have kept inflation steady and low. It is important that monetary policy follows a stable systematic rule in order to deal with the inevitable shocks that periodically hit the economy.

In recent years a lot of your research has focused on issues relating to rules versus discretion in macroeconomic policy making (see Taylor, 1993a, 1993b, 1994). Do any economists still favour a k per cent monetary growth rule?
Aside from Milton Friedman, I think the closest would be Ben McCallum and Allan Meltzer who favour an adapted monetary base rule. Ben and Allan suggest that the monetary base grows at a certain rate which adapts to changes in potential GDP growth.

During the 1950s and 1960s stabilization policy was regarded as a control theory problem, whereas by the mid-1970s, in particular with respect to monetary policy, it was viewed as a game-theoretic problem. What have policy makers learned from the game-theoretic literature?
The importance of establishing credibility. The game-theory literature illustrates the dangers and temptations to change policy. However the earlier work on optimal control had perhaps an even larger impact because it got economists who worked on policy into the habit of thinking about policy as part of a system through a reaction function or feedback rule. What policy makers do today is going to affect what people think policy makers are going to do tomorrow. Thinking about policy as a reaction function or a policy rule came out of that earlier work.

The other thing which had come out of the game-theory literature is the importance of governments having reputations in order to establish their credibility. In May this year the new Labour Government in the UK gave more independence to the central bank. Do you think an independent central bank is a prerequisite for establishing credibility?
Not necessarily, although in certain contexts it is important. You could have a central bank run by the government where the government follows a particular policy rule. For example, even if the central bank is not independent it could follow a fixed money growth rule. However in the context of today's world, where there isn't any one fixed money growth rule which is acceptable, there is no simple way for the government to tell the central bank

exactly what to do in all circumstances. You have to give some degree of authority to policy makers to make choices, so they do need to be independent from the current political environment. Having said this I think we emphasize independence too much relative to accountability. New Zealand, for example, has illustrated the importance of accountability in monetary policy.

What is your view of the recent emphasis given by many governments to inflation targeting?
Inflation targeting is a good idea. As I said before, monetary policy should aim to keep inflation low and stable, and an inflation target helps that and will therefore lead to better economic performance. While the US doesn't have an explicit inflation target most people feel FOMC members have an implicit target somewhere between 1 and 2 per cent; that seems to work nearly as well as having a formal inflation target.

Do you favour a policy target of zero inflation?
Well, I worry about having inflation too low and especially negative inflation. Fluctuations in the nominal rate of interest are limited by zero and you might not get much change in the real interest rate. However, given the bias in the measurement of inflation I see no problem with an inflation target of 1.5 per cent. I get more worried about deflation and that is another important reason to have an inflation target. The Japanese would have done much better over the last five years if they had adopted a zero inflation target. They would have had to increase money growth when inflation dropped below zero and that would have been beneficial for the economy.

Where do you stand on policy with respect to exchange rates?
It depends very much on the country concerned. For the US I am a firm advocate of floating exchange rates and the main reason is monetary independence. One of the reasons that US economic performance has been so good is because monetary policy has been free to do what is right to control inflation and stabilize the economy. When you consider other cases it depends on the relative size of the economy. For a very small open economy a fixed exchange rate seems to make more sense. Now Europe is a much more difficult problem. There are strong political demands for monetary union. However, overall I would emphasize the value of monetary independence. For example, in the UK unemployment has come down and economic performance has improved following greater international monetary independence *vis-à-vis* Germany. If there is monetary union in Europe it has to be recognized that giving up monetary independence could be a problem. The gains in terms of greater credibility feeding off the Bundesbank will hopefully make up for that.

What is your view on the high level of unemployment experienced in Europe since the early 1980s?
That has to do not so much with macroeconomics, but with microeconomics and labour market issues. I know there is a lot of debate and controversy over this subject. While I have not studied European economies as much as the US it strikes me that labour market rigidities in Europe are crucial to explaining the unemployment problem. In a world where technology is changing rapidly greater flexibility in the labour market would make a difference. Of course there are also cyclical changes in unemployment. Although it is very hard to prove I think the rise in unemployment in the UK in the early 1990s was largely cyclical.

POLICY ADVICE

For which administration have you acted as an economic adviser?
I was on the Council of Economic Advisers' staff during the Carter and Ford administrations. I also worked in the Bush Administration as a member of the CEA; that was a political appointment.

In giving advice what aspects of economic theory did you find most useful?
In the broadest sense of economic policy making by far the most useful thing is a firm grasp of basic economic principles. There are a lot of crazy government interventions that are constantly being suggested which basic economic analysis tells you don't make any sense. When it comes to giving advice on more specific macro areas, like monetary policy, then more than a knowledge of basic principles is necessary. For most people macroeconomics is very hard to understand. There you need to have much more background training and experience to understand the different schools and debates.

What lessons did you learn from your time as an economic adviser?
The most important lesson is to focus on economics and not worry about the politics. That may sound a little surprising, but if you make a calculation that a policy will not make it politically it influences what you recommend. In almost all cases I can think of, when I thought too much about the politics rather than the economics, it was a mistake. The second lesson is the need to spend a lot of time learning how to communicate economic ideas to people who have had no prior economic training.

At the round table discussion on 'Applied Economics in Action: The Council of Economic Advisers' at the AEA meeting in January this year Robert Solow suggested that economists act as 'intellectual sanitation workers'. Martin

Feldstein and Joseph Stiglitz also argued that the CEA has a crucial role in representing the national interest as opposed to special interests (see American Economic Review, *May 1997). Do you sympathize with these viewpoints given your experience as an economic adviser?*
Yes, as an economic adviser 90 per cent of your work is putting out fires and keeping bad ideas from happening. As for the national interest I would put it a different way than Stiglitz; I would say that economic advisers are there to represent consumers. For me the principle of letting the market work unless there is a good reason to intervene goes a long way.

When Joseph Stiglitz joined the CEA you suggested that it would make him more sceptical about what governments can do.
(*Laughter.*) Well I think he is a little more sceptical – he now has more examples of government failure – but probably not as much as I would have guessed. Generally speaking, people who go and work in government do get more sceptical about what the government can do.

Do you think that one of the problems economists experience in advising politicians is that very often the advice given is not what politicians want to hear?
No, I have not found that to be the case. Maybe I've been lucky with the people I have chosen to work for (*laughter*). In some cases, of course, politicians will not do what you recommend; but frequently that is not because they don't like it, but because they realize that they can't push it through right now or because it is not going to work politically.

In an article you wrote for the Economic Record *(Taylor, 1989) you stressed that people shouldn't ignore ideas just because they are associated with an approach which is biased either towards or against government intervention. Joan Robinson (1960) many years ago also pointed out that it is foolish to reject economic analysis because of the political doctrines with which it is associated. Did you find that economic advice was ever rejected because it was associated with a left-wing or right-wing view?*
Yes, that is very common. I think we all have a tendency to react that way; to look at the messenger as well as the message. In the political environment there is something else that happens. It makes a difference which side *first* puts forward a view. I remember one case when I first started in the Bush Administration where I suggested indexing capital gains taxation. The proposal was rejected out of hand because at that time it was the opposition's idea. While people clearly take sides in politics, in intellectual pursuits you are much better off carefully listening to what other people have to say regardless of their political views.

Martin Feldstein (1997a) has suggested that the predominant view in 1946 when the CEA was created was one which assumed 'macroeconomic instability and microeconomic insensitivity'. Is the reverse true today?
Well macroeconomic stability has improved, largely as a result of better policies. But I can't believe that micro sensitivity has increased. Maybe we are just more aware of microeconomic sensitivity now. We now have more evidence of it because of all the micro studies of how people respond to changes in taxes for example.

Do you think the UK would gain from having a Council of Economic Advisers?
Well I hesitate to answer your question without giving it a lot of thought because so much depends on the political environment. Certainly in the United States the Council of Economic Advisers has been very useful. One of the advantages of the CEA now is that it is very public and you know who is a member. Having said that it seems to me that there is something valuable in having a group of economists close to the chief executive that he or she can rely on for private advice.

In reality how independent is the Fed from Presidential pressure?
Well there are restrictions which limit the Fed's independence. For example there are issues that the Fed is interested in, such as regulatory power and international policy, which the administration has leverage on. But right now I think it is pretty independent.

The early political business cycle literature, such as the Nordhaus model (1975), suggests that prior to elections governments will try to buy votes by expanding the economy. More recently Alberto Alesina (1989) has suggested that Republicans or right-wing government's tend to give more emphasis to the control of inflation whereas Democrats or left-wing governments give more emphasis to unemployment. Do you feel these are accurate insights?
In recent years there is very little evidence that US Presidents have been able to get the Fed to do whatever they want. For example the Fed raised interest rates during the 1988 election year, the reverse of what political business cycle analysis would predict on the macro side. As for the partisan approach it is true that the Republicans have been more concerned with price stability than the Democrats, but even that has started to change in the United States. Alberto's work may have more applications in Europe.

What is your view of the current US administration's economic record?
The relationship with monetary policy has been good. Other than that I can't really say too much either way. It seems to me that they haven't done very

much. The fiscal stimulus package of 1993 failed. Since then they have got another budget agreement with the co-operation of Congress. I wish they could do more on education, regulation and tax policy. Having said that I would give them high points for not doing bad things, which is 90 per cent of the job.

ECONOMIC GROWTH

Do you agree with the view that economic growth is the part of macroeconomics that really matters?
Certainly in the longer term, for developing poor economies and increasing living standards, growth matters. That is why I have decided to treat economic growth before fluctuations in my introductory economics text (Taylor, 1998a) and I believe more texts will follow that approach in the future.

How do you account for the revival of interest in growth analysis?
Three things. One is that the business cycle is now less of a problem. In the United States we have had only one relatively short recession in the last 15 years. A lot of the freshmen students I teach can't even remember the last recession. The second reason is that growth is more of a problem now, especially since the reduction in productivity growth in the mid-1970s. A third reason is that for a lot of people economic growth is more appealing to teach. It is more straightforward and being an extension of micro is easier for students to understand.

In your intermediate macroeconomics textbook, co-written with Robert Hall (Hall and Taylor, 1997), you have moved growth to the front of the book. That now seems to be the case with a lot of the intermediate macro textbooks.
Bob and I did that in our third edition. It has worked very well for us. Abel and Bernanke (1995), and Mankiw's (1997b) intermediate macro books also have the analysis with growth first. As I mentioned earlier this approach works very well at the introductory level as well.

Do you regard economic growth as a useful bridge when moving from the teaching of microeconomics to macroeconomics?
Yes, in that respect it is very useful. I should add that it is useful in the basic principles market because ideas such as diminishing marginal product are useful in macro as well as micro. In many ways it is even more useful to teach growth first when introducing macro at the principles level because students can understand cyclical fluctuations better once they know about the growth trend in the economy.

What in your view are the most important determinants of growth?
The first step is to distinguish between increases in capital and technology. I think the slowdown in US growth has been due more to non-capital items, which we call technology. Now in terms of the determinants of capital, tax policy is very important in encouraging saving. We know less about total factor productivity growth, but I would go out on a limb and say that education and regulation are the two most important things. We need to keep the amount of regulation low and also improve our education system.

Does inflation damage growth?
Yes, especially at high levels. We don't have very much evidence for low levels of inflation. But another important benefit from low steady inflation is the business cycle effect. By keeping inflation low and preventing it from getting out of hand you run a lot less risk of having recessions.

What do you regard to be the main contribution of endogenous growth theory?
Endogenous growth theory has been useful in bringing to our attention policies that stimulate total factor productivity such as research and education. Total factor productivity, the technology term, is no longer treated as being exogenous. While some people say that we always knew it wasn't really exogenous, the new endogenous growth theory has focused our attention on modelling the process of technological improvement: invention and diffusion of techniques into innovations, and also the role of entrepreneurs and finance.

What can the OECD countries learn from the growth performance of the East Asian Tigers?
A lot of that growth performance has been a process of catching up. However we can all learn from policies which encourage trade, technical research and education and so on. We can also learn about the benefits of having economic growth as the key goal of economic policy. I can remember putting together an economic proposal for Bob Dole where our goal was to raise the growth rate by one percentage point. Once you have a goal of faster growth then you can generate better policies because attention is focused on how that goal is to be achieved.

GENERAL

How healthy is the current state of macroeconomics?
Well I think it is really quite healthy. The big thing that I see now on the research side is bringing sticky prices and wages, and monetary factors, into real business cycle models. That work is very interesting and exciting. The

work on growth theory is also another healthy aspect, although we must not lose the knowledge and interest in the fluctuations side of things. One area though, which I think is quite worrying, is high unemployment in Europe. I wish there could be more focus on that topic. Even though I think of it largely as a microeconomic issue there is still a lot of work that people who think about the whole economy could be doing. On the policy side what I find healthy is the way that central banks are focusing on inflation, following more systematic kinds of rule-like behaviour. I've noticed in the last five years the change in thinking about monetary policy which has been influenced by the research on policy rules. Ever since the rational expectations revolution there has been a tremendous interest in policy rules on the part of academics but much less so by policy makers until recently. When I went to work for the government in 1989 I wanted to bring more attention to that issue. In the first Economic Report of the President we did in 1990 we had a section on policy rules. Since then interest about policy rules has increased dramatically.

What issues are you currently working on?
The application of monetary policy rules and finding ways to reduce the amount of discretion that has led to monetary policy mistakes in the past. I'm doing that partially by simulating my multi-country rational expectations model. I am also looking at US economic history to see the impact of different monetary policy rules. Several years ago (see Taylor, 1993b) I proposed a particular rule for central banks to follow. That rule has received a lot of attention from policy makers which has generated even more interest in policy rules. Because of the questions the rule has raised I am doing more research on such rules. So that is what I'm doing right now.

David C. Colander
(b. 1947)

David Colander is currently Christian A. Johnson Distinguished Professor of Economics at Middlebury College. He is best known for his work on the teaching, history and methodology of economics, the development and advocacy of a market-based anti-inflation plan and more recently the macro foundations of microeconomics.

We interviewed Professor Colander in his office at Middlebury College on 29 October 1997.

BACKGROUND INFORMATION

Why did you decide to study economics at university and thereafter what attracted you to macroeconomics in particular?

I decided to study economics at College because economics gave me the opportunity to go abroad (*laughter*). I was deciding between a Math, Religion and Economics major. I had taken only one course in economics when there were a series of riots at Columbia. I looked for an escape and the economics department allowed me to study at the University of Birmingham in England. As it turned out I took nearly all my undergraduate economics in England. I took a total of three undergraduate courses in economics at Columbia. In my senior year I started taking economics courses at the graduate school, which is how I ended up going to Columbia Graduate School.

What about your interest in macroeconomics?
Frankly I was totally unattracted to macroeconomics. I was a microeconomist. As an undergraduate I had sat in on Gary Becker's lectures. His student William Landes was my graduate teacher in micro. I found microeconomics absolutely fascinating; I was highly attracted to the microeconomics mode of argumentation. Macroeconomics was a conundrum to me. I had problems understanding it. So I took Edmund Phelps's micro foundations course to try and see if that would clear it up, but it did not help. I did my oral examinations in public finance and industrial organization. Although I had done well in Phil Cagan's money course, I was still basically a microeconomist.

I ultimately got into macro because of Bill Vickrey. I was doing a thesis on optimal taxation with Bill and Ned Phelps (optimal taxation was a hot topic at the time). I was doing three essays; I had completed two of them and was in the process of finishing the third when I wrote a little paper called 'The Free Market Solution To Inflation' which I sent to Bill Vickrey. Bill sent me back a letter saying it was brilliant, the best idea he had seen in years. I thought, wow, this is kind of nice because you do not often get a response like that from one of your professors. So I went to see Bill and asked 'if I dump my existing thesis can I get something new out in a year?' and he said 'yes'. Then I went to Ned, who was my other adviser, and said: 'Vickrey thinks I can expand on this paper and get a thesis done in a year, what do you think?' He said something like: 'I expect so'. So they had pretty much signed off on my proposed thesis before I started writing it, which was lucky for me since my new thesis turned out to be pretty awful (*laughter*). It was entitled 'Public Finance Stabilization Policy for an Economy with Simultaneous Inflation and Unemployment'. It was too broad and general, but they let it through. So in my thesis I was looking at inflation and macro issues, but I was still not really a macroeconomist. As I got more and more into these issues I started reading more widely in macro.

Which economists have had a major influence on your own work?
In terms of early economists I would say Thorstein Veblen and Frank Knight; they combine a strange mixture of radical and sound Chicago conservative approaches to economics that I find attractive. Of contemporary economists I think Bill Vickrey played a really important role in a lot that I did. But reading the work of earlier economists was the most important influence.

Which papers and/or books would you identify as having had a major influence on the development of macroeconomics?

The development as it is, or as it should be? (*laughter*). They are two different things.

As it is?
Obviously there is Milton Friedman's (1968) paper and Edmund Phelps's papers (1967, 1968). As macro evolved I think both of those were of central importance. The early work by Franco Modigliani (1944) expanding on the work of John Hicks (1937) played an important role as did Alvin Hansen's early work. But I regard Bob Clower (1965) and Axel Leijonhufvud's (1968) work as really providing the key to the way I think macro should be. That work is not much cited now and is not much read or understood. I also think Paul Davidson's work is important, when he is not too busy saying that he understands Keynes better than everybody else.

METHODOLOGICAL ISSUES

Do you think that an understanding of methodological issues is important for an understanding of current controversies in macroeconomics?
Yes and no. It depends on what level you want to understand it. I am not a methodologist who believes that you should spend any length of time on methodological issues. However, I do think we should think carefully about what we are doing and what questions we are trying to answer. I do not think a lot of people do that. They get into this mode of doing a paper, and of not thinking about the broader questions that give it relevance. There's a lot of needless dotting of 'i's' and crossing of 't's' out there. So in that sense, yes, they should think about methodology. But I am not suggesting they should get into questions such as, 'Are you a post-modernist? Or are you a Popperian?' – that's totally irrelevant. I just ask 'Is what I am doing making sense?' That is the level of my methodological work (*laughter*).

Would you agree with Milton Friedman, who in his famous 1953a paper argued that the realism of assumptions is not important and it is the predictive value of a theory which matters?
It all depends on what level you are doing it. In macroeconomics I think he is totally wrong because in macro we have no way of definitively empirically testing most of the propositions we are making. That is the real difficulty. Where you cannot test the empirical propositions his 'predictive value' method is problematic. In macro you do not have a confirmed theory, what you have is a general understanding. The realism of assumptions for a general understanding is of primary importance because the assumptions become part of that understanding. Assumptions play a role in what you see. So in macro I

think he is totally wrong, even though in some broader sense if economics was a science where you could definitively test propositions I would have much less problem with Friedman's position.

You have talked about Milton Friedman being 'an artist' and the 'art of economics'. What exactly do you mean by the term artist and art in this context? (see Colander, 1995a).
The art of economics goes back to John Neville Keynes, whom Friedman cited when he divided economics into positive and normative economics. Actually Neville Keynes did not do that. He divided economics into positive economics, normative economics and the art of economics. He further said that the art of economics is extraordinarily important because it is the branch of economics concerned with policy issues. The art of economics takes normative economics – which is the study of goals, and positive economics – which is the pure science of economics, and puts them together with reasoned judgement to arrive at policy implications. In the art of economics you take in other variables that you held constant for developing positive economics. So the appropriate methodology for the art of economics is fundamentally different from the appropriate methodology for positive economics. The art of economics in- volves judgement because you are adding in sociological and political variables. You have to do this when talking about policy. Where I have a problem with most of the profession is that they try to combine positive economics with talking about policy, and to draw policy conclusions from models that do not have enough institutional reality from which to draw these policy conclusions.

In your essay 'Confessions of an Economic Gadfly' (1999) you distinguish between what you call the MIT and the Chicago approaches to economics, both of which you are unhappy with. What, if any, is the alternative?
By the Chicago approach I mean the Becker/Friedman approach. My prob- lem with that approach is that they believe the market is the solution to everything. I do not share that view and I do not think it necessarily follows from the theory. While there is a lot of empirical evidence that the market works in a lot of cases, that evidence is not theory. It is based upon the way you look at the world. If they would say that, I would be happy with their approach, and much of what they say.

The MIT approach reduces everything into quasi-formal models. They are not the high-level formal models but rather *ad hoc* models whose conclusions depend upon the assumptions they make. But those assumptions are often based on analytic tractability and not on reasonableness. So they, in my view, often make the model irrelevant. I do not believe simple *ad hoc* models work.

So what is the alternative? I think the answer for policy recommendations is not to use formal models but instead replace them with informal models which make no pretence of being scientific. In effect, I favour the Chicago approach without the Chicago ideology. The answer for formal theory is to take seriously what the issues are and use the mathematics appropriate to answer it. You do not limit yourself to linear dynamics, you allow all possible dynamics to be included; you take into account the complexity of the economy and don't pretend it has a simple structure. Simplicity is not to be found in structure. I think the new work in the science of complexity is an attractive way to do theoretical work within economics. It finds the simplicity in itera-tive dynamics, not in static structure. At this point the complexity approach to theory leaves policy so far removed from what you can say that it has to be done very informally. So I see a much sharper distinction between theoretical work and policy work than the MIT approach allows.

The MIT approach emphasizes formal modelling but you say if a formal model does not make intuitive sense it must be wrong. But if you talk to non-economists, say for example politicians, they often argue the case for restricting free trade in order to protect domestic employment. It makes intuitive sense to some of them. But as economists we know from our formal models that such views are naive and potentially very damaging.
What I mean is that a model has to make *intuitive sense to an educated economist*. I distinguish between common sense and educated common sense. I argue for educated common sense. A person with educated common sense is fully conversant with the best arguments within the literature. It is at that point that common sense becomes relevant. Clearly, if you do not have any training, the common sense thing is to say I do not know what the answer is. People who are making comments about economics without having read and really studied the issues are not using common sense at all. They are being stupid (*laughter*).

How important do you think it is for macroeconomic models to be based on choice-theoretic microfoundations, an approach which became the clarion call of the new classical economists during the 1970s?
It all depends on what you mean by choice-theoretic microfoundations. Clearly there is an interrelationship between micro and macro so in that sense they are necessary. But choice-theoretic foundations which begin without a model of how individuals choose and structure a market do not provide a sensible framework for macroeconomics. It is a sort of abstract nothingness. What I believe is that first of all we need a theory of markets. Why do markets develop and how do they work? It is clear that one of the reasons they are there is to reduce transaction costs, but we don't have a formal theory of markets. The current choice-theoretic frameworks do not provide a satisfactory choice-theoretic framework for me since they assume markets.

That is why I talk about the need for a macro foundation for micro. Once you have that macro foundation – a theory of markets – then you can develop a micro foundation for macro.

Should macroeconomics theory be driven by empirical problems?
Yes and no. Macroeconomic theory is trying to understand how economic systems coordinate a whole bunch of people. How does our economy do that? Will you get certain types of problem? Understanding that has to be involved with empirical issues. However, if your consideration is driven by short-term empirical movements of the economy, you are unlikely to see the important issues. You'll be developing theories of what is essentially noise. Since I believe that theoretical questions have to be very broad-based over long periods, I hesitate to say that theory should be driven by empirical problems because most people interpret 'empirical problems' in a very short-term framework. I see it in a long-term framework.

How important are rhetoric and terminology in macroeconomic debate? Are labels such as 'Neo', 'New', 'Post', significant?
Yes, no, maybe, as in most things (*laughter*). Rhetoric is extremely important. McCloskey has done a nice job of saying, 'look, we are telling stories and we are using metaphors, the metaphors you use can play a big role in how the ideas work out'. As for labels, the labels are done primarily for students. The people who are macroeconomists understand that the distinctions go way beyond the labels. The reason you have labels, and the reason labels are important, is because they provide the initial introduction to students to what the issues and debates are about. But you have to be very careful that pigeonholing does not preclude broader understanding later on.

Do you feel that the main differences between macroeconomists today are over theoretical or empirical issues?
I guess I would say theoretical issues although I know I differ from most people on this point. For me, the big issue is what initial assumptions we make before we go about modelling. I think you have to take the theory of markets first before you can talk about what the macro effect is going to be. We currently assume that markets exist. They exist to reduce transaction costs. How do they do it? How do firms develop? What is our theory of the firm that fits in there? The recent work of Bob Clower and Peter Howitt (1996) is really trying to get at these issues, although Clower has been trying to get at it for 30 years. But the profession has not listened at all and I think that is one of the reasons why Bob is so bitingly sarcastic.

TEACHING MACROECONOMICS

How important do you think it is for undergraduate students of economics to have an awareness of the evolution of ideas?
If the ideas we were teaching were the right ones, probably not all that important. But to the degree that we are teaching ideas which, in my view, limit their vision and say 'this is the truth', then I think it is really important to see how ideas develop and evolve because it opens up the possibility for students to see alternative views. If there is a truth in macro, which I doubt, I do not think we have discovered it. If you do not have a truth in macro then you have to provide students with as many ways of looking at it as possible so they can come to a conclusion on what they think is the correct approach, as opposed to saying 'this is the correct way'.

So you would actually favour subjecting students to a breadth of perspectives and ideas rather than focusing on one particular approach?
Absolutely.

So how do you approach teaching macroeconomics to your own students?
As a teacher you have a duty to teach them what is considered the standard mainstream models. So my students learn all the standard stuff. The difference is that I teach models as logical exercises of the mind. I tell my students the story about callisthenics. As soon as you start a sport the first thing they have you do is callisthenics, you do not immediately go out and play the sport. That is what we do in my classes, callisthenics of the mind because their brains are flabby, just like I am flabby because I do not exercise enough (*laughter*). I regard these exercises of the mind as important. But these exercises are not macroeconomics. They are simply a way of getting your mind to be able to see complicated interrelationships. Unfortunately, all too often, the exercises of the mind end up being portrayed as the macro relationships. So I teach precisely the same macro course that other people do, but I teach it from a different perspective. It is simply a beginning.

Has the move towards producing technically competent graduates who are skilled in maths and econometrics been a retrograde step?
Yes and no. It all depends on what you are trying to do. To the degree you want to produce applied policy economists, it has been retrograde. Students today learn technique but little judgement. The people who can really do math at a high level of formalism often do not have the ability, or the personality, to deal with the loose questions of integrating social issues. The reality is that mathematicians are not especially good at understanding policy issues. By focusing graduate training on math, we have made it unattractive

for broad generalists. What has happened is that we have selected out the broad generalists who would be good at applied policy issues, and replaced them with people who are mathematicians. A few of these mathematicians are brilliant, and they have made some enormous improvements in pure theory. But that improvement has come at a cost in the application of that theory to what is going on. So it helps in one dimension but it hurts in another.

In your 1995b paper in the Journal of Economic Perspectives *you argue that the aggregate demand and aggregate supply model is seriously flawed. Why then do so many eminent macroeconomists actually use this model as a vehicle for teaching in their textbooks?*
Where I said it was flawed was in the introductory courses. What was flawed was the definitions they were providing. They were initially specifying as aggregate demand, an equilibrium curve which was derived from IS–LM analysis. It never was just demand-side phenomena. Then they had to integrate a supply side back into the analysis and in doing so it was unclear what supply curve they were using. Was it a curve derived from the production function, or was it a curve based on institutional structure and frictions? The result was analytically a mess. Lately, because of my complaints, and similar complaints from other people, textbook authors have been much more careful about specifying that they are saying and are specifying aggregate supply and demand in ways that avoid the problem. Why are AS/AD analyses used? When you write a textbook, as I know very well, you face strong pressures to go along with the crowd. Publishers found that teachers were comfortable with AS/AD analysis so they urged their authors to include it. They did, by twisting definitions and misleading students.

You have argued (1988) that new classical macroeconomics fails to pass what you refer to as the 'teachability criteria'. Nevertheless, during the last ten years, many new classical insights have clearly been incorporated into mainstream undergraduate textbooks, both at the principles and intermediate levels. On reflection do you think that your comment was somewhat premature?
No, not at all. I think what has happened is that new classical economics has evolved and now better meets the teachability criteria. If you notice what they do – they move away from models. I do not regard new classical economics to be the driving force in macro anymore. It has blended into new Keynesian economics to give us a very strange combination which comes close to meeting the teachability criteria. I stand on what I said there. What I also said was that new Keynesian economics would much better meet the teachability criteria so there has been a blending of the two, a synthesis, which is what is being taught.

At the January 1997 meeting of the American Economic Association in New Orleans several papers (by Blinder, Blanchard, Solow and Eichengreen) were presented which attempted to answer the question, 'Is there a core of practical macroeconomics that we should all believe in and teach?' What is your answer to that question (see the AER, *May, 1997).*

Yes, I think there is a core but it is not the core that they would necessarily accept (*laughter*). Much of what they said, if they had said it with less certainty, I would not have had a problem with. But what you had there were a group of neo and new Keynesian economists (which have been blended with elements from monetarism) who said, 'Look, we understand most of macroeconomics'. There was no real business cycle theorist there. There was no questioning of the foundations of the mainstream model. There was no Bob Clower there. My view is that real business cycle theory has some important issues to add and that seemed to be missing from those papers. Similarly, some of the ideas Clower has raised were also missing. It was what was left out of the discussion that concerned me.

Does the content of undergraduate macroeconomics textbooks always reflect the direction of macroeconomic research or can it sometimes provide a lead?

It reflects, obviously. It has to because we are providing a service with a textbook. Whenever I try to lead in texts I get dumped on by reviewers.

But do you try and push the emphasis in particular directions, giving a lead reflecting your own preferences?

Of course (*laughter*). When there are new ideas the question is, how do you get those ideas out and get people open to them? I regard textbooks as extraordinarily important. Paul Samuelson once said 'I don't care who writes a nation's laws – or crafts its advanced treatises if I can write its textbooks'. The way textbooks are written is very important as they can influence who becomes an economist. If textbooks present economics in a sterile 'this is the truth' approach, the students who really question ideas will not go into economics. So, in my text, what I try to do is present all the standard stuff in a way that is understandable but then go on to say 'there are lots of other issues here, really interesting ones'. I then briefly try to introduce students to these. I do not pretend to present the truth. I present the same things as other texts but try to force students to think. In doing that what I am trying to do is to change the focus of what economics education is about and how it is presented. But I am very hesitant about putting in material which is too new, so I spend a lot of time thinking how I can get ideas such as the new science of complexity into the text without violating the standard cannons. Thus, in my new edition you will see two pages on the experience curve and a discussion of endogenous comparative advantage. But I have to be very careful. A lot of people who are teaching are far removed from the cutting edge of current research. That's the market. If you can't reduce a new idea to a metaphor that has always made sense to them you can't include it in the text. If you can reduce it to a common sense metaphor, you can get it included. So in my books, even where I have extended beyond the normal discussion, my approach has worked very well especially at lower level schools where they are teaching with some common sense.

You have written quite often, and been critical about, the incentive structure in academia. What are your criticisms of the way that academics operate? (See Colander, 1988, 1994.)

Again this criticism is mainly focused on United States academia although unfortunately Britain is beginning to follow our example. In many ways I found the traditional British way to be very attractive. Academics were given a chance to think for long periods of time about various issues and there was not the pressure to publish relatively unimportant stuff. Here in the US nobody is willing to make judgements about what is published that are independent of the structure of the profession. In other words the approach runs as follows: tenure requires three papers from Column A and two from Column B, and here are the journals in each column. This essentially means that journal editors determine who gets tenure. They know this and they use their power. That leads to people figuring, 'well, how can I get a paper out to fit in at Journal X?' You start focusing totally on how you can get a paper to fit a particular journal and lose sight of doing meaningful research. So you are writing what you think people want to see, not sitting back and reflecting broadly and thinking, 'gee, what really is the problem and how can I best answer it?' The incentive structure is that people have to get tenure by playing the article game. After spending seven years doing that, they have learned by doing, and cannot get back, or very few of them can get back, to looking at the more important broader questions.

In your 'Confessions of an Economic Gadfly' paper (1999) you describe yourself as a 'non-partisan heterodox economist'. Has this made your career as an economist and teacher difficult, enjoyable or both?

Difficult is enjoyable (*laughter*). I suppose my approach is to pick on every-one, including myself, and do not take anything too seriously. I seriously try to understand issues but always be critical. I tend to have problems with many heterodox economists when they start defending their ideas to the death. I also have problems with mainstream economists because they are also too busy defending their ideas instead of trying to be open and saying, 'what is really the best of these ideas?' They forget about what ideas are for.

As a means of communicating ideas do you find it useful to divide macro-economists into different schools or is this misleading?
It depends on for whom. For macroeconomists it is not useful because they know what the distinctions are and what is going on. As I said before the division into schools is done for students and for people being introduced into macro. For that reason the names given are very important. That is why I objected to the new Keynesian terminology of Gregory Mankiw. What he included in new Keynesian was so broad and amorphous that the term was meaningless. It included monetarists and a whole bunch of others. That is why I suggested (1992a) calling it new neo-Keynesian macro, to emphasize its lineage. I now believe that it is time to give up the Keynesian–classical divide. The two have been so merged that it is no longer meaningful. That is when I came up with this Walrasian/post Walrasian division. Unfortunately this new division has not caught on (see Colander, 1996).

If you were to divide economists into schools what would be your classification?
At the moment it would be Walrasian v post Walrasian. The Walrasian school are those economists who will accept modelling the aggregate economy using a concept of a market which does not have a firm foundation. So they just assume that markets exist, and that they work perfectly, and start modelling from there. The post Walrasian position is that before we can start talking about how things would work in a market we need a theory of markets, why they develop, and what is going on there. We currently do not have an acceptable theory of markets so the post Walrasian school includes all those people who are trying to develop one. They include the complexity theorists, particularly those at the Sante Fe Institute, institutionalists, and others such as Clower, all of whom are dealing with those types of questions. So a broad variety of people, from quite different perspectives and backgrounds, are dealing with it. The division creates some strange bedfellows. Imagine Sante Fe economists and institutionalists together! That is very strange but they both do not accept that a market exists independently of individuals setting up a market. How to theoretically include structure into models is a central issue in macro. A distinction of schools based on that distinction makes sense. After you have sorted macro economists out on this question then you can have lots of other divisions, but that is the key division.

But where would someone like Milton Friedman fit in your Walrasian v post Walrasian division?
In many ways I would classify him as a post Walrasian because he is very much against formal theorizing in the way that it has developed. He is a Marshallian. Friedman fits much better in the post Walrasian school than he

would in the Walrasian school, which is why he has separated himself from the new classicals.

KEYNESIAN ECONOMICS

From what you have written you seem to have some affinity and sympathy with the Keynesian end of the macroeconomics spectrum. Is that an accurate representation of your position?

Yes and no. I do not have sympathy with Keynesian economics of the hydraulic variety – I object to that form of Keynesianism that says that we know what policies to follow. What I do have a sympathy for is the idea that it is possible that there may be good reasons why we might want the government to take a policy role in the economy. That is where I have sympathy with Keynesianism. To the degree that Keynesian-style models are based on empirical evidence I find them appealing. Early Keynesians said 'look, nominal wages and prices are relatively fixed, they will change over time, but let's look at the empirical evidence and base our models on that observation'. That makes sense as long as these models are presented as working models and are not presented as formal theoretical models. But Keynesian models were presented as being more than that. That's why I avoided macroeconomics at the beginning of my career. I just could not accept that they were formal scientific models.

What do you think is Keynes's major legacy to economics?

Probably his method, although it has been almost lost. He passed on this Marshallian legacy that economics is really an approach to looking at problems, rather than a way of providing answers. So I consider his methodology to be the most important legacy. I try to pass on that legacy by trying to teach students how to approach problems with a questioning mind. Keynes did that a lot, but much of what he did was related to policy issues relevant for a particular time and place.

Would he have received your vote for a Nobel Prize in economics?
Of course (*laughter*).

POLICY ISSUES AND THEORETICAL DEVELOPMENTS

Initially, in the postwar period Keynesianism was closely associated with fiscalism. What role do you see in the modern world for fiscal policy?

Fiscal policy – by which I mean the degree to which you can vary the budget deficit to influence the level of economic activity – as an effective activist tool just does not exist. That does not mean that the deficit – how big it is and what size it is – does not have a role to play. It does matter. But given current political institutions it is pretty much uncontrollable. You have something that can effect the economy, but you have no way of controlling it.

In the 1970s you were heavily involved with developing new ideas related to anti-inflation plans, the MAP plan. How do you now view that work? (See Lerner and Colander, 1980; Colander, 1992b.)
MAP is an interesting theoretical idea that has possibilities to fundamentally change the institutional structure of the economy to make it operate more efficiently. Politically, it has not a chance in hell of being implemented, and it has large unanswered practical implementation issues. The basic idea of MAP is to create property rights in prices. This was a pure micro approach to inflation that reflected my training as a Chicago economist. How do you get rid of inflation? If you have property rights in prices so that anybody who is raising their price has to find someone else to change their price in the opposite direction – all these are value added prices weighted by the appropriate quantities – then, by definition, you can have no inflation. What does that mean for the aggregate economy?

My initial interest in that question was almost purely theoretical. I regarded this as an interesting way to integrate inflation into aggregate economic models. Bill Vickrey and Abba Lerner, who both became very excited about this idea, saw it as something more practical. So I started to look at these practical issues to see if it would work. I went up to visit Fred Kahn, who was at that time the chief inflation fighter for President Jimmy Carter. He said, 'I have read your stuff but what you want me to do will involve an institutional change much larger than the introduction of the Federal Reserve'. I agreed (*laughter*). He reminded me how in his position he would be 'annihilated' for saying just one wrong word, and asked me whether I thought he was going to have anything to do with something as radical as MAP! And that was in the 1970s. Now the possibility of implementing MAP is even more remote.

Nonetheless I think that understanding MAP gives us insight into how incomes policies might work. The usual view is that incomes policies make the economy less efficient. My argument is that, in theory, an incomes policy makes an economy systematically more efficient by achieving a lower level of equilibrium unemployment. As you expand the economy, you push up the price of raising prices, but you do not cause accelerating inflation. With MAP you have a choice of what level you want the economy to operate at. You also have an actual measure of how much inflationary pressure there is, allowing you to conduct more meaningful monetary policy. MAP gives you an anti-inflationary pressure gauge. You could use the price of MAP credits to base a monetary rule on. I thought then, and I think now, that the idea was neat theoretically. The difficulty I had in explaining this relatively simple idea to macroeconomists, is what lead me to study the profession and its sociology.

During the past decade there has been a renaissance of interest in growth. What is your view of the recent change in orientation in macroeconomics towards economic growth?
I am not opposed to it, but I also do not like the way growth is presented. The Solow growth model is not an especially useful tool for understanding growth or for the teaching of growth. I have been very influenced by the writings of Nathan Rosenberg (1994) who emphasizes the extraordinarily complicated nature of technology and technological decisions and how they influence one another. Most of the important ideas that emerge do not follow directly from planned investment. Investment and capital is only a small part of the growth process. In any growth process there is a cascading effect that fits very well with the complexity point of view. In the macro book I am working on now I really emphasize the Sante Fe approach to growth as a realistic alternative. The Solow growth model works because it has very linear dynamics that always bring you back to the equilibrium growth path. The Sante Fe approach says that there are multiple equilibria out there. The economy can go up a whole number of different growth paths, and *a priori* it is difficult to say which one you will go on. The only way you can get a sense of the growth process is by getting down in the trenches and looking at case studies. I think economists need to make the following distinction: 'Is the market working really well because they inherently work well, or do markets work well because of the institutions we have developed to make them work well'? I think it is the second. If economists are prepared to recognize that institutions are important and evolving, then I have no problem with changing the focus of macro to growth.

An important debate in macroeconomic policy has been the issue of whether or not stabilization policy should be conducted via rules or discretion. Where do you stand in the rules v discretion debate?
I think that the theoretical part of this debate is stupid. People have always understood the distinction between rules and discretion. Time inconsistency is not a new insight. That is why we have had such things as the Gold Standard in the past. Full contingency rules are always preferred to discretion, which is what the time inconsistency work tells us. But, for real world rules of limited contingency that is not helpful. In reality the real debate is about what contingencies to take into account in a rule and how simple a rule we want to make. That is not something we can answer theoretically. That is something which involves judgement. Presenting the issue as a theoretical issue, as opposed to a judgement issue, has misled people.

Does anything remain of what Harry Johnson (1971) called 'the monetarist counter-revolution?'
It has been incorporated into the mainstream. So we do not really talk about it anymore. Mainstream macro is now an amalgamation of views where much of what I consider the essence of Keynesianism has been eliminated. So in a way Friedman's monetarism has won. It is now called new Keynesian macro. In my view Keynesianism does not accept a unique, non-institutionally, non-expectationally dependent, natural rate.

During the 1970s the contributions of new classical economists dominated the agenda of macroeconomic analysis. Do you feel that the work of new classicists such as Robert Lucas has enhanced our understanding of macroeconomic phenomena?
Absolutely. As I said, the neo-Keynesian model, as it existed before the new classical contributions, made a pretence of being scientific without really being scientific. I think that the only thing that changed this complacency was the new classical revolution. They correctly said, 'look, you have made a whole bunch of *ad hoc* assumptions here'. I think it was very important to point that out. Of course, they took macro in a pretty crazy direction, but that is another issue.

What about the later new classical developments inspired by Finn Kydland and Edward Prescott (1982) which identified technological shocks as a predominant source of aggregate fluctuations? Do you think that real business cycle theory will eventually be absorbed into the mainstream?
Absolutely, to the degree that it has some important insights. The important insight as I see it is that short-run supply is constantly changing, so supply issues are really driving what is going on in the economy. However I think the real business cycle theory of supply is absolutely asinine. The intertemporal labour substitution hypothesis does not pass my intuitive understanding test. That is just not the way the labour market works. The relevant supply issues in the type of real world markets that we have – once you have a theory of markets – is that firms have to set prices in order to attract customers, they have to keep those prices relatively constant, given our current institutional structure (that may change as internet commerce develops). To the extent that you have such a market structure, *expected demand plays a fundamental role in short-run supply*. So demand plays a central role in the economy but it is not separate from supply, it operates through supply. If supply adjusts due to expected demand changes this causes demand to change. So you have the interrelated link of the Keynesians but it operates through supply, and expectations of demand. When expectations influence supply the real and illusionary forces become blended and

indistinguishable. Our illusions create our reality. That, in my view, is the central Keynesian insight. Wouldn't it be ironic if that insight is re-introduced to economics via a path through real business cycles?

High rates of inflation and unemployment are regarded as undesirable. Is low inflation and unemployment an achievable goal?
Sure, I think it is totally achievable. Bill Vickrey thought you can go down to 2 per cent unemployment. The issue is whether you want to make the institutional changes which are required to accomplish that goal. To do so you have to introduce an incomes policy, a rather substantial policy like MAP. The political choices are therefore enormous because what it involves is people's freedom to raise their prices. With the MAP plan you take away that freedom because they can only raise prices when it will not lead to inflation. It is a quite different allocation of rights and I doubt if any nation would be willing to accept this sort of change. The reason you do not have discussion of market-based incomes policies, such as MAP, is because they involve enormous changes in power away from insiders and towards outsiders.

Macroeconomic analysis should be able to explain the causes of unemployment. Do you think that the concept of involuntary unemployment is useful and has helped our understanding?
No. The same unemployment can be viewed as voluntary or involuntary depending from which perspective you look at it. What I think is important is whether there are some policies that can eliminate it. Let's say we accept all unemployment as voluntary. Does that mean we should see that unemployment as something good? In my view no. Say I put a gun to your head and say: 'Your money or your life', I suspect you would voluntarily give me your money. But that does not mean that society should allow such actions. Given institutions all results are voluntary to the degree that people accept those institutions. The real unemployment issue is a comparative institutional issue; it is not whether unemployment is voluntary or involuntary.

So what policy prescriptions would you advocate to reduce unemployment?
I see two approaches. One is to make being unemployed less attractive. For example, do away with unemployment insurance. The other way is to take seriously the need to implement an incomes policy. I am very hesitant to advocate specific policy prescriptions. The role of economists is to provide an insight into what the issues are. It is a normative question what level of unemployment we want to push the economy to and that is where politicians have to decide. What economists need to do is explain what types of institutional changes you will be forced to make in order to achieve given goals.

But in the past most incomes policies have involved various unacceptable forms of control.
The MAP plan has no bureaucracy setting prices. It leaves all pricing decisions to firms. It is a market plan. There is no government making any decision on any price. It simply tells firms that as long as they follow the rules of the market, they can do what they want. The rules are that if a firm does not have enough MAP credits it must buy additional ones in the market from a firm that is choosing to lower its prices by an offsetting amount. So in other words you have no government making any decision after the initial property rights are distributed. The market handles it.

Is overall excess demand impossible under your MAP scheme?
Yes, it is impossible as long as the price of MAP credit did not blow up. Excess demand would push the price of MAP credit up causing firms to increase supply. MAP directs an increase in demand to increases in supply and away from increases in nominal price. The MAP credit price would eliminate that excess demand so that there can be no excess demand in this system. So instead of a trade-off between inflation and unemployment you have a trade-off between unemployment and the MAP credit price you want. Excess demand loses its meaning, it is channelled into a constraint of the particular price – the price of raising price.

GENERAL

Is the current state of macroeconomics a cause for concern or do you think we are making steady progress?
I haven't the faintest idea (*laughter*). To the extent that they have not incorporated what they should incorporate, it is not that healthy. But it seems to be going along quite fine, not being on the verge of death or anything

What do you feel will be the future direction of macroeconomics?
I believe that the future lies in a better understanding of the dynamics and complexity of the system. That is where the theoretical movements are operating. Eventually these will have an enormous impact on both how microeconomics and macroeconomics are taught. That is what I see as the real interesting developments. How long will this take to have a real influence? Maybe ten or twenty years, it will be a long time.

In the more immediate future are you planning to run a conference on these issues?

Yes. We are running a conference at Middlebury this year on integrating ideas of complexity into undergraduate textbooks and how, if you take complexity seriously, that would influence the way that economics is taught. Complexity is also the theme at this year's (1998) History of Economics Conference in Montreal, which I am organizing.

What views did earlier economists have on complexity within the history of economics?
Adam Smith had a quite different view and justification for the market than did David Ricardo. Smith was much more sympathetic to this complexity point of view than was Ricardo.

You have argued in your Methodus (1990) *paper that all appraisal of current research by Historians of Thought should make extensive use of interviews. What do you regard as the advantages to be gained from the interview method in research?*
(*Laughter*). That paper was the result of going to History of Thought meetings and hearing a bunch of heterodox economists talk about mainstream economists as if they were dead people. So I said 'look, why spend hours and hours reading their published papers, sorting out what you think is a right or wrong interpretation when this could be sorted out over a phone call?'. You could ask them 'here is my interpretation, what do you think?' When you have such an easy way of asking people what they think it seemed rather stupid to me not to use it (*laughter*). There's far too much writing of papers in our profession and far too little communication.

Have you ever been actively interested in politics and does your political stance influence your economics?
My former wife was quite actively interested in politics. She was one of those Rhodes Scholars who went to Oxford as a stepping stone to bigger things. We got married in Washington and were seen as a couple on the move. A former Chairman of the Council of Economic Advisers gave us our wedding reception. We attended the right cocktail parties, which is where politics really takes place. I quickly discovered that you have to be pleasant to people and not say what you are thinking at those cocktail parties. At that point it became absolutely clear to me that I had no role in politics or policy making circles whatsoever (*laughter*). It also became clear that my first wife and I were incompatible.

Let me be clear. I am not denigrating policy making and politics. Politics requires an understanding of all these issues. Academics are used by politicians because only politicians really understand the extraordinarily complex ways that the policy process works. I am not interested in studying those complex ways, so I have very little to say about specific policies of the type politicians talk about. My interest in policy is more abstract – more visionary and long run.

To translate visionary policies into actual policies you have to understand political issues. Talking about specific policies – when one does not really appreciate all the nuances – is wrong. You have got to specialize in today's world. Economists can say: here are the broad dimensions of the issues and provide a useful perspective, but I do not think economists can come to precise conclusions unless they become politicians too. So I avoid politics. My students are always betting on what political position I might have. Some come out convinced I am a Marxist, others are convinced I am a Libertarian. That pleases me. They do not have the faintest idea where I stand in part because I do not know where I stand myself (*laughter*).

What are your views on Marx's contribution to economics?
I think Marx made some interesting contributions. The problem is Marx was a Ricardian. Marx was limited in the contributions he could make because Ricardo was sending him in the wrong direction (*laughter*). Now, had Marx been a Smithian ...

Do you agree with Keynes that politicians and policy makers are usually the 'slaves of some defunct economist'?
Yes, but I would add an addendum that economists are also the slaves of current politicians (*laughter*).

You exhibit tremendous enthusiasm for economics and an equal enthusiasm for teaching economics. You clearly regard teaching and what we as economists teach as very important. What makes you so enthusiastic about economics?
I think economics has really important things to say. It provides numerous important insights. The market and how it works never ceases to amaze me. You have all these people pushing for their own benefit and somehow it gets organized and the system seems to work. So the same thing that attracted early economists to these issues is what attracts me. When you are amazed at something it is fun to teach other people. You want to show them how beautiful this is.

Do you take an interest in what is going on in Europe and the rest of the world?
Sure. I take an interest in what is going on, but in the same way that I have nothing to say about specific US policies I have nothing specific to say about European policy. I regard the entire world as my laboratory. So, what is

happening in Europe in terms of the unemployment rate is very important. What is happening in Eastern Europe is fascinating. On my sabbatical my wife and I took the kids and went around the world, met with economists, to see what is going on in places like China, to really get a feel for what was going on.

You also spent some time in Bulgaria. Did you learn anything from that?
Well, we were brought over to teach Western economics, and to explain what economic policies Bulgaria should follow. I made it very clear that I did not know what policies to follow because that decision needed a lot more institutional information than I had. But I could say: here is where markets tend to work, and here is where they do not. The political fights within the Universities were over how much the former Marxists would maintain control and how much the control would evolve to others. It was interesting but I do not think my contribution was large.

A key issue at present in Europe is whether or not there should be monetary union. Have you taken any interest in this area? Are you in favour of EMU?
I would have to study the politics of it in much more detail before I could make a judgement. Would EMU have advantages for some countries? Yes, absolutely. Will it have disadvantages for others? Yes, absolutely. Where does one come out on it? I am fairly neutral on that because I have not studied the issue enough. So it really comes down to the same reaction I have to all policy debates which is, yeah, I think I can specify here are the arguments; but to really take a firm policy position I would feel that I have to be part of the political discussions. It is a judgement call. It is not an issue in which economic theory, or previous economic experience, says one side is right, and the other one is wrong. So it fits with my view that economic theory is an organizing principle of how to approach something. It does not provide clear-cut answers.

Supposing you received a telephone call inviting you to Washington as a policy adviser. Would that be attractive?
No. Absolutely not. I cannot stand cocktail parties (*laughter*). Besides there would definitely be no call coming because I am known for saying outrageous things at all the wrong times (*laughter*).

But it is much easier to be a critic than to be the person who actually has to put their head on the line and make a decision. In the final instance someone has to take decisions.
I fully agree. All I am saying is that I am not the person to do it. My interest is in trying to understand issues. I have totally given up all short-run policy

influence. Besides who in their right mind would leave Vermont for Washington (*laughter*).

Olivier Blanchard
(b. 1948)

Copyright: L. Barry Hetherington

Olivier Blanchard is currently Class of 1941 Professor of Economics at Massachusetts Institute of Technology. He is best known for his work on a number of macroeconomic issues including price rigidities, the effects of fiscal policy, the origin of relatively high unemployment in Western Europe, and more recently economic problems associated with transition in Eastern Europe.

We interviewed Professor Blanchard in his office at Harvard University on 30 October 1997, when he was on a year's leave from MIT.

BACKGROUND INFORMATION

Where and when did you first study economics?
I started studying economics in Paris in 1966. But it was not until the events of 1968 that I became truly interested. I stayed in France until 1973 and then came to MIT to study for a PhD, which I received in 1977.

You are known in particular for your work in macroeconomics. What kindled your interest in macroeconomics?
It was largely an accident. I had come to MIT with two goals. The first, modest, one was simply to reconcile and integrate the Marxist historical and

229

neoclassical traditions. After a couple of days, I concluded that that task was probably beyond me (*laughter*). The second was to study development economics. But I found that field in complete disarray – fortunately, things have changed recently and the field is thriving again. Now macroeconomics at that time was very exciting – especially at MIT, with Franco Modigliani, Robert Solow, Stanley Fischer, and one year after I came, Rudi Dornbusch. Rational expectations had just been introduced into macroeconomics and there was a nearly infinite set of issues to revisit with the new tools, a dream for graduate students. *Ex post*, I find macroeconomics more exciting than (nearly) anything else, although I do wonder sometimes how much of that is self-justifying – I don't think I would have had the patience to be, say, a labour economist! I like to think big – although not too big – and macroeconomics fulfils that need well.

Which economists have had an influence on your own work?
In terms of research style, I have been heavily influenced by Bob Solow and by Stanley Fischer. Both of them were my advisers and I have tried to adopt their unpretentious intellectual style. In terms of my approach to macroeconomics, and at a slightly more methodological level, I have been influenced by Rudi Dornbusch, and indirectly by his teacher, Robert Mundell. The message I got from them was look for the central issues, and write the simplest model which captures them: models are about clarifying your thoughts, and explaining them to others. Along the same lines, another name which springs to mind is that of Jim Tobin.

Have you found that your European background has given you a different perspective from American economists on macroeconomic issues and problems?
Probably, but not in any simple way. I chose economics out of social concerns. This motivation was shaped not only by the events of 1968 in France but also by a number of important issues in Europe. And, when it comes to work on macroeconomic issues, I am naturally led to look beyond what is happening in the United States.

EVOLUTION OF MACROECONOMICS

The publication of Keynes's General Theory *shaped the evolution of macroeconomic analysis in the postwar period. What do you regard to be the essential message of the* General Theory?
I am no expert on the *General Theory*. For me the main message is the importance of aggregate demand. In the short run, if aggregate demand is

low, output and employment will also be low. I have always been fascinated by the way Keynes thought about the relationship between saving and investment. I suspect I could have looked at that relation forever and thought about it forever in the old classical way – that the interest rate would clear the market for loanable funds. I regard the conceptual breakthrough provided by Keynes on the relation between saving and investment – that output will do the adjustment – to be absolutely fundamental. Once you see the IS–LM model it becomes obvious how different Keynesian analysis is from the previous way of thinking about things.

The General Theory *grew out of the experience of the Great Depression. Which of the many explanations of the Great Depression do you find most persuasive?*
Again, I am no expert on the Great Depression. My sense is that the Great Depression resulted from an autonomous fall in aggregate demand, with probably an important role for bubbles in the stock market After this, it is important to take account of the negative effects of deflation – the fact that when prices fall it is not necessarily for the better. The main lessons I draw from the Great Depression are that aggregate demand can fall for no obvious reason *ex ante*, and that the adjustment mechanisms which are supposed to get the economy back on its feet can actually produce perverse effects. These two lessons are just as relevant today as they were in the 1930s.

Following the Keynes v Classics debate mainstream macroeconomics gradually evolved into what Samuelson (1955) referred to as the neoclassical synthesis. What went wrong with the neoclassical synthesis?
The neoclassical synthesis basically fell out of favour for two main reasons, one bad and one good. The bad reason is that it had become boring – the breakthroughs provided by Keynes, the IS–LM model, the MPS model had all been worked out, so that, when my generation came to the scene, it appeared that all that remained to do was to clean up details, not a thrilling prospect. I suspect this tends to happen to many paradigms – they can die of old age even if they are right. The good reason was the increasing intellectual tension caused by the reliance, on the one hand, on optimizing behaviour to explain consumption and investment, and, on the other, the unabashed empiricism and lack of underlying theory in explaining price and wage setting.

How important to the development of macroeconomics was the monetarist counter-revolution and in particular the work of Milton Friedman?
I have a sense that Milton Friedman had been put into a corner arguing about the slope of the curves in the standard model and that he didn't really want to be there. He got out of it in his 1967 Presidential Address to the American

Economic Association on the role of monetary policy, and that Address was very important in changing macroeconomics. There is no doubt that he succeeded in changing the dynamics of the field and that his work had a tremendous influence on the next generation of economists, including people like Robert Lucas.

But we don't hear much about monetarism any more. Why has monetarism ceased to be an important force in macroeconomics?
There are two main reasons. First, monetarism essentially focused on only one issue, a bit like the Green Party in politics. If you only concentrate on money you are not going to be able to explain a whole host of other important macroeconomic issues. Second, the main message of monetarism has become part of the common wisdom, and, as such, nearly invisible. I am struck by how stable monetary policy and low inflation are now considered to be an absolute necessity for macroeconomic stability, especially in Europe.

Would you agree that by the mid-1970s a modified mainstream model, incorporating a vertical long-run Phillips curve and the influence of supply-side shocks, could explain the main macroeconomic phenomena of the period, in particular stagflation?
Yes. Although the mainstream model was initially attacked for its inability to explain stagflation, this was not due to a fundamental flaw in the model. The problem had more to do with the unpleasant fact that we rarely have enough imagination to guess what is going to happen next. And we had not thought of the effects of an increase in the price of oil before it happened. Once supply-side shocks and rational expectations were introduced, the mainstream model worked quite well, and has worked well to this day.

Looking back how do you now view the importance of the contributions of Robert Lucas and other leading new classicists in the 1970s to the development of macroeconomics?
The main specific contribution – the introduction of rational expectations – was important both because it made us question all the earlier propositions, and the extent to which these relied on non-rational expectations. Lucas, however, has been much less successful in offering an alternative view to the mainstream. I don't think that, in this respect, the Prescott real business cycle view which took over in the 1980s has been much more successful.

In your intermediate macroeconomics textbook (Blanchard, 1997a) you say that while 'most economists do not believe that the real business cycle approach provides a convincing explanation of major fluctuations in output, the approach has nevertheless proved useful'. In what ways do you feel that the approach has enhanced our understanding of macroeconomics?

That goes back to a number of issues we have been discussing. Lucas convinced the profession of the need to go back to first principles. The real business cycle approach gave us a natural starting point. It has become clear that one cannot stop there, but we now have a structure in which we can introduce imperfections, be it in the goods, the labour, or the credit and financial markets, and see where that leads us. While Keynes gave us a way of thinking about the world but without any specific technical tools, proponents of the real business cycle approach have done just the opposite. They have given us nice tools. It is for us to use them to get somewhere interesting.

Some of your published work features in Robert Gordon's (1990) Journal of Economic Literature *survey of new Keynesian economics, as well as the collection of articles on new Keynesianism edited by Greg Mankiw and David Romer (1991). Do you regard yourself as a new Keynesian economist?*

No. In general I don't like labels. Furthermore, while new Keynesian analysis has clarified our understanding of nominal price and wage setting, beyond that it has not gone very far. Its more general message is that imperfections are important. But while it has given us more plausible theories of how individual price decisions lead to price inertia it has not yet provided us with a coherent vision of the macroeconomy.

Do you think that nominal price rigidity can be successfully explained by menu costs?

My view, expressed in a book co-written with Stan Fischer (Blanchard and Fischer, 1989), is that if you take a conventional neoclassical economy and introduce menu costs you get nowhere. Modern economies are imperfect in many ways and these imperfections, which have nothing to do with menu costs, are essential in understanding goods, labour and credit markets. One of the symptoms of these imperfections is that in many of these markets the relevant prices do not seem to adjust very much to shifts in demand – there are 'real rigidities'. This particular symptom is important because when you combine it with discrete adjustment of individual prices then you get a lot of action. But you really need both types of imperfections; if you just have the second one, menu costs, it doesn't really get you anywhere.

I also think the term 'menu costs' has been a public relations disaster. There is something fundamental about nominal price setting which goes far beyond menu costs. The reason we actually use a numeraire to quote prices is because it is incredibly convenient; for the very same fundamental reason, we do not want to change these quoted prices every five minutes. These two things come together, and are part and parcel of a monetary economy. They imply that not all prices are going to change all the time, so that any change in the price of money is going to involve millions, if not billions, of individual decisions. It is thus no great puzzle that in nearly any stable monetary economy movements in the price level will be sluggish, and that movements in aggregate demand will affect interest rates and output.

Robert Gordon (1990) has identified efficiency wage theory as an important area within new Keynesian economics. What are your views on efficiency wage theory?
Well, while it doesn't add up to a whole theory of wage determination it is one of the important pieces of the whole puzzle. Efficiency wage theory has moved many people away from the competitive labour market paradigm to an alternative model which is more appealing, and has important macroeconomic implications. But there are many other ways to think about wage determination, from individual and collective bargaining, which are likely to be as relevant.

During the past few years there appears to be less division within macroeconomics than was the case, say, five years ago. What do you regard to be the consensus position on the core of macroeconomics today?
As I have written a concluding chapter on this in my textbook I will not risk contradicting myself here (*laughter*). My sense is that there is consensus that in the short run shifts in aggregate demand affect output and that in the medium and long run supply-side factors dominate. Most economists admit that movements in nominal money affect output for some time, although some freely admit that they do not quite know why.

In terms of methodology there is also fairly widespread agreement that we are not going to understand fluctuations without introducing imperfections in a number of markets. We have now moved beyond the real business cycle versus new Keynesian characterization of macroeconomics. For example, Cambridge (USA) has accepted many of the methodological suggestions of the Midwest and the Midwest is moving away from the unreconstructed Ramsey–Prescott model. All this makes macroeconomics even more confusing (*laughter*). But a complete, successful, definitive, integration is just around the corner (*laughter*).

A few years ago (Blanchard, 1992) you made a plea for return to more pragmatic macroeconomics suggesting that macroeconomists had created a 'bewildering array' of 'monsters' which had taken the discipline of macroeconomics away from 'data-oriented research'. Do you think that this development was in part the inevitable result of the incentive to differentiate products within academia?

At the time, I indeed thought that there was too much fascination with modelling, and too little attention to facts. Things have improved. In the end the process of elimination works, and irrelevant or ill conceived stuff eventually disappears. But it is often a slow process.

UNEMPLOYMENT

Do you think that the distinction that many economists used to make between voluntary and involuntary unemployment is still a useful one to make?
No. I agree with Lucas on this. The labour market is a decentralized market, with many jobs and many unemployed workers. In such a market, if you desperately want a job, any job, you typically can get one. But I also believe that when unemployment is 13 per cent, as it is now in France, most of the people do not enjoy being unemployed, and that such a high rate of unemployment reflects a number of market failures. But this is based on abstract reasoning, not on trying to measure involuntary unemployment.

Is there any significant difference between the concept of a natural rate of unemployment and NAIRU?
My own semantics are the following. I think of the natural, or the equilibrium rate of unemployment as a conceptual construct, namely as the rate of unemployment that would prevail if there were no nominal rigidities. I think of the NAIRU as an empirical construct, as the rate of unemployment at which inflation is constant. Under plausible assumptions, the NAIRU actually corresponds to the natural rate, thus providing us with a way of measuring the natural rate by looking at the unemployment–inflation relation.

During the 1980s you wrote a number of papers utilizing the concept of hysteresis to explain the rise of unemployment in Europe (see Blanchard and Summers, 1986, 1987). Are you still as enthusiastic about this approach?
You are catching me at a bad time. My recent work has led me to shift my views somewhat, something I hate to do – at least once the previous views are in print (*laughter*). My current view is that you can go a fairly long way in explaining the rise of unemployment in Europe without hysteresis, far further than I thought when I wrote those papers with Larry Summers. I have a sense that you can explain much of the rise in unemployment in Europe at least up to the mid-1980s by the impact of workers' aspirations not being in line with the realities of the time. Despite the slowdown in productivity growth, wage demands kept increasing, resulting in steadily higher unemployment. The interesting question is why unemployment has remained so high: wage aspirations must now have adjusted, and the price

of oil has fallen. This is where I used to think hysteresis was a natural answer. More recently I have come to the conclusion that there has been something else at work, which in many ways appears quite Marxist! In the same way that there was a wage push by workers until the mid-1980s, there appears to have been a wage pull by firms since the mid-1980s. I am still struggling with the best way of thinking about it. One way is that, since the mid-1980s, firms have reduced labour hoarding, laying workers off and generating more unemployment, as well as generating higher profits (profits are very high in Europe today; profit shares are higher than at any time since the Second World War). If I am right, these higher profits should eventually lead to more capital and more employment; but this may be some time in coming.

So I now believe you can go a long way in explaining why unemployment is still high in Europe without appealing to hysteresis effects. At the same time I continue to believe that once you have had high unemployment for a long time, society changes in many ways, and many of these changes imply a higher equilibrium rate of unemployment. Sociological and psychological changes take place: it becomes OK to be unemployed, OK to use the safety net. There is also often a political economy reaction: faced with high unemployment, governments feel compelled to offer a more generous safety net. All these are potential channels for hysteresis.

Given your analysis what policies would you advocate to reduce the high level of unemployment in Europe?
In many countries, unemployment benefits need to be tightened, employment protection needs to be decreased. However, trying to push reforms of that kind through when starting from a position of high unemployment is neither socially acceptable nor, in our democracies, politically feasible. The right solution would be to use demand policies to trigger growth, and use growth to sustain reforms. Unfortunately, for a country like France, given the constraints of the Maastricht Treaty, there is really no margin for using fiscal and monetary policy. The hope is that growth will come on its own, and allow for a virtuous cycle of growth feeding reforms, and reforms feeding growth. It may happen: after all, profits are high, the firms quite competitive, and if consumers turned optimistic, growth would validate their optimism. On the other hand, it may not.

During recent years unemployment in the UK has fallen quite significantly from its peak of 10.5 per cent in 1993, while unemployment in much of Europe has remained stubbornly high. Do you believe that this recent fall in unemployment in the UK has been the result of policies which have increased labour market flexibility?

No, I take a largely Keynesian view of the recent UK experience. In the UK, unlike the rest of Europe, there has been an old-fashioned expansion which has resulted in a decrease in unemployment. While there are important differences between the UK and continental Europe in terms of labour market structure, the proximate cause of the more recent fall in unemployment in the UK has been expansionary macroeconomic policy. What is interesting is that these circumstances have allowed structural changes to be made, in the right direction, in a number of labour market and welfare programmes. It is exactly the policy mix which I would like to see happen on the other side of the channel.

EUROPEAN MONETARY UNION AND ECONOMIC POLICY

Do you think that European monetary union will proceed on schedule? If so, what form is it likely to take and what are the likely economic consequences?
My sense is that it will almost surely take place on schedule. Given that governments in continental Europe have asked for so many sacrifices in the name of European monetary union, they cannot now turn around and give it up. I am also nearly certain that it will take the form of a large, rather than a small, EMU because countries like Spain, Portugal and Italy are passionate about joining – it is the club that they want to belong to.

This being said, as a macroeconomist I cannot help but worry about the implications of the EMU. The EU is most definitely not an optimal currency area. In my work on US regions I found that the reason the United States worked well as a common currency area – an area composed of the 50 states – was because of labour mobility. In Europe, labour mobility is just not on the cards. So, on macroeconomic grounds, I am against EMU. At the same time I suspect that the microeconomic arguments in favour have been undersold. The fact that many businesses compute costs in the same currency is leading them to think quite differently about location within the European market. Businesses are going to be much more aggressive in locating in some places and relocating from other places. As a result, there is going to be tremendous pressure on governments to unify their legislations, in order to avoid losing one industry or another. This is largely for the good.

Do you think that monetary union will inevitably lead to closer fiscal integration?
No. Furthermore, if you mean by this larger transfers to states which are doing poorly, it is not clear that it should happen. It depends on whether shocks are transitory or permanent. Take again the case of states in the US. Most of the shocks affecting US states are permanent, not transitory – for

example, a good produced in the region becomes obsolete and is no longer in demand. If the Federal government uses fiscal transfers to offset the decline in income in the state, it will also prevent the required adjustment the state must eventually go through: either labour should move out, or wages should decline and make the state competitive. Systematic fiscal transfers in response to permanent shocks will basically lead to welfare programmes for declining states. The lesson applies to countries of the EU just the same: fiscal transfers are a dangerous tool, and are no substitute for wage flexibility and labour mobility. But there is little reason to worry: the political reality is that fiscal transfers across states will remain limited in Europe!

Few economists now advocate an activist discretionary role for fiscal policy to stabilize short-run fluctuations. Do you agree that fiscal policy should be geared to achieving long-run targets rather than stabilization?
When looking at fiscal policy, macroeconomists have become much more aware of public finance issues. Like you, I am struck by the fact that there is so little talk about using fiscal policy for stabilization purposes. In the US that is partly due to the success of monetary policy which is much easier to use than fiscal policy. The other element is the higher level of distrust of governments among economists than there used to be. This is part of a larger evolution in economics. When I was in graduate school, the focus was on what governments should do. The focus is now much more on what governments actually do, and how to tailor policy advice while taking these political realities into account.

The new Labour Government in the UK on being elected immediately established a much greater degree of central bank independence. Is central bank independence important for establishing anti-inflation credibility?
Independence is important, but it is also important how credibility is established once you have independence. I disagree with the prevalent European view that the only way you can establish credibility is to show that you are incredibly tough, care only about inflation, and don't give a damn about output and employment. That view has been extremely costly. In contrast to Europe, in the US Alan Greenspan has shown that credibility can be established while pursuing a responsible and flexible monetary policy.

How do you view the modern political business cycle literature inspired by economists such as Alberto Alesina? (See Alesina, 1989.)
I have learned a lot from the new political economy literature. It has led to a lot of good descriptive work. It has certainly made many of us far more aware of how to shape our recommendations so as to take into account the constraints which come from the political process.

EAST EUROPEAN TRANSITION

What important macroeconomic lessons have you learnt from your work on East European transition? (See Blanchard, 1997b.)
I have first been struck by how you can have very large variations in output which have nothing to do with shifts in aggregate demand or monetary and fiscal policy. I have also been struck at how, in order to understand macroeconomic evolutions, I had to start from microeconomic issues such as governance in state firms, the process and characteristics of privatization, the role of entrepreneurs in private sector growth, the form of the reallocation process and the implications for the nature of unemployment, and so on.

In your American Economic Review paper (Blanchard, 1996) on the theoretical aspects of transition you argue that 'explaining the U-shaped pattern of output is the major theoretical challenge facing economists working in this area'. How do you explain this U-shaped pattern?
In the textbook, removing all distortions leads automatically to an increase in output. In practice, not all distortions are removed. The removal of some makes some problems worse. The required adjustment of some relative prices or relative wages is politically or socially unacceptable. All these are standard second-best arguments. But they have proven to be extremely relevant in explaining the decline in output during transition.

What in your view is the optimal sequencing of policies to ensure a smooth transition from a planned to a market economy?
Explicit second-best models typically deliver ambiguous messages. They rarely deliver big-bang recommendations. For example, do not eliminate all subsidies at once, if the result is such a level of disruptions as to kill the embryonic new private sector. Do not try stabilization if, politically, you are not powerful enough to stop subsidies to state firms. Do not do privatization if price signals are still very noisy. And so on. But, in practice, other considerations dominate sequencing. Governments often have short windows of opportunity. It is wise to use these windows as much as they can be used. It is this tension that makes recommendations as to sequencing or timing so interesting but also so difficult.

ECONOMIC GROWTH

Do you agree with the view expressed by Robert Barro and Xavier Sala-i-Martin (1995) that economic growth is the part of macroeconomics that really matters?

One cannot disagree with the fact that if you want to increase output, then increasing the growth rate by 1 per cent will overwhelm the effect of reducing fluctuations. While this has always been understood, in the past economists thought that their ability to smooth the cycle was substantially better than their ability to generate a 1 per cent increase in growth. So far the more recent work on growth has not led to obvious policy conclusions which would lead to higher growth in the world. At the same time if one has an insight on what affects growth, then one should work on growth rather than fluctuations. Since the mid-1980s Paul Romer and Robert Lucas have stimulated a lot of extremely interesting research in this area.

Recently a number of intermediate textbook writers (for example Hall and Taylor, 1997; Mankiw, 1997a) have moved their discussion of economic growth to the early part of their textbooks. What made you decide to leave your discussion, in its more traditional location, towards the latter part of your textbook? (See Blanchard, 1997a.)
I actually thought very hard about whether to place a discussion of growth before or after a discussion of the short and medium run. I suspect what I ended up doing has lost me some sales (*laughter*). But I did it for very much the same reason I gave in answering your previous question. While growth is a fundamental issue, my mother taught me that you talk about an issue only if you have something to say. When it comes to short-run fluctuations we have models which are amazingly good and powerful – the IS–LM model and the Mundell–Fleming model are just incredible machines, and the man on the street would not do as well as we can do with these models. When it comes to growth we have a nice model, the Solow growth model, which, however, is largely useless as it takes technological progress as unexplained. As economists we can stress the importance of education and research and development for growth, but that is not very different from what the man on the street would say! So I decided to start my discussion of macroeconomics where we know something, the short run, then move to the medium run, and only then to talk about the long run which is extremely interesting but about which we still have so few insights.

One final question. What areas are you currently working on?
Since 1990, I have spent much of my time working on transition in Eastern Europe. I am fascinated by the interplay both between micro and macro issues, and between economics and politics. In the last year, I have also returned to unemployment. I am focusing on what I call 'medium run' evolutions, these decade-to-decade movements in unemployment, capital shares, capital–output ratios, that are neither business cycle movements, nor steady state growth. This should keep me busy for some time.

Franco Modigliani
(b. 1918)

Franco Modigliani is currently Institute Professor Emeritus of Economics and Finance at the Massachusetts Institute of Technology. He is best known for his seminal contributions to macroeconomic and monetary theory, the theory of saving and the theory of corporate finance. In 1985 he was awarded the Nobel Prize in Economics: 'For his pioneering analyses of saving and of financial markets'.

We interviewed Professor Modigliani in his office at MIT on 31 October 1997.

BACKGROUND INFORMATION

As an undergraduate you initially studied law. Why did you switch to studying economics?
I would say it was largely by chance as I recount in my autobiography, which I am writing at the moment. My father, who was a well-known paediatrician, died very young and everyone expected me to follow in his footsteps. Although my mother expected me to become a doctor, when I went to register for medicine I realized that I could not stand the sight of blood (*laughter*). So I decided that to train to become a doctor was not a good idea. I also remember an episode relating to my father, a man of very nice humour. He

used to tell the story that our name, Modigliani, came from a town called Modigliani, which is above Bologna, and that the emblem of the town was a sow with a suckling pig which he thought was a great expression of useful economic activity (*laughter*). So I decided to try economics. I actually registered in law because there was no economics school as such at that time at the University of Rome, only a business school. So I went into law and in my second year there was a national competition, actually a set of competitions launched by the university students, one of which was in economics. I participated because I had plenty of time to waste. Law was not very taxing, all you had to do was cram in the last month before the exams and so I entered the competition. In addition, because it was useful for me to make some money, I translated German articles for one of the libraries, actually the Association of Commerce Library, and the articles were all about price control because that was the big issue in Germany at that time. The competition that was announced that year was about price controls, so I was already an expert on the subject (*laughter*). I won first prize and everybody said 'well, evidently you have great promise in economics'. It was an interesting piece, in the sense that what I essentially said was unfavourable to price controls. Under fascism you were supposed to say price controls were wonderful. The position I took was quite clever because I said that price control is really quite good if it imitates closely the market mechanism (*laughter*).

You reacted against the fascist regime in Italy. Were you ever attracted to Marxist ideas in economics?

No, never. I have never had much acquaintance with Marxist economics. It is one of the areas in my history of economic thought that I have been lacking. My opposition to the regime was not based on the class struggle but on the fact that I disapproved of what they were doing. My father was against the regime but as he died when I was only 13 I only knew very vaguely that he was against it because he told us he had voted against in the plebiscite in 1929. Then I joined the youth organization, when I was a student, because they had a skiing section and I loved to go skiing. But I began to be very upset with the war in Abyssinia, the Ethiopian war. I felt this was a great injustice despite all the propaganda. This view was then reinforced following the aggression against Spain, when the fascists gave their support to the side of Franco. Because of this I felt completely revolted and then I became in principle opposed to the regime, but not as a member of any organized group. After winning the national competition in economics I became secretary for organizing the next year's competition. All the Littori, the previous years' prize winners, were invited to Palermo, and there I met a group of people who were violently anti-fascist. Among them was a man who later became very well known in a rather sombre way. He was the man who led a group of resistance fighters that ambushed a German detail. His name was Alicata. As a result the Germans executed 300 civilians.

So, at that time I began to have some more formal relations with the anti-fascist group. Although I was never very active in the group I felt very strongly against fascism. So I began to apply for scholarships in the United States to give me a chance to leave Italy. I had just married and the whole family came to America. I began studying at the New School in New York and by that time I had no doubt that I wanted to study economics. I did not know the work of Keynes yet. When I arrived in New York in 1939, on the last boat from Europe, it was clear that it would not be possible to return to Europe because by the time we landed the war had begun. In that first year I made three great discoveries in economics. The first was Jacob Marshak, my teacher and mentor, from whom I learned my style. Second, he introduced me to mathematical economics. He told me I had promise but that I couldn't progress unless I studied some mathematics – so I did it and greatly enjoyed it. Then finally he introduced me to Keynes and Schumpeter, but what struck me most was Keynes.

THEORETICAL DEVELOPMENTS: KEYNES AND KEYNESIANISM

Do you recall when you first read the General Theory *and what your first impressions were of the book?*
Well the answer I can give is not very good because I read Hicks's IS–LL article before I read Keynes. So by the time I read Keynes I knew what to look for. But I remember being struck by the breadth of ideas and by the many side issues which turn out to be very important. One proposition that I always love is the statement in chapter 19 that if trade unions were really capable of reducing money wages so as to ensure full employment we could have in effect monetary policy conducted by the trade unions instead of the central bank (*laughter*).

The interpretation of the General Theory *provided by John Hicks in 1937 had immense influence on the course of the Keynesian Revolution. Do you think Hicks's paper was a good interpretation of Keynes's work?*
Yes, a truly outstanding one. But in my autobiography I give a different interpretation of Keynes and I think that my interpretation is much easier for the layman to understand. The first step of my Keynesian construction is to forget about liquidity preference. It is an exceedingly important concept but at first forget about it – just say that the demand for money depends on output times price, XP, and is proportional to it, say $Md = kPX$. Then if prices are flexible the

money market is cleared (*Md = M*) by the price level. But if prices are rigid the money market is cleared by output *X*, and hence by unemployment. That is a different view but I think it is very understandable. The great contribution of Keynes was to explain the mechanism by which an excess demand for money leads to a contraction of output, and there you need liquidity preference and the multiplier. Then you can see that unemployment is not a disequilibrium mechanism but an equilibrating mechanism for clearing the money market.

Your 1944 Econometrica *paper was also tremendously influential. How do you view that contribution now?*
Looking back I feel I could have done a much better job (*laughter*). Now I would have done something different. Of course I feel I was absolutely right in saying that the essence of Keynesian economics is wage rigidity. That is Keynes! We also know that the empirical evidence demonstrates the importance of *downward* wage rigidity. Actually Keynes could have said that wages do not fall, but instead continue to rise no matter what unemployment you have. The whole European experience of the 1970s and the 1980s is one in which unemployment continues to increase and is accompanied by rising nominal wages. So I still feel that this is the fundamental issue. If you do not have wage rigidity you have the classical model.

When you wrote that 1944 paper how aware were you of the Pigou effect argument?
The Pigou effect argument was not considered at all in that paper because essentially consumption was not a function of wealth. The Pigou argument only comes into effect when consumption is a function of wealth. However, I am very proud that I disposed of the Pigou argument once and for all in my paper on the life cycle hypothesis. The second paper (1980) has a whole section devoted to showing that the Pigou effect does not exist and that the reason it does not exist is because it is a transitory effect. It is true that you can make people wealthier by a one time deflation. But the effect is transitory and you do not solve the problem. What you need is *not* a one time fall but a *continuous fall or deflation.* But even that will not work because people cannot fail to see that the deflation means that the real interest rate is higher and therefore you lose on investment what you might gain in consumption. So it essentially does not exist and this is what we showed in the Modigliani–Brumberg paper, the one that was not published until 1980. We completed the paper before Richard Brumberg died in 1955, but when he died I was so upset that I did not look at it again for a long time. It was only finally published in my collected papers, pretty much in its original form.. The Pigou effect turned out to be a diversion which for a while was appealing, but its effects are transient and cannot be made permanent.

There are numerous interpretations of Keynes's General Theory. *What do you regard to be the main or essential message to come out of the* General Theory*?*

The one I mentioned before, namely that when prices are rigid and if there is insufficient (real) money, a fall in output or unemployment is the mechanism that clears the money market – that I think is the fundamental message. Of course the shortage can be eliminated through an expansion of the money supply. Also important is how a shortage of money leads to a contraction and here you need liquidity preference because the effect of the shortage is to raise interest rates. You also need the investment function because the effect of higher interest rates is to reduce investment. Furthermore you need the multiplier because when you reduce investment you reduce income. I regard these as tremendously important contributions which were needed to arrive at the main message of the *General Theory*. I like to equate Keynes with Einstein. Einstein also had to do a lot of preliminary work to finally get to a fundamental result. I think that in the teaching of Keynes from now on I will use my new approach because then you understand the role of each mechanism. The fact that the demand for money depends on the interest rate *per se* is of no interest, it was more or less known, and what consequence does it have if you have price flexibility, none! It does not mean that you will get unemployment. It is only when it is combined with the rigidity of wages, and an investment function and multiplier, that you really get the important message.

Why do you think there are so many different interpretations of the General Theory*?*

I do not really have a good answer to your question. I have always assumed everyone fully agreed with my view except by way of emphasis (*laughter*). Because of limiting cases and so on you can take one of these mechanisms and do a great deal with that mechanism and say that liquidity preference, for example, is the most important concept. I am not sure what other interpretations there are.

What about the work of Robert Clower (1965) and Axel Leijonhufvud (1968)? Did you find their interpretations convincing or interesting?

Not very much. I have always had a great deal of difficulty understanding the idea of notional demand. I did not think that this really made any important or essential contribution to our understanding of Keynes.

Robert Lucas is very critical of the General Theory. *In Arjo Klamer's (1984) book Lucas expresses the view that he finds the* General Theory *almost incomprehensible. What do you think causes that kind of reaction?*

It is very different with rational expectations because if rational expectations were true there would be no wage rigidity and no Keynes. So the Lucas contributions lead to a very different non-Keynesian position because you have to find some other cause of instability. Wage rigidity is very simple and it is a fact of fife. These people have to find all kinds of other reasons, such as equilibrium business cycle ideas. Of course I have always believed in the equilibrium business cycle and I have even written a couple of papers about the forces that do tend to impart cyclical behaviour to the economy – fundamentally stock-flow relations – that have that implication. This is made easier with rigid wages. In that sense these developments do not surprise me. But to say that all unemployment can be accounted for without wage rigidity, that is of course where I completely disagree with new classical economists. These people have not shown this and will never be able to do it. They will never be able to explain to me why Europe now has 9, 10, 12 per cent unemployment while the United States has 5 per cent. In the 1960s Europe had 3 per cent unemployment while we in the United States had 5 per cent and Europe had lower unemployment down to the mid-1980s. So Europe has changed enormously while we have not. Now that is due to wage rigidity combined with the actions of the German Bundesbank, a combination of effects, namely rigid wages and an incompetent monetary policy coming out of Germany.

What do you mean by incompetent monetary policy?
They do not understand Keynes, nor for that matter do they understand economics. Fundamentally, if you do not have enough money, and wages are not very flexible, you are never going to get full employment. So I think that is the actual explanation. All the other explanations that people try to give are basically worthless.

Keynes was very much concerned with unemployment in the 1920s and 1930s. How would you explain European unemployment in the 1990s?
I have written a couple of articles on this. One is my 1994 Tinbergen Lecture 'The Shameful Rate of Unemployment in the EMS: Causes and Cures' (1996). I say it is shameful because it is due to poor policy. I go over about seven different explanations that are given and eventually I find that none of them can explain what is happening in Europe. Some explanations are stupid, such as those blaming technological progress. We know that is nonsense because in the United States we never had such high unemployment and technological progress is very rapid here. Another explanation is to blame unemployment on the competition coming from the emerging economies. Again this effect is felt all over the world and yet European unemployment is much higher than in the United States or most other developed countries. So there are a whole series of completely stupid explanations of unemployment. Then there are a

couple that have some value. I agree that an explanation which has some value is that based on the rigidity of the labour contract. Employers have great problems firing people for economic reasons. That is a deterrent to hiring, and it particularly affects young people. If there is a low rate of labour turnover you do not have new people coming in taking up jobs so young people never come in and youth unemployment is very high. But the reason why that is not a sufficient explanation of unemployment is that there is enormous diversity of unemployment within countries. Take Italy for example. In the north the unemployment is probably down to 5 per cent, which is close to full employment. In the south unemployment at the moment is 30 per cent and among young people it is much higher. I was recently in the island of Sardinia where youth unemployment gets up to around 50 per cent. The rigidity is exactly the same because they work with the same unions and under the same contracts. So that cannot be the whole explanation. Although rigidities have declined, if anything unemployment has kept rising. So while reducing rigidities would help, it is not a sufficient or complete explanation.

Do you regard Keynes to have been a great economic theorist worthy of a Nobel Prize?
(*Laughter*) That is a very good question. First of all I regard him as one of the greatest economists of all time. Absolutely. His was a completely novel conception of the monetary mechanism, one that says you clear markets by unemployment. This is very important in the kind of world that we live in today. Now it may be that two centuries ago wages were very flexible and therefore that solved the problem, but in today's world his was a most important contribution. Now about receiving the Nobel Prize, that is a different matter because you have to remember that the Swedes have a very strong mind of their own. It is conceivable that they would not have liked Keynes (*laughter*). I think they would actually because if anything they would probably say *déja vu*, because the initial work on the multiplier concept actually started in Sweden. So I think they would have given Keynes a Nobel Prize, I am pretty sure of that. However, I also think they were wrong not to give a Nobel Prize to the British economist, Joan Robinson, who clearly deserved an award. But, for whatever reason, they decided she would not get one. At the moment I think they are really amiss at not having given one to Edmund Malinvaud, the French economist. He is really a very remarkable man and I think they have given the prize to people with lesser qualifications. So you never know, but Keynes was so great that you could not pass him by (*laughter*). Does anyone doubt that?

Well in previous interviews David Laidler doubted if Keynes would have received the first Nobel Prize in 1969 while Charles Plosser thought that without the work of John Hicks an award to Keynes would have been unlikely – he attributes the influence of Keynes to the IS–LM framework. Robert Lucas does not believe that the General Theory *is a book that students should read but did agree that Keynes would have been an early recipient of the award (see Snowdon, Vane and Wynarczyk, 1994).*

The point about Hicks is really funny (*laughter*). Certainly Hicks did a lot for Keynes, there is no question about that, but Keynes did even more for Hicks (*laughter*). You mention Lucas. The opinion that Lucas has of Keynes is very understandable because Lucas has a logical framework which is absolutely fine. I would say that he deserved the Nobel Prize for having completed the model of rational behaviour. Before Lucas the model was incomplete because expectations were outside the model. Then with the help of my paper with Emile Grunberg (1954) he has formalized the notion of rational expectations. It is not very convincing because if you go into it in detail there are great problems with his model, the problem of the heterogeneity of views. You see Lucas assumes everyone has the same model, then the rational expectation is the one that maps into itself given that model. But if we have different models there is a huge problem. For example, Lucas could never explain the sharp break in the stock market which simply comes from the fact that people have different views and some views dominate the others. But from a logical point of view it is a consistent construction. The problem is that it does not apply to the real world. People do not have rational expectations and there is plenty of evidence which shows this. I have a paper published in 1979 in which I show that the stock market does not know how to value stocks because the nominal interest rate was used to capitalize the real stream and the error lasted for years. Therefore, the market was too low. Since I am foolhardy I went against the fashion of the time which said the market is always right and I published the paper saying that the market was half as high as it should be and in the next four years the market doubled as inflation fell. So my view is that an economist should distinguish between a paradigm from which you start and reality. Rationality is an excellent paradigm from which to start because it has the advantage of a unique answer. If you say I am emotional or I am altruistic it does not tell you very much about what I will do. If you say you are rational then you know what maximization means. But once you have done that you should be able to admit and know when the world does not behave according to the paradigm and see the implications. My complaint about Lucas is that he does not do that and in particular wage rigidity cannot be reconciled with rational expectations because if everyone had rational expectations everyone would know that by taking lower nominal wages they would end up with the same real wage and more employment. Therefore why not take cuts in the nominal wage? The point is people do not believe that if they take a lower wage the consequence will be more employment for everybody.

With rational expectations wages must be flexible and the reason why they are not falling is for some other, God knows what, reason. Then of course Keynesian problems do not exist, so who cares. In other words, in a world of flexible wages there would be no need for Keynes. But since they are in fact rigid or worse all the time, if that is due to some reason other than 'Lucas irrationality', that other reason must be there all the time and you may as well say that wages *are* rigid and therefore Keynesian analysis applies.

STABILIZATION POLICY

During the 1950s and 1960s, in the heyday of the neoclassical synthesis, how did you view the stabilizing role of fiscal and monetary policy?
I very much agreed to it, that both could be used and should be used as I argued in my 1976 AEA Presidential Address (Modigliani, 1977). My support was proved by the fact that I agreed to build the model for the Federal Reserve, the so-called FMP model. It was built in the 1960s, about 1966, and it was to be used for stabilization purposes. So I certainly believed that you could use that model. I have since come to agree that you have to be careful, the Lucas critique has some value, things are not that stable. I also agree with Friedman that even if you have a good model you do not know exactly what will happen if you do certain things, there are lags and so on and so forth. But I still think it was a useful framework for policy analysis and performance. I have built four such models, one for the United States, one for Italy, one for Spain and one for Sweden. In the case of Italy I was in charge of the model for many years, in the case of Spain and Sweden I was a visitor for a while and instructed people on their construction. I still believe in both policies, fiscal and monetary, though the emphasis may have shifted towards giving priority to monetary policy (the appropriate real money supply).

What impact did the Friedman and Schwartz (1963) volume, A Monetary History of the United States, *have on your own thinking? Did it influence you?*
I am completely convinced by the thesis that the Federal Reserve played a major role in both the intensity and length of the Great Depression. Also in taking lessons from that I also believe there are situations where monetary policy may become ineffective. The famous Keynesian liquidity trap case, which I think is really not a relevant one in most situations, may become relevant.

So is it your view that monetary policy can normally have powerful effects?
I have the conviction that if the central bank pursues the wrong policy it can have horrible effects. The interesting thing is that it can have damaging

effects even if wages are very flexible. Take the case of Germany where wages are said to be still rising too fast and the authorities are going to raise interest rates. Suppose they are successful and wages and prices do decline. They can still keep high interest rates by reducing the money supply, no matter how flexible wages are. Central banks can do a lot of harm, as they are doing now in Europe. So I recognize the existence of stabilization policy and anti-stabilization policy (*laughter*). That is what the Germans are doing, destabilizing their economy.

In the early postwar years Keynesianism was often identified with fiscalism. Do any Keynesians still believe in an activist role for fiscal policy?
Of course stabilization policy usually means a combination of fiscal and monetary policy. Now with the work that I have done on the economics of the budget deficit, beginning with an article in the *Economic Journal* in 1961, I have become convinced that one should not use fiscal policy except cyclically. Fiscal policy should not be used as a permanent device because it has undesirable consequences for the future. Because it can reduce investment, monetary policy should therefore be the main weapon in terms of influencing investment. Fiscal policy can help primarily through the influence of built-in stabilizers. Occasionally some additional amount of stimulus may be used but this should be transitory. The main weapon for stabilization policy is monetary policy.

What were your thoughts on Friedman's critique of the conventional view of the Phillips curve in his 1968 AER *paper?*
I think that Milton Friedman's Presidential Address was a very important paper. I think of the vertical Phillips curve as providing a very good example of Thomas Kuhn's notion of changing paradigms. When a new paradigm comes in you forget the old one very quickly and you cannot understand how you could ever have believed the old one. The changing view of the Phillips curve is a very good example of a paradigm change. When I first read that paper I did have to rub my eyes a couple of times (*laughter*). But after that it became a very credible story, especially on the inflationary side. I am not convinced that model works on the deflationary side. If you have too much unemployment, will inflation decline to the point where it becomes negative? I do not believe that will happen, although it is not impossible. I think zero inflation is possible. But anyway that is a minor point and certainly when the economy is on the up side I think that if you try to push demand too far you will get accelerating inflation. So I learned a lot and wrote one of the early articles about measuring the non-inflationary rate of unemployment (see Modigliani and Papademos, 1975). There is now a bit of a controversy about terminology. Have you talked to Tobin?

Yes, a few years ago, in 1993.
He has this mania about pointing out that the expression non-inflationary rate of unemployment is wrong because accelerating inflation is not increasing inflation. Essentially accelerating inflation is a second derivative, inflation is a first derivative, the rate of change of prices. Anyway I called it NIRU, non-inflationary rate of unemployment, then it became NAIRU. My name was probably better (*laughter*).

You mention James Tobin. In a recent paper (1995) he has actually commented that Friedman's 1968 paper is 'very likely the most influential article ever published in an economics journal'. Would you accept that comment?
What is the beginning of the ever? (*laughter*) In that era, yes, I would agree, but Friedman also went on to say other things in that paper that were not right and there were also the important contributions of Edmund Phelps. It was a very important idea and Phelps deserves as much credit. They changed an important paradigm because up until then the Phillips curve had been very widely accepted. Now you have to understand that in some sense a very important first step had already been made by Richard Lipsey (1960) who introduced a lag on the rate of inflation. Because after all what is the Friedman statement, it is that the coefficient of the lag is 1. So potentially we already had a very unstable system. For the same rate of unemployment you would get more and more inflation.

Do you agree with Thomas Mayer (1997) that 'much of moderate monetarism has been absorbed into the mainstream of macroeconomics'?
Yes, I hope so. If you are talking about the importance of money, I always believed that anyway (*laughter*). I have always put money at the centre from the very beginning so I have never been surprised by this. But to say it is the only important variable is wrong and the facts have confirmed this to be the case. Milton is remarkable for supporting the idea of how stable velocity is by changing the concept of money each time that velocity becomes unstable (*laughter*). So he has tried them all, and then he goes back to try them again, and there is always one concept of money that eventually works (*laughter*). The trouble is which one. So I do not think that at this point in time people accept that by maintaining a stable rate of growth of the money supply all will be well. I do not think Milton's *k* per cent rule has any standing anymore. I think I won that particular debate (*laughter*). Having said that, there were people who did not believe that money was important. Maybe some of them have been converted, I do not know. Some of them may belong to the Marxian fringe to whom the whole debate does not mean much. My article of 1944, as I explain in my autobiography, was prompted by continuous arguing with Abba Lerner who was really an extreme Keynesian. He believed that

investment was driven by animal spirits and that monetary policy was useless because all it could do was change interest rates and they had no effect on investment. Lerner thought that the only thing you could use to stabilize aggregate demand was fiscal policy. Lerner developed this famous notion that the only purpose of taxation is to prevent inflation (*laughter*). You do not tax to pay for public expenditure, the only purpose of fiscal policy is to maintain stability of the price level. For economists like that, and there certainly have been many, I think that they may have learned something from monetarism including the fact that, on the whole, the stability of the relationship between output and money is greater than one would have expected. The whole discussion and exchange that I and Albert Ando had with Meiselman and Friedman in the early 1960s was a little silly because they and us were using very elementary methods. But in the end that debate did show that both fiscal and monetary policy matter, which is really what I have always believed .

But what about the Lucas, Sargent and Wallace policy ineffectiveness proposition and the distinction between anticipated and unanticipated money which Lucas, in his Nobel Lecture (1996), suggests is one of the most important postwar developments in macroeconomics?
If monetary policy really has no effect because the market is perfectly self-equilibrating then there is some truth to the fact that for it to have any real effect it must be unanticipated and disequilibrating because it creates unexpected effects disrupting the self-equilibrating mechanism. Then you might say that the best thing to do is to avoid surprises by having a very even keel. But I disagree with all of that because if you have wage rigidity then you do need active policy to maintain full employment. So the whole issue really boils down to, who really believes that wages are perfectly flexible? From this angle there is of course another interesting and important contribution, that of Stanley Fischer (1977) with respect to wage contracts. Well if wage contracts create a problem my question always is, why not get rid of them? If everybody understands the consequences of wage rigidity then get rid of contracts because they cause unemployment.

What is your preferred way of modelling expectations? Do you think rational expectations is the best hypothesis we have?
No. I believe, as I mentioned before, that it is a good paradigm to start from. The old way of modelling expectations in terms of what has happened in the past, adaptive expectations, even sophisticated models of that kind are a good approximation, but in many cases can be improved upon by allowing for additional information. I am now working on a model of stock market bubbles and I find I have to use a fairly complex model. Essentially it involves the past, it also involves asking how irrational is the price. So it is certainly

not backward looking, it is forward looking. I think that the simple elegant notion of mapping into yourself really is a useful shortcut. It gives you another rule, like taking a simple lag of the past, which students love because it is mathematically very easy to manipulate. We have learned a lot from the general notion of rational expectations. Remember that Lucas was originally at Carnegie Mellon University and his work was preceded by two other important contributions which also came out of Carnegie Mellon. First there was the 1961 paper by John Muth, a student of mine, who essentially said that people cannot be that irrational, they cannot just form expectations in such a mechanical way that would make them lose all the time. Then there was also our even earlier contribution, the Modigliani–Grunberg (1954) proposition, that there is an expectation that maps into itself. But in general I think the future way to model expectations will involve considering the rational expectations mechanism as one possibility. Clearly if you try to use that hypothesis in the stock market you will find that it provides very unsatisfactory answers because any price can be justified. But most people do not have a model of the economy and the evidence is that wages are rigid. So the future has in store a more flexible kind of mechanism which allows for irrationalities, probably ones that cannot easily be exploited.

In the past 15 years or so the work of the real business cycle school has been very influential. Do you find their arguments in anyway persuasive?
Well I have never been very excited by it because I have seen this kind of idea before. I understand very well that there exists a real cycle that is independent of money, prices and so on, that would exist on its own. So I do not find anything particularly exciting in this literature.

What about the new Keynesian developments, the attempt to improve the supply side of Keynesian models and to find better micro foundations for wage and price rigidities?
Well it is very important first of all to distinguish between nominal and real rigidity. Nominal wages are certainly not rigid in an upwards direction, they are very flexible. For example, during a severe inflation wages could be changing by 10 per cent a day. What is inflexible is real wages and that can be a big problem because to the extent that trade unions can impose a real wage, for example, through indexation, then you can have situations where the real wage is too high and this gets in the way of achieving full employment. Once you have indexation the central bank can no longer control the real money supply and therefore loses control of the economy. I think in general the new Keynesian work is interesting. Gregory Mankiw is one of those people who is brilliant but not very rigorous and he has made a number of bloopers. The insider–outsider models of real wage rigidity are extremely important, espe-

cially the contributions of Assar Lindbeck and others. The insiders do not really give a damn if there is unemployment (*laughter*). That is because they make sure that they are protected. A famous case is in Italy where the unions kept pushing up real wages and unemployment began to rise. The rank and file workers began to get concerned. So in order to be able to keep pushing wages up they created a special unemployment system. Nobody cared about those who had never been employed. But for the insiders, if they became unemployed, they could claim 90 per cent of the regular wage. They were not supposed to be working but in fact did, in the black market, and so it got to be a very privileged position to be in. So the insider–outsider model is a very important part of the unemployment story. There is no effective competition from the people who are out of work, the outsiders. We need to let the real wage be determined by the market by ensuring that the path of nominal wages is fixed in advance. That is what they have done in Italy since 1973. And the path of prices is also agreed in principle. Once you have that, the central bank can concentrate on employment because they do not have to worry that prices will rise. That I think is the real future, and Europe will have to develop that especially if there is a monetary union. In that case policy will have to be co-ordinated. There will have to be a unified wage policy, but not in the sense that all people have the same real wage or the same growth of real wage. It will depend on how productivity changes. More advanced countries will probably have less growth than countries that are developing. This has to be built into the mechanism but at the moment the only unions which are in favour of that are the Italian unions with whom I have worked, and I have helped to persuade them to accept this kind of arrangement.

EUROPEAN ISSUES

Currently the economic debate in Europe is dominated by the issue of EMU. Are you an enthusiast for European Monetary Union?
My answer to this is very simple. So far the march towards the euro has been a disaster which can be measured by constantly rising unemployment. Monetary policy has been dictated by the strongest central bank which is the Bundesbank. I see the combination of a dominant central bank and bad monetary policy as a recipe for disaster. Now the question arises as to what will happen if they move to a new European Central Bank. Will it be dominated by the Bundesbank or will it be able to develop an intelligent policy? In particular will they be able to get out of this naive and completely stupid notion that the central bank should only worry about inflation? The central bank's main concern should be with employment, making sure that there is

no perverse effects on inflation. To a large extent that is a characteristic of the present British system. There it is understood that if wages and prices are rising too fast there will be a more restrictive policy which will cause some increase in unemployment. I think that is the correct way to operate monetary policy. If there is one important thing that we have learned it is that the price level is largely exogenous, it is not affected significantly by unemployment and is therefore difficult to reach with stabilization policies. Stabilization policies mainly affect employment. Now by exogenous I mean the same thing that Keynes meant. The price level is given historically and then it evolves in directions which depend somewhat on history, somewhat on tradition, somewhat on the aggressiveness of the unions and so on. In the postwar period we have had very aggressive unions who have tried to push nominal wages up creating inflation or unemployment or both. I think we have got to understand that to get a stable macroeconomic system we have to get labour to agree to a nominal wage policy, and I think that is the future way forward. Textbooks in the future will not say that the price level is determined by the money supply but that the money supply is determined by the price level.

With respect to the issue of unemployment do European policy makers have any lessons to learn from the experience of the United States labour market? There are two distinct issues here. One is, to what extent the labour practices in Europe v the United States are the sources of the differentials in unemployment. The more generous unemployment compensation and arrangements available in Europe do reduce the cost of being unemployed and therefore do reduce the incentive to try and get employment. However it is very important to note that differences in the unemployment compensation system have always existed. It has always been the case that Europe has had much more generous unemployment arrangements than in America and yet unemployment was lower in Europe than here in the period from the 1960s to the mid-1980s. So the great differential rise cannot be explained by this factor. Why does unemployment keep rising? It is not enough to say unemployment is higher now than it used to be. On the other hand, the flexibility of the labour contract does have something to do with unemployment in Europe. People in the United States are prepared to accept lower wage jobs. What they should develop are systems where people who get lower wages get some form of compensation through a negative income tax or equivalent arrangement. Let some workers be paid less because they are less productive, but as human beings those people are entitled to keep a reasonable standard of living relative to the rest. It would also help to reduce social security charges on new entrants to the labour force; this would encourage employment. On the whole the structure of the American labour market has indicated that you can get good results from more flexibility. But my personal feeling is that the downsizing movement went much too far. We used to say that employers try to avoid firing people if they think a recession is a temporary situation, because if you take into account the goodwill of your workforce, as well as the hiring and firing costs, it is cheaper to keep them and have them paint the factory. I do not think that the downsizing experience will be repeated because many employers are now regretting it. It is hard to replace good employees.

GENERAL

Have you ever been tempted to write a principles of economics textbook like Samuelson?
Well I have co-authored a textbook but not a basic principles of economics textbook. I have a textbook in finance, two volumes in fact, an undergraduate and graduate text, but I have never been tempted to write an introductory textbook. The reason I agreed to write the finance textbook is because Frank Fabozzi took the initiative. We discussed all the chapters and he is very knowledgeable, much more in some areas than I am. The framework was jointly decided. He did most of the writing and I went over it. I do not feel that I can write a textbook alone because writing does not come easy to me. So I have the basic ideas and I work them out with someone else. Paul Samuelson is always joking 'now Franco, tell me who are all these people who write articles with you, who is that Samuelson?' (*laughter*). I have written two articles with Paul and recently I have been writing articles with my granddaughter, who works at Morgan Stanley, which gives me a great deal of pleasure. We have developed a measure of risk adjusted returns which has come to be known as M squared, Modigliani Modigliani (*laughter*). So writing with other people makes it easier for me. They also keep pushing me otherwise I would delay forever. But I do not think I would ever write an introductory textbook unless somebody very inspiring came along and said 'let's do it together'. Then it might be conceivable.

Your work has been very influential in three main areas, macroeconomic theory and policy, the consumption function and the theory of finance. Where do you feel your most important contribution has been or do you regard all three as equally important?
It is very hard to say. In the area of macroeconomics my contribution was significant in trying to clarify what was important and special about Keynes. But I do not think I opened up a new paradigm. In the other two areas I did. In the area of consumption there is no doubt that people now think about consumption and saving in life-cycle terms. While people may criticize it or

develop it further, there is no doubt that it has changed the way that people think about saving and consumption behaviour. Before my contributions all economists could say was people save because they are rich, that is all, which among other things is not true, especially if we are talking about countries rather than individuals. People used to generalize and say if rich people save more then rich countries will have high savings ratios. Now we know why people save, the fundamental concept is the smoothing of consumption. Once you have that idea you can insert all kinds of modifications and draw out all kinds of implications. For example, a student of mine has shown that if there are gross imperfections in the borrowing market, if people are not allowed to borrow to buy a home or automobile, then the effect is to increase saving because it postpones consumption, as you have to accumulate. Even though you may consume the same amount over your lifetime the timing is different. There is evidence that one of the main reasons for low saving in the United States is the existence of a very advanced market for credit. But, fundamentally the life-cycle idea has given us a meaningful way of looking at consumption and saving behaviour. There has been a definite change of paradigm in that area. The same thing is true of the Modigliani–Miller theorem. Again people know this theorem, they criticize it and say it does not apply to the real world but it has fundamentally changed the way people think about finance. Going back to the macroeconomics area I think that the work I have done on the economics of deficits is also important because it has helped to clarify a variety of issues which are very easy to confuse. For example, when is a deficit bad and when is it useful? I am also proud of the fact that any propositions I make, I always test.

How did you feel when you were awarded the Nobel Prize in 1985?
The first thing I said to my wife was why me, it is luck (*laughter*). I still believe there was a great deal of luck involved because at the time I was awarded the prize there must have been at least ten people that could have received it. They have a list and sometimes they can be original in the people that they pick and produce surprises. They do not necessarily stick to the mainstream and have chosen economic historians, finance people, a public-choice theorist and so on, so you never know. So it is luck in that sense. But as you can imagine I was very happy because it is a great privilege. People are generally very surprised when you tell them that you have a Nobel Prize because they think that it is the end of the world. I sometimes tell people that Nobel Prize winners are to the scientific establishment what cardinals are to the church. They are figures who command reverence (*laughter*) and benevolence (*laughter*). That is very nice.

Edward C. Prescott
(b. 1940)

Edward Prescott is currently Professor of Economics at the University of Chicago. He is best known for his highly influential work on the implications of rational expectations in a variety of contexts and more recently the development of stochastic dynamic general equilibrium theory. Professor Prescott is widely acknowledged as being a leading advocate of the real business cycle approach to economic fluctuations.

We interviewed Professor Prescott in Chicago, in his hotel room, on 3 January 1998, while attending the annual conference of the American Economic Association.

BACKGROUND INFORMATION

Where and when did you first study economics?
I first studied economics as a graduate student at Carnegie-Mellon in 1963, which was then the Carnegie Institute of Technology. As an undergraduate I initially started out as a Physics major – back then it was the *Sputnik* era and that was the glamorous field. I had two boring laboratory courses, which I didn't enjoy, so I transferred into Math.

What was it about economics that attracted you?

258

Having transferred from Physics to Math I first considered doing Applied Math – I got my degree in Operations Research. Then I went to an interdisciplinary programme and it seemed to me that the smartest, most interesting people were doing Economics. Bob Lucas was a new Assistant Professor when I arrived at Carnegie-Mellon. My mentor though was Mike Lovell, a wonderful person.

Apart from Bob Lucas and Mike Lovell did any of your other teachers stand out as being particularly influential or inspirational?
Sure. Morie De Groot, a great Bayesian statistician.

With respect to your own research which economists have had the greatest influence?
I would say Bob Lucas. Also Finn Kydland, who was a student of mine – perhaps my two most important papers were written with Finn (Kydland and Prescott, 1977, 1982).

For over twenty years you have had a very productive relationship with Finn Kydland. When did you first meet Finn Kydland?
My first position after leaving Carnegie-Mellon was at the University of Pennsylvania. When I came back to Carnegie-Mellon Finn was an advanced graduate student there, ready to work on research. We had a very small economics programme with approximately seven faculty members and seven students. It was a good programme where students worked quite closely with faculty members. Bob Lucas and I had a number of joint students – unlike Bob I didn't scare the students (*laughter*).

DEVELOPMENT OF MACROECONOMICS

You have already mentioned that Bob Lucas was very influential on your own thinking. Which other economists do you regard as being the most influential macroeconomists since Keynes?
Well if you define growth as being part of macroeconomics Bob Solow has to be up there. Peter Diamond, Tom Sargent and Neil Wallace have also been very influential.

What about Milton Friedman?
Well I know Bob Lucas regards Friedman as being incredibly influential to the research programme in the monetary area. Friedman's work certainly influenced people interested in the monetary side of things – Neil Wallace, for example, was one of Friedman's students. But I'm more biased towards

Neil Wallace's programme, which is to lay down theoretical foundations for money. Friedman's work in the monetary field with Anna Schwartz (1963) is largely empirically orientated. Now when Friedman talked about the natural rate – where the unit of account doesn't matter – that is serious theory. But Friedman never accepted the dynamic equilibrium paradigm or the extension of economic theory to dynamic stochastic environments.

You were a graduate student at a time when Keynesianism 'seemed to be the only game in town in terms of macroeconomics' (Barro, 1994). Were you ever persuaded by the Keynesian model? Were you ever a Keynesian in those days?
Well in my dissertation I used a Keynesian model of business cycle fluctuations. Given that the parameters are unknown I thought that, maybe, you could apply optimal statistical decision theory to better stabilize the economy. Then I went to the University of Pennsylvania. Larry Klein was there – a really fine scholar. He provided support for me as an Assistant Professor, which was much appreciated. I also had an association with the Wharton Economic Forecasting group. However after writing the paper on 'Investment under Uncertainty' with Bob Lucas (*Econometrica*, 1971), plus reading his 1972 *Journal of Economic Theory* paper on 'Expectations and the Neutrality of Money', I decided I was not a Keynesian (big smile). I actually stopped teaching macro after that for ten years, until I moved to Minnesota in the spring of 1981, by which time I thought I understood the subject well enough to teach it.

BUSINESS CYCLES

The study of business cycles has itself gone through a series of cycles. Business cycle research flourished from the 1920s to the 1940s, waned during the 1950s and 1960s, before again witnessing a revival of interest during the 1970s. What were the main factors which were important in regenerating interest in business cycle research in the 1970s?
There were two factors responsible for regenerating interest in business cycles. First, Lucas beautifully defined the problem. Why do market economies experience recurrent fluctuations of output and employment about trend? Second, economic theory was extended to the study of dynamic stochastic economic environments. These tools are needed to derive the implications of theory for business cycle fluctuations. Actually the interest in business cycles was always there, but economists couldn't do anything without the needed tools. I guess this puts me in the camp which believes that economics is a tool-driven science – absent the needed tools we are stymied.

Following your work with Finn Kydland in the early 1980s there has been considerable re-examination of what are the stylized facts of the business cycle. What do you think are the most important stylized facts of the business cycle that any good theory needs to explain?

Business cycle-type fluctuations are just what dynamic economic theory predicts. In the 1970s everybody thought the impulse or shock had to be money and were searching for a propagation mechanism. In our 1982 *Econometrica* paper, 'Time to Build and Aggregate Fluctuations', Finn and I loaded a lot of stuff in our model economy in order to get propagation. We found that a prediction of economic theory is that technology shocks will give rise to business cycle fluctuations of the nature observed. The magnitude of the fluctuations and persistence of deviations from trend match observations. The facts that investment is three times more volatile than output and consumption one-half as volatile also match, as does the fact that most business cycle variation in output is accounted for by variation in the labour input. This is a remarkable success. The theory used, namely neoclassical growth theory, was not developed to account for business cycles. It was developed to account for growth.

Were you surprised that you were able to construct a model economy which generated fluctuations which closely resembled actual experience in the US?

Yes. At that stage we were still searching for the model to fit the data, as opposed to using the theory to answer the question – we had not really tied down the size of the technology shock and found that the intertemporal elasticity of labour supply had to be high. In a different context I wrote a paper with another one of my students Raj Mehra (Mehra and Prescott, 1985) in which we tried to use basic theory to account for the difference in the average returns on stock and equity. We thought that existing theory would work beforehand – the finance people told us that it would (*laughter*). We actually found that existing theory could only account for a tiny part of the huge difference.

How do you react to the criticism that there is a lack of available supporting evidence of strong intertemporal labour substitution effects?

Gary Hansen (1985) and Richard Rogerson's (1988) key theoretical development on labour indivisibility is central to this. The margin that they use is the number of people that work, not the number of hours of those that do work. This results in the stand-in or representative household being very willing to intertemporally substitute even though individuals are not that willing. Labour economists using micro data found that the association between hours worked and compensation per hour was weak for full-time workers. Based on these observations they concluded that the labour supply elasticity is small.

These early studies ignore two important features of reality. The first feature of reality is that most of the variation in labour supply is in the number working – not in the length of the workweek. The second important feature of reality ignored in these early studies is that wages increase with experience. This suggests that part of individuals' compensation is this valuable experience. Estimates of labour supply are high when this feature of reality is taken into account. The evidence in favour of high intertemporal labour supply elasticity has become overwhelming. Macro and micro labour economics has been unified.

Many prominent economists such as Milton Friedman (see Snowdon and Vane, 1997b), Greg Mankiw (1989) and Lawrence Summers (1986) have been highly critical of real business cycle models as an explanation of aggregate fluctuations. What do you regard as being the most serious criticisms that have been raised in the literature against RBC models?

I don't think you criticize models – maybe the theory. A nice example is where the Solow growth model was used heavily in public finance – some of its predictions were confirmed, so we now have a little bit more confidence in that structure and what public finance people say about the consequences of different tax policies. Bob Lucas (1987) says technology shocks seem awfully big and that is the feature he is most bothered by. When you look at how much total factor productivity changes over five-year periods and you assume that changes are independent, the quarterly changes have to be big. The difference between total factor productivity in the US and India is at least 400 per cent. This is a lot bigger number than if in say a two-year period the shocks are such that productivity growth is a couple per cent below or above average. This is enough to give rise to a recession or boom. Other factors are also influential – tax rates matter for labour supply and I'm not going to rule out preference shocks either. I can't forecast what social attitudes will be, I don't think anybody can – for example, whether or not the female labour participation rate will go up.

In your 1986 Federal Reserve Bank of Minneapolis *paper, 'Theory Ahead of Business Cycle Measurement', you concluded that attention should be focused on 'determinants of the average rate of technological advance'. What in your view are the main factors that determine the average rate at which technology advances?*

The determinants of total factor productivity is *the* question in economics. If we knew why total factor productivity in the US was four times bigger than in India, I am sure India would immediately take the appropriate actions and be as rich as the US *(laughter)*. Of course the general rise throughout the world has to be related to what Paul Romer talks about – increasing returns and the increase in the stock of usable knowledge. But there is a lot more to total factor productivity, particularly when you look at the relative levels across countries or different experiences over time. For example, the Philippines and Korea were very similar in 1960 but are quite different today.

How important are institutions?
Very. The legal system matters and matters a lot, particularly the commercial code and the property rights systems. Societies give protection to certain groups of specialized factor suppliers – they protect the *status quo*. For example, why in India do you see highly educated bank workers manually entering numbers into ledgers? In the last few years I have been reading quite a lot about these type of issues. However there seem to be more questions than answers (*laughter*).

When it comes to the issue of technological change are you a fan of Schumpeter's work?
The old Schumpeter, but not the new (*laughter*). The new suggests that we need monopolies – what the poor countries need is more competition, not more monopolies.

In your 1991 Economic Theory *paper, co-authored with Finn Kydland, you estimated that just over two-thirds of postwar US fluctuations can be attributed to technology shocks. A number of authors have introduced several modifications of the model economy, for example Cho and Cooley (1995). How robust is the estimate of the contribution of technology shocks to aggregate fluctuations to such modifications?*
The challenge to that number has come from two places. First, the size of the estimate of the intertemporal elasticity of labour supply. Second, are technology shocks as large as we estimated them to be? You can have lots of other factors and they need not be orthogonal – there could be some moving in opposite directions that offset each other or some moving in the same direction that amplify each other. Are the shocks that big? Marty Eichenbaum (1991) tried to push them down and came up with a 0.005 number for the standard deviation of the total factor productivity shocks. My number is 0.007. I point out to Marty that Ian Fleming's secret agent 005 is dead. Agent 007 survives (*laughter*).

How do you view the more recent development of introducing nominal rigidities, imperfect credit markets and other Keynesian-style features into RBC models?
I like the methodology of making a theory quantitative. Introducing monopolistic competition with sticky prices has been an attempt to come up with a

good mechanism for the monetary side. I don't think it has paid off as much as people had hoped, but it is a good thing to explore.

The new classical monetary-surprise style of models developed in the 1970s by Lucas, Sargent, Wallace and others were very influential. When did you first begin to lose faith in that particular approach?
In our 1982 paper Finn and I were pretty careful – what we said was that in the post-war period if the only shocks had been technology shocks, then the economy would have been 70 per cent as volatile. When you look back at some of Friedman and Schwartz's (1963) data, particularly from the 1890s and early 1900s, there were financial crises and associated large declines in real output. It is only recently that I have become disillusioned with monetary explanations. One of the main reasons for this is that a lot of smart people have searched for good monetary transmission mechanisms but they haven't been that successful in coming up with one – it's hard to get persistence out of monetary surprises.

How do you now view your 1977 Journal of Political Economy *paper, co-authored with Finn Kydland, in which monetary surprises, if they can be achieved, have real effects?*
Finn and I wanted to make the point about the inconsistency of optimal plans in the setting of a more real environment. The pressure to use this simple example came from the editor – given the attention that paper has subsequently received, I guess his call was right (*laughter*).

What do you regard to be the essential connecting thread between the monetary-surprise models developed in the 1970s and the real business cycle models developed in the 1980s?
The methodology – Bob Lucas is the master of methodology, as well as defining problems. I guess when Finn and I undertook the research for our 1982 piece we didn't realize it was going to be an important paper. *Ex post* we see it as being an important paper – we certainly learnt a lot from writing it and it did influence Bob Lucas in his thinking about methodology. That paper pushed the profession into trying to make macroeconomic theory more quantitative – to say how big things are. There are so many factors out there – most of them we have got to abstract from, the world is too complex otherwise – we want to know which factors are little and which are significant.

Turning to one of the stylized facts of the business cycle. Does the evidence suggest that the price level and inflation are procyclical or countercyclical?
Finn and I (Kydland and Prescott, 1990) found that in the US prices since the Second World War have been countercyclical, but that in the inter-war period

they were procyclical. Now if you go to inflation you are taking the derivative of the price level and things get more complex. The lack of a strong uniform regular pattern has led me to be a little suspicious of the importance of the monetary facts – but further research could change my opinion.

What is your current view on the relationship between the behaviour of the money supply and the business cycle?
Is it okay to talk about hunches? (*laughter*). My guess is that monetary and fiscal policies are really tied together – there is just one government with a budget constraint. In theory, at least, you can arrange to have a fiscal authority with a budget constraint and an independent monetary authority – in reality some countries do have a high degree of independence of their Central Bank. Now I've experimented with some simple closed-economy models which unfortunately get awfully complicated, very fast (*laughter*). In some of those models government policy changes do have real consequences – the government 'multipliers' are very different from those in the standard RBC model. Monetary and fiscal policy are not independent – there is a complex interaction between monetary and fiscal policy with respect to debt management, money supply and government expenditure. So I think that there is a rich class of models to be studied and as we get better tools we are going to learn more.

One of the main features of Keynesianism has always been the high priority given by its advocates to the problem of unemployment. Equilibrium business cycle theory seems to treat unemployment as a secondary issue. How do you think about unemployment?
When I think about employment it is easy because you can go out and measure it – you see how many hours people work and how many people work. The problem with unemployment is that it is not a well-defined concept. When I look at the experience of European economies, like France and Spain, I see unemployment as something to do with the arrangements that these societies set up. Unemployment, particularly among the young, is a social problem. Lars Ljungqvist and Tom Sargent (1998) are doing some very interesting work on this question and that is something I want to study more.

Given that your work has provided an integrated approach to the theory of growth and fluctuations, should we perhaps abandon the term 'business cycle' when we refer to aggregate economic fluctuations?
Business cycles are in large part fluctuations due to variations in how many hours people work. Is that good language or not? I think I'll leave that for you to decide (*laughter*). I'm sympathetic to what your question implies, but I can't think of any better language though right now.

METHODOLOGY

You are known as a leading real business cycle theorist. Are you happy with that label?
I tend to see RBC theory more as a methodology – dynamic applied general equilibrium modelling has been a big step forward. Applied analyses that people are doing now are so much better than they used to be. So in so far as I am associated with that, and have helped get that started, I am happy with that label.

Do you regard your work as having resulted in a revolution in macroeconomics?
No – I have just followed the logic of the discipline. There has been no real dramatic change, only an extension, to dynamic economics – it takes time to figure things out and develop new tools. People are always looking for the revolutions – maybe some day some revolution will come along, but I don't think I'll sit around and wait for it (*laughter*).

What role have calibration exercises played in the development of real business cycle models?
I think of the model as something to use to measure something. Given the posed question we typically want our model economy to match reality on certain dimensions. With a thermometer you want it to register correctly when you put it in ice and in boiling water. In the past economists have tried to find *the* model and that has held them back. Today people don't take the data as gospel, they look at how the data is collected. So it has forced people to learn a lot more about government statistics on the economy.

How important was Lucas's (1980b) paper on 'Methods and Problems in Business Cycle Theory' in your development of the calibration approach?
It's hard to recall exactly – I saw his vision more clearly later on. Back then I kept thinking of trying to find the model, as opposed to thinking of economic theory in terms of a set of instructions for constructing a model to answer a particular question. There never is a right or wrong model – the issue is whether a model is good for the purpose it is being used.

Kevin Hoover (1995a) has suggested that 'the calibration methodology, to date, lacks any discipline as stern as that imposed by econometric methods'. What happens if you have a Keynesian and a real business cycle model which both perform well? How do you choose between the two?
Well let's suppose you work within a Keynesian theoretical framework and it provides guidance to construct models, and you use those models and they

work well – that's success, by definition. There was a vision that neoclassical foundations would eventually be provided for Keynesian models but in the Keynesian programme theory doesn't provide much discipline in constructing the structure. A lot of the choice of equations came down to an empirical matter – theory was used to restrict these equations, some coefficients being zero. You notice Keynesians talk about equations. Within the applied general equilibrium approach we don't talk about equations – we always talk about production functions, utility functions or people's ability and willingness to substitute. We are not trying to follow the physicist in discovering the laws of motion of the economy, unlike Keynesians and monetarists. Keynesian approaches were tried and put to a real test and to quote Bob Lucas and Tom Sargent (1978), in the 1970s Keynesian macroeconometric models experienced 'econometric failure on a grand scale'.

To what extent is the question of whether the computational experiment should be regarded as an econometric tool an issue of semantics?
It is pure semantics. Ragnar Frisch wanted to make neoclassical economics quantitative – he talked about quantitative theoretical economics and quantitative empirical economics, and their unification. The modern narrow definition of econometrics only focuses on the empirical side.

Lawrence Summers (1991) in a paper on 'Scientific Illusion in Empirical Macroeconomics' has argued along the lines that formal econometric work has had little impact on the growth of economic knowledge, whereas the informal pragmatic approach of people like Friedman and Schwartz (1963) has had a significant effect. Are you sympathetic to Summers's view?
In some ways I'm sympathetic, in others I'm unsympathetic – I think I'll hedge (*laughter*). With regard to representing our knowledge in terms of the likelihood of different things being true, so that as we get more observations over time we zero in on the truth, it doesn't seem to work that way.

GROWTH AND DEVELOPMENT

Since the mid-1980s many eminent economists have turned their attention to the issue of economic growth. Are we any closer to explaining why there has been a lack of convergence between rich and poor countries?
The new growth and development literature, which was touched off by Paul Romer (1986) and Bob Lucas (1988), is very exciting. We now know that standards of living were more or less constant from the beginning of civilization until the industrial revolution, then something changed. When I compare countries in the East (China, India, Japan and so on) with those in the West

they were about the same in 1800 in terms of per capita GDP – by 1950 the West was almost ten times richer, now it is only about four times richer. So I do see signs of convergence. Divergence occurred when modern economic growth started. In China, for example, the peasants were equally well off in 2 AD as they were in 1950 – today they are a lot better off. The process of modern economic growth started earlier in Japan – even so they didn't do all that well until the postwar period. Japan's relative position to England or the United States in 1870 was about the same as it was in 1937. Even per capita income growth in Africa is now taking place at the same rate as in the rich countries – they should be growing much faster and I expect that they soon will start to catch up. Furthermore when you look at countries like India, Pakistan, Indonesia and the Philippines, they are now growing faster than the rich industrial countries. So I believe that there will be a lot of convergence over the next 50 years, in the same way that there has been a lot of convergence over the last 50 years – it all depends upon how you look at the data.

The endogenous growth literature has led to a re-opening of the debate relating to the role of government in promoting economic growth. What role do you see for the government?
My interest is in the problem of the poor countries, like India. In those countries it is important to let things happen and not protect the *status quo*. For example, there are some bizarre licensing practices in India. Once things start happening, they can happen pretty fast and there can be rapid development.

How do you account for the revival of interest in development economics?
People pushed the paradigm as far as the old tools would allow it to go. Now a new generation has come along and have sought to advance it a little bit further. Exciting theoretical developments as well new data sets are key to the revival of interest. People like Kravis, and more recently Summers and Heston (1991), have done a major service to the profession by providing new data.

GENERAL

If you were asked to teach macroeconomics to intermediate undergraduates how would you go about the task?
Basically I concentrate on the Solow growth model, with factors paid their marginal product and consider the two key decisions: consumption–saving and labour–leisure. In discussing monetary issues I follow some basic simple intertemporal model with people holding assets – Neil Wallace and his students have developed some pretty good material that can be used. The hard

thing about teaching macro to undergraduates is that the textbooks are not that good – there is a need for a Paul Samuelson. Samuelson is an artist, he brought undergraduates pretty well up to the level of the state of knowledge in the profession. Now there is a big gap.

Most of your work has involved research which has pushed back the frontiers of knowledge in economics. Have you ever thought about writing a basic principles of economics textbook or an intermediate macro textbook?
Writing this type of book requires a special talent – if I had this talent I would give it some serious thought. I don't (*laughter*).

Have you ever been asked to be an economic adviser in Washington?
No (*laughter*). I get too excited – you have to be calm and have the right style. You also have to be a good actor as well as being a good economist. So again I've never been tempted – maybe if I had the ability I might have been asked.

Are you optimistic about the future of macroeconomics?
Yes – I think a lot of progress has been made and will continue to be made.

What issues or areas are you currently working on?
I always work on a variety of issues in the hope that one will break (*laughter*). I've recently completed a couple of papers (Parente and Prescott, 1997; Prescott, 1998). One paper is on economic development for a monograph on barriers to riches – I use game theory to construct an explicit model economy where a particular set of monopoly rights can give rise to large differences in total factor productivity. The other paper is on financial economics, considering why there occurs such a big jump in the value of firms associated with mergers. I also want to look more fully at the issue of the relationship and interaction between monetary and fiscal policy I hinted at earlier.

Robert M. Solow
(b. 1924)

Robert Solow is currently Institute Professor Emeritus of Economics at the Massachusetts Institute of Technology. In addition to his seminal work on growth theory and capital theory, he is well known for his development and championing of neo-Keynesian economics. In 1987 he was awarded the Nobel Prize in Economics: 'For his contributions to the theory of economic growth'.

We interviewed Professor Solow in Chicago, in his hotel room, on 4 January 1998, while attending the annual conference of the American Economic Association.

BACKGROUND INFORMATION

When did you first decide to study economics?
Well there is a story to that. I came to Harvard College in 1940 as a 16-year-old freshman with no intention of studying economics; I did not even know what economics was. At that point I thought I might be a biologist but I proved to be no good at that so I started off as a major in general social science. I studied subjects like elementary economics, psychology, sociology and anthropology. The reason I was interested in social science was just the circumstances of the time. Remember it was 1940, the Depression was just

over, and the war had just begun. In 1942, after two years, I quit Harvard College and joined the army, which seemed more important to me then. In 1945 I returned to education and I said to the girl I left behind and who has been my wife ever since, 'you majored in economics; was it interesting?'. When she said yes I decided to give it a try. At the time I was under pressure to choose something to study because I was discharged in August and the school term was due to start in September. I was still an undergraduate. Anyway, it turned out all right. So the reason I studied economics was related both to my general interest in what was happening – why society was not working so well in the 1930s and 1940s – and to sheer desperation because I had to do something in a hurry.

As a student which of your teachers inspired your interest in economics?
Mainly Wassily Leontief, who taught me for one course, even before I joined the army. In those days Harvard College had a tutorial system and every student majoring in economics had a member of the faculty assigned to him as a tutor. We met once a week and it was obviously an imitation of the Oxford and Cambridge system. Wassily was my tutor and I really learnt my economics from him; he was undoubtedly the main person who inspired my interest in economics. The only other teacher in those days who really caught my imagination was Dick Goodwin, who had been my teacher in the elementary economics course that I had taken in 1940–41. I hit it off with him very well. After the war when I came back I studied more economics with him.

Which economists have had the greatest influence on the direction that your own work has taken?
Since I completed my PhD degree, Paul Samuelson and Jim Tobin – both very good friends – are the people whose way of doing economics I admired and still admire. They were representatives of what I now (I did not see it then) think of as the new style of doing economics after the war. Economics went from being a sort of cultural subject to a model building subject, and I liked that. Paul Samuelson and Jim Tobin were the people who for me exemplified that new approach. The other name I would mention, but not from a personal contact point of view, only from his work, was Lloyd Metzler. I read Metzler's work after I had read Samuelson's (1939) multiplier–accelerator papers. Metzler's (1941, 1947) papers on inventory cycles and 'Wealth, Saving and the Rate of Interest' (1951) were absolutely splendid. I did not know Lloyd Metzler very well because he had gone off to Chicago by then and later he suffered a terrible brain tumour. After that he was no longer the real Lloyd Metzler.

The next question is one we also asked James Tobin, Milton Friedman, Franco Modigliani and Robert Lucas. In 1987 you were awarded the Nobel Prize for your contributions to the analysis of economic growth. On a personal level how did you feel and react to that award?

Well, I can describe the facts. The telephone rang at 6 a.m. and I got out of bed to answer it. Our first thought, obviously, was that something had happened to one of the kids. I guess I knew that about that time the Swedish Academy was making its decision. All my friends had been telling me for years that I might very well get that award, but with friends like that you don't need enemies (*laughter*). But I really was not focused on the possibility of being awarded the prize. Then I heard a Swedish voice and it gradually penetrated what the phone call was about. Someone asked me if I would be willing to go to Stockholm to accept the prize and I of course allowed that I could manage it. Then when I put down the phone I said probably the stupidest short sentence I have uttered in my life. I said to my wife 'let's go back to sleep' (*laughter*). But there was no possibility of that because the phone started ringing continuously.

Who were the people calling you?

Reporters, my colleagues and anyone who had heard about it, even at 6.30 a.m. So I was very excited, who wouldn't be. I thought it was absolutely wonderful. It was nice to think that in 1987, some 30 years after I had written those couple of papers, someone thought that my work was worthy of such an award. Of course MIT fixed up a press conference and I had a struggle getting my clothes on as the phone was ringing that much. One of my colleges, Dick Eckaus, even turned up at the door, how he managed that I do not know. I managed to talk to my kids on the phone and my son John, who is himself an economist, gave me a piece of advice that not only stood me in terrifically good stead throughout that time, but also gave me a way of handling questions. As I was chatting to John he said 'Dad try not to say anything stupid about the stock market' (*laughter*). So whenever I was asked a question about the stock market I was able to quote my son. All that people want to ask you about is the stock market and the only way not to say anything stupid is not to say anything (*laughter*). But it was good fun and at the press conference I had the time of my life.

ECONOMIC GROWTH

The whole issue of economic growth has seen a regeneration of interest in recent years and many prominent economists like Robert Barro and Xavier Sala-i-Martin (1995) regard it as the part of macroeconomics that really matters. There seems to have been a neglect of Nobel Prize awards in this area, so do you anticipate that this relative neglect will be rectified in the future given the importance of growth for human welfare?

Well I would not describe it as a relative neglect. I think that what looks like neglect is actually something quite different. They started the Nobel Prize awards in economics in 1969, and, unlike Physics or Chemistry, which had been going for years, there was a long backlog of people who were clearly of that calibre, if you have that kind of prize. Therefore it was only natural to start picking them up in turn. There are exceptions. Some people came out of order, for example Ken Arrow (deservedly) came early in the awards but even he was paired with John Hicks who was old by then. In 1987 when I got the award nobody born later than me had yet been given the prize, so in a way it is still just rolling up the carpet from the old end. My view is that if growth theory, the empirical analysis of growth, and ideas connected with them, continue to be popular, the subject will attract the best people in the profession. And yes, there surely will be more awards in this area. By the way I do not know how you count Arthur Lewis and Ted Schultz, who were interested in economic development – Ted Schultz in a very different way – but Arthur Lewis contributed that famous 1954 paper on 'Economic Development with Unlimited Supplies of Labour'. So I would not say that there has been a neglect, I would say the timing has been natural. There are likely to be more surprises, coming at a slightly greater rate than the past, because we are now getting up to contemporary people, to economists who were doing their work fairly recently. Since 1987 there has been a real outburst of work on growth so there will be more awards in that area.

Your 1956 and 1957 papers have clearly had a profound impact on the direction of research in the area of economic growth. Can you tell us what were the main influences which led you into that research and which generated those papers?

Yes, I do recall what led me to that research. I became interested in growth for three main reasons. First, in the early 1950s everybody was interested in economic development, for the obvious reason that most of the population of the world was living in poor economies. I was passively interested in economic development, but I have never been actively interested – in a research way – in what happens in underdeveloped countries. But I got to thinking about development issues and I had read Arthur Lewis. I knew I was not going to work on development issues, but it did get me interested in the general area of economic growth. Then Paul Samuelson and I had started thinking about what later became Dorfman, Samuelson and Solow (1958), the book on Linear Programming. That was the second factor. In the course of that research we thought about the Von Neumann and Ramsey models. So from the optimization and linear programming end and the idea of using programming theory to deal with intertemporal optimization, I also got interested in growth. The third influence was my reading of the work of Harrod and Domar; but I guess my reaction to their ideas was a little different from some other economists. I was suspicious of the Harrod–Domar model for reasons which I have occasionally explained. It occurred to me that if the world works in the way suggested by their model then the history of capitalism would have been much more erratic than it has been. If Harrod–Domar was a good macro model for the long run then it is impossible to explain, to my mind, how contained economic fluctuations have been, how you can draw a trend and look at fluctuations around that trend, and how those fluctuations stay 3–4 per cent either side of trend, except for a few major depressions. I thought that there must be a way of modelling growth that does not have the knife-edge property of the Harrod–Domar model. Those were the influences which led me to the 1956 paper.

You mentioned Arthur Lewis in your answer. His model was described as a classical rather than neoclassical model. Do you think that the classical economists made any important lasting insights on the issue of economic growth?
When you say classical economists do you mean Smith, Ricardo and Mill and so on?

Yes.
If so, that is not where I got any intellectual help, for a number of reasons. First, I am not very well read in the History of Economic Thought. I know the potted versions of Smith, Ricardo and Mill, but I would never trust myself to have a deep thought about classical economics. I have looked back to see if there was anything that I missed, and I would say that apart from Mill on the stationary state, and Ricardo to a certain extent as Mill's predecessor, I did not find much there other than vague ideas. They were obviously interested in the long run but that does not butter any parsnips really. The relationship of diminishing returns to the stationary state, especially in Mill, obviously has some relationship to the work I was doing in the mid-1950s. That paid off a lot. On the other hand the obvious thing on the negative side is that Ricardo at the beginning, and Mill a little later on in the course of the industrial revolution, were thinking about the long run and yet the notion that growth can be maintained by technological improvements did not seem to occur seriously to either of them.

Was your 1956 paper accepted for publication straight away?
Yes. I can pinpoint when I was working on it, it was in 1955. I sent it to the *Quarterly Journal of Economics* and they accepted it right away. Writing

papers is very hard for me; and so throughout my whole career I have only written papers when I thought that either I had something really serious to say, or I had to produce a paper for a Festschrift or something like that. In the latter case anything intellectually respectable would do. But the papers that I write of my own free will are usually pretty serious, otherwise it is not worth the effort, because I really do not like doing it.

Earlier you mentioned the growth of interest in development economics which took off as a research area during the 1950s. Why did development economics emerge during this period as a separate branch of economics from growth theory?
Why did it happen that way? Well I am going to offer a suggestion but it is not original to me. I guess it comes originally from Paul Krugman of MIT. On the whole the personality types in the profession who became interested in economic development were not model builders. They were collectors of data and generalizers from rough empirical data, like Simon Kuznets; or they were like Ted Schultz, really deeply into underdeveloped agriculture, or they were people interested in history and backwardness for its own sake. That sort of temperament is not suited to model building. Growth theory, *par excellence*, yielded to model building. So even Arthur Lewis, whom I mentioned earlier, thought of his 1954 paper as a minor sideline to his book *The Theory of Economic Growth* (1955). The people who got interested in the theory of economic growth were interested in model building.

When we talked to James Tobin in 1993 he remarked that the really good papers in economics always contain a surprise. Were you surprised to find that the steady-state rate of growth is independent of the saving rate?
Oh yes. I wrote that up right away and wanted to publish it in spite of my dislike of writing papers. I thought it was a real shocker. It is not what I expected at all, and by the way when I did the 1957 paper on technical change I also expected a different answer from the one that I found. I expected that the main source of growth would be capital accumulation because that is what everyone talked about and I had heard that all my life as a student. Those were both real surprises.

That 1957 paper inspired a vast literature on growth accounting with contributions from economists such as Denison, Kendrick, Jorgenson, Maddison and others. After 40 years of work what have we learned about the sources of economic growth?
I think we have learned a great deal, not compared with what might be learned, but compared to what we have learned in other areas of macroeconomics. The notion that technical change or the residual accounts for much

more of growth than you would expect, much more of productivity increase than capital accumulation, has stood up. Where it has not stood up – as in the work of Alwyn Young (1995), Jong Il Kim and Larry Lau (1994), Sue Collins and Barry Bosworth (1996) on the four Asian tigers – it has been fascinating and you actually learn a lot (assuming it is all true of course) that they have recorded staggeringly rapid growth but not in the same way as the historical capitalist economies. That basic distinction between capital accumulation and the residual has proved to be very informative. We have also learned a lot about the importance of human capital, as distinct from tangible capital, but the relative importance of each is still not settled. You still find what look like perfectly sound empirical papers which come up with conflicting results about the importance of human capital, depending on the time period, the model and other factors especially the way 'human capital' is measured. I was delighted to learn after the fact that in my 1957 paper, at the very beginning, I said that what I called technical change included a lot of things such as human capital, although I did not have that language then. But the work on growth accounting, beginning with Edward Denison and then continuing on, has taught us a great deal about the nature of growth. I would say that the fact that the growth of the current advanced industrial economies only owes a little to the exploitation of natural resources is very interesting and this too has come out of growth accounting methods.

In 1970 your book, Growth Theory: An Exposition *was published. Following that, for the next 16 years, the interest of macroeconomists in the issue of economic growth, or more accurately growth theory, went into relative decline. Why do you think that happened?*
I think it happened because the profession ran out of ideas and you cannot maintain interest in any subject simply on the basis of looking more and more closely into the existing ideas. Edward Denison was still writing his books during this period, all of which I read and admired. But there were no new ideas. The merit of the contributions from Paul Romer (1986) and Bob Lucas (1988) – I do not know how to divide it up between them – is that they renewed interest in the subject by bringing in new ideas. That always attracts people to any branch of economics and I presume the same thing is true of chemistry. So it was just a case of intellectual diminishing returns. Around 1970 we simply ran out of new ideas.

The first paper on endogenous growth in the new phase of interest in economic growth was Paul Romer's (1986) 'Increasing Returns and Long-Run Growth'. What do you think inspired the new research? Was it the convergence controversy issue which also emerged about the same time with the contributions of Abramovitz (1986) and Baumol (1986)?

Well you are going to have to ask Lucas and Romer that question.

Okay, we will ask Paul Romer that question when we interview him tomorrow.

I would have said, just from the second-hand evidence of reading their papers, that the convergence issue was more of a stimulus to Bob Lucas than it was to Paul Romer. It may have influenced Paul Romer as well, but I do not remember anything in that 1986 paper which suggests that, though I could easily have forgotten. I am inclined to think that Paul Romer had an idea, found it exciting and followed it. But Lucas gave more signs of having been fascinated by the international comparisons.

What are your views on the convergence issue? Your 1956 model predicts conditional convergence and this prediction seems to fit reasonably well to a group of countries, a 'convergence club'. Yet there are other poor countries which are showing little sign of catching up with the rich industrialized countries.

I have no independent thoughts on this at all. I just read the literature, not all of it because there is so much. But I read enough of it to develop opinions and these go roughly like this. First of all I am at heart very suspicious of all this international cross-section research. I read it, sometimes it is interesting and sometimes it is not, but in the back of my mind there is always a question as to whether I should believe it. The fundamental reason why I am dubious about it is that there is no solution to the inverse causation issue. The more right-hand-side variables that go into those regressions, the more they seem to me to be just as likely the consequences of success or failure of long-term economic growth, as the cause. The second reason I am suspicious is that I learned from Ross Levine at the World Bank a long time ago that most of those results are not robust. They do not stand up if you make minor variations. The third reason I am suspicious is that I keep asking myself, do I really believe that there is a surface out there in space whose axes are labelled with all the things Robert Barro and company put on them? Do I believe that there is such a surface, and countries or points on that surface could in principle move from one place to another on it and then move back to where they began by changing their form of government or by having more or fewer assassinations? A small voice says maybe, but I would not bet anything on the existence of that surface. So I am dubious about that whole line of research. If you look at it as a pure time-series problem, the way Danny Quah (1993) does, if you look at conditional convergence – and conditional convergence is the only version of this that makes sense – then the evidence does look more or less as if there really is something to the distinction between growth and development. There is a group of countries, which for one reason or another, do not catch onto the railroad train as it goes by and I am inclined to attribute that to their lacking some institutional infrastructure, some sociological infrastructure, whatever. If I had to throw in with one camp or the other I would support the convergence club.

Another factor which has contributed to the reawakening of interest in the growth issue has been the so-called productivity slowdown which began in the late 1960s/early 1970s. Do you believe there was a productivity slowdown and if so what were the possible causes?

Yes, I do believe that there was a productivity slowdown. All the debate about price indices does not seem to me to produce a convincing case against the observation that there has been a productivity slowdown. There is no reason to suppose that if you made the same corrections on price indices before 1970 you would not have at least as much overstatement of inflation. So I think there was a productivity slowdown, I think it had an international character, it happened as much in Japan as it did in the US, and I think that as far as anyone can tell at least half or more of it is a mystery still. But when I say mystery I think we should distinguish between two senses of the word inexplicable (or mystery, for that matter). When I say something is inexplicable or a mystery I could mean that I cannot pin down in detail the causes of the phenomenon. But inexplicable may also mean that it is utterly shocking!!! How could such a thing happen? I think the productivity slowdown is inexplicable only in the first of those two senses. There is nothing in any piece of growth economics, theoretical or empirical, which says that the rate of growth of the residual is an invariant, that it cannot change from one period of time to the next. We know by the usual backward extrapolation that there cannot have been productivity growth at 1 or 2 per cent a year forever or else Oliver Cromwell would have been crawling around in skins. By the way, this goes back to a significant analytical issue. When I say that in my work in the 1950s I treated technical change as exogenous, that does not mean that I really believed at the time that it had no internal economic causes. In the very same papers I always treated population growth as exogenous, but I did know about Malthus, and there is clearly a connection between economic development and demographic patterns. What I meant by saying something is exogenous was that I do not pretend to understand this, I have nothing worthwhile to say on this so I might as well take technical change as given for reasons which are inexplicable in the first sense I mentioned before. I do not know what the determinants of technical change are in any useful detail. But technical change is not inexplicable in the second sense. I am not shocked to learn that productivity growth after 1973 is slower than before 1973, nor would I have been shocked in this sense if it had been higher.

If we take a longer-term view, going back a hundred years or so, perhaps the bigger puzzle is the above trend productivity performance of the postwar period up until the 1970s.

Exactly. I do believe that. It is a hypothesis that makes sense to me; and I can even tell a story that makes sense to explain it. But keep in mind that I am, so to speak, estimating one parameter with one degree of freedom, so there is no real test being made. The story I tell myself is as follows: From 1930 to 1947 or so, a certain amount of technological change and other improvements in productive knowledge were taking place, but could not be incorporated into the real economy, first because of the Great Depression and then because of the war. So beginning around 1950 the world had a 20-year backlog of technological improvements to incorporate into practice. After 1950 this began to happen. That seems to make perfectly good sense; but I do not believe that it is possible to test the hypothesis because there is nothing to compare it with.

Are there any strong theoretical or empirical reasons for believing that moderate inflations of less than 10 per cent have any significant adverse effects on economic growth?

I am not up on all the literature on this topic. But what I have gathered is that, at least empirically, the evidence is that rapid inflation is unconditionally bad for economic growth, but relatively slow inflation, even perhaps averaging 10 per cent annually, has no visible correlation with economic performance. I doubt that theory compels that view; but I can easily imagine that theory would be compatible with that view.

The modern phase of endogenous growth theory has now been with us for just over ten years. What do you think have been the most important developments or insights which have emerged from this research programme? Have we learned anything useful?

Less than I had hoped. My own opinion, which I think is now shared by Paul Romer, is that the early developments – the so called AK models which simply amounted to saying, let us assume that there are exactly constant returns to the collection of accumulatable factors of production, human and physical – all that led nowhere because it was not robust theory. It is very unlikely that growth could happen that way. If you adopt the AK view, it is the simplest thing in the world to say: I can show you how reducing a tax on capital will increase the growth rate, or I can show you how making leisure less attractive will increase the growth rate. But that sort of stuff went nowhere and added no real insights because it rested entirely on a linearity which is so unlikely to be true. But then when you start asking questions about what *does* govern the accumulation of technical knowledge, how could you model the accumulation of human capital, then you begin to get into really interesting issues. That is what I like about all that literature.

The current crisis involving the so-called 'Asian Tiger' economies is making big news. Their success in the past has been identified with, amongst other factors, export performance. What in your view is the relationship between foreign trade and growth? Has the East Asian growth 'miracle' been export led?

Well I am uncertain about the relationship between trade and growth. Empirically there does seem to be a relationship. I have lots of friends who have worked on this empirically and while their results differ, and some of them come up empty handed, it appears that openness to trade favours economic performance. It is a bit less clear, at least in the literature I have read, what the source of that relationship is. The very important distinction needs to be made between factors that have growth effects and factors that have level effects. Imagine exponential growth as a linear trend on semi-log paper. You can ask: are there forces that take a country's trend line and lift it without changing its slope, a level effect, shifting the trend roughly parallel? It is clear that anything that improves economic efficiency can do that. So trade which increases economic efficiency can almost certainly do that. If what you are looking for is something that will change the slope of the trend line, the rate of growth, then sheer efficiency gains from trade cannot do that except temporarily, not over a very long period of time. The only way you can make sense of trade having an effect on the long-term growth rate is not so much whether the country is export led, but whether the country is in contact with the rest of the world.

So the important factor for growth is the degree of openness of an economy?

Yes, openness in general and especially the will and the capacity to pick up new technology and new ideas from the rest of the world. I am absolutely clear that a positive impact from trade on efficiency and the level of output happens, and that those countries that went in for export-led growth rather than import substitution integrated themselves with the world economy and learned things. Some of it they learned from transplants, from direct foreign investment and multinationals. But whether or not there are any cases of really long-term changes in growth rates as a consequence of trade is I think very uncertain. I can easily imagine a country breaking out from being an underdeveloped stagnant economy and getting on the growth train as a result of trade. That I can easily see. But whether a country that is already growing at the same sort of rate as the OECD economies can improve its *growth rate* over a period of many decades by virtue of openness or trade, that seems to me to be unproved.

There were some interesting papers published in the first issue of the Journal of Economic Growth *(1996) by Robert Barro, Alberto Alesina and others on the relationship between democracy and economic growth, and political instability and economic growth. Barro, for example, suggests that the best way we can help poor countries is to export our economic system to them and, if as a result, their economies improve, they will tend to become more democratic. In other words economic freedom, by promoting economic growth, will eventually lead to more democratic outcomes in today's poor countries. Have you looked at this literature and developed any ideas on these issues?*

That gets into questions that are too big for little old me (*laughter*). But my reaction to that kind of literature has always been as follows. I can easily see that if you compare a democratically organized country with a country which is really tightly oligarchically organized, then the democratically organized economy is going to tap the bigger store of entrepreneurship, whereas the oligarchs in the non-democratic countries pretty soon give up any entrepreneurial pretensions they ever had in favour of wine, women and song or whatever (*laughter*). There is also the question of whether you can run a modern economy in a tightly authoritarian regime or whether these are incompatible. What happens next in China is going to be the big example of this dilemma. I can understand this kind of difference. But the notion that if you could take roughly democratic countries and order them on a scale from zero to one, that going from 0.5 to 0.6 on a measure of democracy gets you a big or detectable difference in growth rate or even the level of output, that seems to be much less likely.

The greens and environmentalists are always warning everyone that the costs of economic growth will eventually outweigh the benefits. Do you ever worry about the environmental consequences of growth? Can the world sustain OECD levels of output per capita for China, South Asia, Africa and Latin America?

Yes, I worry first of all that rapid population growth will begin to encroach on the possibilities of improving productivity and on the environment. Furthermore, one of my sons is interested in these issues professionally; he likes to say that China is made of coal, that China is just one large coal deposit. Now if they were simply to burn that coal, while it might not have any effect on the growth rate of GDP as we measure GDP, it would certainly have a big effect on the growth of some rough welfare equivalent of GDP. Yes, of course I worry about these things. I worry more about that than I do about resource exhaustion, simply because we seem to be a lot further from resource exhaustion. By the way, I do think that the issue of the relationship between economic growth and the environment is, to put it crudely, probably going to boil down to a race between technology and pollution. We do not have much of a grip on the likely outcome of that issue and possibly cannot get much of a grip on it. It is foolish to be a fatuous optimist on these issues, but it is equally foolish to believe that we have come to the end of our capacity to overcome resource limitations technologically.

THE DEVELOPMENT OF MODERN MACROECONOMICS

It is now some 15 years since your interview with Arjo Klamer. At that time you identified yourself as being a Keynesian. Are you still happy with the label of being a Keynesian economist?
Yes, I am. I interpret being a Keynesian economist in a particular way and this is important. I am not someone who believes that everything that is said in the *General Theory of Employment, Interest and Money* (to the extent that you can figure out what is being said) is true, or that everything that is true or interesting about macroeconomics fits into that framework. I think that there are two types of vision or temperament in macroeconomics. First of all, there are macro-economists who want to establish a canonical model, and then answer whatever question they are interested in by using that model. Whether it be the effect of fiscal policy on inflation or whatever, you use the model and find an answer by applying that model. That is one group. Another group of macroeconomists thinks that macroeconomics is a complicated subject, and what is more, what happens to be true changes from time to time as institutions change and firms and people react to changes. In this view, what macroeconomics ought to be is a collection of models each of which focuses on one or two of the macroeconomic mechanisms that might be operating out there. So when you come to a problem like the effect of fiscal policy on inflation, you ask yourself, now which of the models that I know or that my colleagues know, is likely to throw some light on this issue. The Keynesian part of the profession, so to speak, tends to fall into that second group. The other group, I do not know what to call them, but they have come to be known as real business cycle theorists and new classical economists, represents the other approach. They think that there ought to be a true model, and then you just spin out its implications. Now I am definitely in that second group of tinkerers and eclectics. The other thing that being a Keynesian economist means to me is that I ask myself the following question. Can I name or think of mechanisms, detectable in the real world, that make for wage and price stickiness and make for very slow adjustment to real shocks? Well, I can think of dozens of them. I feel no impulse, which the anti-Keynesian group feels, to say: no, I must not admit that; what I must do is find some way in which greed and rationality together will lead precisely to these mechanisms. They may look to a poor jerk like Solow like some imperfections that are just sitting out there; but they are really the higher perfection,

very likely the optimal institutional response, given informational constraints and so on. I just do not feel that impulse. It seems to me that this is not a worthwhile enterprise.

You are known as a neoclassical economist as well as a Keynesian economist. Does this produce any underlying tension?
None at all. My best stab at a description of the world is that over long periods of time it adjusts toward some sort of neoclassical equilibrium, though definitely not a simple competitive equilibrium, but in the short-to-medium run it exhibits many rigidities and multiplicities that make it behave more the way Keynes described. I seem to remember that Bob Lucas (1981b) once wrote that this view is illogical. I think I know what he had in mind; but I think it is wrong. My belief is that it is bad economics to stick rigidly to a single model. I enjoy sailing small boats. I know I can sail in the short run as if the earth is flat, and make occasional adjustments so that a long voyage will take account of curvature.

It is not inconceivable that Keynes could still have been alive in 1969 when the first Nobel Prize was awarded: he would have been in his mid-80s. If that had been the case do you think he would have been awarded the first prize and if so what would the citation have been?
That gets into barnyard questions. If the Nobel Prize in economics was awarded not by Swedes, but by some other group, then I think that Keynes might very well have been chosen. I do not say that in any derogatory way. If I had been a Swedish economist, I would have said: 'What is so special about this guy?' You can read what we now call Keynesian-type ideas in the work of Lindahl, Ohlin, Myrdal, Lundberg and others. But I think that Keynes was in fact a big improvement on the Stockholm way of doing macroeconomics, because it was much easier to generate transparent models out of the *General Theory*. So I would have voted for him and the citation would have said something like: Keynes is someone whose work allows, permits, demands, attention to those forces that created the Great Depression of the 1930s. While he did not provide a complete understanding of that phenomenon, any more than modern astronomers understand the big bang (that is an empty comparison since I don't know beans about any of that), he did draw attention to a big problem and he provided usable tools for addressing this remarkable event so that we could learn something about it. All our talk about automatic stabilizers, just for example, derives from his ideas. He was, as Pigou said, the first real macroeconomist.

Another area which you have been associated with in macroeconomics has been the various controversies surrounding the Phillips curve. Recently Robert

Leeson (1997b) had an interesting paper published which discusses your well-known 1960 paper co-authored with Paul Samuelson. Leeson talks at length about the 1959 AEA conference where you presented that paper and also refers to the various background debates which were taking place with regard to anti-inflation policy. What do you recall about the context in which that paper was prepared and given?

Yes, Leeson has sent me some of his manuscripts and I have read some of them. He writes too long a paper for my taste, so I do not get to read them all. But his description of events in that paper does not correspond to my recollection. My recollection goes like this: here is this paper written by Bill Phillips. I read it, Paul read it, we talked about it. How could you resist a paper that seemed to be able to organize data over more than a century of British history? I am talking now about how we got to write our paper. We began thinking about it and asking ourselves: do we believe this story? Upon investigation we discovered there was not anything remotely so neat about US data. But if you read the data sympathetically you came upon the possibility of a Phillips-like interpretation, but without the stability suggested by the British data. There had not then been much American writing about the Phillips curve because his paper only came out in November 1958, and it was 1959 when we wrote ours. We were just curious; and we were trying to understand inflation, slow or creeping inflation as it was called in those days. We were looking especially at the period between 1953 and 1958 and we thought the Phillips curve provided some help in understanding slow inflation. We did not start from debates relating to incomes policy. Leeson casts all this as some sort of dark drama of conflicting ideas and personalities, and that does not correspond at all to my recollection.

Let us turn to the important contribution of Milton Friedman with his 1968 paper on the expectations-augmented Phillips curve. James Tobin (1995) has suggested that this paper, 'The Role of Monetary Policy', is 'very likely the most influential article ever published in an economics journal'. Do you share Tobin's assessment?

I do not know how you can make that judgement but it is certainly right up there in the top twenty.

As far as we can trace it Friedman first brought up this idea of the expectations-augmented Phillips curve in a debate that he had with you in April 1966. This was a debate on the role of wage and price guideposts (see Friedman, 1966; Solow, 1966). How did you react to this idea?

Well, I took it in. But the 1960 paper that Samuelson and I wrote actually already said something about expectations. We said that this apparently stable relationship between wage or price inflation and unemployment could be systematically upset by induced expectational changes. We did not ask if that was likely to happen or what it would do to macro theory if it did happen, but we were aware of it. However we did not see it as being as central as it became later. I have to say that I am always uncomfortable with arguments in economics that rest heavily on expectations, not because I think that they are not important but because it is a kind of all purpose alibi. Since you do not ever see expectations, you can always invent an expectations story that will explain nearly any sequence of events, and that is too easy.

It is now some 25 years since Bob Lucas brought rational expectations into macroeconomics. Is it the best expectations hypothesis we have?
The big intellectual advantage of rational expectations is that it is definite. The complement of rational expectations is a very large grab-bag. I think that sort of problem explains why Herb Simon's (1957) notion of 'bounded rationality' has never caught on despite its obvious truth. It is too indefinite; it does not tell you what to *do*. My impression is that there are some applications where rational expectations is empirically appropriate. But I believe that theories of the labour market or of macroeconomic general equilibrium built on rational expectations have proved to be empirically unsatisfactory. There has not been much experimentation with other specific hypotheses about the formation of expectations. It is intrinsically very difficult to make such tests anyway because they have to be so indirect. We do not observe expectations themselves.

Where do you now stand in the rules v discretion debate in the conduct of stabilization policy?
I stand where I have always stood. I have not changed my mind at all. My view is that, first of all, you cannot in practice have a rules-run monetary or fiscal policy. There are occasions when the temptation to fudge on the rule is just so great, and the penalty for not doing it may be so great, that the central bank will fudge. They will of course cover themselves, and say they are really obeying a rule but are just doing it in nine dimensions instead of eight dimensions, or some other escape valve. So I do not really think that it is a practical proposition. Secondly, the rules side of that debate comes fundamentally from distrust of democratic government and, in principle, I do not distrust democratic government. Some governments I distrust more that others but I am certainly not prepared to say everyone is feeding at a trough somewhere and if you allow the central bank discretion, the central bank will misuse it. Nicky Kaldor used to say that if you really are convinced that central bankers make inflation, then shoot them if there is inflation, that will stop them. That probably violates their constitutional rights. But my impression of central bankers and many people in government is that they are trying

to do the best they can and I do not see any reason to tie them down that completely. I suppose that even a believer in rules will agree that occasions will arise when departure from the rule would be a good thing; the down side is that then the central bank will feel free to violate the rule when doing so would be a mistake. Possibly so; but that calls for a complicated cost–benefit analysis. More to the point, I think the whole distinction is much overblown. A sensible rule, like John Taylor's (1993b, 1994), describes what a sensible central bank would be doing anyway.

Since the CEA was formed in 1946 economists' views of the role of fiscal policy have changed considerably. In particular the short-run stabilizing role of fiscal policy has been downgraded relative to monetary policy and the important role for fiscal policy is now seen to be mainly in terms of its role in promoting economic efficiency and long-term objectives such as growth. Do you agree with this interpretation and if so does it mean that the discretionary stabilizing role of fiscal policy, associated with orthodox Keynesianism, is dead?

I am going to state an American's view about America; but I think at least some of it applies to Europe as well. Discretionary fiscal policy seems to be paralysed for two reasons. First, the median voter seems to be hooked on public services that he or she does not want to pay for. Indiscriminate tax reduction is always popular. So fiscal policy has become a one-way street. But intelligent fiscal stabilization has to be able to move both ways, roughly symmetrically. This situation is obviously a recipe for trouble. Secondly, it is hard to invent and negotiate a neutral fiscal package. Any tax-expenditure change will have allocational and distributional effects. Lobbyists descend, and legislators listen. Any outcome, good or bad, will take a long time to negotiate. So timely fiscal stabilization seems to be very unlikely. Mind you, monetary policy also has allocational and distributional effects. But the institutional framework allows quick action, accompanied by mystificatory talk. So monetary policy gets the stabilization job by default. This is a lot better than nothing (which is what the Europeans have accomplished for themselves). But it leaves problems. One instrument can achieve one target, with luck; but we find ourselves trying to load every policy target on to the central bank, and that won't do.

You said in response to an earlier question that you do not in principle distrust democratic government. Are you therefore critical of economists such as William Nordhaus (1975) and Alberto Alesina (1989) who have stressed the potentially distorting influence on macroeconomic targets and instruments of opportunistic and ideological political behaviour?

I have just answered that question implicitly: no, I accept that those who are trying to think systematically about the biases in discretionary policy are thinking about something important. When I said that I do not distrust democratic government, I did not mean that I believe democratic government to be free of opportunism, bias, vested interest and distortion. I meant two things. The first is that policy by rule does not escape that difficulty. Someone has to choose the rule; and choice by undemocratic means will likely be even more subject to vested interest and opportunism. I had in mind also that the circumstances of an economy or a society change over time. Those changed circumstances have to be reflected in policy. And I believe that democratic government is the best way for those changes to be negotiated. People eventually figure out if they are being well or poorly served by economic policy. In the meantime swindles and foolishness occur, but that's life.

A central feature of orthodox Keynesian economics was the idea that unemployment could be involuntary. As a Keynesian do you still feel that involuntary unemployment is a useful concept in macroeconomics given that many prominent macroeconomists such as Robert Lucas (1978a) and Milton Friedman (see Snowdon and Vane, 1997b) would prefer to bury the idea for good?
I think that Keynes's use of the particular phrase was a bad move. The words, the semantics, always suggest a nonsensical question: do you choose to be unemployed? Compared with what? But you can take the definition that is actually there in the *General Theory*, and loosen it up so it says that someone is involuntarily unemployed if he or she would be prepared to work at a job that he or she knows how to do, at the going wage, and cannot find employment. That is good enough for me. You will notice that by this definition a person can be involuntary unemployed and employed at the same time. If you take an inferior job you can still be an involuntary unemployed skilled worker. That seems to me to be a centrally important idea. Macroeconomics is not primarily about unemployed bodies but about idle capacity.

Your 1979 paper on efficiency wages was very influential. To what extent do you think that efficiency wage theory has provided a plausible explanation of involuntary unemployment as an equilibrium phenomenon?
The phrase 'efficiency wage theory' covers a number of different hypotheses. My own favourite involves morale considerations in a major way. (Some extensive and very important observational work by Truman Bewley seems to confirm that.) It seems to me that the class of efficiency wage theories is very important and very useful, because they give an account of equilibrium unemployment in which employers help to enforce the equilibrium. It is hard to believe that observed real wages are always close to what a clean spot market would generate, and informal mechanisms seem more important than formal ones like trade-union bargaining, and so on.

The current unemployment experience in Europe has attracted the attention of many economists, not least because that experience contrasts markedly with the experience of unemployment in the US economy since the 1980s. In the Summer 1997 issue of the Journal of Economic Perspectives *Horst Siebert argues that 'institutional changes affecting Europe's labour market over the last twenty years are a main reason for Europe's poor labour market performance'. Do you accept this view of the contrasting US and European experiences with unemployment?*

The character of European labour markets is almost certainly an important factor in the prolonged high unemployment experienced by France and Germany. So I would agree with Horst Siebert's careful sentence. But too many Europeans stop right there. It does not follow, logically or empirically, that 'labour-market rigidity' is the whole story, and in fact I am convinced that it is not. I do not see how one can avoid the conclusion that the large European economies have bent themselves out of shape trying to meet the Maastricht criteria, and in the course of doing so have generated quite a lot of straightforward inadequate-aggregate-demand unemployment. It cannot be sensible policy to hamstring fiscal policy and monetary policy simultaneously. I have not done the work to tell me if Keynesian unemployment accounts for five points of the French total or more or less. But there is plenty of evidence that it is not trivial. There is also probably some truth in hysteresis arguments, and the Europeans have dredged themselves in hysteresis by now.

In your recently published debate with John Taylor, Inflation, Unemployment and Monetary Policy *(MIT Press, 1998) you present a strong case for what you call 'exploratory monetary policy' as long as there is uncertainty about the natural rate of unemployment, a concept you describe as 'theoretically and empirically as soft as a grape'. With US unemployment currently (January 1998) running at less than 5 per cent do you feel that the views you expressed in that book have been vindicated?*

Yes I do. I realize those are famous last words; I certainly do not believe in any 'new paradigm' nonsense. The current honeymoon may not last, and in any case there clearly are limits to how tightly we or anyone can safely run the economy. The difficulty is to know where they are. If inflation starts to pick up, I will be the first to urge that the Fed backtrack cautiously, just as it advanced cautiously. I certainly think that recent events have tended to confirm that 'exploratory' idea. There is little or nothing to support the conventional 'irreversible trap' picture.

At last year's AEA conference in New Orleans you contributed a paper in the session on 'Applied Economics in Action: The Role of the Council of Economic Advisers' (Solow, 1997a). In that paper you described the CEA as a body whose main role could be described as that of an 'intellectual sanitation worker'. What exactly did you mean by that and was this a view formed as a result of personal experience at the CEA?

I meant that my experience as a staff member of the CEA (and this has been expressed by others with similar experiences) has taught me that perhaps the main contribution that the Council makes is to shoot down bad ideas before they take root. In any democratically elected government there are agencies of the government that represent specific interests. There is a labour department, an agricultural department, and so on. The people in those agencies are forever proposing projects or ideas whose main outcome is that it helps their constituents, or at least it makes them look good to their constituents. Most of those ideas are bad ideas; they will not achieve what they are supposed to achieve, or their cost–benefit ratios are very unfavourable. Someone has got to squelch them before they get a foothold, and that is what we were forever doing. We were forever turning up at inter-agency meetings and saying, no that is not the way things go. And then you tell your client, who for the CEA is the President, this is a really bad idea, do not encourage it. If he listens, great. That is what I meant. But I also went further than that because I think that one of the really important functions of economics in general is to knock down silly ideas. It is not just inside government that silly ideas surface and become popular. You can pick up the *Wall Street Journal* or the *New York Times* or the *San Francisco Chronicle* any day and find a lousy idea in it . Let me give you an example that frustrates the hell out of me right now. If you have been reading the US newspapers you know that because the Federal budget may turn into surplus, given the way it is measured, there are influential people who say, oh we can now do things with the surplus. I do not mind that in principle. A democratic country has to use its resources in a way that corresponds to voters' preferences. But I thought that some years ago we had finally got across the idea that the balance of the budget is an endogenous variable, and you should be looking at the balance of the budget at some fixed level of capacity utilization. But nobody remembers that anymore. I have not read anybody saying that the budget may go into surplus but as of x per cent unemployment there is still a deficit of a half a per cent of GDP or so. It is that kind of lesson which just seems to have vanished. So we have to go back and teach them again.

You frequently defend the mainstream in economics from critiques launched by economists such as Bob Lucas, who are new classical in their approach, as well as more heterodox critics such as Bob Clower and David Colander. Do you see yourself as a representative of the mainstream position in macro-economics, or for that matter economics in general?

Yes, I guess I am a mainstream economist. I feel most comfortable with the centre of the literature. Economics is a very complicated subject, there are a lot of aspects to it and there are a lot of different ways of looking at macro-economics. But we seem to do best if we stick to what can be deduced from standard theory. I am always prepared to accept a new idea if it is a good one. The notion that there is some new paradigm out there is possible, but I have not seen any real overturning of the standard mainstream view.

So if we have a good understanding of the basic demand and supply model, the IS–LM, AD–AS model and the Solow growth model we can go a long way?
That will take you a long way. And in that order by the way.

Your early interest in sociology seems to have had a lasting impact on your views. From reading some of your work it seems to have given you a broader perspective than most economists, particularly when it comes to looking at the operation of the labour market. For example, in your book The Labour Market as a Social Institution *(1990) you draw attention to the importance of the issue of 'fairness' when it comes to looking at how the labour market actually works. George Akerlof and Janet Yellen (1988, 1990) have also made this point in several papers relating to efficiency wages. Would macroeconomists in general benefit from taking a broader perspective, especially when it comes to labour market issues?*
Obviously I think so. But you do not need to have been a student of Talcott Parsons, as I once was, to come to that realization. I do not see how any reasonable observer could believe that wages and employment in advanced economies approximate the outcome of a purely competitive spot market. I might say much the same thing about the market for loans or for fashion goods, for example. But the labour market is certainly the key case, both because it is so pervasive and because it is so close to the surface that considerations like equity, status and normed behaviour play an important role in determining actual outcomes. Art Okun's (1981) concept of the 'customer market' (further developed by Ian McDonald, 1992) makes it thoroughly believable that other markets would be more understandable if they were analysed from this broader point of view. I should say explicitly that this is definitely not a brief for 'softness' or vagueness in macroeconomics (or elsewhere). What I am after are *models*, good solid models, that incorporate (and even parameterize) these considerations and the institutional realities that embody them. Unfortunately academic sociology and social psychology do not usually provide reliable insights in a form that would be useful to an economic modeller. Of course, they are engaged in frying their fish, not ours.

Do you see any signs of an emerging consensus in macroeconomics?
Actually I do. A year ago Al Harberger asked me to organize a session at the AEA convention, and I did so under the general title: Is there a core of

practical macroeconomics that we should all believe? There were four very short papers, plus a fifth by me. I very carefully chose very able, reasonably pragmatic people from both ends of the spectrum. Let us call them the real-business-cycle end and the neo-Keynesian end. I really wanted to counter the cheap nihilistic view that macroeconomics is no damn good, just a bunch of ideological prejudices expressed in algebra. You can read the papers (Solow et al., 1997). It worked out even better than I had dared to hope because there turned out to be quite a lot of common ground among Marty Eichenbaum, John Taylor, Olivier Blanchard, Alan Blinder and me. You might say that I cooked that outcome by leaving out the really strong-minded people. Of course I did. You do not expect *everyone* to agree about an intrinsically complex and uncertain subject like macroeconomics. We need those strong-minded extremists who stick to a doctrinaire line and say common sense be damned. We do not have to believe them, God help us, but they perform a useful function in keeping us wishy-washy sheep in the broad middle honest. I only wanted to show that the broad middle has some coherence.

What sort of issues are you currently working on?
Well, not much. I am going on 74 years old and travelling a lot, as you have noticed. I do not have a long, active research agenda at the moment, although I would like to get back to one if I can. I still intend to do work in macroeconomics. The main thing that I want to work further on is what macroeconomics looks like when it takes imperfect competition seriously. Frank Hahn and I wrote an approximately unreadable book (1995) which was published a couple of years ago. There we made an attempt to outline how you might make a macro model that takes imperfect competition seriously, and possibly also takes increasing returns seriously, because increasing returns to scale are a standard reason why competition is imperfect. We might have done reasonably well in that particular chapter, but we did not carry the model nearly far enough. In particular we did not develop it to the point where you could sensibly ask what the appropriate values are for the main parameters, if the model is to be roughly in the ball park for the US, British or German economy. I would like to go back and develop that model further. I also have a couple of ideas on growth theory but that is another story.

Paul M. Romer
(b. 1955)

Copyright: Anne Knudsen

Paul Romer is currently Professor of Economics at Stanford University. He is best known for his very influential contributions to the field of economic growth which have led to the renaissance of economic growth analysis and, in particular, the development of endogenous growth models.

We interviewed Professor Romer in Chicago, in his hotel room, on 5 January 1998 while attending the annual conference of the American Economic Association.

BACKGROUND INFORMATION

Where and when did you first begin to study economics?
I was a math and physics major at the University of Chicago. I took my first economics course in my senior year because I was planning to go to law school. I did well in the class and the professor encouraged me to go on to graduate school to study economics. Economics offered some of the same intellectual appeal as physics – it uses simple mathematical models to understand how the world works – and in contrast to physics, it was an area of academic study where I could actually get a job.

In some ways staying at the University of Chicago was attractive because it had a very exciting economics department but I had already been there for four years. Even though I had had very little Chicago economics training I did not think it was a good idea to spend my whole career as a student in one place, so I started in the PhD programme at MIT. There I met my wife who was just visiting for a year from Queens University in Canada. After two years at MIT we went back to Queens to finish her final year of training in medicine. That was when I started working on growth. At the end of that year I transferred to Chicago, where my wife had a fellowship position, and completed my PhD. I finished my PhD and entered the job market in 1982 – my thesis is actually dated 1983 because it took me a year to polish it up.

As a student did you find any of your teachers to be particularly influential or inspirational?

Well, Sam Peltzman was the professor who encouraged me to switch my career path from law to economics. I shudder to think what my life would have been like if he hadn't asked to talk with me after the midterm and I had gone on to law school. It is an episode that I try to keep in mind – that professors can be very influential, and a little bit of attention to your students as people can make a big difference in their lives.

Besides having saved me from a life in the law, Sam was also an excellent teacher. He was the first person to show me that you could take very simple tools – demand curves or indifference curves – and derive surprising insights about how the world works. Having mentioned Sam, I should also mention some other very good teachers that I had. Donald McCloskey, now Deirdre McCloskey, was the second person I had for economics. Donald, like Sam, took economics very seriously. Together, they gave me an excellent introduction to the subject. I should also mention that at Chicago, they did not offer what is known as a 'principles' course, the watered-down, mind-numbing survey course that most universities offer as a first course in economics. At Chicago, they started right off at the intermediate microeconomics level. So I had the enormous advantage of starting off with challenging, intellectually coherent material and first-rate teachers. I was very fortunate.

Later in graduate school, when I was back at Chicago, Bob Lucas and Jose Scheinkman had a big influence on my style and the way I look at the world. They set a standard for rigour and discipline – zero tolerance for intellectual sloppiness – that I have aspired to ever since. But probably the best year of graduate school was the year I spent at Queens University because I had a lot of interaction with the faculty there. Normally as a graduate student you do not really get that much time to sit and talk with members of the faculty as colleagues. At Queens I had more of that kind of experience. Some of the people I talked with intensively during that year – Russell Davidson and James McKinnon – are terrific economists and had a big effect on my career.

DEVELOPMENT OF MACROECONOMICS

Are there any particular papers or books that you would identify as having a major influence on the development of macroeconomics?
For me that's too broad a question. I could list all the usual suspects, people like Keynes, and so on. I'd be more comfortable describing the contributions that have influenced my own work.

Tell us about the influences on your own research interests.
Bob Lucas brought a style to macroeconomics that had a big impact on a whole generation of people, including me. There are several papers that exemplify this style. One is his 1972 *Journal of Economic Theory* paper on 'Expectations and the Neutrality of Money'. Another would be his 1978 *Econometrica* paper 'Asset Prices in an Exchange Economy'. But his 1971 *Econometrica* paper, 'Investment Under Uncertainty,' written with Edward Prescott, is probably the best example because it really brought to the forefront and crystallized for macroeconomists the connection between what we did in macroeconomics and what the rest of the profession had been doing in general equilibrium theory. In that paper Lucas and Prescott used the connection between solving optimization problems and equilibria that has become such a powerful tool in modern macroeconomics. That 1971 paper builds on the work of people like Cass (1965) and Koopmans (1965) who had been working in growth theory, and this basic approach for characterizing dynamic equilibria can be traced all the way back to Frank Ramsey's (1928) paper. Still, Lucas and Prescott took this approach much further into the core of macroeconomics. If all you have seen is the theory of investment as developed by the macro modellers and presented by the macro textbook writers, this paper is like a flash of lighting in the night that suddenly shows you where you are in a much bigger landscape.

You mentioned the influence of Bob Lucas's work. What do you think has been the lasting impact of his work, particularly the work he carried out in the 1970s for which he was awarded the Nobel Prize?
I think the deeper impact of Lucas's contributions has been on the methodology of the profession. He took general equilibrium theory and operationalized it so that macroeconomists could calculate and characterize the behaviour of the whole economy. Just as Peltzman and McCloskey took intermediate microeconomics seriously, Lucas took general equilibrium theory seriously. Many of the people doing general equilibrium theory for a living did not really seem to believe in what they were doing. They gave the impression that it was a kind of mathematical game. Economists working in trade and growth had shown us how we could use general equilibrium models, but they were

not ready to bring dynamics and uncertainty into the analysis. It was econo-mists working first in finance, then in macroeconomics, who took the theory seriously and showed economists that fully specified dynamic models with uncertainty had real implications about the world. A very important result of that methodological shift was a much greater focus on, and a much deeper understanding of, the role of expectations. But this is only part of the deeper methodological innovation. You still wouldn't know it from reading text-books, but to research professionals, it finally is clear that you can't think about the aggregate economy using a big supply curve and a big demand curve.

One of the ironies in this revolution in thinking is that the two people who did the most to bring it about, Lucas and Robert Solow ended up at swords' points about the substantive conclusions that this methodology had for macro-economic policy. Solow's work has also had a huge impact on the profession, pushing us in the same direction. His work on growth also persuaded econo-mists to take simple general equilibrium models seriously. Many people recognize the differences between Lucas and Solow over macro policy ques-tions, but fail to appreciate the strong complementarity between their work at the methodological level. If Joan Robinson had won the day and banished the concept of a production function from professional discourse, Lucas and Prescott could never have written 'Investment Under Uncertainty'.

During the 1980s, the real business cycle approach to aggregate fluctuations developed in parallel with new growth theory. How do you view that work, in particular the way it has sought to integrate the analysis of fluctuations and growth?
A lot of the progress in economics still comes from building new tools that help us understand very complicated systems. As a formal or mathematical science, economics is still very young. You might say it is still in early adolescence. Remember, at the same time that Einstein was working out the theory of General Relativity in physics, economists were still talking to each other using ambiguous words and crude diagrams.

To see where real business cycle theory fits in, you have to look not just at its substance and conclusions but also at how it affected the methodological trajectory I was talking about before. You can think of a hierarchy of general equilibrium models – that is models of the whole economy. At the top you have models of perfect competition, which are Pareto optimal so that you can solve a maximization problem and immediately calculate the behaviour of the economy. Then, at the next level down, you have a variety of models with some kind of imperfection – external effects, taxes, nominal money, or some kind of non-convexity. In many cases you can find a way to use some of the same maximization tools to study those dynamic models even though their equilibria are not Pareto optimal. This is what Lucas did in his 1972 paper 'Expectations and the Neutrality of Money'. Formally it is like an external effect in that model. It is also what I did in my first paper on growth.

The real business cycle guys went one step further than Lucas or I did in trying to simplify the analysis of aggregate economies. They said, 'We can go all the way with pure perfect competition and pure Pareto optimality. We can even model business cycles this way. Doing so simplifies the analysis tremendously and we can learn a lot when we do it.' My personal view – and increasingly the view of many of the people like Bob King who worked in this area – is that at a substantive level real business cycle theory simplifies too much. It excludes too many elements that you need to understand business cycles. This doesn't mean that the initial work was bad. It just means that we are now ready to go on to the next stage and bring back in things like predetermined nominal prices. Methodologically this work helped us refine our tools so we'll do a better job of understanding predetermined prices when we bring them back into the model.

We frequently make progress in economics by seeming to take a step backwards. We assume away real problems that people have been working on in vague and confused ways, strip things down to their bare essentials, and get a better handle on the essentials using some new tools. Then we bring the complications back in. This is what Solow was doing, and what drove Robinson to distraction, when he modelled the production structure of an economy using an aggregate production function. Later we brought back many of those complications – irreversible investment, limited *ex post* substitution possibilities, and so on – back into the model. The real business cycle theorists did the same kind of thing, and during the simplification phase, they also made people mad.

ECONOMIC GROWTH

In Lucas's (1988) paper 'On the Mechanics of Economic Development' he comments that once you start to think about growth it is hard to think about anything else. In the introduction of their textbook Economic Growth *Robert Barro and Xavier Sala-i-Martin (1995) argue that economic growth is the part of macroeconomics that really matters. In the light of these comments by very influential macroeconomists do you think that, on reflection, economists have in the past spent too much time trying to understand business cycles?*
That is almost right. Remember that we experienced major macroeconomic calamities in the inter-war period. These depressions were sufficient to wipe out 30 to 40 years' worth of growth. Economists who grew up during this era certainly didn't have any trouble thinking about something else besides long-run growth. They naturally focused on avoiding those calamities.

So I don't think that you can make the statement that focusing on growth is more important in some absolute sense than focusing on stabilization. What I think is correct is that we now know how to avoid the kind of catastrophic events that we saw in the UK in the 1920s and in the US in the 1930s. Those were both major mistakes in monetary policy and we now know how to avoid them. We also know how to avoid the disruptive hyperinflations of the inter-war era. Recently, we have even developed better monetary rules for avoiding the less disruptive but still costly inflation of the 1970s. Once you have learnt to avoid those kinds of problems, growth stands out as the most important remaining issue on the agenda.

I do believe that there was a period in the 1960s and 1970s, when macroeconomists were spending too much time looking at business cycles – the smaller cycles and fluctuations which characterized the postwar period – and too little time on growth. We should have kept working on stabilization policy, but we should also have worked on the determinants of long-run growth. Adjusting the balance is what my career has been all about.

When I teach students I try very hard to get them to get this balance right. I give them an analogy about a runner who is trying to train for a marathon. Asking whether growth is more important than stabilization is like asking whether conditioning is more important than putting on a tourniquet when the runner starts bleeding. In a sense the training and the technique of running really are what wins races. But if the runner is bleeding to death, it is pretty silly to lecture her about getting in better shape.

But now, when we look at the allocation of the profession's intellectual resources today, we are in a situation where we can learn more about how to make minor adjustments in the amplitude of cycles or in the trend rate of growth. Faced with that trade-off, it is very clear that small improvements in the trend rate of growth can have far greater effects on the quality of life and this area has been understudied.

Looking back, one of the reasons why economists avoided questions about growth was that our tools were not sufficiently well developed. Purely technical or mathematical issues about the existence of a solution to an infinite horizon maximization problem, transversality conditions, knife-edge behaviour and explosive growth deterred economists from asking the right kind of substantive questions about long-run growth. Now that our tools are better, we have been able to set those issues aside and make progress on the substantive questions.

The classical economists were very concerned with long-run issues such as growth. Did you find any inspiration for your work by going back and looking at the contributions of the classical economists and other early work on growth?

I did spend some time thinking about that, reading Adam Smith and Alfred Marshall. For example, I read the 1928 paper by Allyn Young, which builds on Marshall's work. I think it is in the same issue of the *Economic Journal* as Ramsey's paper. So there was a period where I spent a couple of years trying to sort out the connections between what Young and Smith were saying and what I was trying to say. I did that for a while and enjoyed it, then I stopped doing it. I am not sure I would recommend it as a research strategy for a young person but it can be interesting and instructive.

When I started working on growth I had read almost none of the previous literature. I started very much from a clean sheet of paper and only later went back to try and figure out what other people had said. I think that in a lot of cases that is the right way to do it. If you devote too much attention to ancestor worship, you can get trapped and lose the chance to see things from a new perspective. Of course, in economics, your ancestors are still around, occupying positions of power in the profession, and they are not always happy when someone comes along and tries to take a fresh look at things.

During the whole period from the marginalist revolution in the 1870s through to the mid-1950s economists were mainly concerned with microeconomic developments and managing the birth of macroeconomics during the Great Depression. Then the issue of economic growth came back onto the scene during the 1950s. One of the puzzles is that during the period when growth theory made great advances, with the contributions of Solow in 1956 and 1957, the field of development economics seemed to evolve as an almost separate area of interest. Why did that dichotomy happen?

I am probably going to sound like a broken record here, repeating my message over and over, but the divide was methodological. The growth guys talked math; the development guys still talked words. They diverged further and further apart because they could not understand each other. It was less the differences in the substantive questions they were asking, than the tools they were selecting to try and address them.

Wasn't it more the case that development economists actually wanted and needed to say something about policy issues?

There was an element of that. As I said about the real business cycle theorists, sometimes you have to take a step back and simplify to make progress developing new formal tools. This is hard to do when you are in the thick of the process of trying to offer policy advice.

If you go back and read Smith, Marshall or Young, you have to be struck by what an incredibly wrenching transformation the economics profession has gone through, from operating as a purely verbal science to becoming a purely mathematical one. Remember that Allyn Young's paper came out at the same time, even in the same issue, as Frank Ramsey's. Ramsey was using tools like the calculus of variations that physicists had been using for decades. But economists were still having trouble with basic calculus. Jacob Viner needed help from his draftsman to get the connection right between long-run and short-run average cost curves. Nowadays economists use math that is as sophisticated and as formal as the math that physicists use. So we went through a very sharp transition in a relatively short period of time. As we learned how to use mathematics we made some trade-offs. You could think of a kind of production possibility frontier, where one axis is tools and the other axis is results. When you shift effort towards the direction of building tools you are going to produce less in the way of results. So the development guys would look at Solow and say, 'What you are producing has no useful content for policy makers in the development world, you guys are just off in mathematical space wasting time while we are out here in the real world making a difference.' The tool builders should have responded by explaining the intertemporal trade-off between results and tool building and that as a result of this work we can give better policy advice in the future. Overall the right stance for the profession as a whole is one where we approve of the division of labour, where the people who specialize in those different activities can each contribute and where we do not try and force the whole profession into one branch or the other. Ideally we should keep the lines of communication open between the two branches.

Let us turn to Robert Solow's contributions. What do you see as being the main strengths and weaknesses of the Solow growth model? Some economists like Greg Mankiw (1995b) would prefer to modify the Solow model rather than follow the endogenous growth path.
When it was introduced, the Solow model made several very important contributions to economics and progress in this tool building direction. It was a very important demonstration of how you could take general equilibrium theory and apply it and say things about the real world. As I suggested before, Solow helped persuade us that there are ways to think about the equilibrium for the whole economy, using simple functional forms and simplifying assumptions, and get some important conclusions out of that. It is a very different style of general equilibrium theory from that of Arrow and Debreu and their more abstract work that was going on at the same time. Remember that Solow and Samuelson had to engage in vicious trench warfare about this time with Cambridge, England, to make the world safe for those of us who wanted to use the concept of a production function.

At the substantive level – which I think is where your question was directed – the strength of Solow's model was that he brought technology explicitly into the analysis in both his empirical paper and his theoretical paper. He had an explicit representation for technology, capital and labour. Those are the three elements that you have to think about if you want to think about growth. That was the good part. The downside was that because of the constraints imposed on him by the existing toolkit, the only way for him to talk about technology was to make it a public good. That is the real weakness of the Solow model. What endogenous growth theory is all about is that it took technology and reclassified it, not as a public good, but as a good which is subject to private control. It has at least some degree of appropriability or excludability associated with it, so that incentives matter for its production and use. But endogenous growth theory also retains the notion of nonrivalry that Solow captured. As he suggested, technology is a very different kind of good from capital and labour because it can be used over and over again, at zero marginal cost. The Solow theory was a very important first step. The natural next step beyond was to break down the public good characterization of technology into this richer characterization – a partially excludable nonrival good. To do that you have to move away from perfect competition and that is what the recent round of growth theory has done. We needed all of the tools that were developed between the late 1950s and the 1980s to make that step.

Let me place the other strand of growth in context, the so-called AK versions of endogenous growth. In these models, technology is just like any other good – we might put another label on it and call it human capital or we can call it generalized capital – but technology is treated as being completely analogous with physical capital. I think that approach actually represented a substantive step backwards compared to the Solow model. The AK models are actually less sophisticated than the Solow model because those models do not recognize that technology is a very different kind of input. As I suggested above, I also disagree with the real business cycle methodology that says 'Let us do everything with perfect competition'. Before, you could argue that there was no alternative, but that's no longer true. We have perfectly serviceable dynamic general equilibrium models with monopolistic competition and there is no reason not to use them if they capture important features of the world.

There is still a group that says 'Let's just treat technology as pure private good and preserve perfect competition'. Then there is another group of economists who, like Mankiw, say that technology is different, but we can treat it as a pure public good just as Solow did. I think that both of these positions are mistaken. There are incredibly important policy issues where the pure private good characterization and the pure public good characterization of technology are just completely off the mark.

Wasn't your earlier work, as exemplified in your 1986 paper, more concerned with increasing returns than the determinants of technology change?

You have to look between the lines of that paper at what was going on at the methodological level, because remember, methodological and formal issues had been holding everything up. The logical sequence in my 1986 paper was to say that as soon as you think about growth, you have to think about technology. As soon as you think about technology, you have to confront the fact that there is a built-in form of increasing returns – technically, a nonconvexity. Notice that is all there in Solow's model. If you look at $AF(K, L)$ you have got increasing returns in all the relevant inputs A, K and L. So up to this point, Solow and I are on the same track. You have to think of technology as a key input and one that is fundamentally different from traditional inputs. As soon as you think about that, you face increasing returns or nonconvexities. Then you have to decide how to model this from a methodological point of view. Solow said treat it as a public good. There are two variants of that. One is that it comes from the sky and is just a function of time. The other is that the government could publicly provide it. I think Solow had both of those in mind and it does not really matter which you specify. What I wanted was a way to have something where there are some increasing returns but also some private provision. I wanted to capture the fact that private individuals and firms made intentional investments in the production of new technologies. So in this sense, the paper was very much about technological change. To allow for private provision, I used the concept of Marshallian external increasing returns. This lets you describe an equilibrium with price-taking but still allows you to have nonconvexities present in the model. That was a first provisional step. It was a way to capture the facts: there is some private control over technology, there are incentives that matter, and there are increasing returns in the background. What happened between 1986 and 1990 was that I worked hard at the mathematics of this and persuaded myself that the external increasing returns characterization was not right either – just as the public goods assumption of Solow was not right.

Whenever you write down theories you make approximations, you take short cuts. You are always trading off the gains from simplicity against the losses in our ability to describe the world. The public good approximation was a reasonable first step, but we needed to keep working and improve on it. The external increasing returns approximation was something of an improvement but the later monopolistic competition version (Romer, 1990) was the one which really gets about the right trade-off between simplicity and relevance.

Since Solow's (1957) paper there has been a huge literature on growth accounting. What do you think have been the main substantive findings from this research?

The general progression in that area has been to attribute a smaller fraction of observed growth to the residual and a higher fraction to the accumulation of inputs. The way that literature started out was a statement that technology is extremely important because it explains the bulk of growth. Where we are now is that technology does not explain, all by itself, the majority of growth. Initially, we overstated its importance when we claimed that technological change explained 70 per cent of growth all by itself. But there are some people who would like to push this further and say there is really no need to understand technology, because it is such a small part of the contribution to growth. They argue that we can just ignore it. That is a non sequitur. It does not follow logically. We know from Solow, and this observation has withstood the test of time, that even if investment in capital contributes directly to growth, it is technology that causes the investment in the capital and indirectly causes all the growth. Without technological change, growth would come to a stop.

When we spoke to Bob Solow yesterday he explained why he made technology exogenous in his model. It was simply due to his lack of understanding of the causes of technological change.
That is a reasonable provisional strategy when you are dealing with a complicated world.

A great deal of attention during the past decade or so has been focused on the so-called convergence issue. At the same time your first important endogenous growth paper was published in 1986, Moses Abramovitz and William Baumol also had papers published that drew attention to this catch-up and convergence debate. This controversy continues to draw research interest, for example, in a recent issue of the Journal of Economic Perspectives *Lant Pritchett (Summer, 1997) has a paper entitled 'Divergence, Big Time'. When we talked to Edward Prescott two days ago he was reasonably confident that convergence would eventually occur. Did this important debate influence your own thinking about growth and what are your views on this area of research?*
It is very important to keep clear what the facts are. The facts are that over the time horizon that people have looked at the data, say from 1950 to the present, there is very little evidence of overall convergence. Everybody agrees about this, even if it is not always stated up front. People who describe this tendency for countries to converge are saying that if everything else were the same – if you hold all the right variables constant – then there would be a tendency for countries to converge. For example, this is one of the key results in Robert Barro's work. This is really just a refined statement of the convergence club interpretation articulated by Baumol. If you look at countries that have the same values for these variables, then they tend to converge. But it is also true that in the background, the overall progress towards reduced disper-

sion in per capita incomes has been very modest. Pritchett was making a useful background point. If you go back before 1950, it must be the case that there was a period where incomes diverged quite a bit – some countries moved very rapidly ahead as others were left behind. At that time, the overall distribution of income widened for a period of time. More recently, in the postwar years, the overall distribution has been roughly constant.

So why do we care about this issue? First you might care about it from a human welfare point of view, or an income distribution point of view. On those grounds there is some reason for pessimism – we really have not made that much progress in the last 30 or 40 years. You might also care about it because you think it might help you discriminate between different theories of growth – which ones are right and which are wrong. Many people have asserted that this process of conditional convergence – everything else equal, incomes converge – is consistent with a pure Solow style model, that is, one where knowledge is a public good, all technology is a public good. So they say the evidence is consistent with the public good model of technology. That statement is correct but the evidence is also completely consistent with a model where technology is not a public good. In this interpretation, the technology gap model, flows of technology between countries is what drives the convergence process. In this explanation, the convergence you see is catching up with technology, not just catching up in the stock of capital per worker. Under the Solow model as interpreted by Mankiw and others, technology is already the same everywhere in the world. It is a public good that is in the air like a short-wave radio broadcast, so under this model there is no room for technological catch-up. It still mystifies me that people try to justify this model in the face of direct evidence about the importance of technology flows. But they certainly use the conditional convergence evidence to back up their position.

So I do not think that the convergence controversy has helped us discriminate between the different models. As a result, I think a great deal of the attention that the convergence controversy has generated has been misplaced. Prescott's assertion is that he does not think that we are going to see continued divergence. I think he is probably right about that. I personally think that these flows of technology between countries are very important forces in the big convergence episodes that we have seen. If you look at a country like Japan and ask what lies behind its very rapid convergence with the leading nations of the world, then the transfer of technology was a critical part of the process. There are grounds for optimism, looking ahead. If we can get the right institutions in place in these developing countries, the same process of flows of technologies could be unleashed and we really could see some narrowing of worldwide income inequality. If you weight it by countries the situation looks worse than if you weight it by people, at least during the last ten years. This is because the process of catching up in China will make a huge difference to the overall picture. And China is a good illustration of what is wrong with the public good model. China had a high savings rate before the reform era. What's most different now in the sectors of manufacturing where China has been so successful, has been the flow of technology into China via direct foreign investment. Reforms that changed the incentives that foreign firms faced to bring technology and put it to work in China.

Did you ever look at the work of economists such as Gunnar Myrdal (1957) and Nicholas Kaldor (1970) who tended to reject the equilibrating properties of the neoclassical model in favour of the forces of cumulative causation? In their models a lack of convergence is no surprise.
It interested me in the same way that Allyn Young interested me. I wanted to see how much there was in common between what I and what they were thinking. But it is very hard to tell, quite frankly, when you go back and read economics that is stated in purely verbal terms. There is always the danger that you read between the lines and say, oh, they had it exactly right – here is this mathematical model which shows what they were thinking. But that is usually based on a charitable reading and one that ignores some of the ambiguities and confusions. I wrote a paper like that at one point interpreting Allyn Young's paper, so one could probably do that for some of the other economists in this area. For example the big push paper by Murphy, Shleifer and Vishny (1989) did this for some of this literature. So the right conclusion to make is that these were very smart people and they did have some good ideas, but they were working with very crude tools. I guess I would describe ancestor worship as a research strategy as probably an unproductive one (*laughter*). But as a consumption activity it is something that can be fun.

Well we want to keep you on the topic of ancestors for a moment. Given that your research has concentrated heavily on the influence and determinants of technological change and the importance of R&D, has the work of Joseph Schumpeter ever influenced your ideas?
No, I can honestly say that it has not. Schumpeter coined some wonderful phrases like 'creative destruction' but I did not read any of Schumpeter's work when I was creating my model. As I said, I really worked that model out from a clean sheet of paper. To be honest, the times when I have gone to try and read Schumpeter I have found it tough going. It is really hard to tell what guys like Schumpeter are talking about (*laughter*).

Too many words and not enough math?
Yes, and words are often ambiguous.

That problem has also been the source of confusion and the various conflicting interpretations of Keynes's General Theory.

Yes, right. Paul Krugman (1994b) has a nice article talking about the big push idea in development economics. When you state it now in mathematical terms, the way Murphy, Shleifer and Vishny did, you see how clearly the idea can be expressed and you wonder why someone had not done it before. I think that what it shows is that economists now are the beneficiaries of a lot of development of mathematical modes of thinking and analysis and it seems very easy to us now because we have those tools to work with. Before these techniques were available it was really very tough.

Let us go back to the issue of nonrivalry and excludability with reference to the growth of knowledge and technological change. How do you get the balance right between encouraging technological change by using incentives and yet making the new ideas and discoveries available to the rest of society? There is a trade-off problem here with respect to patent rights.

Sure. What's interesting about this question is that it is not resolved. If you take traditional private goods that are excludable and rival, we know what the best institutional arrangement is: strong property rights and anonymous markets. That's all you need. This is a remarkably important insight that economists must still communicate to the rest of the world. If people understood it, there would not be so much resistance to pricing roads, pollution or water in agriculture. Non-economists are still slow to understand how powerful the price mechanism is for allocating and producing rival goods.

But when you come to nonrival goods, we do not know what the right institutions are. It is an area that I think is very exciting because there is a lot of room for institutional innovation. One strategy is to work out a rough trade-off where you allow patent rights but you make them be narrow and have a finite duration. You would allow partial excludability – less than full but stronger than zero excludability. We often talk as if that is the general solution. But in fact, this is not the general solution. You have to break the question down by type of nonrival good. There are some nonrival goods like the quadratic formula or pure mathematical algorithms that traditionally have been given no property rights whatsoever. There are other forms of nonrival goods like books. You will get a copyright for this book of interviews, which is a very strong form of protection. The text that you write and my words – you can take them and put a copyright on them so that nobody else can re-use them. I can not even re-use my own words without getting permission from you (*laughter*). So that is a very strong form of intellectual property protection. What we need is a much more careful differentiation of different types of nonrival goods and an analysis of why different institutional structures and degrees of property protection are appropriate for different kinds of goods.

Patent rights or legal property rights are only a part of the story. We create other mechanisms, like subsidies for R&D. We create whole institutions like universities which are generally nonprofit and government supported, that are designed to try and encourage the production of ideas. The analysis of institutions for nonrival goods is more subtle than many people realize.

For example, I have argued that it is very important to distinguish human capital from ideas – they are very different types of economic goods. Human capital is just like capital or land. It is an ordinary private good. I agree with Gary Becker on this. I think a lot of claims about human capital externalities are wrong. Nevertheless, when people conclude that we should not have any government subsidies for the production of human capital, I disagree. Why is that? It is because human capital is the crucial input into producing ideas. If you want to encourage the production of ideas, one way is to subsidize the ideas themselves. But another way is to subsidize the inputs that go into the production of ideas. In a typical form of second-best analysis, you may want to introduce an additional distortion – subsidies for scientists and engineers – to offset another – the fact that the social returns from new ideas are higher than the private returns. You create a much larger pool of scientists and engineers. This lowers the price of scientists and engineers to anybody who wants to hire their services to produce new ideas.

So in general, the optimal design of institutions is an unresolved problem. We have seen a lot of experimentation during the last 100 years. I have made the claim that the economies that will really do well in the next 100 years will be the ones that come up with the best institutions for simultaneously achieving the production of new ideas and their widespread use. I am quite confident that we will see new societal or institutional mechanisms that will get put in place for encouraging new ideas.

Research into economic growth has extended into a large number of other interesting areas in recent years. For example Alberto Alesina and Dani Rodik (1994) have explored the relationship between inequality and growth, Robert Barro (1996), Alberto Alesina and others (1996) have explored the relationships between democracy, political stability and growth. How do you view this work? Can we help poor countries more by exporting our economic systems than our political systems as Barro has suggested?

Let me back up a little here. One of the disciplines that formal economic theory forces on you is that you must start with an explicit conceptual framework. For example, Marshallian analysis makes us think about supply v demand when we look at the world. General equilibrium theory forces us to split the world into preferences and the physical opportunities available to us. That split is really important and I always try to get my students to think about it when they approach a question. What do people in your model want? What are the production possibilities that are available to them?

All of growth theory has been operating under the physical opportunities question side of the model. We describe the physical opportunities as physical objects like raw materials and then you start to think about ideas as recipes for rearranging these objects. When you start to think about democracy and politics, you have to start addressing the other side of the model. What is it that people want? What drives their behaviour? If you expand the concept of preferences and say that it is everything that is inside of peoples' heads, it includes all kinds of things that sociologists and psychologists talk about: tastes, values and norms, and so on. When you start to talk about the connections between economic growth and democracy you really have to start inquiring into these issues. Barro's assertions are based on some empirical generalizations and they are fine as far as they go, but what is missing there is any kind of theoretical understanding of the connection between economic development and political structures. This is not just a problem in economics. It is also a deep problem in political science. There are many fundamental issues that have not been addressed in political science. To begin with, why does anybody bother to vote? The standard theory that political scientists have is that people go and vote because they have a stake in the outcome and they want to influence the outcome so it goes their way – less taxes and more transfers, and so on. That theory contradicts itself as soon as you state it because the probability that any one voter will be decisive in an election is so trivial that the cost of going to the polls just dwarfs any possible expected gain that anyone could get from going to the poll.

So I would just assert a cautionary note here. There is a little bit of empirical evidence that suggests a connection between the level of income and democracy, but we really face an almost total theoretical vacuum in studying this question. We are unlikely to make much progress until we have some theoretical foundations that force us to think clearly about the issues involved.

Another controversial area that has received much attention in the economic development literature is the relationship between foreign trade and growth. This is especially topical given the current crisis, which has spread throughout the 'Asian Tiger' economies that are often held up as prime examples of export-driven growth. As economists we can easily envisage an effect on the level of GDP coming from trade, but can trade influence the rate of growth? There are two mechanisms here. From a development point of view the main thing you want to think about is this process of catching up. The key role for trade is that it lets developing countries get access to ideas that exist in the rest of the world. I tell my students that in the advanced countries of the world, we

already know everything that we need to know to provide a very high standard
of living for everybody in the world. It is not that we lack physical resources, it
is not a lack of mass or matter that makes people in India and China poor. What
makes them poor is that they do not have access to the knowledge and ideas
that we have already worked out in North America, Europe and Japan for doing
all the things that we do in the modern economy. The trick to make them better
off is just to get that knowledge flowing into those countries. Much of it is very
basic knowledge – like how do you operate a distribution system so that clothes
get from a factory to a store shelf so that someone can buy a shirt when they
want one. How do you make sure that food does not spoil and is distributed to
the right locations at the right times? How do you implement quality control
systems in a manufacturing process? This is all basic knowledge but it is the
stuff that raises living standards. A lot of that knowledge can be put to work in
poor countries if they allow the right kinds of trade. Direct foreign investment
from multinationals, in particular, is important for getting quick access to these
kinds of ideas.

There is also a second issue. If you take the rich economies, OECD
countries for example, the larger the market the bigger the incentives are to
develop new ideas. So free trade in very large market areas creates greater
incentives for innovation and therefore leads to more technological progress.
If you don't think that this is true, just ask yourself how much innovation
would be taking place in Silicon Valley if products made there had to be sold
just in the US, or just in California, or just in Santa Clara County? Some, to
be sure, but a lot less than we see right now.

So trade matters for catching up. It also matters for sustaining growth in
the leading countries.

*Since growth is so important to the improvement of living standards it is
inevitable that governments will try and influence the growth rate. What
should the role of government be with respect to growth? In particular what
role do you see for monetary and fiscal policy here?*
On monetary policy it is a bit like the distinction I talked about before –
stopping the bleeding v getting in shape. There is a certain amount of emer-
gency medicine that governments have to be prepared to engage in. A lot of
that amounts to an injunction to do no harm. It helps enormously if policy
makers just keep from screwing up the way they did in the inter-war period.
But a sensible monetary policy only creates the opportunity for growth to
happen; it does not make it happen. On the fiscal side, a government has to be
able to pay its bills and it must keep from taxing income at such high rates
that it severely distorts incentives.

There are other policies that also matter. Some of those involve creating a
legal framework. What kind of institutions matter if you are in the United

States? Venture capital, fluid capital markets – think of all the things that help a company like Intel come into existence and grow into a huge force. The government did not have to do anything very active but it did have to put in place structures that permitted venture capital, a new-issue stock market and so forth. Beyond that there are measures related to human capital. There is a role for government there. The modern university, as it emerged in the United States in the last century, is one that is very focused on training and practical problem-solving. It is subsidized by the government. As I said before, subsidizing human capital is a very important way to indirectly subsidize technological change. So the modern university is an example of the kind of institution that the government can support.

I should add the caveat that many of the direct roles that people articulate for the government are not justified. A lot of people see endogenous growth theory as a blanket seal of approval for all of their favourite government interventions, many of which are very wrong-headed. For example, a lot of the discussion about infrastructure is just wrong. Infrastructure is to a very large extent a traditional physical good and should be provided in the same way that we provide other physical goods, with market incentives and strong property rights. A move towards privatization of infrastructure provision is exactly the right way to go. The government should be much less involved in infrastructure provision. So that is one area where I disagree with some of the wild-eyed interventionists. Another is the notion that the government should directly subsidize particular research programmes to produce particular kinds of ideas. If you compare that mechanism with the mechanism of subsidizing human capital and letting the market mechanism allocate where the human capital goes and what ideas get developed, the human capital-based approach works better. Selecting a few firms and giving them money has obvious problems. How do bureaucrats get access to all the decentralized information they need if they are to decide which projects should be supported? How do you keep rent-seeking and pork barrel politics from dominating the allocation process?

A great deal of thought has been given to the design of institutions to avoid non-trivial rates of inflation. However the relationship between inflation performance and growth performance is far from clear, especially at low rates of inflation. How do you read the evidence on this issue?
Inflation is somewhat damaging and it is probably a non-linear relationship, so the higher the rate of inflation gets the more damaging it is likely to be.

Is this due to the greater variability of inflation at higher rates?
At least partly. The variability and the higher rates both make the damage grow more than linearly. There is no trade-off, fundamentally, between growth

and inflation and therefore no reason not to aim at very low levels of inflation from a growth perspective. The best place to be is at a very low level of inflation and there is no reason to accept, say, 10 per cent inflation because we think we can get some benefit in terms of long-run growth. So if you are trying to do the best job you can on growth you basically want to aim for whatever the consensus is on minimal inflation. That will vary between zero and 2 or 3 per cent at the moment. It may not be too harmful to be up at 6 per cent instead of 2 or 3, but if it is harmful at all, why accept even that.

During the early 1970s a great deal of interest was stirred up by the book Limits To Growth *(Meadows et al., 1972). Since then the environmental movement has become increasingly influential. Do you ever think or worry about the environmental impact of growth or the possibility of resource limitations on growth? Can the rest of the world expect to enjoy the same living standards currently enjoyed in the OECD economics without generating an environmental catastrophe?*

Environmental problems are real problems. They are cases where our current institutional structures do not put prices on physical objects that should have prices on them. When you do not have prices on fish in the sea, market incentives cause fishermen to overfish. We know that we either need to institute a price mechanism or some regulatory system that has the same effect as a price mechanism. We will face a big challenge if, for example, human sources of carbon dioxide prove to be too much for the carrying capacity of the atmosphere. We are going to have trouble implementing a worldwide price or a regulatory system to deal with this, but we will need to do it.

However, all this is very different from saying that there are long-run limits to growth. The way to think about limits is to ask, 'What does it mean to say that our standards of living are higher now or that we have more income now than we had one hundred years ago?'. It does not mean that we have more mass, more pounds or kilos of material. What it means is that we took the finite resources that are available here on earth and just rearranged them in ways that made them more valuable. For example, we now take abundant silicon and we rearrange it into microchips that are much more valuable. So the question is: how much scope is there for us to take the finite amount of mass here on earth and rearrange it in ways that people will find more valuable? Here, you can make a strong case that the potential is virtually unlimited. There is absolutely no reason why we cannot have persistent growth as far into the future as you can imagine. If you implement the right institutions, the type of growth might take a slightly different form than what we anticipated. If carbon dioxide turns out to be a really big problem and we implement institutions which raise the price of carbon emissions, then cars will get smaller. Or we might drive cars somewhat less frequently, or we might rely on video conferencing, instead of driving automobiles, to meet with family and so on. We could shift to much greater reliance on renewable biomass or photovoltaics as a primary source of energy. We have the technology to do this right now. It's a more expensive way to generate electricity than burning oil and coal, but if income per capita is five to ten times higher 100 years from now, paying a bit more for energy will be a minor issue.

The bottom line is that there are pollution and other environmental problems that we will need to address. But these problems will not stop microchips from getting faster, hard disc storage densities from continuing to get higher, new pharmaceuticals from being introduced, new communications technologies from emerging, new methods for distributing goods like overnight delivery and discount retailing from emerging. All those processes will continue in the rich countries and will spread to the poor countries. In the process, the standards of living will go up for everyone.

In looking at the postwar economic growth performances of Germany and Japan compared to the UK do you think there is anything in Mancur Olson's (1982) argument, developed in his book The Rise and Decline of Nations, *that societies which have been stable for a long time such as the UK develop organizations for collective action which are harmful to economic efficiency and dynamism?*

His conjecture is interesting, but to evaluate it we have to come back to the discussion we had earlier about production possibilities versus preferences. What Mancur tried to do was bring back into the discussion some theory about what is going on inside someone's head. He wanted to do this so he could understand the political dynamics that influence policy decisions about universities, regulations, rent-seeking and so on. Those are important questions both from a development perspective and from a long-run growth perspective for advanced countries like the UK. These are important issues, but when we think about them it is important to distinguish between assertions about the physical world and assertions about what goes on inside someone's head. Anytime you bring politics into the discussion you are crossing that divide. At that point it is always important to remind oneself that we know very little about this area. Mancur is relying on a few empirical generalizations. He looks at historical episodes where something like a revolution or a war frees things up and then you see rapid growth. He has also looked at the general process of the growth slowdown. History is never a completely reliable guide for these kinds of questions because we do not have very many observations and the current circumstances are always different from the past. I always caution someone like Mancur to be honest about the extent of our ignorance in this area, although I encourage economists to think about these questions. Just saying that the physical world presents us with enormous opportunities for growth does not mean that we will necessarily organize ourselves and take advantage of them as rapidly as we could.

Moses Abramovitz (1986), your colleague at Stanford University, has stressed the importance of what he calls 'social capability' in the catch-up process. Differences among countries' productivity levels create a potential for catch-up providing the follower countries have the appropriate institutions and technical competence. Can we operationalize a concept like social capability?
Social capability is one of those vague terms like social capital that I think would benefit from the kind of clarification that you are forced to engage in when you write down a mathematical model. It could be something that you understand in this physical opportunity side of the theoretical framework. For example, you can think of human capital as a key complementary input for technology. So just as physical capital by itself cannot explain much – neither land nor labour can themselves produce corn, but the two of them together can – it could be that human capital is the key complement for ideas or knowledge just as land is complementary to labour. Just bringing in physical capital from the rest of the world will not work if you do not have the human capital there to work with it.

You could also interpret social capability in a broader sense. You could ask whether a country has a political or social ethic or a set of norms that lets markets operate, that encourages risk taking, that supports the rule of law as opposed to either corruption or purely discretionary negotiations. You can interpret social capability in that broader sense and there are some important issues there. But when you do this, you have to recognize that you are theorizing about what goes on in someone's head.

A great deal of research and effort has been put into investigating the existence, causes and consequences of the productivity slowdown in the US and other advanced industrial countries. What is your personal interpretation of the findings from this research?
When I talk to students and with people from outside the university, I try to be honest about our ignorance. It is always very tempting for economists to claim more than they know. We do not know what happened with the productivity slowdown in two senses. First, I don't think we know for sure what the basic facts are. The quality of the data is such that we cannot speak with authority and answer the question about what has happened over time to the rate of growth of productivity. Second, even if there was a slowdown we do not know the reasons with any confidence. In a recent paper with Kevin Murphy and Craig Riddell (Murphy, Riddell and Romer, 1998) I have started looking at the labour market evidence which suggests to me that technologi-

cal change has proceeded at a pretty rapid but steady pace for the last three or four decades, neither slowing down nor speeding up. This calls into question some of the interpretation of the output data that we have, which does suggest that there has been a big slowdown. But all of the inferences here have to be quite tentative. You have to be realistic about what you can expect. It could be that when we get the hard numbers we will conclude that there was a productivity slowdown and we may never completely understand why it happened. I have never claimed that endogenous growth theory is necessarily going to be able to predict or explain precisely all the things that we observe. The economy is a very complicated beast and the goal for us should not be to predict within a few tenths of a percentage point the rate of growth, prospectively or retrospectively. The real test is, does the theory give us some guidance in constructing institutions that will encourage growth? Does it help us understand what kinds of things led to difference between the growth performance of the UK and the US in the last 100 years? If the theory gives us that kind of guidance then it has been successful and can help us design policies to improve the quality of people's lives and that is an extremely important contribution.

Where do you think the direction of research into economic growth is likely to go next or where should it go next?
I have referred a couple of times to the process of crossing the divide from thinking only about the physical opportunities to thinking about what goes on in someone's head. Once we do that more systematically, we can begin to understand the choices that individuals and societies make about growth. I believe that we already know the policies that would speed up growth in a country like India. What we need to know is why individual and collective decision procedures in India keep them from implementing these policies. This should be the next item on the research agenda.

Mark Blaug
(b. 1927)

Mark Blaug is currently Professor Emeritus at the University of London and the University of Buckingham, and Visiting Professor at the University of Exeter, UK. He is best known for his work on the economics of education, methodology and the history of economic thought.

We interviewed Professor Blaug in his son's office at the University of Leeds on 1 May 1998.

BACKGROUND INFORMATION

Where and when did you first study economics?
I took my first course in economics at the University of California, Berkeley in 1947. But my interest in economics actually developed in high school in America. I am a Dutchman who went to the United States during the middle of World War Two. In my last year in high school I had a teacher who taught a course in Commerce – which was how economics was taught in high school at that time, it was never called economics. She took all the best students in the class, of which I was one, to a Henry George School of Social Science in New York where we heard a lecture on Henry George and were given a free copy of his book *Progress and Poverty* (1879). I was about 17 when I read the book and I thought it was really terrific – in fact I was completely bowled

over by it. After that I decided I wanted to study economics. I ended up at the University of California, Berkeley where I took my first course in economics, by which time I was a Marxist. I learned from Marxism economic determinism, that nothing is more important than the economic foundations of society. Unfortunately the more economics I learned the less I believed in Henry George or Karl Marx. Having said that I should add that, even today, I have never completely gotten over the effect of the radicalism of George and Marx and as a result I think I am a better economist for it.

Were any of your teachers particularly influential in kindling your interest in economics?
Well I ended up doing my undergraduate course at Queens College in New York and my first teacher in the history of economic thought there was Joseph Soudek. Soudek was known for an incredible article he wrote on Aristotle and Aristotle's economics. I was about 20 when I first read the article and I found that it went completely over my head. However, it did give me my first taste of scholarship. I realised that for Soudek to have written such an article he would need to be able to read Greek, think about translations and interpretations of texts and so on. That prompted me to want to learn more about the history of economic thought so that one day I could really come to grips with that kind of analysis. After Queens I went to graduate school at Columbia University where I had a couple of very influential teachers. In particular George Stigler – who later became my PhD supervisor – had a terrific influence on me, both in terms of economics and his whole style of writing. Although I have tried I have never been able to be as funny as he was.

INTERVIEWS

Your (1990) book on John Maynard Keynes: Life, Ideas, Legacy *included a number of interviews you conducted with eminent economists. Other economists, most notably Arjo Klamer (1984), have also used interviews as a means of communicating ideas and highlighting contrasting visions. What do you regard to be the main strengths and weaknesses of interviews, as a means of illuminating the nature of disagreement within economics?*
That is a very tricky question. If you look at my quote on the back cover of Arjo Klamer's (1984) book you will see that I love that book. I am widely enthusiastic about conversations and interviewing as a technique for interesting readers in economics, especially if it leads people to read the articles that the economists talk about. The more you know about economics the more fascinating such conversations become because you are able to read into

them all sorts of things. Furthermore the insights into the personality of the economists, while strictly speaking irrelevant to the validity of their views, also lend an extra dimension of interest and help bring the subject matter to life. To digress, I love classical music and have had many discussions with people about the personalities of great composers. Now some people will say that they don't like Wagner because he was such a son of a bitch. While that is fundamentally irrelevant to his music, nevertheless you can't help thinking about whether his personality is reflected in his music and how odd it is that such an unpleasant person could have produced such great works of art. There is a very subtle line between asserting that the lives of creators make their creative works more interesting and judging creative work entirely by the personality of the creator. To return to your question. If the only economics you ever read is interviews with economists then it is not the way to learn about the subject. It is, however, a terrific way of sparking interest in reading more and also thinking about the personality of the economists concerned.

Now Arjo Klamer went on from that book, along with Deirdre McCloskey, to develop a kind of methodology of rhetoric – that all social science is nothing but conversation – suggesting that all you can really do in methodology is lay down rules for polite and constructive conversation. Well, I don't buy that. In my view there is more to social science that just polite conversation between informed individuals. I do agree, of course, that all writing and discourse has a rhetorical element and can be thought of as a kind of sophisticated conversation. However, Klamer and McCloskey have attempted to turn this almost into a meta-theory, a methodological view of looking at economics. To me that seems over the top.

Tobin (1988) has suggested that good papers in economics contain surprises. Were there any surprises for you in the answers given by the economists in the series of interviews we conducted?

Well, I know quite a lot about virtually all the economists you interviewed. I was though quite surprised by Paul Romer's answers. I do not know Paul Romer personally and I don't know anyone who knows him. So I read your interview with him absolutely fresh and was quite surprised by the views expressed. I hadn't appreciated from reading his papers what a down-the-line Chicago new classical macroeconomist he basically is. In that respect the interview lends an interesting extra dimension to his work. But given my knowledge of virtually all the other economists you interviewed their answers confirmed what I already believed. That's especially true of your interviews with Friedman, Lucas, Clower and Tobin. I was, for example, a colleague of Tobin's in my young days at Yale, so I know a hell of a lot about him.

METHODOLOGY

Your methodological writings have played an important role in the revival of interest in the methodology and philosophy of economics. In your (1992) book the Methodology of Economics *you argue that 'the methodology that best supports economists striving for substantive knowledge of economic relationships is the philosophy of science associated with the names of Karl Popper and Imre Lakatos. To fully attain the idea for falsifiability is, I still believe, the prime* desideratum *in economics.' What has led you to this particular view?*

I got into Popper, Popperianism and falsifiability in the late 1960s/early 1970s having only slowly begun to realize that I had picked up such ideas from personal contact with Stigler and also Friedman much earlier, without realizing where these ideas had come from. Stigler in all his lectures in graduate school and all his writing, without actually naming Popper, really exemplified the view that ultimately you have to judge economic theories in terms of their empirical falsifiability. That view occurs almost repeatedly in practically everything he ever wrote and I just took it in without realizing that in the 1960s it was quite a far-out view, methodologically speaking. When I first read Friedman's (1953a) paper on 'The Methodology of Positive Economics' – which has had such a deep influence on modern economics – it totally convinced me. Now that paper can be read on various levels and I now regard it as a sort of vulgar Mickey Mouse Popperianism in the sense that assumptions don't matter, the only thing that matters is prediction. When you actually read Popper you realize that he is much more sophisticated than that. Popper never said that assumptions don't matter and that nothing else matters except prediction. When you read Friedman's paper relatively uncritically, which is what I first did when I was young, you pick up a hard down-the-line vulgar Popperianism. Certainly when I began to read Popper seriously in the 1960s my view about falsifiability became much more sophisticated. After that I got into Lakatos, who I knew personally and who became a very good friend of mine. Now Lakatos is even more sophisticated than Popper in that falsifiability is never interpreted as a single refutation in rejecting a theory. With Lakatos you have to consider a whole series of refutations before you reject a theory and even then you only reject theories in the light of alternative competing theories. So by the mid-1970s I had become what Lakatos called a sophisticated falsificationist. That was the kind of thinking that went into my 1980 book.

Did it surprise you that the book did so well?
Very much so. When I wrote that book methodology was then, and is even now, not highly regarded by economists. It certainly was not considered a

prestige area of research. Today the mainstream position on methodology is to begin by saying: I have no use for methodology; I don't like methodological pronouncements; who are these philosophers of social science telling me how to do economics? Most economists then move on to express views about what constitutes good or bad economics which are in fact, ironically, methodological views. For example, Frank Hahn has perfected this formula of starting an article by saying that methodology is a bitter pill to swallow; that he doesn't want to be told how to do economics; that people who can't do economics write books on methodology and so on. Then he goes on to express all sorts of views – like he doesn't like monetarism or new classical economics, and so on – which are all methodological views. He never sees the contradiction between despising something which he then uses for the purposes of validating pronouncements. So when I wrote that book I realized that most economists had a very low opinion of methodology. I was genuinely surprised when the book did so well. Now some people have said it produced a revival of interest in methodology. It certainly produced a great increase in writing about methodology – there have now been four or five textbooks on methodology since then. Looking back I see an enormous drift of opinion – I have become a kind of Neanderthal methodologist who people use as a whipping boy in the first paragraph of their articles, saying that there are very few down-the-line falsificationists, other than Terence Hutchison and Mark Blaug and that these two guys stick to their guns and really think that one refutation and the theory should be rejected. They seldom take back such slurs not just on myself and Hutchison but also on Popper. While Popper has all sorts of limitations he never encouraged the idea that a theory that has been refuted once, twice and so on should be immediately rejected. I now find myself in the amusing position of being the bad old man of methodology (*laughter*). But I go back to the fact that despite there having been a revival of interest in methodology, it is still amazing how frequently economists express dislike with the whole notion of methodology. It is also amazing how much widespread confusion exists over the meaning of the word – methodology means the logic of method, the principles on which we appraise competing theories in any subject, not the method itself. Economists very often start any kind of statistical exercise by saying my methodology, when what they really mean is my method.

You mentioned Friedman earlier and what you regard as his vulgar Mickey Mouse Popperianism. Nevertheless we presume you would agree with Friedman who, when we interviewed him, stressed that in his opinion 'the right kind of theory is one that makes predictions that are capable of being contradicted'. Yes, absolutely. If it were very easy to unambiguously evaluate the predictions of economic theories then we could indeed say that the realism of assumptions do not matter. But unfortunately it is very difficult to even agree on what economic theories may predict and it is even more difficult to unambiguously appraise the predictions to see whether the theory is being successfully refuted or not. In consequence we do have to worry about the realism of assumptions. It is also true that if all theories, including economic theories, had a tight deductive structure you could say that if a theory predicts correctly the assumptions must have been predictably accurate, otherwise it would have been impossible to find accurate predictions. But again unfortunately the journey from assumptions to predictions – which is what a theory is – almost never involves a tight deductive structure. In fact that journey is very messy. When you actually look at what follows from the assumptions it is frequently very difficult to decide whether A, B, C or D follows from the assumptions. The fact is that theories only loosely relate assumptions to predictions. In consequence it is very important in appraising a theory to look at the assumptions made and worry about their descriptive accuracy. Friedman's view is that the realism of assumptions don't matter and that all that matters is prediction – that would be fine if it were easy to actually appraise predictions.

When we asked Franco Modigliani about his views on Friedman's (1968) famous AER *paper he replied that he thought 'of the vertical Phillips curve as providing a very good example of Thomas Kuhn's notion of changing paradigms'. What are your views of Kuhn's approach to explaining the evolution of economic science and do you think Modigliani's example is a good one?*
There is obviously something to the idea of scientific research, including economic research, being guided by paradigms – if by a paradigm you mean a world view, a general conception of how the world works. There is no doubt that the belief in a vertical long-run Phillips curve and the idea of a natural rate of unemployment is guided by a paradigm in which markets clear fairly quickly. If you talk about unemployment, in the same way that you talk about prices, then you should look at long-run equilibrium values. In that sense the idea of market clearing is a kind of master paradigm that not only lies behind Friedman–Lucas–Sargent–Wallace type macroeconomics but also the whole of microeconomics. The essence of Keynesian economics is the attempt to break that paradigm. In a nutshell Keynesian economics rejects the market clearing–full employment paradigm which lay behind the whole of economics for perhaps 100, some would even say 150–200, years before the Keynesian revolution. Keynes rejected the idea that a capitalist economy tends automatically to revert to full employment when disturbed and that the only disagreement amongst economists is how long it takes. Keynes rejected the idea that there is a self-restorative power in a capitalist economy. That is why

even after 60 years you still find people with right-wing political views who become very distraught and red in the face about Keynes. They realize that Keynes rejected that basic kind of paradigm and that he provided an invitation for some kind of government action, which people with right-wing pro-market views find insupportable. Modigliani's example is one which is often made by commentators on modern macroeconomics. With Friedman's paper you get an extraordinary reversal to the full employment paradigm. That is made all the more fascinating by the fact that Friedman, who started it all, never went as far as Lucas, Sargent and Wallace, who all carried Friedman's views much further. Friedman has never endorsed the idea that the vertical long-run Phillips curve is restored almost instantaneously. He has always insisted that there is a negatively inclined short-run Phillips curve. I hand it to him that he is one of the few modern macroeconomists who is willing to put a time period on the difference between the short-run and long-run Phillips curve – even though he has hedged as to whether it is 12–18 months, or 3–5 years. I very much admire the fact that he has been willing to put his money where his mouth is. One of the most irritating things about economists, particularly macroeconomists, is that many propositions are put forward which are, truly speaking, timeless – they involve the concept of logical time and not real or historical time. We are almost never told how long it actually takes for disequilibrium adjustments to converge on equilibrium, particularly in macroeconomics. It is all very well for people to argue about whether the Phillips curve is negatively inclined or vertical, but the real question is how long does it take for the vertical Phillips curve to emerge. You can read right through, as I have done, the writings of Lucas, Sargent and Wallace and the word 'instantaneous', or 'almost instantaneous' occurs many times, but no time period is ever put on what that means. What does instantaneous or almost instantaneous mean? Does it mean one week, one month, two months, whatever? It makes an enormous amount of difference to the question of whether you can influence real output and employment by demand management.

Do you think that if students had an understanding of methodological issues they would be in a better position to understand current controversies in macroeconomics?
I am, of course, deeply convinced of that – if I wasn't I wouldn't have spent years reading and writing about methodology (*laughter*). I have a certain difficulty in understanding why not only students but also economists tend to have an antipathy to methodology. I guess I'm the kind of person who is psychologically inclined to be a true believer – I fell for Henry George, Karl Marx and outside of economics Sigmund Freud. However, I also have an inbuilt scepticism which stops me believing at the last minute. Although I had a

religious upbringing I achieved atheism by the age of 15. I have always been someone who would like to believe in gods but scepticism always breaks through. Whenever I receive ideas and study them the first thing that I always ask myself is: Do I believe this? Is this true? How do I know whether it is true? I can't imagine how people can resist asking the methodological question of whether a theory is true; asking what reasons they have for believing in a theory. I find it amazing that students do not ask themselves whether, for example, they believe that markets are self-equilibrating. For me, teaching methodology is an attempt to make students think about the truth value of ideas such as this and the reasons we have for believing such ideas in economics. It is also very important to show students that there is nothing special about economics – as a social science it raises the same questions as all scientific ideas, namely questions of validity, the likeness theories have to truth. So I do believe that students should be taught methodology which of course they are, but not explicitly. It is impossible to teach elementary economics without subtly imparting all kinds of views about the truth. The concept of equilibrium, for example, which is at the heart of all economics, is methodologically a very difficult idea. We should be making students think about the correspondence of the concept of equilibrium, that we illustrate by two curves crossing each other, and the determination of a price in reality.

I also passionately believe that you have got to teach economics historically. In macroeconomics, for example, you start with Keynes, progress through to Friedman, Lucas and so on, so that you study the history of modern macroeconomics. People tend to only associate the history of economic thought with the eighteenth and nineteenth centuries. A paper published last week is part of the history of economic thought. If students had far more of a sense, right from their first course, that economics is evolving continuously and that there are important methodological issues to be addressed, then the subject would be much more accessible to them. Increasingly economics is taught as a set of techniques, a technical body of ideas, quasi-mathematical ideas with the result that students find the subject forbidding and cannot understand what it relates to. So I believe in methodological and historical teaching, in conjunction.

When we interviewed Bob Solow he suggested that 'there are two types of vision or temperament in macroeconomics'. One group of economists, the real business cycle theorists and new classical economists 'want to establish a canonical model and then answer whatever question they are interested in by using that model'. The other group of economists, where he locates himself, take a more pragmatic/eclectic approach and they use whatever model throws light on some issue. Is that the way you see the divide?
Well I doubt whether it is simply a contrast in style. One can't deny that economics has become increasingly technical and arcane under the influence

of people like Lucas, which I find distressing. That has left people who are much more pragmatic and eclectic, and who are fundamentally interested in the questions to which economics is addressed, rather than the technical character of economics itself, high and dry and in a minority. All the older-generation economists you have interviewed fall into that group. Bob Solow (1997c) recently wrote an article entitled 'How Did Economics Get That Way and What Way Did It Get?' in which he notes that some people say that economics has become increasingly abstract, unrealistic and unconcerned with policy issues. He then goes on to say that he doesn't think that is true, rather economics has become more technical which is something completely different. However, in my view, economics hasn't just become more technical. In the last 15–20 years economists have made a virtue of technique and technicality as an end in itself. Graduate students love the work of economists such as Lucas, Sargent, Kydland and Prescott. Even econometrics has surrendered to this search for technique. Econometrics has become extremely technical and more and more concerned with theoretical, rather than applied, econometrics. The old ideal that econometrics would somehow test economic hypotheses and help the process of validation of economic theories has more or less gone out of the window. What is very alarming is that we now often find econometric departments separate from economics departments. This is a terrible development.

Bob Clower remarked to us that 'we are supposed to be a science not a branch of mathematics' and that 'a lot of people treat economics as if it were a branch of mathematics and then translate into words'. You clearly sympathize with Clower's viewpoint.
Absolutely. Economics has become like social mathematics in the sense that words like prices, markets and commodities appear in it but actually have nothing to do with real prices, real markets and real commodities – they are just points in mathematical space. Deirdre McCloskey (1996), in one of the few pieces by her that I really like, said it very well in that economists increasingly look to the maths department for their ideals, not to the physics department. Phil Mirowski says that economists suffer from physics envy – we don't, we suffer from maths envy. If you talk to physicists the thing they really care about is experiments and experimental evidence. If you ask them where is the rigorous model that developed these results, they say to hell with the model we've got all these laboratory experiments to demonstrate the results. That is much more the kind of style of economics that I would like to see. Economics as a branch of applied mathematics doesn't really strike me as being very interesting – I'd rather do mathematics (*laughter*).

When we interviewed Milton Friedman he expressed the view that 'economics has increasingly become an arcane branch of mathematics rather than dealing with real economic problems'.

I completely agree with Friedman on that point. It's an odd thing that I have always been 180 degrees away from Friedman's political views – I am not a strong pro-marketeer and I don't share his general political outlook – but I really like the way he does economics. In particular I very much admire the fact that, unlike most modern economists, he has actually used history rather than regression as a way of validating economic hypotheses. One should never forget when talking about the desirability of confronting theories with empirical evidence that most people immediately think that you mean econometrics. I also mean looking at comparative historical experience and I regard Friedman and Schwartz's (1963) *Monetary History of the United States* as a tremendous contribution to our understanding of the role of money in economic systems. It is one of the tragedies of modern economics that this style of empirical research, via history, has never really been picked up. While the Friedman and Schwartz book has been endlessly criticized it really has not been extended, refined, developed and applied to other areas.

Many economists that we have interviewed, such as Stanley Fischer (1994), have cited the Friedman and Schwartz volume as having had a very important influence on them. Bob Lucas (1994b) has also singled that book out because of its influence.

Well I wish Lucas, who originally studied as a history student, would do more of that kind of research (*laughter*).

Ironically Lawrence Summers (1991) has expressed the view that formal econometric work has had little impact on the growth of economic knowledge, whereas the informal pragmatic approach of people like Friedman and Schwartz has had a significant effect.

Paul Samuelson once remarked to Stanley Fischer, something along the lines, that his greatest disappointment in economics was that the high hopes he had for econometrics, when he was young, had never been realized and that econometrics hasn't sorted out different economic theories. It is the same point that Larry Summers made. Indeed, it has been extraordinarily disappointing that the development and refinement of econometrics far from having helped economists to choose between competing economic theories has actually complicated the choice. That does not mean that we should reject econometrics which I still think is immensely important for economists to grapple with. It is a puzzle why econometrics has apparently led us down the garden path into a greater and greater morass – it is ever more difficult to either support or refute economic theories by econometric results.

In your 1994b essay 'Confessions of an Unrepentant Popperian' you conclude that 'there has been much theoretical progress in twentieth century economics' and 'there has also been some empirical progress'. So you wouldn't attribute much of that progress to the increasing sophistication of econometric techniques?

No I wouldn't. There have been more and more attempts to survey and add up the econometric evidence on particular propositions. For example, if you ask what are the econometric results on Ricardian equivalence it turns out to be highly ambiguous – we have had something like five or six econometric papers which support it but we've also had fourteen or fifteen which refute it. Even Barro himself acknowledges that the evidence is extremely mixed. Now the attempt to add up the evidence, and ask whether it is mixed or not, is an extremely worthwhile exercise – we ought to be continuously surveying the econometric evidence for particular economic propositions. If the evidence is extremely ambiguous and it is impossible to know, for example, whether Ricardian equivalence holds then we ought to say that again and again, and not just teach it as a fascinating proposition about rational expectations and the relation between taxes and expenditure over infinite horizons for a representative agent. So often when we teach Ricardian equivalence we turn it into a technical issue yet it is extremely important to know whether it holds or not – if it does it has a tremendous effect on everything we say about fiscal and monetary policy.

One final question on methodology before we move on to the historical evolution of macroeconomics. How would you summarize the major methodological divides than can be identified in our collection of interviews with leading macroeconomists?

Well in methodology itself, aside from the interviews, the major divide is that falsifiability is now pooh-poohed by most people who write about methodology and increasingly they go in for rhetoric, the methodology of conversation, constructivism, post-modernism – it has various names but it amounts to a kind of relativism, that we never really know anything and we can't decide between theories in terms of evidence. It's an attempt to open your mind to all possibilities – anything goes. Very little of that is reflected in the interviews you've conducted. In the conversations you've had it seems to me that you can identify two methodologies. One is a kind of generalized expression that empirical evidence is important but then a failure to actually take it very seriously in choosing between theories – what I call innocuous falsificationism. Economists say that theories should be confronted by evidence to see whether it can be refuted but they never really take that approach all that seriously. You find that reflected in a lot of your interviews. Then you find one other point of view, which I find extremely alarming, and which was most clearly expressed in Lucas's (1980b) article 'Methods and Problems in Business Cycle Theory'. In that article he says that economic theories are themselves like a laboratory and that we can test theories by examining the technical formal properties of theories. We take a modular representation of a theory and then we adjust the model, and this is like a kind of mental laboratory. As such it virtually amounts to rejecting empirical evidence and turning economics, strictly speaking, into mathematical models and contrasts between different mathematical models – the only way you ever relate theory to evidence is via calibration. When you have models that produce results which track the evidence the emphasis is on the formal properties of the models themselves. That is very alarming because it makes it easier to make theories which are foolproof against the empirical evidence. It really is a denial of refutability and falsifiability, an anti-falsifiability methodology which Lucas hints at but never really explicates fully.

HISTORICAL EVOLUTION OF MACROECONOMICS

In your well-known book Economic Theory in Retrospect *(1997a) you provide a comprehensive survey of the evolution of economic analysis. Who do you regard as the most important contributors to what we now call macroeconomics prior to Keynes?*

Macroeconomics before Keynes, during the whole of the nineteenth and early twentieth centuries, was the quantity theory of money, a theory concerned with the determination of the level of prices, which is an aggregate idea. The quantity theory addresses an aggregate question by considering the flow of expenditure in the light of increases in the stock of money – it is essentially a macroeconomic analysis. When you look, for example, at Fisher's (1911) *Purchasing Power of Money* – one of the great classic statements of the quantity theory of money – it is about the relation between aggregate quantities. We think of macroeconomics since Keynes as being about employment and real output. The most influential macroeconomist before Keynes was Knut Wicksell. Wicksell's (1898) second major book *Interest and Prices* and particularly the doctrine of the relationship between the real rate of interest – or what he called the natural rate of interest, a term later used by Friedman in the context of unemployment – and the money rate of interest acts to account for booms and depressions. Ludwig von Mises picked it up and turned it into the so-called Austrian theory of business cycles, which all through the 1930s was the main rival of Keynes. It is an extraordinary thing that most modern students of macroeconomics have never heard of Mises and only tangentially of Friedrich von Hayek. It was one of Keynes's master strokes in the *General Theory* hardly to ever refer to Hayek and the Austrian theory of business cycles, a theory he was fundamentally attacking. As a result it has been obliterated. Yet it is extremely useful to teach students a little bit of the Austrian theory of business cycles, particularly the view that Mises developed that the business cycle is a natural phenomenon of the capitalist economy. In the Austrian view a depression is a purge of the system and if you try and do something about it and attempt to purge unemployment you make things worse by inhibiting the boom that naturally comes out of the slump. The paradigm that the capitalist system is automatically self-restorative produces a *laissez-faire* view of business cycles – a view which Schumpeter also expressed – which was dominant before 1936. It would make a lot more sense to students when we teach them Keynes if we told them a bit about the Austrian view. Anyway Wicksell is an absolutely central figure in early twentieth-century theories of the business cycle. Aside from Wicksell you need only add Dennis Robertson who developed a variant of real business cycle theory in the 1910s and 1920s. In that view the business cycle is produced basically by the technology of the capitalist economy. Kydland and Prescott make you recall this tradition of real business cycle theory, even though their theory is very different.

Who do you regard as the most influential macroeconomists since Keynes?
Well obviously Friedman – his 1967 Presidential Address to the American Economic Association is easily the most influential paper on macroeconomics published in the postwar era. Friedman has scored twice, once with his methodology paper and once with his paper on the role of monetary policy. He and Ronald Coase are right up there, at the top of the citation index, as economists who have made it with a couple of brilliant articles (*laughter*). Obviously Lucas has been very important, although personally I don't like new classical macroeconomics and I don't believe in rational expectations. But if you are talking about influence then there is simply no question – Friedman and Lucas. If the Nobel Prize was given for influence – which by the way it only ever is now and again – they were right to give it to Lucas. One of the puzzles about the Nobel Prize is that we do not know the grounds on which it is awarded. We are not privy to the discussion and the criteria seem to change from year to year. Sometimes it is given for a lifetime contribution; sometimes for work that has revolutionized the subject; sometimes for sustained work valued by a group within the profession. But they have also given it to some economists who have had little influence. If the prize was awarded solely on the criterion of influence then Joan Robinson would have been a most worthy recipient – imperfect competition, apart from everything else she ever did, has had an incredible influence on modern microeconomics.

When we talked with Bob Lucas he told us that he thought Joan Robinson would have been awarded the first Nobel Prize in Economics.
I was surprised by that.

He also expressed the view that Keynes would have been an early recipient if he had still been alive when the prize was first awarded in 1969. However, when we asked him whether students of macroeconomics should still read the General Theory *he replied no. Do you think that it is important for students to read the* General Theory*?*
I believe they should look at parts of it, but certainly not the entire book. It is an incredibly difficult book and it has become even more difficult as the years have passed. It is now much more difficult for us to read the *General Theory* than it was in 1936. The book goes all over the place – it has four or five different arguments leading to more or less the same kind of conclusions. Students find it very difficult and confusing as it is so much out of touch with the kind of macroeconomics that they now learn. You could ask: why should students read even parts of the *General Theory*? Well, because at some point they should realize, or be made to think about the fact, that very influential books are often very difficult and confusing when you go back and read them. That can be said not just of Keynes's works but also of Marx's and Ricardo's writings. Even Smith's (1776) *Wealth of Nations* goes all over the place even though it is beautifully written. It's often hard to decide what Smith really meant. But that is the history of ideas and the nature of the beast. The same often holds when you read more recent articles which have also been so influential. If, for example, you get students to read Friedman's 1967 Presidential Address they puzzle over why they can't find the vertical long-run Phillips curve in the paper. So I think students should read the *General Theory* selectively and dip into it. You know Lucas does more than suggest that students shouldn't read the *General Theory* he virtually disparages the book – he literally says that Keynes's style of reasoning is so messy and not technically up to par that we can do it all much better now. Well that I don't buy because as confusing as it is, the *General Theory* is also a real work of genius. Everyone of the four or five strands of argument in it is capable of being developed into a kind of economics.

Lucas acknowledges that the General Theory *is 'an unusually important book' in particular because it emphasized that depressions 'can be solved within the context of a liberal democracy without having to resort to centralized planning'. Bob Clower suggested to us that Keynes was 'in his way an incredible conman' and that it was the polemics and his mastery of the English language that helped win people over.*

I think Keynes was rhetorically very self-conscious. He really thought about how to sell his ideas to his fellow economists. He thought very carefully about the structure of the *General Theory* and did some extraordinarily strange things in terms of exposition. If Clower meant, by saying Keynes was a conman, that he tried to sell a bill of goods, then yes he did. Keynes thought about how to market the *General Theory* to his fellow economists and communicate effectively with them. McCloskey should have used the example of Keynes in her book on rhetoric. Keynes is a wonderful example of conscious rhetorical analysis. Whether Keynes got it right or wrong he had an enormous influence.

Paul Romer suggested to us that 'when you go back and read economics which is stated in purely verbal terms' that 'there is always a danger that you read between the lines'. Romer talks about the danger of 'ancestor worship'. Well strongly mathematically inclined economists tend to disparage economists who write largely in words. One is perfectly aware of the enormous ambiguity of words. By way of contrast economists who like writing prose tend to disparage the mathematical style adopted by many economists because while economics which is mathematically expressed is precise and rigorous, it is also extraordinarily narrow. Unfortunately when you try and express social science mathematically many of the ideas that you want to tackle, and problems you want to address, have to be set aside because they can't be expressed precisely and rigorously. Mathematics is a tool and modern mathematical economists, while they try to make the most of that tool, think it is a very limited tool. Economics is about trade-offs and one of the fundamental trade-offs in methodology is between rigour and relevance. As an individual economist you have to decide whether you want to be rigorous and precise, even though the issues and problems you are addressing are largely irrelevant, or whether you want to address issues and problems which are important and relevant, even though you do so in an imprecise and less rigorous manner. Somewhere along the line you have to decide as an individual economist whether you want to be rigorous, precise and unrealistic, or relevant even if imprecise and less rigorous. It wouldn't matter at all if some people choose to be mathematical economists and the rest of us got on with addressing practical policy problems. What is alarming is when the people who play one end of the trade-off – the rigorous end of the spectrum – come to dominate the profession. You can divide almost all the economists you interviewed along this spectrum, with Lucas, Prescott and Romer clearly at the mathematical end.

Why do you think that the intellectual lead within macroeconomics passed from the UK to the USA in the early postwar period? Friedman suggests that

it had a great deal to do with the strong Keynesian orthodoxy established at Cambridge University.
I do not think it has anything fundamental to do with the intellectual evolution of economics within the two countries. Essentially it was, and still is, a matter of numbers, particularly student numbers. As I am always telling European economists the American system has 6000 institutions of higher education with more than 5 million students. To focus on just one number, every year America produces some 500–600 completed PhDs in economics, a third of whom according to Lee Hansen seek employment in academia. You get employment in academia through publication of articles in the top twenty journals. So you have something like 200 PhD students in economics every year all pulling articles out of their PhDs. There is no country in Europe, or for that matter all European countries together, which produce 50 completed PhDs in economics. Of those there are about 20 which are written in English and can compete within the American market. So it is hardly any wonder that more research output comes out of the United States. This same reasoning applies across the Social Sciences. The output is like a great locomotive – an avalanche!

Do you have fears that the Research Assessment Exercise (RAE) in the UK has pushed our own higher education institutions into a publication rat-race?
Sure. I am sorry to say that I avidly supported the RAE exercise eight to ten years ago. I now realize that you can only emphasize research output in an American-style system with differentiated salaries among a large number of institutions. American higher education institutions range from the best in the world – the likes of Harvard and Chicago – to colleges that intellectually rank below the average Indian college. The American system is extraordinarily heterogeneous with fantastic salary differences. Robert Barro, for example, has just been offered \$300 000 a year to go to Columbia, while at the bottom end of the scale many American universities pay their professors \$40 000–50 000 a year. What we have done in the UK with the RAE is overemphasize research in a system which has no real pay differentials. This has produced a mad scramble for institutions to poach people for their research output. I only hope that we can undo the bad we've done. We did not think things through and there has been too much de-emphasis on teaching.

Milton Friedman suggested to us that 'every science every 10 or 20 years has to have a new fad or it goes dead'. David Colander has often talked about the need for new ideas to satisfy what he calls the 'article criteria' if they are to catch on within academia. Do you agree with these views?
David Colander is always saying that with all these new PhD students coming out we need a kind of economics that can be replicated very easily. He

explains the development of economics in terms of easily replicable research programmes. Retrospectively it sounds like a clever explanation, but I am not convinced that you can explain developments in macroeconomics by appealing to fads and fashions. Was rational expectations just a new fad?

Friedman was referring to real business cycle theory when he made that remark.
Well we have had real business cycle theory now. Does this mean that something new is about to come around the corner? I am not convinced that it is. What other fads have there been?

Beginning in the mid-1980s we have had the new Keynesian contributions with their emphasis on providing more solid microfoundations for Keynesian macroeconomics. Do you think it has added much to our understanding of Keynesian ideas?
It has certainly added to our insights into the working of markets, but to a certain extent that research has been misdirected. It has tried to square Keynes's macroeconomics with the neoclassical rational-choice framework. Yes, we do need to find out why labour markets do not clear when aggregate demand falls. But if you are willing to suspend the belief that behaviour is always rational the research effort might yield more fruitful results. New Keynesians resort to efficiency wage and insider-outsider theories to account for the rigidity of real wages. Those kinds of intellectual handstands and fantastic acrobatics have occurred because we will not give up the idea of well-defined preferences and people maximizing utility all the time. If we worked a little harder on constructing a more descriptively realistic conception of economic behaviour we would naturally develop more adequate microfoundations for macromodels.

What is your view of the area of macroeconomics which has been developed by economists such as Alberto Alesina in recent years? He clearly believes that macro analysis must take into account the impact of political distortions.
Yes I welcome the entire development associated with political business cycle theory. I think that it has been a really fruitful development coming out of Keynesian macroeconomics. If you are going to practise demand management then you do have to worry a great deal about the fact that it is practised by governments who have their own electoral interests and ideological preferences. It is amazing how quickly this field has developed since the original Nordhaus view appeared in the literature. Although I haven't worked on, or taken a keen interest in, this line of research I do think it is a very important development. It also emphasizes the links between politics and economics, and helps us bring economics closer to one of our natural sister social sci-

ences. I particularly welcome that because it provides an opportunity to de-emphasize the technical side of economic theory – the more we take an interest in the political aspects of macroeconomics the less we will be inclined to worship at the altar of technique.

Since the mid-1980s there has been a revival of interest in economic growth in large part inspired by the work of Romer and Lucas. Some of the work on endogenous growth theory highlights the importance of human capital. Given that you have spent a lot of time in less developed countries as a consultant, and have also worked in the area of the economics of education, what are your impressions of this work?

Well, I think that it is wonderful to put growth back at the centre of the stage. Nevertheless I am alarmed by how much of this new growth theory skips blithely over some very difficult questions which have never been properly established. While the ideas that human capital and R&D generate externalities which make growth endogenous have been around for a long time, they have never really been empirically substantiated. The new growth theory, for example, ignores a lot of empirical research undertaken in the 1960s and 1970s on the externalities of human capital. It is also excessively technical, concerned far more with model building than substantiating the empirical foundations for particular beliefs.

I was a member of a working party for the Dearing Committee where amongst other things we looked at the private and social rate of return on investment in higher education in Britain. At present the social rate of return is about 7 per cent which is also approximately the cut-off rate that the Treasury uses for appraising investment in the public sector. So it appears that the social rate of return to higher education in Britain is just about right, justifying no further expansion of expenditure on higher education. A lot of people asked: what about the externalities, they are not included in that social rate of return? As a result we spent a lot of time looking to see what evidence there is that there are externalities from higher education in Britain. The general conclusion we came to was that no one has ever been able to quantify the externalities from higher education in Britain, or for that matter anywhere else. Furthermore it is not certain that even if we could that the number would be anything other than zero. Where is the evidence that human capital generates externalities that makes growth endogenous? While the new growth theory has raised a lot of interesting technical ideas relating to the influence of economies of scale, externalities, R&D and so on, none of these are ever pinned down very precisely. Of course I believe that growth is endogenous but I don't think that the new theory has even begun to substantiate that. So full marks for giving a new prominence to growth. I have just finished reading Greg Mankiw's (1997b) new principles textbook. It is a lovely book

and he emphasizes the importance of growth, but it is still too much concerned with the old disease of formalism, writing down a model which makes
growth endogenous. That isn't the problem. The problem is to show that
empirically we have very good reasons for believing that growth is actually
an endogenous engine.

Do we really know much more than Adam Smith about economic growth?
What we do know is 200 more years of comparative experience with growth
than Adam Smith had. We have been able to observe the growth experiences
of the communist world, East Asia and the other developing countries as well
as the continued growth of the OECD economies. Smith had to spend 150
pages of Book Three of the *Wealth of Nations* to demonstrate to his readers
that there had been growth between 1600 and 1776 because he knew that
most people in the eighteenth century believed that the standard of living had
stood still for 175 years. Indeed many people thought that material living
standards had fallen and had never recovered from the Black Plague. While I
do believe that we now know more than Adam Smith, it is still rhetorically
effective to ask that question (*laughter*).

What are you currently working on?
I'm still working on methodological appraisal. Now in order to appraise you
have to know the theory that you are appraising. Lately I've been reading a
lot of evolutionary economics and thinking about whether it is the new way
to go. I am more interested in economics today than I was when I first started
studying the subject – it is a fascinating subject. When I read things I still
wonder: Is it true? Can I put my hand on my heart and say I believe this?

*Don't you find that the boundaries of the subject are moving out so fast that it
is virtually impossible to stay in touch with what is going on? The more you
read the more you realize what you don't know.*
In a way yes, that is perfectly true. But the questions become even more
interesting. When I look at the sky at night I find it more fascinating than a
believer in God because they know where the stars come from. Because I do
not believe that God put them there makes it even more mystifying and
fascinating. I find economics the same and I am becoming increasingly
concerned about where economics should be going and how it should develop. Having said that there are some very important basic ideas in economics
which are incredibly useful: decisions at the margin; cost–benefit analysis;
the trade-off between inflation and unemployment and so on. The exact
nature of the trade-off between inflation and unemployment remains one of
the central ideas in macroeconomics. It is invaluable for thinking about
questions of macroeconomic policy. I am still persuaded by the Keynesian

idea that the capitalist economy is a cornucopia, that it is always threatening to produce more goods than can ever be sold; and that it has weak recovery powers without a stimulus to aggregate demand. If that is Keynesian economics then I am a Keynesian economist.

References

Abel, A.B. and B.S. Bernanke (1995), *Macroeconomics*, 2nd edn, New York: Addison Wesley.

Abel, A.B., B.S. Bernanke and R. McNabb (1998), *Macroeconomics*, European edn, New York: Addison Wesley.

Abraham, K.G. and J.C. Haltiwanger (1995), 'Real wages and the business cycle', *Journal of Economic Literature*, September.

Abramovitz, M. (1956), 'Resource and output trends in the United States since 1870', *American Economic Review*, May.

Abramovitz, M. (1986), 'Catching up, forging ahead, and falling behind', *Journal of Economic History*, June.

Ades, A. and R. Di Tella (1997), 'The new economics of corruption: a survey and some new results', *Political Studies*.

Aghion, P. and P. Howitt (1998), *Endogenous Growth Theory*, Cambridge, MA: MIT Press.

Akerlof, G.A. and J.L. Yellen (1985), 'A near-rational model of the business cycle, with wage and price inertia', *Quarterly Journal of Economics*, Supplement.

Akerlof, G.A. and J.L. Yellen (1988), 'Fairness and unemployment', *American Economic Review*, May.

Akerlof, G.A. and J.L. Yellen (1990), 'The fair wage–effort hypothesis and unemployment', *Quarterly Journal of Economics*, May.

Akerlof, G.A., W.T. Dickens and G.L. Perry (1996), 'The macroeconomics of low inflation', *Brookings Papers on Economic Activity*.

Akhtar, M.A. (1995), 'Monetary policy goals and central bank independence', *Banca Nazionale Del Lavoro Quarterly Review*, December.

Aldcroft, D.H. (1993), *The European Economy, 1914–1990*, 3rd edn, London: Routledge.

Alesina, A. (1987), 'Macroeconomic policy in a two-party system as a repeated game', *Quarterly Journal of Economics*, August.

Alesina, A. (1988), 'Macroeconomics and politics', *National Bureau of Economic Research Macroeconomics Annual*.

Alesina, A. (1989), 'Politics and business cycles in industrial democracies', *Economic Policy*, April.

Alesina, A. (1994), 'Political models of macroeconomic policy and fiscal reforms', in S. Haggard and S. Webb (eds), *Voting for Reform*, Oxford: Oxford University Press.

Alesina, A. (1995), 'Elections, party structure, and the economy' in J.S. Banks and E.A. Hanushek (eds), *Modern Political Economy: Old Topics, New Directions*, Cambridge: Cambridge University Press.

Alesina, A. and R. Gatti (1995), 'Independent central banks: low inflation at no cost?' *American Economic Review*, May.

Alesina, A. and R. Perotti (1995a), 'The political economy of budget deficits', *IMF Staff Papers*, March.

Alesina, A. and R. Perotti (1995b), 'Fiscal experiences and adjustments in OECD economies', *Economic Policy*, October.

Alesina, A. and R. Perotti (1996a), 'Fiscal discipline and the budget process', *American Economic Review*, May.

Alesina, A. and R. Perotti (1996b), 'Reducing budget deficits', *Swedish Economic Policy Review*, Spring.

Alesina, A. and R. Perotti (1997a), 'Fiscal adjustments in OECD countries: composition and macroeconomic effects', *IMF Staff Papers*.

Alesina, A. and R. Perotti (1997b), 'The welfare state and competitiveness', *American Economic Review*, December.

Alesina, A. and R. Perotti (1998), 'Economic risk and political risk in fiscal unions', *Economic Journal*, July.

Alesina, A. and D. Rodik (1994), 'Distributive politics and economic growth', *Quarterly Journal of Economics*, May.

Alesina, A. and H. Rosenthal (1995), *Partisan Politics, Divided Government and the Economy*, Cambridge: Cambridge University Press.

Alesina, A. and N. Roubini (1992), 'Political cycles in OECD economies', *Review of Economic Studies*, October.

Alesina, A. and N. Roubini, with G.D. Cohen (1997), *Political Cycles and the Macroeconomy: Theory and Evidence*, Cambridge, MA: MIT Press.

Alesina, A. and J. Sachs (1988), 'Political parties and the business cycle in the United States, 1914–1984', *Journal of Money, Credit, and Banking*, February.

Alesina, A. and E. Spolare (1997), 'On the number and size of nations', *Quarterly Journal of Economics*, November.

Alesina, A. and L.H. Summers (1993), 'Central bank independence and macroeconomic performance: some empirical results', *Journal of Money, Credit, and Banking*, May.

Alesina, A. and G. Tabellini (1987), 'Rules and discretion with non-coordinated monetary and fiscal policies', *Economic Inquiry*, October.

Alesina, A. et al. (1996), 'Political instability and growth', *Journal of Economic Growth*, June.

Alesina, A., R. Perotti and J. Tavares (1998), 'The political economy of fiscal adjustments', *Brookings Papers on Economic Activity*.

Alt, J..E. and A. Alesina (1996), 'Political economy: an overview' in R.E. Goodin and H.D. Klingerman (eds), *A New Handbook of Political Science*, Oxford: Oxford University Press.

Arestis, P. (1997), *Money, Pricing, Distribution and Investment*, London: Macmillan.

Arestis, P. and M. Sawyer (1998), 'Keynesian economic policies for the new millennium', *Economic Journal*, January.

Arrow, K.J. (1962), 'The economic implications of learning by doing', *Review of Economic Studies*, June.

Artis, M., P. Mizen and Z. Kontolemis (1998), 'Inflation targeting: what can the ECB learn from the recent experience of the Bank of England', *Economic Journal*, November.

Backhouse, R.E. (1995), *Interpreting Macroeconomics: Explorations in the History of Macroeconomic Thought*, London: Routledge.

Backhouse, R.E. (1997a), 'The rhetoric and methodology of modern macroeconomics' in B. Snowdon and H.R. Vane (eds), *Reflections on the Development of Modern Macroeconomics*, Cheltenham: Edward Elgar.

Backhouse, R.E. (1997b), *Truth and Progress in Economic Knowledge*, Cheltenham: Edward Elgar.

Backus, D. and J. Driffill (1985), 'Inflation and reputation', *American Economic Review*, June.

Bakhshi, H., A.G. Haldane and N. Hatch (1997), 'Quantifying some benefits of price stability', *Bank of England Quarterly Bulletin*, August.

Ball, L. (1994), 'What determines the sacrifice ratio?' in N.G. Mankiw (ed.), *Monetary Policy*, Chicago, IL: University of Chicago Press.

Ball, L. and D. Romer (1991), 'Sticky prices as co-ordination failure', *American Economic Review*, June.

Barro, R.J. (1974), 'Are government bonds net wealth?', *Journal of Political Economy*, November/December.

Barro, R.J. (1976), 'Rational expectations and the role of monetary policy', *Journal of Monetary Economics*, January.

Barro, R.J. (1979), 'Second thoughts on Keynesian economics', *American Economic Review*, May.

Barro, R.J. (1989), 'New classicals and Keynesians, or the good guys and the bad guys', *Schweiz Zeitschrift für Volkswirtschaft und Statistik*.

Barro, R.J. (1991), 'Economic growth in a cross section of countries', *Quarterly Journal of Economics*, May.

Barro, R.J. (1994), 'Interview with Robert Barro' in B. Snowdon, H.R. Vane and P. Wynarczyk, *A Modern Guide To Macroeconomics: An Introduction to Competing Schools of Thought*, Aldershot: Edward Elgar.

Barro, R.J. (1995), 'Inflation and economic growth', *Bank of England Quarterly Bulletin*, May.

Barro, R.J. (1996), 'Democracy and growth', *Journal of Economic Growth*, March.

Barro, R.J. (1997), *Determinants of Economic Growth*, Cambridge, MA: MIT Press.

Barro, R.J. and D.B. Gordon (1983), 'Rules, discretion and reputation in a model of monetary policy', *Journal of Monetary Economics*, July.

Barro, R.J. and H.I. Grossman (1976), *Money, Employment and Inflation*, New York: Cambridge University Press.

Barro, R.J. and X. Sala-i-Martin (1991), 'Convergence across states and regions', *Brookings Papers on Economic Activity*.

Barro, R.J. and X. Sala-i-Martin (1995), *Economic Growth*, New York: McGraw-Hill.

Baumol, W.J. (1986), 'Productivity growth, convergence and welfare: what the long-run data show', *American Economic Review*, December.

Bean, C. (1998), 'The new UK monetary arrangement: a view from the literature', *Economic Journal*, November.

Beaud, M. and G. Dostaler (1995), *Economic Thought Since Keynes: A History and Dictionary of Major Economists*, Aldershot: Edward Elgar.

Bernanke, B.S. (1983), 'Non-monetary effects of the financial crisis in the propagation of the Great Depression', *American Economic Review*, June.

Bernanke, B.S. (1995), 'The macroeconomics of the Great Depression: a comparative approach', *Journal of Money, Credit and Banking*, February.

Bernanke, B.S. and K. Carey (1996), 'Nominal wage stickiness and aggregate supply in the Great Depression', *Quarterly Journal of Economics*, August.

Bernanke, B.S. and F. Mishkin (1992), 'Central bank behaviour and the strategy of monetary policy: observations from six industrialised countries', *National Bureau of Economic Research Macroeconomics Annual*.

Bernanke, B.S. and F.S. Mishkin (1997), 'Inflation targeting: a new framework for monetary policy', *Journal of Economic Perspectives*, Spring.

Bernanke, B.S. and M. Woodford (1997), 'Inflation forecasts and monetary policy', *Journal of Money, Credit, and Banking*, November.

Beveridge, W.H. (1944), *Full Employment in a Free Society*, London: Allen and Unwin.

Blanchard, O.J. (1983), 'Price asynchronization and price level inertia' in R. Dornbusch and M.H. Simonsen (eds), *Inflation Debt, and Indexation*, Cambridge, MA: MIT Press.

Blanchard, O.J. (1984), 'The Lucas critique and the Volcker deflation', *American Economic Review*, May.

Blanchard, O.J. (1986a), 'The wage price spiral', *Quarterly Journal of Economics*, August.

Blanchard, O.J. (1986b), 'Reagonomics', *Economic Policy*, October.

Blanchard, O.J. (1990), 'Why does money affect output? A survey' in B.M. Friedman and F.H. Hahn (eds), *Handbook of Monetary Economics Vol. II*, Amsterdam: North Holland.

Blanchard, O.J. (1992), 'For a return to pragmatism' in M. Belongia and M. Garfinkel (eds), *The Business Cycle: Theories and Evidence*, London: Kluwer Academic Publishers.

Blanchard, O.J. (1996), 'Theoretical aspects of transition', *American Economic Review*, May.

Blanchard, O.J. (1997a), *Macroeconomics*, New Jersey: Prentice Hall.

Blanchard, O.J. (1997b), *The Economics of Post-Communist Transition*, Oxford: Oxford University Press.

Blanchard, O.J. (1997c), 'Is there a core of usable macroeconomics?', *American Economic Review*, May.

Blanchard, O.J. and S. Fischer (1989), *Lectures on Macroeconomics*, Cambridge, MA: MIT Press.

Blanchard, O.J. and L.F. Katz (1997), 'What we know and do not know about the natural rate of unemployment', *Journal of Economic Perspectives*, Winter.

Blanchard, O.J. and N. Kiyotaki (1987), 'Monopolistic competition and the effects of aggregate demand', *American Economic Review*, September.

Blanchard, O.J. and M. Kremer (1997), 'Disorganization', *Quarterly Journal of Economics*, November.

Blanchard, O.J. and L.H. Summers (1986), 'Hysteresis and the European unemployment problem', *National Bureau of Economic Research Macroeconomics Annual*.

Blanchard, O.J. and L.H. Summers (1987), 'Hysteresis in unemployment', *European Economic Review*, February/March.

Blanchard, O.J. and L.H. Summers (1988), 'Beyond the natural rate hypothesis', *American Economic Review*, May.

Blanchard, O.J. and M.W. Watson (1984), 'Bubbles, rational expectations, and financial markets' in P. Wachtel (ed.), *Crises in the Economic and Financial Structure*, Lexington, MA: Lexington Books.

Blaug, M. (1990), *John Maynard Keynes: Life, Ideas, Legacy*, London: Macmillan in association with the Institute of Economic Affairs.

Blaug, M. (1991a), *The Historiography of Economics*, Aldershot: Edward Elgar.

Blaug, M. (1991b), 'Second thoughts on the Keynesian revolution', *History of Political Economy*, Summer.

Blaug, M. (1992), *The Methodology of Economics: Or, How Economists Explain*, 2nd edn, Cambridge: Cambridge University Press.

Blaug, M. (1994a), 'Recent biographies of Keynes', *Journal of Economic Literature*, September.

Blaug, M. (1994b), 'Why I am not a constructivist: confessions of an unrepentant Popperian' in R.E. Backhouse (ed.), *New Directions in Economic Methodology*, London: Routledge.

Blaug, M. (1994c), 'Not only an economist – autobiographical reflections of a historian of economic thought', *American Economist*, Fall.

Blaug, M. (1997a), *Economic Theory in Retrospect*, 5th edn, Cambridge: Cambridge University Press.

Blaug, M. (1997b), *Great Economists Before Keynes*, 2nd edn, Cheltenham: Edward Elgar.

Blaug, M. (1998), *Great Economists Since Keynes*, 2nd edn, Cheltenham: Edward Elgar.

Bleaney, M. (1996), 'Central bank independence, wage bargaining structure and macroeconomic performance in OECD countries', *Oxford Economic Papers*, January.

Blinder, A.S. (1986), 'Keynes after Lucas', *Eastern Economic Journal*, July–September.

Blinder, A.S. (1987), *Hard Heads, Soft Hearts: Tough-Minded Economics for a Just Society*, New York: Addison Wesley.

Blinder, A.S. (1988a), 'The fall and rise of Keynesian economics', *Economic Record*, December.

Blinder, A.S. (1988b), 'The challenge of high unemployment', *American Economic Review*, May.

Blinder, A.S. (1991), 'Why are prices sticky? Preliminary results from an interview study', *American Economic Review*, May.

Blinder, A.S. (1992a), 'A Keynesian restoration is here', *Challenge*, September/October.

Blinder, A.S. (1992b), 'Deja vu all over again' in M. Belongia and M. Garfinkel (eds), *The Business Cycle: Theories and Evidence*, London: Kluwer Academic Publishers.

Blinder, A.S. (1997), 'Is there a core of practical macroeconomics that we should all believe?', *American Economic Review*, May.

Blitch, C.P. (1995), *Allyn Young: The Peripatetic Economist*, Basingstoke: Macmillan.

Bordo, M.D. (1986), 'Explorations in monetary history: a survey of the literature', *Explorations in Economic History*, October.

Bordo, M.D. (1989), 'The contribution of *A Monetary History of the United States, 1867–1960* to monetary history' in M.D. Bordo (ed.), *Money, His-*

tory, and International Finance: Essays in Honour of Anna J. Schwartz, Chicago, IL: University of Chicago Press.

Bordo, M.D., E.U. Choudhri and A.J. Schwartz (1995), 'Could stable money have averted the great contraction?', *Economic Inquiry*, July.

Bordo, M.D., C. Goldin and E.N. White (1998), *The Defining Moment: The Great Depression and the American Economy in the Twentieth Century*, Chicago, IL: University of Chicago Press.

Borensztein, E. and J.D. Ostry (1996), 'Accounting for China's growth performance', *American Economic Review*, May.

Brandolini, A. (1995), 'In search of a stylised fact: do real wages exhibit a consistent pattern of cyclical variability?', *Journal of Economic Surveys*.

Breit, W. and R.W. Spencer (1997), *Lives of the Laureates*, 3rd edn, Cambridge, MA: MIT Press.

Briault, C. (1995), 'The costs of inflation', *Bank of England Quarterly Bulletin*, February.

Broadberry, S.N. (1991), 'Unemployment' in N.F.R. Crafts and N.W.C. Woodward (eds), *The British Economy Since 1945*, Oxford: Clarendon Press.

Brunner, K. (1968), 'The role of money and monetary policy', *Federal Reserve Bank of St. Louis Review*, July.

Brunner, K. (1981), 'Understanding the Great Depression' in K. Brunner (ed.), *The Great Depression Revisited*, Boston: Martinus Nijhoff.

Bruton, H.J. (1998), 'A reconsideration of import substitution', *Journal of Economic Literature, June*.

Budd, A. (1998), 'The role and operations of the Bank of England Monetary Policy Committee', *Economic Journal*, November.

Burton, J. (1981), 'Positively Milton Friedman' in J.R. Shackleton and G. Locksley (eds), *Twelve Contemporary Economists*, London: Macmillan.

Cagan, P. (1956), 'The monetary dynamics of hyperinflation' in M. Friedman (ed.), *Studies in the Quantity Theory of Money*, Chicago, IL: University of Chicago Press.

Calomiris, C.W. (1993), 'Financial factors in the Great Depression', *Journal of Economic Perspectives*, Spring.

Calomiris, C.W. and C. Hanes (1995), 'Historical macroeconomics and American macroeconomic history' in K.D. Hoover (ed.), *Macroeconometrics: Developments, Tensions, and Prospects*, Boston, MA: Kluwer Academic Publishers.

Calomiris, C.W. and D.C. Wheelock (1998), 'Was the Great Depression a watershed for American monetary policy?' in M.D. Bordo, C. Goldin and E.N. White (eds), *The Defining Moment: The Great Depression and the American Economy in the Twentieth Century*, Chicago, IL: University of Chicago Press.

Carvalho, F.J.C.D. (1995/96), 'The independence of central banks: a critical assessment of the arguments', *Journal of Post Keynesian Economics*, Winter.

Cass, D. (1965), 'Optimum growth in an aggregative model of capital accumulation', *Review of Economic Studies*, July.

Cecchetti, S. (1992a), 'Stock market crash of October 1929' in P. Newman, M. Milgate and J. Eatwell (eds), *The New Palgrave Dictionary of Money and Finance*, London: Macmillan.

Cecchetti, S.G. (1992b), 'Prices during the Great Depression: was the deflation of 1930–1932 really anticipated?', *American Economic Review*, March.

Chappell, H.W., T.M. Havrilesky and R.R. McGregor (1993), 'Partisan monetary policies: Presidential influence through the power of appointment', *Quarterly Journal of Economics*, February.

Cho, J.O. and T.F. Cooley (1995), 'The business cycle with nominal contracts', *Economic Theory*, June.

Choudri, E.U. and L.A. Kochin (1980), 'The exchange rate and the international transmission of business cycle disturbances', *Journal of Money, Credit, and Banking*, November.

Clower, R.W. (1952a), 'Professor Duesenberry and traditional theory', *Review of Economic Studies*.

Clower, R.W. (1952b), 'Mr. Graff's producer–consumer theory: a restatement and correction', *Review of Economic Studies*, October.

Clower, R.W. (1964), 'Monetary history and positive economics', *Journal of Economic History*, September.

Clower, R.W. (1965), 'The Keynesian counter-revolution: a theoretical appraisal' in F.H. Hahn and F.P.R. Brechling (eds), *The Theory of Interest Rates*, London: Macmillan.

Clower, R.W. (1967), 'A reconsideration of the microfoundations of monetary theory', *Western Economic Journal*, December.

Clower, R.W. (ed) (1969), *Monetary Theory: Selected Readings*, Harmondsworth: Penguin.

Clower, R.W. (1971), 'Theoretical foundations of monetary policy' in G. Clayton, J.C. Gilbert and R. Sedgwick (eds), *Monetary Theory and Monetary Policy in the 1970s*, London: Oxford University Press.

Clower, R.W. (1975), 'Reflections on the Keynesian perplex', *Zeitschrift fur Nationalökonomie*.

Clower, R.W. (1994), 'The fingers of the invisible hand', *Brock University Review*, April.

Clower, R.W. (1995), 'Axiomatics in economics', *Southern Economic Journal*, October.

Clower, R.W. and P. Howitt (1996), 'Taking markets seriously: groundwork for a post Walrasian macroeconomics' in D. Colander (ed.), *Beyond*

Microfoundations: Post Walrasian Macroeconomics, New York: Cambridge University Press.

Clower, R.W., G. Dalton, M. Harwitz and A. Walters (1966), *Growth Without Development: An Economic Survey of Liberia*, Evanston, IL: Northwestern University Press.

Coddington, A. (1976), 'Keynesian economics: the search for first principles', *Journal of Economic Literature*, December.

Colander, D. (1984), 'Was Keynes a Keynesian or a Lernerian?', *Journal of Economic Literature*, December.

Colander, D. (1988), 'The evolution of Keynesian economics: from Keynesian to new classical to new Keynesian' in O.F. Hamouda and J.N. Smithin (eds), *Keynes and Public Policy After Fifty Years, Vol. 1: Economics and Policy*, Aldershot: Edward Elgar.

Colander, D. (1990), 'Form and content in appraising recent economic developments', *Methodus: Bulletin of the International Network For Economic Method*, December.

Colander, D. (1992a), 'The new, the neo and the new neo', *Methodus: Bulletin of the International Network For Economic Method*, June.

Colander, D. (1992b), 'A real theory of inflation and incentive anti-inflation plans', *American Economic Review*, May.

Colander, D. (1994), 'Visions, judgement and disagreement among economists', *Journal of Economic Methodology*, June.

Colander, D. (1995a), 'Is Milton Friedman an artist or a scientist?', *Journal of Economic Methodology*, June.

Colander, D. (1995b), 'The stories we tell: a reconsideration of the AS/AD analysis', *Journal of Economic Perspectives*, Summer.

Colander, D. (ed.) (1996), *Beyond Microfoundations: Post Walrasian Macroeconomics*, New York: Cambridge University Press.

Colander, D. (1998), 'Macroeconomics: was Vickrey ten years ahead?', *Challenge*, September/October.

Colander, D. (1999), 'Confessions of an economic gadfly' in M. Szenberg (ed.), *Passion and Craft: Economists at Work*, Ann Arbor: University of Michigan Press.

Colander, D. and D. Daane (eds) (1994), *The Art of Monetary Policy*, London: M.E. Sharpe.

Colander, D.C. and H. Landreth (eds) (1996), *The Coming of Keynesianism to America: Conversations with the Founders of Keynesian Economics*, Cheltenham: Edward Elgar.

Collins, S.M. and B.P. Bosworth (1996), 'Economic growth in East Asia: accumulation versus assimilation', *Brookings Papers on Economic Activity*.

Cooley, T.F. (1997), 'Calibrated models', *Oxford Review of Economic Policy*, Autumn.

Cooley, T.F. and G.D. Hansen (1997), 'Unanticipated money growth and the business cycle reconsidered', *Journal of Money, Credit, and Banking*, November.

Cooley, T.F. and E.C. Prescott (1995), 'Economic growth and business cycles' in T.F. Cooley (ed.), *Frontiers of Business Cycle Research*, Princeton, NJ: Princeton University Press.

Cooper, R. and A. John (1988), 'Coordinating coordination failures in Keynesian models', *Quarterly Journal of Economics*, August.

Crafts, N.F.R. (1995), 'Exogenous or endogenous growth? The Industrial Revolution reconsidered', *Journal of Economic History*, December.

Crafts, N. (1996a), 'Macroeconomic policies in historical perspective' in M. Mackintosh, V. Brown, N. Costello, G. Dawson, G. Thompson and A. Trigg (eds), *Economics and Changing Economies*, London: International Thomson Business Press.

Crafts, N. (1996b), 'Post-neoclassical endogenous growth theory: what are its policy implications?', *Oxford Review of Economic Policy*, Summer.

Crafts, N. (1996c), 'Deindustrialisation and economic growth', *Economic Journal*, January.

Crafts, N. and G. Toniolo (eds) (1996), *Economic Growth in Europe Since 1945*, Cambridge: Cambridge University Press.

Cross, R. (ed) (1995), *The Natural Rate of Unemployment: Reflections on 25 Years of the Hypothesis*, Cambridge: Cambridge University Press.

Cross, R. (1996), 'The natural rate: an attractor for actual unemployment, or an attractee?', *Scottish Journal of Political Economy*, August.

Crucini, M.J. and J. Kahn (1996), 'Tariffs and aggregate economic activity: lessons from the Great Depression', *Journal of Monetary Economics*, December.

Cukierman, A. (1992), *Central Bank Strategy, Credibility and Independence*, Cambridge, MA: MIT Press.

Cukierman, A. (1994), 'Central bank independence and monetary control', *Economic Journal*, November.

Danthine, J.P. (1997), 'In search of a successor to IS–LM', *Oxford Review of Economic Policy*, Autumn.

De Long, J.B. (1988), 'Productivity growth, convergence and welfare: comment', *American Economic Review*, December.

De Long, J.B. (1996), 'Keynesianism, Pennsylvania Avenue style: some economic consequences of the Employment Act of 1946', *Journal of Economic Perspectives*, Summer.

De Long, J.B. (1999, forthcoming), *Slouching Towards Utopia?: The Global Economy in the Twentieth Century*.

Denison, E.F. (1974), *Accounting for United States Economic Growth, 1929–1969*, Washington, DC: The Brookings Institution.

Diamond, P.A. (1982), 'Aggregate demand management in search equilibrium', *Journal of Political Economy*, October.

Dimand, R.W. (1995), 'Irving Fisher, J.M. Keynes, and the transition to modern macroeconomics' in A.F. Cottrell and M.S. Lawlor (eds), *New Perspectives on Keynes*, Durham: Duke University Press.

Dixon, H.D. (1997), 'The role of imperfect competition in new Keynesian economics' in B. Snowdon and H.R. Vane (eds), *Reflections on the Development of Modern Macroeconomics*, Cheltenham: Edward Elgar.

Dorfman, R., P.A. Samuelson and P.M. Solow (1958), *Linear Programming and Economic Analysis*, New York: McGraw-Hill.

Dornbusch, R., S. Fischer and R. Startz (1998), *Macroeconomics*, 7th edn, New York: McGraw-Hill.

Domar, E.D. (1947), Expansion and employment', *American Economic Review*, March.

Doyle, C. and M. Weale (1994), 'Do we really want an independent Central Bank?' *Oxford Review of Economic Policy*, Autumn.

Easterly, W. and R. Levine (1997), 'Africa's growth tragedy: policies and ethnic divisions', *Quarterly Journal of Economics*, November.

Eichenbaum, M. (1991), 'Real business cycle theory: wisdom or whimsy?', *Journal of Economic Dynamics and Control*, October.

Eichenbaum, M. (1997), 'Some thoughts on practical stabilization policy', *American Economic Review*, May.

Eichengreen, B. (1992a), 'The origins and nature of the Great Slump revisited', *Economic History Review*, May.

Eichengreen, B. (1992b), *Golden Fetters: The Gold Standard and the Great Depression, 1919–1939*, New York: Oxford University Press.

Eichengreen, B. and J. Sachs (1985), 'Exchange rates and economic recovery in the 1930s', *Journal of Economic History*, December.

Eijffinger, S. and M.V. Keulen (1995), 'Central bank independencies in another eleven countries', *Banca Nazionale Del Lavoro Quarterly Review*, March.

Fabozzi, F.J. and F. Modigliani (1996), *Capital Markets, Institutions and Instruments*, 2nd edn, New Jersey: Prentice Hall.

Fackler, J.S. and R.E. Parker (1994), 'Accounting for the Great Depression: a historical decomposition', *Journal of Macroeconomics*, Spring.

Fagerberg, J. (1994), 'Technology and international differences in growth rates', *Journal of Economic Literature*, September.

Farmer, R.E.A. (1997), 'Money in a real business cycle model', *Journal of Money, Credit, and Banking*, November.

Feldstein, M. (1992), 'The Council of Economic Advisers and economic advising in the United States', *Economic Journal*, September.

Feldstein, M. (1997a), 'The Council of Economic Advisers: from stabilization to resource allocation', *American Economic Review*, May.

Feldstein, M. (1997b), 'The political economy of the European economic and monetary union: political sources of an economic liability', *Journal of Economic Perspectives*, Fall.

Feldstein, M. (1997c), 'EMU and international conflict', *Foreign Affairs*, November/December.

Fischer, S. (1977), 'Long-term contracts, rational expectations, and the optimal money supply rule', *Journal of Political Economy*, February.

Fischer, S. (1988), 'Recent developments in macroeconomics', *Economic Journal*, June.

Fischer, S. (1990), 'Rules versus discretion in monetary policy' in B.M. Friedman and F.H. Hahn (eds), *Handbook of Monetary Economics Vol. II*, Amsterdam: North Holland.

Fischer, S. (1993), 'The role of macroeconomic factors in growth', *Journal of Monetary Economics*, December.

Fischer, S. (1994), 'Interview with Stanley Fischer' in B. Snowdon, H.R. Vane and P. Wynarczyk, *A Modern Guide to Macroeconomics: An Introduction to Competing Schools of Thought*, Aldershot: Edward Elgar.

Fischer, S. (1995a), 'Central bank independence revisited', *American Economic Review*, May.

Fischer, S. (1995b), 'The unending search for monetary salvation', *National Bureau of Economic Research Macroeconomics Annual*.

Fischer, S. (1996), 'Robert Lucas's Nobel Memorial Prize', *Scandinavian Journal of Economics*, March.

Fischer, S. et al. (1988), 'Symposium on the slowdown in productivity growth', *Journal of Economic Perspectives*, Fall.

Fisher, I. (1911), *The Purchasing Power of Money*, New York: Macmillan.

Fisher, I. (1933), 'The debt–deflation theory of Great Depressions', *Econometrica*, October.

Forder, J. (1998), 'Central bank independencies – conceptual clarifications and interim assessment', *Oxford Economic Papers*, July.

Frey, B.S. and F. Schneider (1978), 'A politico-economic model of the United Kingdom', *Economic Journal*, June.

Friedman, B.M. (1988), 'Lessons of monetary policy from the 1980s', *Journal of Economic Perspectives*, Summer.

Friedman, B.M. and K.N. Kuttner (1996), 'A price target for U.S. monetary policy? Lessons from the experience with money growth targets', *Brookings Papers on Economic Activity*.

Friedman, M. (1948), 'A monetary and fiscal framework for economic stability', *American Economic Review*, June.

Friedman, M. (1953a), 'The methodology of positive economics' in M. Friedman, *Essays in Positive Economics*, Chicago, IL: University of Chicago Press.

Friedman, M. (1953b), 'The case for flexible exchange rates' in M. Friedman, *Essays in Positive Economics*, Chicago, IL: University of Chicago Press.

Friedman, M. (1953c), 'The effects of a full-employment policy on economic stability: a formal analysis', in M. Friedman, *Essays in Positive Economics*, Chicago, IL: University of Chicago Press.

Friedman, M. (1956), 'The quantity theory of money – a restatement', in M. Friedman (ed.), *Studies in the Quantity Theory of Money*, Chicago, IL: University of Chicago Press.

Friedman, M. (1959), *A Program for Monetary Stability*, New York: Fordham University Press.

Friedman, M. (1966), 'What price guideposts? Comments' in G.P. Schultz and R.Z. Aliber (eds), *Guidelines, Informal Controls and the Market Place: Policy Choice in a Full Employment Economy*, Chicago, IL: University of Chicago Press.

Friedman, M. (1968), 'The role of monetary policy', *American Economic Review*, March.

Friedman, M. (1969), *The Optimum Quantity of Money and Other Essays*, Chicago, IL: Aldine.

Friedman, M. (1970a), *The Counter-Revolution in Monetary Theory*, IEA Occasional Paper No. 33, London: Institute of Economic Affairs.

Friedman, M. (1970b), 'A theoretical framework for monetary analysis', *Journal of Political Economy*, March/April.

Friedman, M. (1972), 'Comments on the critics', *Journal of Political Economy*, September/October.

Friedman, M. (1975), *Unemployment Versus Inflation? An Evaluation of the Phillips Curve*, IEA Occasional Paper No. 44, London: Institute of Economic Affairs.

Friedman, M. (1977), 'Nobel lecture: inflation and unemployment', *Journal of Political Economy*, June.

Friedman, M. (1982), 'Monetary policy: theory and practice', *Journal of Money, Credit, and Banking*, February.

Friedman, M. (1991), 'Old wine in new bottles', *Economic Journal*, January.

Friedman, M. (1992), *Money Mischief: Episodes in Monetary History*, New York: Harcourt Brace Jovanovich.

Friedman, M. (1993), 'The plucking model of business fluctuations revisited', *Economic Inquiry*, April.

Friedman, M. and A.J. Schwartz (1963), *A Monetary History of the United States, 1867–1960*, Princeton, NJ: Princeton University Press.

Friedman, M. and A.J. Schwartz (1982), *Monetary Trends in the United*

States and the United Kingdom: Their Relation to Income, Prices and Interest Rates, 1867–1975, Chicago, IL: University of Chicago Press.

Galbraith, J.K. (1972), *The Great Crash, 1929*, 3rd edn, Boston: Houghton Mifflin.

Galbraith, J.K. (1997), 'Time to ditch the NAIRU', *Journal of Economic Perspectives*, Winter.

Garratt, D. (1995), 'Qualifications to political business cycle models', *Journal of Interdisciplinary Economics*.

George, H. (1879), *Progress and Poverty*, published 1929 New York: Schalkenback Foundation.

Gerrard, B. (1991), 'Keynes's *General Theory*: interpreting the interpretations', *Economic Journal*, March.

Gerrard, B. (1995), 'The scientific basis of economics: a review of the methodological debates in economics and econometrics', *Scottish Journal of Political Economy*, May.

Gerrard, B. (1996), 'Review article: competing schools of thought in macroeconomics – an ever-emerging consensus?', *Journal of Economic Studies*.

Goodhart, C.A.E. (1994a), 'Game theory for central bankers: a report to the Governor of the Bank of England', *Journal of Economic Literature*, March.

Goodhart, C.A.E. (1994b), 'What should central banks do? What should be their macroeconomic objectives and operations?', *Economic Journal*, November.

Gordon, R.J. (1975), 'Alternative responses to external supply shocks', *Brookings Papers on Economic Activity*.

Gordon, R.J. (1981), 'Output fluctuations and gradual price adjustment', *Journal of Economic Literature*, June.

Gordon, R.J. (1982), 'Price inertia and policy ineffectiveness in the United States, 1890–1980', *Journal of Political Economy*, December.

Gordon, R.J. (1990), 'What is new-Keynesian economics?', *Journal of Economic Literature*, September.

Gordon, R.J. (1997), 'The time-varying NAIRU and its implications for economic policy', *Journal of Economic Perspectives*, Winter.

Gordon, R.J. (1998), *Macroeconomics*, 7th edn, New York: Addison Wesley.

Gordon, R.J. and J.A. Wilcox (1981), 'Monetarist interpretations of the Great Depression: an evaluation and critique' in K. Brunner (ed.), *The Great Depression Revisited*, Boston: Martinus Nijhoff.

Green, J.H. (1996), 'Inflation targeting: theory and policy implications', *IMF Staff Papers*, December.

Greenspan, A. et al (1996), 'Symposium on achieving price stability', *Federal Reserve Bank of Kansas City*.

Griliches, Z. (1994), 'Productivity, R&D, and the data constraint', *American Economic Review*, March.

Grossman, G.M. and E. Helpman (1994), 'Endogenous innovation in the theory of growth', *Journal of Economic Perspectives*, Winter.

Haberler, G. (1958), *Prosperity and Depression*, 4th edn, Cambridge, MA: Harvard University Press.

Hadri, K., B. Lockwood and J. Maloney (1998), 'Does central bank independence smooth the political business cycle in inflation? Some OECD evidence', *Manchester School*, September.

Hahn, F.H. and R.M. Solow (1995), *A Critical Essay on Modern Macroeconomic Theory*, Cambridge, MA: MIT Press.

Haldane, A.G. (1998), 'On inflation targeting in the United Kingdom', *Scottish Journal of Political Economy*, February.

Hall, R.E. (1996), 'Robert Lucas, recipient of the 1995 Nobel Memorial Prize in Economics', *Scandinavian Journal of Economics*, March.

Hall, R.E. and C.I. Jones (1997), 'Levels of economic activity across countries', *American Economic Review*, May.

Hall, R.E. and C.I. Jones (1999, forthcoming), 'Why do some countries produce so much more output per worker than others?', *Quarterly Journal of Economics*.

Hall, R.E. and J.B. Taylor (1997), *Macroeconomics*, 5th edn, New York: W.W. Norton.

Hall, T.E. and J.D. Ferguson (1998), *The Great Depression: An International Disaster of Perverse Economic Policies*, Ann Arbor: University of Michigan Press.

Hamilton, J.D. (1986), 'On testing for self-fulfilling speculative price bubbles', *International Economic Review*, October.

Hamilton, J.D. (1987), 'Monetary factors in the Great Depression', *Journal of Monetary Economics*, March.

Hamilton, J.D. (1992), 'Was the deflation during the Great Depression anticipated? Evidence from the commodity futures market', *American Economic Review*, March.

Hammond, J.D. (1996), *Theory and Measurement: Causality Issues in Milton Friedman's Monetary Economics*, Cambridge: Cambridge University Press.

Hansen, A.H. (1949), *Monetary Theory and Fiscal Policy*, New York: McGraw-Hill.

Hansen, A.H. (1953), *A Guide to Keynes*, New York: McGraw-Hill.

Hansen, G.D. (1985), 'Indivisible labour and the business cycle', *Journal of Monetary Economics*, November.

Hansen, G.D. and E.C. Prescott (1993), 'Did technology shocks cause the 1990–1991 recession?', *American Economic Review*, May.

Hansen, L.P. and J.J. Heckman (1996), 'The empirical foundations of calibration', *Journal of Economic Perspectives*, Winter.

Harberger, A.C. (1998), 'A vision of the growth process', *American Economic Review*, March.

Harcourt, G.C. and P.A. Riach (eds) (1997), *A 'Second Edition' of The General Theory*, London: Routledge.

Harrod, R.F. (1939), 'An essay in dynamic theory', *Economic Journal*, June.

Harrod, R.F. (1948), *Towards a Dynamic Economics*, London: Macmillan.

Harrod, R.F. (1951), *The Life of John Maynard Keynes*, London: Macmillan.

Hartley, J.E., K.D. Hoover and K.D. Salyer (1997), 'The limits of business cycle research: assessing the real business cycle model', *Oxford Review of Economic Policy*.

Hartley, J.E., K.D. Hoover and K.D. Salyer (eds) (1998), *Real Business Cycles: A Reader*, London: Routledge.

Havrilesky, T.M. (1993), *The Pressures of Monetary Policy*, Norwell: Kluwer Academic Publishers.

Hayek, F.A. (1933), *Monetary Theory and the Trade Cycle*, London: Jonathan Cape.

Heilbroner, R.L. (1989), *The Making of Economic Society*, 8th edn, New Jersey: Prentice Hall.

Hibbs, D.A. (1977), 'Political parties and macroeconomic policy', *American Political Science Review*, December.

Hicks, J. (1933), 'Equilibrium and the cycle', in J. Hicks, *Collective Essays on Economic Theory, Vol. II, Money, Interest and Wages*, Oxford: Basil Blackwell.

Hicks, J.R. (1937), 'Mr Keynes and the "classics": a suggested interpretation', *Econometrica*, April.

Hicks, J.R. (1939), *Value and Capital*, Oxford: Oxford University Press.

Hicks, N. and P. Streeten (1979), 'Indicators of development: the search for a basic needs yardstick', *World Development*.

Hines, A.G. (1971), *On the Reappraisal of Keynesian Economics*, London: Martin Robertson.

HMSO (1944), *Employment Policy*, Cmnd 6527, London: HMSO.

Hodrick, R.J. and E.C. Prescott (1997), 'Postwar U.S. business cycles: an empirical investigation', *Journal of Money, Credit, and Banking*, February.

Hoover, K.D. (1984), 'Two types of monetarism', *Journal of Economic Literature*, March.

Hoover, K.D. (1988), *The New Classical Macroeconomics*, Oxford: Basil Blackwell.

Hoover, K.D. (ed.) (1992), *The New Classical Macroeconomics*, Aldershot: Edward Elgar.

Hoover, K.D. (1995a), 'Facts and artifacts: calibration and the empirical assessment of real business-cycle models', *Oxford Economic Papers*, January.

Hoover, K.D. (1995b), 'Relative wages, rationality and involuntary unemployment in Keynes's labour market', *History of Political Economy*, Winter.

Hoover, K.D. (ed.) (1995c), *Macroeconometics: Developments, Tensions, and Prospects*, Boston, MA: Kluwer Academic Publishers.

Hoover, K.D. and S.J. Perez (1994), 'Post hoc ergo propter hoc once more: an evaluation of "Does monetary policy matter?" in the spirit of James Tobin', *Journal of Monetary Economics*, August.

Howitt, P.W. (1990), *The Keynesian Recovery*, Oxford: Philip Allan.

Hu, Z.F. and M.S. Khan (1997), 'Why is China growing so fast?', *IMF Staff Papers*, March.

Hume, D. (1752), 'Of Money', and 'Of Interest' in *Essays Moral, Political and Literary*, reprinted in 1963, London: Oxford University Press.

Hunt, D. (1989), *Economic Theories of Development: An Analysis of Competing Paradigms*, New York: Harvester Wheatsheaf.

Hutchison, M.M. and C.E. Walsh (1998), 'The output–inflation tradeoff and central bank reform: evidence from New Zealand', *Economic Journal*, May.

Hylleberg, S. and M. Paldam (1991), 'New approaches to empirical macroeconomics', *Scandinavian Journal of Economics*, June.

Jenkins, M.A. (1996), 'Central bank independence and inflation performance: panacea or placebo?', *Banca Nazionale Del Lavoro Quarterly Review*, June.

Johnson, H.G. (1971), 'The Keynesian revolution and the monetarist counter-revolution', *American Economic Review*, May.

Jones, C.I. (1998), *Introduction to Economic Growth*, New York: W.W. Norton.

Jones, H.G. (1975), *An Introduction to Modern Theories of Economic Growth*, Southampton: Nelson.

Jonsson, P.O. (1997), 'Underconsumption vs. co-ordination failure: explanations of gluts in pre-Keynesian economics', paper presented at the *History of Economics Society Conference*, Charleston, South Carolina.

Jordan, J.L. et al. (1993), 'Milton, money and mischief: symposium and articles in honour of Milton Friedman's 80th birthday', *Economic Inquiry*, April.

Joyce, M. (1997), 'Inflation and inflation uncertainty', *Bank of England Quarterly Bulletin*, August.

Kahn, R.F. (1929), *The Economics of the Short Period*, unpublished Fellowship Dissertation, Cambridge; published in 1989, London: Macmillan.

Kahn, R.F. (1931), 'The relation of home investment to unemployment', *Economic Journal*, June.

Kaldor, N. (1970), 'The case for regional policies', *Scottish Journal of Political Economy*, November.

Kalecki, M. (1943), 'Political aspects of full employment', *Political Quarterly*, October–December.

Keynes, J.M. (1912), *Indian Currency and Finance*, London: Macmillan.

Keynes, J.M. (1919), *The Economic Consequences of the Peace*, London: Macmillan.

Keynes, J.M. (1921), *A Treatise on Probability*, London: Macmillan.

Keynes, J.M. (1923) *A Tract on Monetary Reform*, London: Macmillan.

Keynes, J.M. (1926), *The End of Laissez-Faire*, London: Hogarth Press.

Keynes, J.M. (1930), *A Treatise on Money*, London: Macmillan.

Keynes, J.M. (1931), 'The consequences to the banks of the collapse of money values', in *Essays in Persuasion*, published 1963 New York: W.W. Norton.

Keynes, J.M. (1933a), 'National self-sufficiency', *The Yale Review*, June.

Keynes, J.M. (1933b), *Essays in Biography*, London: Macmillan.

Keynes, J.M. (1936), *The General Theory of Employment, Interest and Money*, London: Macmillan.

Keynes, J.M. (1937), 'The General Theory of Employment', *Quarterly Journal of Economics*, February.

Keynes, J.M. (1940), *How to Pay For the War*, London: Macmillan.

Kim, J.-I. and L.J. Lau (1994), 'The sources of economic growth of the East Asian newly industrialized countries', *Journal of the Japanese and International Economies*.

King, M. (1997), 'The inflation target five years on', *Bank of England Quarterly Bulletin*, November.

Klamer, A. (1984), *The New Classical Macroeconomics: Conversations with New Classical Economists and their Opponents*, Brighton: Harvester Wheatsheaf.

Klenow, P.J. and A. Rodriguez-Clare (1997), 'Economic growth: a review essay', *Journal of Monetary Economics*, December.

Koopmans, T.C. (1965), 'On the concept of optimal economic growth' in *The Econometric Approach to Development Planning*, Amsterdam: North Holland.

Kouri, P.J.K. (1986), 'Franco Modigliani's contributions to economics', *Scandinavian Journal of Economics*.

Krueger, A.O. (1994), 'Lessons from developing countries about economic policy', *American Economist*, Spring.

Krueger, A.O. (1997), 'Trade policy and economic development: how we learn', *American Economic Review*, March.

Krugman, P. (1994a), *Peddling Prosperity: Economic Sense and Nonsense in the Age of Dimished Expectations*, New York: W.W. Norton.

Krugman, P. (1994b), 'The fall and rise of development economics' in L. Rodwin and D.A. Schon (eds), *Rethinking the Development Experience:*

Essays Provoked by the Work of O. Hirschman, Washington, DC: Brookings Institution; Cambridge, MA: Lincoln Institute of Land Policy.

Krugman, P. (1996), *Pop Internationalism*, Cambridge, MA: MIT Press.

Krugman, P. (1998), 'Two cheers for formalism', *Economic Journal*, November.

Kydland, F.E. and E.C. Prescott (1977), 'Rules rather than discretion: the inconsistency of optimal plans', *Journal of Political Economy*, June.

Kydland, F.E. and E.C. Prescott (1982), 'Time to build and aggregate fluctuations', *Econometrica*, November.

Kydland, F.E. and E.C. Prescott (1990), 'Business cycles: real facts and a monetary myth', *Federal Reserve Bank of Minneapolis Quarterly Review*, Spring.

Kydland, F.E. and E.C. Prescott (1991a), 'The econometrics of the general equilibrium approach to business cycles', *Scandinavian Journal of Economics*.

Kydland, F.E. and E.C. Prescott (1991b), 'Hours and employment variation in business cycle theory', *Economic Theory*, January.

Kydland, F.E. and E.C. Prescott (1996), 'The computational experiment: an econometric tool', *Journal of Economic Perspectives*, Winter.

Laidler, D.E.W. (1992), 'Issues in contemporary macroeconomics' in A. Vercelli and N. Dimitri (eds), *Macroeconomics: A Survey of Research Strategies*, Oxford: Oxford University Press.

Laing, D. (1993), 'A signalling theory of nominal wage inflexibility', *Economic Journal*, November.

Lakatos, I. (1978), *The Methodology of Scientific Research Programmes*, Cambridge: Cambridge University Press.

Landes, D.S. (1990), 'Why are we so rich and they so poor?', *American Economic Review*, May.

Landes, D.S. (1998), *The Wealth and Poverty of Nations: Why Some Are So Rich and Some So Poor*, New York: W.W. Norton.

Lange, O. (1942), 'Say's Law: a restatement and criticism' in O. Lange, F. McIntyre and T.O. Yutema (eds), *Studies in Mathematical Economics and Econometrics*, Chicago, IL: University of Chicago Press.

Leeson, R. (1994a), 'A.W.H. Phillips M.B.E. (Military Division)', *Economic Journal*, May.

Leeson, R. (1994b), 'A.W.H. Phillips, inflationary expectations and the operating characteristics of the macroeconomy', *Economic Journal*, November.

Leeson, R. (1997a), 'The trade-off interpretation of Phillips's dynamic stabilization exercise', *Economica*, February.

Leeson, R. (1997b), 'The political economy of the inflation–unemployment tradeoff', *History of Political Economy*, Spring.

Leeson, R. (1997c), 'The eclipse of the goal of zero Inflation', *History of Political Economy*, Fall.

Leeson, R. (1998), 'Phillips' econometric policy evaluation critique and the prediction of stagflation generated by his model', Unpublished Paper.

Leeson, R. (ed.) (1999), *A.W.H. Phillips: Collected Works in Contemporary Perspective*, Cambridge: Cambridge University Press.

Leijonhufvud, A. (1968), *On Keynesian Economics and the Economics of Keynes*, London: Oxford University Press.

Leijonhufvud, A. (1981), *Information and Co-ordination: Essays in Macroeconomic Theory*, Oxford: Oxford University Press.

Lekachman, R. (1969), *The Age of Keynes*, Harmondsworth: Pelican.

Lerner, A.P. (1944), *The Economics of Control*, New York: Macmillan.

Lerner, A. and D. Colander (1980), *MAP: A Market Anti-Inflation Plan*, New York: Harcourt Brace Jovanovich.

Lewis, W.A. (1954), 'Economic development with unlimited supplies of labour', *Manchester School of Economics and Social Studies*, May.

Lewis, W.A. (1955), *The Theory of Economic Growth*, London: Allen and Unwin.

Lindbeck, A. (1985), 'The prize in economic science in memory of Alfred Nobel', *Journal of Economic Literature*, March.

Lindbeck, A. (1998), 'New Keynesianism and aggregate economic activity', *Economic Journal*, January.

Lindbeck, A. and D. Snower (1986), 'Wage setting, unemployment, and insider–outsider relations', *American Economic Review*, May.

Lipsey, R.G. (1960), 'The relationship between unemployment and the rate of change of money wage rates in the UK, 1862–1957: a further analysis', *Economica*, February.

Ljungqvist, L. and T.J. Sargent (1998), 'The European unemployment dilemma', *Journal of Political Economy*, June.

Lohmann, S. (1992), 'Optimal commitment in monetary policy: credibility versus flexibility', *American Economic Review*, March.

Long, J.B. and C.I. Plosser (1983), 'Real business cycles', *Journal of Political Economy*, February.

Lucas, R.E. Jr (1972), 'Expectations and the neutrality of money', *Journal of Economic Theory*, April.

Lucas, R.E. Jr (1973), 'Some international evidence on output–inflation tradeoffs', *American Economic Review*, June.

Lucas, R.E. Jr (1975), 'An equilibrium model of the business cycle', *Journal of Political Economy*, December.

Lucas, R.E. Jr (1976), 'Econometric policy evaluation: a critique' in K. Brunner and A.H. Meltzer (eds), *The Phillips Curve and Labour Markets*, Amsterdam: North Holland.

Lucas, R.E. Jr (1978a), 'Unemployment policy', *American Economic Review*, May.

Lucas, R.E. Jr (1978b), 'Asset prices in an exchange economy', *Econometrica*, November.

Lucas, R.E. Jr (1980a), 'The death of Keynesian economics: issues and ideas', *University of Chicago*, Winter.

Lucas, R.E. Jr (1980b), 'Methods and problems in business cycle theory', *Journal of Money, Credit and Banking*, November.

Lucas, R.E. Jr (1981a), 'Rules, discretion and the role of the economic adviser' in R.E. Lucas Jr, *Studies in Business Cycle Theory*, Oxford: Basil Blackwell.

Lucas, R.E. Jr (1981b), 'Tobin and monetarism: a review article', *Journal of Economic Literature*, June.

Lucas, R.E. Jr (1981c), *Studies in Business Cycle Theory*, Oxford: Basil Blackwell.

Lucas, R.E. Jr (1987), *Models of Business Cycles*, Oxford: Basil Blackwell.

Lucas, R.E. Jr (1988), 'On the mechanics of economic development', *Journal of Monetary Economics*, July.

Lucas, R.E. Jr (1990), 'Why doesn't capital flow from rich to poor countries?', *American Economic Review*, May.

Lucas, R.E. Jr (1993), 'Making a miracle', *Econometrica*, March.

Lucas, R.E. Jr (1994a), 'Interview with Robert Lucas' in B. Snowdon, H.R. Vane and P. Wynarczyk, *A Modern Guide to Macroeconomics: An Introduction to Competing Schools of Thought*, Aldershot: Edward Elgar.

Lucas, R.E. Jr (1994b), 'Review of Milton Friedman and Anna J. Schwartz's *A Monetary History of the United States, 1867–1960*', *Journal of Monetary Economics*, August.

Lucas, R.E. Jr (1996), 'Nobel lecture: monetary neutrality', *Journal of Political Economy*, August.

Lucas, R.E. Jr and E.C. Prescott (1971), 'Investment under uncertainty', *Econometrica*, September.

Lucas, R.E. Jr and T.J. Sargent (1978), 'After Keynesian macroeconomics' in *After the Phillips Curve: Persistence of High Inflation and High Unemployment*, Boston, MA: Federal Reserve Bank of Boston.

Lucas, R.E. Jr and T.J. Sargent (eds) (1981), *Rational Expectations and Econometric Practice*, Minneapolis: University of Minnesota Press.

Maddison, A. (1991), *Dynamic Forces in Capitalist Development*, Oxford: Oxford University Press.

Maddison, A. (1997), 'The nature and functioning of European capitalism: a historical and comparative perspective', *Banca Nazionale Del Lavoro Quarterly Review*, December.

Malinvaud, E. (1977), *The Theory of Unemployment Reconsidered*, Oxford: Basil Blackwell.

Mankiw, N.G. (1985), 'Small menu costs and large business cycles: a macroeconomic model of monopoly', *Quarterly Journal of Economics*, May.

Mankiw, N.G. (1989), 'Real business cycles: a new Keynesian perspective', *Journal of Economic Perspectives*, Summer.

Mankiw, N.G. (1990), 'A quick refresher course in macroeconomics', *Journal of Economic Literature*, December.

Mankiw, N.G. (1991), 'Comment on J.J. Rotemberg and M. Woodford: markups and the business cycle', *National Bureau of Economic Research Macroeconomics Annual*.

Mankiw, N.G. (1992), 'The reincarnation of Keynesian economics', *European Economic Review*, April.

Mankiw, N.G. (1995a), 'Foreword' to R.J. Barro and X. Sala-i-Martin, *Economic Growth*, New York: McGraw-Hill.

Mankiw, N.G. (1995b), 'The growth of nations', *Brookings Papers on Economic Activity*.

Mankiw, N.G. (1997a), *Macroeconomics*, 3rd edn, New York: Worth.

Mankiw, N.G. (1997b), *Principles of Economics*, New York: Dryden Press.

Mankiw, N.G. and D. Romer (eds) (1991), *New Keynesian Economics*, Cambridge, MA: MIT Press.

Mankiw, N.G., D. Romer and D.N. Weil (1992), 'A contribution to the empirics of economic growth', *Quarterly Journal of Economics*, May.

Marris, R. (1991), *Reconstructing Keynesian Economics with Imperfect Competition: A Desk Top Simulation*, Aldershot: Edward Elgar.

Marshall, A. (1890), *Principles of Economics*, 1st edn, 8th edn 1929, London: Macmillan.

Mas, I. (1995), 'Central bank independence: a critical view from a developing country perspective', *World Development*.

Mauro, P. (1995), 'Corruption and growth', *Quarterly Journal of Economics*, August.

Mauro, P. (1998), 'Corruption: causes, consequences and agenda for further research', *Finance and Development*, March.

Mayer, T. (1990a), *Monetarism and Macroeconomic Policy*, Aldershot: Edward Elgar.

Mayer, T. (1990b), *The Political Economy of American Monetary Policy*, New York: Cambridge University Press.

Mayer, T. (1993), *Truth versus Precision in Economics*, Aldershot: Edward Elgar.

Mayer, T. (1997), 'What remains of the monetarist counter-revolution?' in B. Snowdon and H.R. Vane (eds), *Reflections on the Development of Modern Macroeconomics*, Cheltenham: Edward Elgar.

McCloskey, D. (1996), *The Vices of Economists – The Virtues of the Bourgeoisie*, Chapter 3, Amsterdam: Amsterdam University Press.

McDonald, I.M. (1992), *Macroeconomics*, New York: John Wiley.

McKenzie, L.W. (1998), 'Turnpikes', *American Economic Review*, May.

Meadows, D.H. et al. (1972), *The Limits to Growth*, London: Earth Island Limited.

Mehra, R. and E.C. Prescott (1985), 'The equity premium: a puzzle', *Journal of Monetary Economics*, March.

Meier, G.M. (ed.) (1994), *From Classical Economics to Development Economics*, New York: St. Martin's Press.

Meltzer, A.H. (1988), *Keynes's Monetary Theory: A Different Interpretation*, Cambridge: Cambridge University Press.

Metzler, L.A. (1941), 'The nature and stability of inventory cycles', *Review of Economics and Statistics*, August.

Metzler, L.A. (1947), 'Factors governing the length of inventory cycles', *Review of Economics and Statistics*, February.

Metzler, L.A. (1951), 'Wealth, saving and the rate of interest', *Journal of Political Economy*, April.

Millard, S., A. Scott and M. Sensier (1997), 'The labour market over the business cycle: can theory fit the facts?', *Oxford Review of Economic Policy*, Autumn.

Minford, A.P.L. (1985), *Unemployment: Cause and Cure*, Oxford: Basil Blackwell.

Minford, A.P.L. (1997), 'Macroeconomics: before and after rational expectations' in B. Snowdon and H.R. Vane (eds), *Reflections on the Development of Modern Macroeconomics*, Cheltenham: Edward Elgar.

Miron, J.A. (1994), 'Empirical methodology in macroeconomics: explaining the success of Friedman and Schwartz's *A Monetary History of the United States, 1867–1960*', *Journal of Monetary Economics*, August.

Mishkin, F.S. (1982), 'Does anticipated monetary policy matter? An econometric investigation', *Journal of Political Economy*, February.

Modigliani, F. (1944), 'Liquidity preference and the theory of interest and money', *Econometrica*, January.

Modigliani, F. (1961), 'Long-run implications of alternative fiscal policies and the burden of the national debt', *Economic Journal*, December.

Modigliani, F. (1977), 'The monetarist controversy or, should we forsake stabilization policies?', *American Economic Review*, March.

Modigliani, F. (1986), *The Debate Over Stabilization Policy*, Cambridge: Cambridge University Press.

Modigliani, F. (1988a), 'The monetarist controversy revisited', *Contemporary Policy Issues*, October.

Modigliani, F. (1988b), 'Reagan's economic policies: a critique', *Oxford Economic Papers*, September.

Modigliani, F. (1996), 'The shameful rate of unemployment in the EMS: causes and cures', *De Economist*, October.

Modigliani, F. and R. Brumberg (1954), 'Utility analysis and the consumption function: an interpretation of cross-section data' in K.K. Kurihara (ed.), *Post-Keynesian Economics*, New Brunswick, NJ: Rutgers University Press.

Modigliani, F. and R. Brumberg (1980), 'Utility analysis and aggregate consumption functions: an attempt at integration' in A. Abel (ed.), *The Collected Papers of Franco Modigliani, Vol. 2, The Life Cycle Hypothesis of Saving*, Cambridge, MA: MIT Press.

Modigliani, F. and R.A. Cohn (1979), 'Inflation, rational valuation and the market', *Financial Analysis Journal*, March–April.

Modigliani, F. and E. Grunberg (1954), 'The predictability of social events', *Journal of Political Economy*, December.

Modigliani, F. and L.D. Papademos (1975), 'Targets for monetary policy in the coming year', *Brookings Papers on Econonic Activity*.

Modigliani, F. et al. (1998), 'An economist's manifesto on unemployment in the European Union', *Banca Nazionale Del Lavoro Quarterly Review*, September.

Moggridge, D.E. (1995), 'The diffusion of the Keynesian revolution: the Young and the Graduate Schools' in A.F. Cottrell and M.S. Lawlor (eds), *New Perspectives on Keynes*, Durham: Duke University Press.

Murphy, K., C. Riddell and P.M. Romer (1998), 'Wages, skills and technology in the United States and Canada' in E. Helpman (ed.), *General Purpose Technologies*, Cambridge, MA: MIT Press.

Murphy, K.M., A. Shleifer and R.W. Vishny (1989), 'Industrialization and the big push', *Quarterly Journal of Economics*, May.

Murphy, K.M., A. Shleifer and R.W. Vishny (1991), 'The allocation of talent: implications for growth', *Quarterly Journal of Economics*, May.

Murphy, K.M., A. Shleifer and R.W. Vishny (1993), 'Why is rent-seeking so costly to growth?', *American Economic Review*, May.

Muscatelli, A. (1998), 'Optimal inflation contracts and inflation targets with uncertain central bank preferences: accountability through independence?', *Economic Journal*, March.

Muth, J.F. (1961), 'Rational expectations and the theory of price movements', *Econometrica*, July.

Myrdal, K.G. (1957), *Rich Lands and Poor: The Road to World Prosperity*, New York: Harper and Row.

Nelson, R.R. and P.M. Romer (1996), 'Science, economic growth, and public policy', *Challenge*, March/April.

Nelson, R.R. and G. Wright (1992), 'The rise and fall of American technological leadership: the postwar era in historical perspective', *Journal of
Economic Literature*, December.

Newcomb, S. (1885), *Principles of Political Economy*, New York: Harper &
Bros.

Nickell, S. (1997), 'Unemployment and labour market rigidities: Europe
versus North America', *Journal of Economic Perspectives*, Summer.

Nordhaus, W.D. (1975), 'The political business cycle', *Review of Economic
Studies*, April.

Nordhaus, W.D. (1994), 'Policy games: co-ordination and independence in
monetary and fiscal policy', *Brookings Papers on Economic Activity*.

North, D.C. (1990), *Institutions, Institutional Change and Economic Performance*, Cambridge: Cambridge University Press.

Oakley, A. (1990), *Schumpeter's Theory of Capitalist Motion: A Critical
Exposition and Reassessment*, Aldershot: Edward Elgar.

Obstfeld, M. (1997), 'Europe's gamble', *Brookings Papers on Economic
Activity*.

Obstfeld, M. and K. Rogoff (1996), *Foundations of International Macroeconomics*, Cambridge, MA: MIT Press.

Okun, A. (1962), 'Potential GNP: its measurement and significance', *Pro-
ceedings of the Business and Economics Statistics Section of the American
Statistical Association*, Washington, DC: ASA.

Okun, A. (1981), *Prices and Quantities: A Macroeconomic Analysis*, Oxford:
Basil Blackwell.

Olson, M. (1982), *The Rise and Decline of Nations*, New Haven, CT: Yale
University Press.

Olson, M. Jr (1996), 'Distinguished Lecture on Economics in Government:
Big bills left on the sidewalk: why some nations are rich, and others poor',
Journal of Economic Perspectives, Spring.

Ostroy, J.M. and R.M. Starr (1974), 'Money and the decentralization of
exchange', *Econometrica*, November.

Pack, H. (1994), 'Endogenous growth theory: intellectual appeal and empirical shortcomings', *Journal of Economic Perspectives*, Winter.

Parente, S.L. and E.C. Prescott (1992), 'Technology adoption and the mechanics of economic development' in A. Cukierman, Z. Hercowitz and L.
Leiderman (eds), *Political Economy, Growth, and Business Cycles*, Cambridge, MA: MIT Press.

Parente, S.L. and E.C. Prescott (1993), 'Changes in the wealth of nations',
Federal Reserve Bank of Minneapolis Quarterly Review, Spring.

Parente, S.L. and E.C. Prescott (1997), 'Monopoly rights: a barrier to riches',
Federal Reserve Bank of Minneapolis Staff Report 236, July.

Patinkin, D. (1956); *Money, Interest and Prices: An Integration of Monetary and Value Theory*, Evanston, IL: Row Peterson.

Patinkin, D. (1978), 'The process of writing *The General Theory*: a critical survey' in D. Patinkin and J.C. Leith (eds), *Keynes, Cambridge and the General Theory*, Toronto: University of Toronto Press.

Patinkin, D. (1982), *Anticipations of the General Theory? and Other Essays on Keynes*, Chicago, IL: University of Chicago Press.

Patinkin, D. (1990), 'On different interpretations of the *General Theory*', *Journal of Monetary Economics*, October.

Pearce, K.A. and K.D. Hoover (1995), 'After the revolution: Paul Samuelson and the textbook Keynesian model' in A.F. Cottrel and M.S. Lawlor (eds), *New Perspectives on Keynes*, Durham: Duke University Press.

Perkins, D.H. (1988), 'Reforming China's economic system', *Journal of Economic Literature*, June.

Perkins, D.H. (1994), 'Completing China's move to the market', *Journal of Economic Perspectives*, Spring.

Phelps, E.S. (1967), 'Phillips curves, expectations of inflation and optimal unemployment over time', *Economica*, August.

Phelps, E.S. (1968), 'Money wage dynamics and labour market equilibrium', *Journal of Political Economy*, August.

Phelps, E.S. (1994), *Structural Slumps: The Modern Equilibrium Theory of Unemployment, Interest and Assets*, Cambridge, MA: Harvard University Press.

Phelps, E.S. and J.B. Taylor (1977), 'Stabilizing powers of monetary policy under rational expectations', *Journal of Political Economy*, February.

Phelps, E.S. and G. Zoega (1998), 'Natural-rate theory and OECD unemployment', *Economic Journal*, May.

Phillips, A.W. (1958), 'The relationship between unemployment and the rate of change of money wages rates in the United Kingdom, 1861–1957', *Economica*, November.

Pierce, J.L. (1995), 'Monetarism: the good, the bad, and the ugly', in K.D. Hoover and S.M. Sheffrin (eds), *Monetarism and the Methodology of Economics: Essays in Honour of Thomas Mayer*, Aldershot: Edward Elgar.

Pigou, A.C. (1936), 'Mr J.M. Keynes's *General Theory of Employment, Interest and Money*', *Economica*, May.

Plosser, C. (1994), 'Interview with Charles Plosser' in B. Snowdon, H.R. Vane and P. Wynarczyk, *A Modern Guide to Macroeconomics: An Introduction to Competing Schools of Thought*, Aldershot: Edward Elgar.

Poole, W. (1988), 'Monetary policy lessons of recent inflation and disinflation', *Journal of Economic Perspectives*, Summer.

Posen, A. (1998), 'Central bank independence and disinflationary credibility: a missing link', *Oxford Economic Papers*, July.

Prescott, E.C. (1986), 'Theory ahead of business cycle measurement', *Federal Reserve Bank of Minneapolis Quarterly Review*, Fall.

Prescott, E.C. (1988), 'Robert M. Solow's neoclassical growth model: an influential contribution to economics', *Scandinavian Journal of Economics*.

Prescott, E.C. (1996), 'Interview with Edward C. Prescott', *The Region*, September.

Prescott, E.C. (1998), 'Needed: a theory of total factor productivity', *International Economic Review*, August.

Pritchett, L. (1997), 'Divergence, big time', *Journal of Economic Perspectives*, Summer.

Proudman, J. and S. Redding (1997), 'The relationship between openness and growth in the United Kingdom: a summary of the Bank of England growth project', *Bank of England Quarterly Bulletin*, November.

Purvis, D.D. (1982), 'James Tobin's contributions to economics', *Scandinavian Journal of Economics*.

Quah, D. (1993), 'Galton's fallacy and tests of the convergence hypothesis', *Scandinavian Journal of Economics*, December.

Quah, D.T. (ed.) (1995), 'Business cycle empirics: calibration and estimation', *Economic Journal*, November.

Radelet, S. and J.D. Sachs (1998), 'The East Asian financial crisis: diagnosis, remedies, prospects', *Brookings Papers on Economic Activity*.

Ramsey, F. (1928), 'A mathematical theory of saving', *Economic Journal*, December.

Rebelo, S. (1991), 'Long-run policy analysis and long-run growth', *Journal of Political Economy*, June.

Robbins, L. (1934), *The Great Depression*, London: Macmillan.

Robinson, J. (1933), *The Economics of Imperfect Competition*, London: Macmillan.

Robinson, J. (1960), *Collected Economic Papers, Vol. 2*, Oxford: Basil Blackwell.

Rogerson, R. (1988), 'Indivisible labour, lotteries and equilibrium', *Journal of Monetary Economics*, January.

Rogerson, R. (1997), 'Theory ahead of language in the economics of unemployment', *Journal of Economic Perspectives*, Winter.

Rogoff, K. (1985), 'The optimal degree of commitment to an intermediate monetary target', *Quarterly Journal of Economics*, November.

Rogoff, K. and A. Sibert (1988), 'Equilibrium political business cycles', *Review of Economic Studies*, January.

Romer, C.D. (1990), 'The great crash and the onset of the Great Depression', *Quarterly Journal of Economics*, August.

Romer, C.D. (1992), 'What ended the Great Depression?', *Journal of Economic History*, December.

Romer, C.D. (1993), 'The nation in depression', *Journal of Economic Perspectives*, Spring.

Romer, C.D. and D.H. Romer (1989), 'Does monetary policy matter? A new test in the spirit of Friedman and Schwartz', *National Bureau of Economic Research Macroeconomics Annual*.

Romer, D. (1993), 'The new Keynesian synthesis', *Journal of Economic Perspectives*, Winter.

Romer, D. (1996), *Advanced Macroeconomics*, New York: McGraw-Hill.

Romer, P.M. (1986), 'Increasing returns and long-run growth', *Journal of Political Economy*, October.

Romer, P.M. (1987a), 'Growth based on increasing returns due to specialization', *American Economic Review*, May.

Romer, P.M. (1987b), 'Crazy explanations for the productivity slowdown', *National Bureau of Economic Research Macroeconomics Annual*.

Romer, P.M. (1989), 'Capital accumulation in the theory of long-run growth' in R.J. Barro (ed.), *Modern Business Cycle Theory*, Cambridge, MA: Harvard University Press.

Romer, P.M. (1990), 'Endogenous technological change', *Journal of Political Economy*, October.

Romer, P.M. (1993), 'Idea gaps and object gaps in economic development', *Journal of Monetary Economics*, December.

Romer, P.M. (1994a), 'The origins of endogenous growth', *Journal of Economic Perspectives*, Winter.

Romer, P.M. (1994b), 'New goods, old theory, and the welfare costs of trade restrictions', *Journal of Development Economics*.

Romer, P.M. (1995), 'The growth of nations: a comment on Mankiw', *Brookings Papers on Economic Activity*.

Romer, P.M. (1996), 'Why, indeed, in America? Theory, history, and the origins of modern economic growth', *American Economic Review*, May.

Rosenberg, N. (1994), *Exploring the Black Box: Technology, Economics and History*, Cambridge: Cambridge University Press.

Rostow, W.W. (1960), *The Stages of Economic Growth*, Cambridge: Cambridge University Press.

Ryan, C. and A.W. Mullineux (1997), 'The ups and downs of modern business cycle theory' in B. Snowdon and H.R. Vane (eds), *Reflections on the Development of Modern Macroeconomics*, Cheltenham: Edward Elgar.

Sachs, J.D. and A.M. Warner (1995), 'Economic reform and the process of global integration', *Brookings Papers on Economic Activity*.

Sachs, J.D. and A.M. Warner (1997), 'Fundamental sources of long-run growth', *American Economic Review*, May.

Samuelson, P.A. (1939), 'Interactions between the multiplier analysis and the principle of acceleration', *Review of Economics and Statistics*, May.

Samuelson, P.A. (1948), *Economics*, New York: McGraw-Hill.

Samuelson, P.A. (1955), *Economics*, 3rd edn, New York: McGraw-Hill.

Samuelson, P.A. (1983), 'The Keynes centenary: sympathy from the other Cambridge', *Economist*, 25 June.

Samuelson, P.A. (1997), 'Credo of a lucky textbook author', *Journal of Economic Perspectives*, Spring.

Samuelson, P.A. and R.M. Solow (1960), 'Analytical aspects of anti-inflation policy', *American Economic Review*, May.

Sargent, T.J. (1982), 'The ends of four big inflations' in R.H. Hall (ed.), *Inflation: Causes and Effects*, Chicago, IL: University of Chicago Press.

Sargent, T.J. (1993), *Rational Expectations and Inflation*, New York: Harper Collins.

Sargent, T.J. and N. Wallace (1975), 'Rational expectations, the optimal monetary instrument, and the optimal money supply rule', *Journal of Political Economy*, March/April.

Sargent, T.J. and N. Wallace (1976), 'Rational expectations and the theory of economic policy', *Journal of Monetary Economics*, April.

Schultze, C.L. (1996), 'The CEA: an inside voice for mainstream economics', *Journal of Economic Perspectives*, Summer.

Schwartz, A.J. (1981), 'Understanding 1929–1933' in K. Brunner (ed.), *The Great Depression Revisited*, Boston: Martinus Nijhoff.

Sen, A. (1998), 'Mortality as an indicator of economic success and failure', *Economic Journal*, January.

Shapiro, C. and J. Stiglitz (1984), 'Equilibrium unemployment as a discipline device', *American Economic Review*, June.

Shaw, G.K. (1992), 'Policy implications of endogenous growth theory', *Economic Journal*, May.

Shaw, G.K. (1997), 'How relevant is Keynesian economics today?' in B. Snowdon and H.R. Vane (eds), *Reflections on the Development of Modern Macroeconomics*, Cheltenham: Edward Elgar.

Shleifer, A. and R. Vishny (1993), 'Corruption', *Quarterly Journal of Economics*, August.

Siebert, H. (1997), 'Labour market rigidities: at the root of unemployment in Europe', *Journal of Economic Perspectives*, Summer.

Simon, H.A. (1957), *Models of Man: Social and Rational*, New York: Wiley.

Sims, C.A. (1996), 'Macroeconomics and methodology', *Journal of Economic Perspectives*, Winter.

Skidelsky, R. (1992), *John Maynard Keynes, Vol. 2, The Economist as Saviour, 1920–1937*, London: Macmillan.

Skidelsky, R. (1996), *Keynes*, Oxford: Oxford University Press.

Smaghi, L.B. (1998), 'The democratic accountability of the European Central Bank', *Banca Nazionale Del Lavoro Quarterly Review*, June.

Smith, A. (1776), *An Inquiry into the Nature and Causes of the Wealth of Nations*, edited by R.H. Campbell and A.S. Skinner, 1976 Oxford: Clarendon.

Smith, B.D. (1994), 'Mischief and monetary history: Friedman and Schwartz thirty years later,' *Journal of Monetary Economics*, August.

Smith, D. (1997), 'Independence Day', *Sunday Times*, 11 May.

Snowdon, B. (1997), 'Politics and the business cycle', *Political Quarterly*, July.

Snowdon, B. and H.R. Vane (1995), 'New Keynesian economics today: the empire strikes back', *American Economist*, Spring.

Snowdon, B. and H.R. Vane (1996), 'The development of modern macroeconomics: reflections in the light of Johnson's analysis after twenty-five years', *Journal of Macroeconomics*, Summer.

Snowdon, B. and H.R. Vane (eds) (1997a), *A Macroeconomics Reader*, London: Routledge.

Snowdon, B. and H.R. Vane (1997b), 'Modern macroeconomics and its evolution from a monetarist perspective: an interview with Professor Milton Friedman', *Journal of Economic Studies*.

Snowdon, B. and H.R. Vane (1997c), 'Politics and the macroeconomy: endogenous politicians and aggregate instability' in B. Snowdon and H.R. Vane (eds), *Reflections on the Development of Modern Macroeconomics*, Cheltenham: Edward Elgar.

Snowdon, B. and H.R. Vane (1998), 'Transforming macroeconomics: an interview with Robert E. Lucas Jr.', *Journal of Economic Methodology*.

Snowdon, B. and H.R. Vane (1999, forthcoming), 'The new political macroeconomics', *American Economist*.

Snowdon, B., H.R. Vane and P. Wynarczyk (1994), *A Modern Guide to Macroeconomics: An Introduction to Competing Schools of Thought*, Aldershot: Edward Elgar.

Solow, R.M. (1956), 'A contribution to the theory of economic growth', *Quarterly Journal of Economics*, February.

Solow, R.M. (1957), 'Technical change and the aggregate production function', *Review of Economics and Statistics*, August.

Solow, R.M. (1966), 'The case against the case against the guideposts' in G.P. Schultz and R.Z. Aliber (eds), *Guidelines, Informal Controls and the Market Place: Policy in a Full Employment Economy*, Chicago, IL: University of Chicago Press.

Solow, R.M. (1970), *Growth Theory: An Exposition*, Oxford: Clarendon Press.

Solow, R.M. (1979), 'Another possible source of wage stickiness', *Journal of Macroeconomics*, Winter.

Solow, R.M. (1980), 'On theories of unemployment', *American Economic Review*, March.

Solow, R.M. (1982), 'Some lessons from growth theory' in W.F. Sharpe and C.M. Cootner (eds), *Financial Economics: Essays in Honour of Paul Cootner*, Englewood Cliffs: Prentice Hall.

Solow, R.M. (1986), 'What is a nice girl like you doing in a place like this? Macroeconomics after fifty years', *Eastern Economic Journal*, July–September.

Solow, R.M. (1990), *The Labour Market as a Social Institution*, Oxford: Basil Blackwell.

Solow, R.M. (1994), 'Perspectives on growth theory', *Journal of Economic Perspectives*, Winter.

Solow, R.M. (1997a), 'It ain't the things you don't know that hurt you, it's the things you know that ain't so', *American Economic Review*, May.

Solow, R.M. (1997b), 'Is there a core of usable macroeconomics we should all believe in?', *American Economic Review*, May.

Solow, R.M. (1997c), 'How did economics get that way and what way did it get?' *Daedalus*, Winter.

Solow, R.M. (1997d), *Learning from 'Learning by Doing': Lessons for Economic Growth*, Stanford, CA: Stanford University Press.

Solow, R.M. (1998), 'How cautious must the Fed be?' in R.M. Solow and J.B. Taylor, *Inflation, Unemployment, and Monetary Policy*, Cambridge, MA: MIT Press.

Solow, R.M. and J.B. Taylor (1998), *Inflation, Unemployment, and Monetary Policy*, Cambridge, MA: MIT Press.

Solow, R.M. et al. (1997), 'Is there a core of practical macroeconomics that we should all believe?', *American Economic Review*, May.

Staiger, D., J.H. Stock and M.W. Watson (1997), 'The NAIRU, unemployment and monetary policy', *Journal of Economic Perspectives*, Winter.

Stein, H. (1969), *The Fiscal Revolution in America*, Chicago, IL: University of Chicago Press.

Stein, H. (1986), 'The Washington economics industry', *American Economic Review*, May.

Stein, H. (1994), *Presidential Economics: The Making of Economic Policy from Roosevelt to Clinton*, 3rd edn, Washington, DC: AEI Press.

Stein, H. (1996), 'A successful accident: recollections and speculations about the CEA', *Journal of Economic Perspectives*, Summer.

Steindl, F.G. (1996), *Monetary Interpretations of the Great Depression*, Ann Arbor: University of Michigan Press.

Steindl, F.G. (1998), 'The decline of a paradigm: the quantity theory and recovery in the 1930s', *Journal of Macroeconomics*, Fall.

Stewart, M. (1986), *Keynes and After*, 3rd edn, Harmondsworth: Penguin.

Stiglitz, J. (1997), 'Reflections on the natural rate hypothesis', *Journal of Economic Perspectives*, Winter.

Summers, L.H. (1986), 'Some skeptical observations on real business cycle theory', *Federal Reserve Bank of Minneapolis Quarterly Review*, Fall.

Summers, L.H. (1991), 'The scientific illusion in empirical macroeconomics', *Scandinavian Journal of Economics*.

Summers, R. and A. Heston (1991), 'The Penn World Table (Mark 5): an expanded set of international comparisons, 1950–88', *Quarterly Journal of Economics*, May.

Svensson, L.E.O. (1996), 'The scientific contributions of Robert E. Lucas, Jr.', *Scandinavian Journal of Economics*, March.

Svensson, L.E.O. (1997a), 'Optimal inflation targets, "conservative" central banks, and linear inflation contracts', *American Economic Review*, March.

Svensson, L.E.O. (1997b), 'Inflation forecast targeting: implementing and monitoring inflation targets', *European Economic Review*, June.

Swan, T.W. (1956), 'Economic growth and capital accumulation', *Economic Record*, November.

Szenberg, M. (ed) (1992), *Eminent Economists: Their Life Philosophies*, Cambridge: Cambridge University Press.

Tavelli, H., G. Tullio and F. Spinelli (1998), 'The evolution of European central bank independence: an updating of the Masciandaro and Spinelli Index', *Scottish Journal of Political Economy*, August.

Taylor, J.B. (1979), 'Staggered wage setting in a macro model', *American Economic Review*, May.

Taylor, J.B. (1982), 'Establishing credibility: a rational expectations viewpoint', *American Economic Review*, May.

Taylor, J.B. (1983), 'Union wage settlements during a disinflation', *American Economic Review*, December.

Taylor, J.B. (1989), 'The evolution of ideas in macroeconomics', *Economic Record*, June.

Taylor, J.B. (1993a), *Macroeconomic Policy in a World Economy: From Econometric Design to Practical Operation*, New York: W.W. Norton.

Taylor, J.B. (1993b), 'Discretion versus policy rules in practice', *Carnegie Rochester Conference Series on Public Policy*, Amsterdam: North Holland.

Taylor, J.B. (1994), 'The inflation–output variability tradeoff revisited' in J. Fuhrer (ed.), *Goals, Guidelines and Constraints Facing Monetary Policy Makers*, Boston: Federal Reserve Bank of Boston.

Taylor, J.B. (1995), 'Changes in American economic policy in the 1980s: watershed or pendulum swing?', *Journal of Economic Literature*, June.

Taylor, J.B. (1997), 'A core of practical macroeconomics', *American Economic Review*, May.

Taylor, J.B. (1998a), *Economics*, 2nd edn, New York: Houghton Mifflin.

Taylor, J.B. (1998b), 'Monetary policy guidelines for employment and inflation stability' in R.M. Solow and J.B. Taylor, *Inflation, Unemployment,
and Monetary Policy*, Cambridge, MA: MIT Press.

Temin, P. (1976), *Did Monetary Forces Cause the Great Depression?*, New
York: W.W. Norton.

Temin, P. (1989), *Lessons From the Great Depression*, Cambridge, MA: MIT
Press.

Temin, P. (1993), 'Transmission of the Great Depression', *Journal of Economic Perspectives*, Spring.

Temple, J. (1999), 'The new growth evidence', *Journal of Economic Literature*, March.

Thygesen, N. (1977), 'The scientific contributions of Milton Friedman',
Scandinavian Journal of Economics.

Tobin, J. (1955), 'A dynamic aggregative model', *Journal of Political Economy*,
April.

Tobin, J. (1958), 'Liquidity preference as behaviour towards risk', *Review of
Economic Studies*, February.

Tobin, J. (1970), 'Money and income: post hoc ergo propter hoc?', *Quarterly
Journal of Economics*, May.

Tobin, J. (1972), 'Friedman's theoretical framework', *Journal of Political
Economy*, September/October.

Tobin, J. (1977), 'How dead is Keynes?', *Economic Inquiry*, October.

Tobin, J. (1980a), 'Are new classical models plausible enough to guide policy?',
Journal of Money, Credit, and Banking, November.

Tobin, J. (1980b), *Asset Accumulation and Economic Activity*, Oxford: Basil
Blackwell.

Tobin, J. (1981), 'The monetarist counter-revolution today: an appraisal',
Economic Journal, March.

Tobin, J. (1987), *Policies for Prosperity: Essays in a Keynesian Mode*, in
P.M. Jackson (ed.), Brighton: Wheatsheaf.

Tobin, J. (1988), 'Comment' on David Romer's paper on 'What are the costs
of excessive deficits?', *National Bureau of Economic Macroeconomics
Annual*.

Tobin, J. (1993), 'Price flexibility and output stability: an old Keynesian
view', *Journal of Economic Perspectives*, Winter.

Tobin, J. (1995), 'The natural rate as new classical economics' in R. Cross
(ed.), *The Natural Rate of Unemployment: Reflections on 25 Years of
Hypothesis*, Cambridge: Cambridge University Press.

Tobin, J. (1996), *Full Employment and Growth: Further Keynesian Essays on
Policy*, Cheltenham: Edward Elgar.

Tobin, J. (1997), 'An Overview of *The General Theory*', *Cowles Foundation
Paper* No. 947.

United States Government (1946), *Employment Act of 1946*, Washington, DC: Government Printing Office.

United States Government, Congress (1946), *Committee of Conference Report: A Bill Declaring a National Policy on Employment, Production, and Purchasing Power, and for Other Purposes*, Washington, DC: Government Printing Office.

Vercelli, A. (1991), *Methodological Foundations of Macroeconomics: Keynes and Lucas*, Cambridge: Cambridge University Press.

Vickers, J. (1998), 'Inflation targeting in practice: the UK experience', *Bank of England Quarterly Bulletin*, November.

Waller, C.J. and C.E. Walsh (1996), 'Central-bank independence, economic behaviour, and optimal term lengths', *American Economic Review*, December.

Walsh, C. (1993), 'Central bank strategies, credibility and independence: a review essay', *Journal of Monetary Economics*, November.

Walsh, C. (1995a), 'Optimal contracts for central bankers', *American Economic Review*, March.

Walsh, C. (1995b), 'Recent central-bank reforms and the role of price stability as the sole objective of monetary policy', *National Bureau of Economic Research Macroeconomics Annual*.

Walsh, C.E. (1998), *Monetary Theory and Policy*, Cambridge, MA: MIT Press.

Weitzman, M.L. (1996), 'Hybridizing growth theory', *American Economic Review*, May.

White, E.N. (1990), 'The stock market boom and crash of 1929 revisited', *Journal of Economic Perspectives*, Spring.

Wickens, M. (1995), 'Real business cycle analysis: a needed revolution in macroeconometrics', *Economic Journal*, November.

Wicksell, K. (1898), *Interest and Prices*, translated by Richard Kahn for the Royal Economic Society 1936, reprinted 1962 New York: Augustus Kelley.

Williamson, S.D. (1996), 'Real business cycle research comes of age: a review essay', *Journal of Monetary Economics*, August.

Woglin, J.M. (1997), 'The evolution of economic policymaking in Africa', *American Economic Review*, May.

Wooley, J.T. (1994), 'The politics of monetary policy: a critical review', *Journal of Public Policy*.

World Bank (1998/99), 'Knowledge for development', *World Development Report*.

Yellen, J.L. (1984), 'Efficiency wage models of unemployment', *American Economic Review*, May.

Young, A. (1928), 'Increasing returns and economic progress', *Economic Journal*, December.

Young, A. (1992), 'A tale of two cities: factor accumulation and technical change in Hong Kong and Singapore', *National Bureau of Economic Research Macroeconomics Annual*.

Young, A. (1995), 'The tyranny of numbers: confronting the statistical realities of the East Asian growth experience', *Quarterly Journal of Economics*, August.

Zahka, W.J. (1992), *The Nobel Prize Economics Lectures: A Cross-Section of Current Thinking*, Brookfield, VT: Ashgate.

Index

Asian Tiger economies 64, 74, 280

calibration 41–3, 135, 156, 266
central bank independence 52–7, 200–201, 238
consensus in macroeconomics 87–9, 121, 160, 290–91
convergence 72, 267–8, 277–8, 302–4
Council of Economic Advisers 23–5, 202–4, 289
credibility 200

development economics 66–7, 268, 275

East European transition 64, 239–40
economic growth 8–9, 60–87, 160–62, 205–6, 239–40, 272–82, 296–313
efficiency wage theories 113, 234, 287
empirical macroeconomic research 43–4
endogenous growth theory 76–81, 276, 279, 299–301, 305–6
European Monetary Union 55–6, 104, 140–41, 164, 175–6, 227, 237–8, 254–5
expectations
  adaptive 31, 131
  rational 109, 131, 252–3, 285

fairness in the labour market 114, 290
fiscal policy 119, 138–9, 198–9, 238, 249, 250, 286

Great Depression 2, 10–21, 125, 198, 231

hysteresis effects 113, 235–6

imperfect competition 46, 111
incomes policy 101, 111
inflation
  costs of 51–2

costs of reducing 38, 109–10
  in 1970s 5, 33
  targeting 58, 201
insider/outsider theories 113
intertemporal labour substitution effects 154, 261–2

Keynesian economics 21–30, 91–5, 125–7, 147–9, 167–8, 179–87, 243–9
  central propositions 27–8, 93
Keynes's *General Theory* 2, 13, 15, 22, 92, 94–5, 108, 110, 125–6, 148, 149, 179–82, 230–31, 243–4, 327–8

Lucas critique 36–7, 154, 196

menu costs 46, 113, 198, 233–4
methodological issues 135–7, 155, 159, 210–13, 266–7, 317–25
microfoundations of macroeconomics 29–30, 96, 107, 120, 136, 159, 212–13
monetarism 8, 16–17, 30–34, 128–32, 149–51, 187–8, 232, 251–2
monetary policy 199–200, 249

NAIRU 32, 97, 103, 113, 235
natural rate of unemployment 31–2, 97, 113, 122, 130, 158, 235
neoclassical growth theory 68–74
neoclassical synthesis 26, 93–4, 108, 231
new classical macroeconomics 34–8, 108–10, 133–5, 152–5, 188–9
new Keynesian macroeconomics 44–7, 98, 157
new political macroeconomics 47–50, 170–74, 330–31
Nobel Prize in Economics 9, 94, 127, 142–3, 148–9, 164–5, 247–8, 257, 272, 283

Printed and bound by CPI Group (UK) Ltd, Croydon, CR0 4YY

16/04/2025

14658488-0005